Discover Sacramento and the Gold Country

Who would believe that California's state capital is still an undiscovered gem? Long bypassed by motorists bound for greener pastures, Sacramento deserves a second look. The capital city is home to a colorful legacy of politics, modern art, music, fine dining, and countercultural movements.

Sacramento is a town always caught in the crucible of clashing styles and personalities—where politicians in tailored suits pedal beach cruisers alongside hipsters in pegged jeans and where movie stars discover a second life as governors. An urban renaissance has remade the historic Midtown, East Sacramento, and downtown neighborhoods into a vibrant, multicultural metropolis packed with bistros and cutting-edge museums.

With some of the best weather in the country—Sacramento is sunny nearly 80 percent of the time—you can walk, bike, hike, or stroll to the city's gleaming State Capitol Building and 40-acre Capitol Park. Just 45 minutes outside of Sacramento, the Auburn State Recreation Area waits on the banks of the mighty American River with horseback riding, swimming, rafting, and hiking on more than 100 miles of trails. You can catch a world-renowned jazz festival in the morning and ride white-water rapids by the afternoon. Or simply take cover under an endless green

canopy of valley oaks, elms, and maples; Sacramento claims to have more trees per capita than any city in the world.

Prospectors first discovered gold here in 1848, and the Gold Rush pioneers who poured in left behind dozens of boomtowns with rugged brick storefronts and gabled Victorian mansions. Gas lamps and saloons were as common as the waves of forty-niners searching for the next mother lode. This rough and storied past lives on in Sacramento's Gold Country, a gorgeous 130-mile-long belt of award-winning wineries, world-class bistros, and historic museums deep in the Sierra Nevada foothills. Today, modern-day "prospectors" search for antiques, explore underground caves, raft tumbling white water, luxuriate at private inns in renovated farmhouses, and discover a secluded yet booming wine region.

Join the region's ambitious foodies, visionary vintners, and outdoor adrenaline-seekers in embracing California's rejuvenated capital: Sacramento, the gateway to adventure.

Planning Your Trip

▸ WHERE TO GO

Grass Valley both offer quaint downtowns rife with mining museums and quirky shops. Cool off in the clear and cold Yuba River at South Yuba River State Park or venture to the other side of I-80 and the Auburn State Recreation Area, where mountain biking, horseback riding, and numerous hiking trails

Sacramento

Sacramento is the political heart of California and home of the State Capitol. Old Sacramento encourages visitors to ride steamboats and admire the historic brick buildings by day, and cruise the bars and restaurants by night. Midtown's nightlife offers a thriving live music scene as well as packed bars and clubs that inject a vibrant energy into the city's soul. Urban adventures continue in the American River Parkway, a vast playground for hiking, boating, and fishing. Not bad for an old railroad town built on steel and gold.

The Northern Gold Country

This beautiful high country is a rugged Shangri-la for outdoor recreation. The neighboring Gold Rush towns of Nevada City and

IF YOU HAVE . . .

- **ONE WEEKEND:** Visit Sacramento, exploring the Midtown and Old Town neighborhoods.
- **FIVE DAYS:** Add Grass Valley and Nevada City in the Northern Gold Country.
- **ONE WEEK:** Add Placerville and Apple Hill and continue exploring the Northern Gold Country.
- **TWO WEEKS:** Add the Southern Gold Country, starting in Amador County and heading south to Jamestown in Tuolumne County.

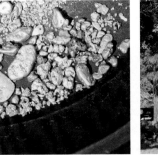

Gold!

Apple Hill

California State Capitol

await. Placerville is your base for exploring the orchards and wineries of delightful Apple Hill or the churning white-water river canyons that plunge through Coloma. History buffs can stand on the very spot where James W. Marshall found gold nuggets at Marshall Gold Discovery State Historic Park.

The Southern Gold Country

The Mediterranean landscape that lies between Amador and Calaveras Counties is the Napa Valley of the Gold Country. Beautiful, bucolic hillsides softly roll south from the Shenandoah Valley through Sutter Creek, past Jackson, and into the untamed ravines surrounding Angels Camp. Some insist that Amador County wineries are the best in California, producing finely balanced zinfandel, syrah, and barbera while bubbling over with country hospitality. Farther south,

Justice has been served at the Placer County courthouse since 1898.

The tractor at Fitzpatrick Winery and Lodge runs on biofuel.

Murphys is riddled with miles of spooky caverns far beneath the topsoil. Outdoors adventurers can go white-water rafting and gaze up at the soaring greenery in Calaveras Big Trees State Park. Mining ruins and artifacts left over from generations of prospectors pepper Tuolumne County. Visit real working locomotives at Railtown 1897 State Historic Park in Jamestown, take a carriage ride through the living Gold Rush town of Columbia in Columbia State Historic Park, or retrace the footsteps of Mark Twain during the writer's 19th-century travels in these parts.

▶ WHEN TO GO

Sacramento's climate means you'll rarely experience frigid winters or humid summers. On the flip side, it can be sweltering between June and September. The best time to visit is between March and May, when the city's trees explode with flowers and bright new leaves. Fall is also a special time, when temperatures begin to cool and Sacramento's urban forest turns shades of glowing red and gold. Winter is fairly mild compared to other parts of the country, but still cold. Perhaps the only time when Sacramento is unpleasant might be mid-December through mid-February, when trees are bare and the rain falls in sheets, though more optimistic locals grab their skis or snowboards to plow the Sierra Nevada slopes.

the California Assembly

Nevada County ranch

the Broad Street Inn, Nevada City

► BEFORE YOU GO

One of the first things you should do is reserve accommodations. Staying in Sacramento on short notice usually isn't a problem, thanks to the sheer volume of lodgings spread throughout town. But unless you plan ahead, it can be nearly impossible to score quaint foothill lodgings where innkeepers may have only half a dozen rooms. Book at least three or four months in advance for accommodations in the Gold Country or risk missing out on your first choices.

Getting to Sacramento is easy: The airport, train station, and many freeways link the capital to San Francisco and the Bay Area. Within Sacramento, the light-rail and bus system together blanket the city with cheap transport options; for anything in between there are taxis and pedicabs. The Gold Country, however, is more difficult. A car is absolutely necessary for traveling between small foothill towns that may be miles away from each other. Some form of public transportation exists in each town, but this is mostly for commuters heading into Sacramento on weekdays.

If you're traveling to Sacramento during spring or fall, it can still be warm during the day so wear layers and bring a light coat for the cooler evenings. You'll also want a good pair of walking shoes. Despite Sacramento's sunny reputation, winters in the Gold Country can be frigid. If you intend to visit between November and March, bring warm clothing to prepare for what Mother Nature might toss your way.

Two of Old Sac's hardest workers take five.

Old Town Auburn

Explore Sacramento and the Gold Country

▶ THE BEST OF SACRAMENTO

Sacramento is an easy destination to visit in a long weekend. Most of the must-see attractions are close together, so it doesn't take much effort to immerse yourself in the capital's potent brew of history and political theater.

Day 1

Base yourself in Old Sacramento. In the morning, rise early and grab breakfast at Fox and Goose Pub and Restaurant. This British-style pub grills the best omelette in town, with freshly baked muffins on the side. After breakfast, everything begins and ends with the State Capitol. First, arrive early to catch the California Legislature in session, then take a tour of the State Capitol Museum to see the re-created offices of past statesmen. Head out through the sprawling emerald grounds of Capitol Park and pay your respects at the somber Vietnam Veterans Memorial.

Lawmakers love to shout and grumble at the Capitol, but sometimes real policy gets made on the white paper napkins at Frank Fat's Chinese restaurant. Stop here for lunch, then walk across the Capitol Mall to K Street; make sure to pass the powder-gray spires of the Cathedral of the Blessed Sacrament. In the stately Elks Tower, ride the elevator to the 14th floor for wine-tasting at Rail Bridge Cellars Penthouse Lounge with a stunning bird's-eye view of downtown.

After sampling the wine and crow's nest

California's State Capitol and surrounding Capitol Park

Cathedral of the Blessed Sacrament

panorama, head to Ella Dining Room and Bar to splurge on dinner, or chow down on grass-fed beef patties at Burgers and Brew in the Historic R Street District. Catch an indie flick or live performance at the majestic Crest Theatre downtown. Afterward, cross the street to finish the evening with drinks and cool beats at ultra-swanky District 30 or hip KBAR.

Day 2

Spend the morning exploring Old Sacramento. Spend at least an hour wandering through the California State Railroad Museum, then board an actual steam train for a jaunt along the Sacramento River. After riding the rails, return to Old Sac for a juicy burger and fries at the iconic Fanny Ann's Saloon.

Walk off that meaty burger with a stroll down Front and Second Streets. Pop into Evangeline's for some fun shopping or load up on homemade fudge at The Sacramento Sweets Co. Take a break from the packed cobblestoned streets and spend the afternoon at the Crocker Art Museum; one of the Golden State's largest collections of California artwork hangs here.

As the museum curators get ready to go home, head back over to Old Sacramento as the day's last light shines on the Delta King steamboat. Grab dinner at the Rio City Cafe on the riverfront and watch lights from the Tower Bridge twinkle in the water.

Day 3

Don't let a weekend go by without cruising through Sacramento on two wheels. Rent a bicycle for the day at City Bicycle Works in Midtown and pedal over to East Sacramento for a healthy breakfast of whole grain pancakes or soy chorizo at Orphan. After licking your plate clean, order a cup of Naked Coffee and go for a light stroll in McKinley Park.

Now that the caffeine is pumping through your veins, hop on your bike and pedal

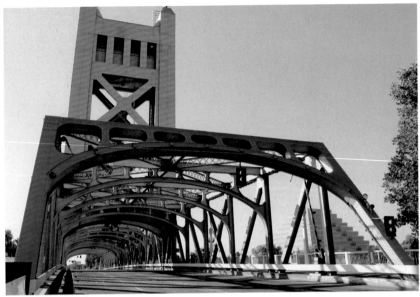

Tower Bridge

through bucolic East Sacramento toward the American River Parkway. Ride a few miles up- or downriver before heading back to East Sacramento. Make sure to pass through Ronald Reagan's old neighborhood in the Fabulous Forties. After that bike ride, pop into Juno's for a sandwich or gobble down a plate of fish-and-chips at Bonn Lair. After lunch, head over to Midtown and visit one of Sacramento's original buildings at Sutter's Fort State Historic Park. Docents dressed as blacksmiths and mountain men re-create life inside John Sutter's imposing adobe 1840s rancho. Hang a left outside the gate and find out more about the Golden State's native people at the California State Indian Museum.

Pedal back into Midtown for great Italian food at Paesano's or go a little fancier at Mulvaney's B&L. The night is still young, so get tickets for a Broadway-style show at the Wells Fargo Pavilion or catch a play at Capital Stage or B Street Theatre. Celebrate the end of a long day with cocktails at Kasbah Lounge.

▶ THE BEST OF THE GOLD COUNTRY

After exploring the city, head to the Sierra Nevada foothills for this weeklong adventure. The region is still rugged, but with a modern flair, and visitors can enjoy everything from river rafting and mountain biking to cosmopolitan restaurants and charming bed-and-breakfasts.

This road trip starts in Nevada City, 61 miles north of Sacramento in the Northern Gold Country, and travels from north to south crossing major highways and traversing winding backroads. Make sure to bring a good map and take note of driving distances; try to avoid doubling back over routes and instead keep moving north to south.

SACRAMENTO ON WHEELS

All aboard for Sacramento's wheeled adventures!

The wheel transformed Sacramento from a swampy river outpost into a proud metropolis. Today, visitors can find all kinds of fascinating and fun wheeled transport.

- At the **California State Railroad Museum,** sit in restored cars from the old Sacramento Valley Railroad and ride a steam train through Old Town.

- On the **Sacramento RiverTrain,** visitors enjoy three-hour jaunts into the Central Valley on an immaculate diesel train.

- A famous paddle-wheeled steamboat, the **Delta King**, now sits permanently moored to Sacramento's embarcadero in Old Town. Today, visitors can eat, drink, or sleep at this restaurant and hotel.

- If it's sailing up the Sacramento River you want, book an afternoon passage with **Hornblower Historic River Cruises** to chug up and down Old Sacramento's waterfront.

- In **Old Sacramento,** travel in horse-drawn carriages that clip-clop their way down the city's cobblestoned streets while the driver regales you with stories about Sacramento's bawdy past.

- Visit **Nevada City** in December to ride through the streets in style during the town's **Victorian Christmas,** a street fair where top hats and roasted chestnuts become en vogue.

- The flat landscape and tree-lined streets of Sacramento make a tour through the **Midtown** neighborhood an easy pedal. Guides are available from **Fast Eddie Bike Tours**.

- Take a self-guided tour along 23 miles of the **American River Parkway** and stop for a picnic by the water.

- Comedy tour company **Hysterical Walks** takes people on gyroscope-aided spins up and down **River Walk Park** or zips through downtown and Old Sacramento for a laugh-out-loud adventure.

the historic Nevada Theatre

Day 1

From Sacramento, head north to the Victorian mining town of Nevada City. Check in to the luxurious Emma Nevada House, where you can chill out later in your antique soaking tub. If the weather is warm enough, lace on some hiking boots and visit the spooky mining ruins at Malakoff Diggins State Historic Park. Listen to how eerily quiet it is as you wander past glowing turquoise pools left over from 19th-century hydraulic mining. On the way out, stop at the ghost town of North Bloomfield and wonder where everyone went. If it's too hot for a hike, drive west to cool off in the South Yuba River State Park where you can splash around near the world's longest single-span covered bridge.

After building up an appetite, drive into Nevada City's downtown for gourmet po'-boy sandwiches at Matteo's Public or a Hillbilly Burger at Lefty's Grill. Walk off lunch by strolling around the town's illustrious commercial district and quirky shops. Buy tickets for an evening show inside the austere brick walls of the Nevada Theatre, where cultural luminaries from Mark Twain to The Second City comedy troupe have performed. After the show, celebrate with a steak dinner at Friar Tuck's or savor the region's best Japanese food at Sushi in the Raw. For dessert, walk down to Treats for handmade ice cream with locally grown organic ingredients.

Day 2

Wake up early and enjoy a good breakfast at South Pine Café, but don't get bogged down—today's a big day. Take a short jaunt to Grass Valley and explore Empire Mine State Historic Park, home of the most productive strike in the Gold Country. Spend time in the vast courtyard inspecting rows of powerful mining equipment before roaming through acres of green lawns, rose gardens, and towering pine trees to the majestic Bourn Cottage.

Thanks to your early start, there should

be plenty of time for a hike through the park's rugged outskirts. Follow the Hardrock Trail as it retraces an old rail line and keep an eye out for machinery rusting in the woods. After your hike, jump back behind the wheel and head south on Highway 49 to downtown Auburn. Pick up some sandwiches to go at Little Belgium Deli and Beer Bar and rent a mountain bike at Atown Bikes, then keep going south to the Auburn State Recreation Area. Two forks of the American River converge in this deep river canyon, making it a playground for adrenaline junkies. Mountain bikers can plunge down an old stagecoach route to the Lower Clementine Trail.

Return the rental bike in Auburn and check in to a hotel for a shower. For dinner, head over to Old Town Auburn below the restored 19th-century Placer County courthouse. Splurge on gourmet American cuisine at Carpe Vino, or stay simple with burgers at Auburn Alehouse.

Day 3

Time to hit the road again, but first make sure to wolf down a country breakfast at either Katrina's Cafe or Sweetpea's. Don't overdo it though, because today you're going white-water rafting on the American River. Many guided trips are based out of Coloma, where numerous guide companies can meet your needs. Depending on skill level, more advanced rafters should book a half-day river trip on the Middle Fork of the American River, while newcomers might want to try the calmer South Fork.

Whew, you made it! After burning your adrenaline on the river, make a beeline to the peaceful Coloma Country Inn to clean up. Devour some grilled flatbread or chocolate chipotle prawns for dinner at Café Mahjaic and then crash hard back at the inn.

Day 4

In the morning, visit Marshall Gold Discovery State Historic Park and take the

Carpe Vino is housed in an Old West saloon.

RECREATION: THE NEW GOLD

The American River Parkway is a 23-mile-long playground for outdoor fun.

A "New Gold Rush" begins whenever visitors flock to the Sierra Nevada foothills for something fresh and exciting. This time it's outdoor recreation, something found in abundance in Sacramento and the Gold Country.

- Twenty-three miles of urban wilderness follow the **American River Parkway**'s course from its confluence with the mighty Sacramento up to Folsom in the lower foothills. Along the way, the paved **Jedediah Smith Bike Trail** bends along wide bluffs, levees, and through oak woodlands above the river, making a fantastic place for jogging and cycling.

- The 4.8-mile-long expanse of Folsom Lake at the **Folsom Lake State Recreation Area** has plenty of open water for wakeboarding, Jet Skiing, and fishing as well as hiking and mountain biking trails around the northeast corner of the lake. Folsom Lake also has several **campgrounds** that offer families a chance to hang out on the waterfront.

- A slice of heaven awaits at the **Auburn State Recreation Area** between Auburn and Cool. Visitors will enjoy swimming, horseback riding, or zipping dirt bikes through the off-road park. Mountain biking is extremely popular on trails like **Quarry Road** and **Lower Clementine.**

- Once North America's largest riparian wilderness, the **Cosumnes River Preserve** still attracts 250 species of birds every year during migration season. Bring binoculars and comfortable hiking shoes for a stroll around the park as you pass vernal pools, seasonal wetlands, and oak woodlands.

- From Downieville to Sonora, plunge through diabolical Class II-V rapids on **white-water rafting trips.** The most popular trip is the **South Fork of the American River** near Coloma, the site of the first noteworthy gold discovery in 1848.

- The best single-track **mountain biking** in California just might be in **Downieville.** Mountain bikers start at the Sierra Buttes, where they begin a 17-mile charge back to town.

Hanford House Inn

Gold Discovery Loop Trail to the very spot where James W. Marshall found nuggets shining in the American River near Sutter's Mill. The discovery sparked the Gold Rush, inspiring ore-hungry prospectors to strike out for the Sierra Nevada foothills.

Back in the car, head over to Old Hangtown, otherwise known as downtown Placerville, for burgers at The Shoestring or gourmet pizza at The Heyday Café. Take a stroll up historic Main Street to burn off those calories and snap a photo of Placerville's iconic Hangman's Tree mannequin strung high above the sidewalk.

From Placerville, travel south through the Shenandoah Valley to Sutter Creek, which continues Amador County's parade of stellar wineries with a murderer's row of killer wines right in downtown. Book a room at Hanford House Inn, then step onto Main Street to explore the long thoroughfare packed with art galleries and quirky boutiques. For dinner, enjoy a relaxed vibe at Susan's Place

for Mediterranean-fusion cuisine. Wrap up the evening with a show at the lively Sutter Creek Theatre before heading back for a romantic evening at the inn.

Day 5

Get ready for some underground adventures in the Southern Gold Country. Migrate south to the famous town of Angels Camp, and if you're in town during the Calaveras County Fair and Jumping Frog Jubilee, buy a ticket and join in the fun. Descend into the Jungle Room at California Caverns or listen to the haunting sounds emitted by Moaning Cavern. Before heading out of town, grab delicious homemade sandwiches from the Pickle Barrel or try the burritos at Sidewinders in downtown Angels Camp.

Continue south to the twin towns of Columbia and Sonora. Pan for gold, ride a stagecoach, watch a blacksmith at work, or down some sarsaparilla at Columbia State

Columbia State Historic Park

Historic Park, a re-created mining camp in Tuolumne County and one heck of a family adventure. For your last evening in the Gold Country, stay the night at swanky Barretta Gardens Inn in Sonora and chow down on farmstead produce at the endearingly rustic Diamondback Grill before saying so long to the foothills.

► WINE COUNTRY ROAD TRIP

Almost every corner of the Gold Country now has wineries and tasting rooms offering homegrown estate vino to visitors. Fun and unpretentious, these wineries often feature vintners working in their own tasting rooms, where you'll experience vintage foothills hospitality while sipping Rhône and Bordeaux varietals. Along the way, enjoy a few side trips to Gold Rush ruins or a short hike to breathe in the pine-scented air of the Sierra Nevada high country.

Apple Hill

In the Northern Gold Country, El Dorado County's wineries are especially known for finely balanced syrah, barbera, cabernet

Fruit trees are everywhere in Apple Hill.

FAMILY FUN

the entrance to Fairytale Town in Land Park

Traveling with children can be a fun and memorable experience in Sacramento and the Gold Country. There's a whole range of things to do all over the region.

- Sacramento's largest developed park is bristling with kid-friendly activities. **Land Park** has eight ball fields, a stocked trout pond, and several playgrounds spread over 166 acres. Families can feed giraffes at the **Sacramento Zoo** or explore *two* children's theme parks: the whimsical **Fairytale Town** and **Funderland.**

- Even the biggest kid will never stop loving the big locomotives and gleaming dining cars on display at the **California State Railroad Museum.**

- In the Southern Gold Country near

Jamestown, visitors can tour a locomotive workshop at **Railtown 1897 State Historic Park** and watch the engineers drive puffing steam engines.

- Pumpkins, pony rides, and hay mazes are sure to get any kid excited, and you will find all three at **Apple Hill,** an area filled with apple orchards and vineyards that fling open their doors for months of weekend harvest fairs.

- In the Southern Gold Country, kids will dig the vine-like formations in the Jungle Room at **California Caverns,** near Angels Camp. Go underground at **Mercer Caverns** near Murphys or stop by **Moaning Cavern** near Vallecito, where a mysterious grumble emits whenever water seeps into the cave.

sangiovese wine grapes at Fitzpatrick Winery and Lodge

sauvignon, and zinfandel. Start by exploring Apple Hill, near Placerville, where vineyards mingle with fruit trees high in the foothills. Follow the Apple Hill Scenic Drive to visit numerous orchards and sample fresh produce, apple cider doughnuts, and homemade apple pies. Along the way, make sure to visit family-owned vintners like Madroña Vineyards, Lava Cap Winery, and Boeger Winery. Spend the night back in Placerville at the adorable Albert Shafsky House and get spruced up for dinner at Cascada.

Fair Play

For jaw-dropping scenery with a glass of wine, get ready to dig Fair Play in southern El Dorado County. Barely a town, Fair Play is a rugged backcountry community that produces damn good wine. Often ignored by most day-trippers enthralled with Amador's wine scene, Fair Play is really the next big thing in Gold Country wine.

Make your first stop at Miraflores, named by *Wine Spectator* as a place to watch. That esteemed publication also thinks Cedarville Vineyards is leading a "taste revolution" in the foothills, but you'll need to make an appointment first. Take a lunch break at Gold Vine Grill in Somerset, then help your digestion with more foothill vino from Skinner Vineyards, produced by arguably one of California's most storied winemaking clans. There's a gorgeous view of the vineyards and surrounding hillsides, but it's hard to top Fitzpatrick Winery and Lodge for scenery. Make this place your last stop and crash here for the night after trying the Irish-themed wine.

BEST WEEKEND GETAWAYS

Union Inn, Volcano

Sometimes, you just need to run for the hills. The following Gold Country towns and villages make a perfectly romantic weekend getaway.

- **Nevada City:** A smattering of Victorian town houses and gaslit lamps give this foothill burg a Dickensian flair. Drop off your bags at the delightfully cozy **Emma Nevada House** and spend an afternoon browsing quirky gift shops and art galleries on Broad Street.

- **Grass Valley:** More Norman Rockwell than Charles Dickens, Grass Valley boasts a rugged brand of Americana straight from the 1950s. Grab a room with your sweetie at **Annie Horan's B and B** and make a date with the luxurious claw-foot tub.

- **Volcano:** Volcano is a tiny hamlet tucked way back in the far reaches of Amador County where you can truly get lost among the towering oak forests and one-lane country roads. Reserve comfy lodgings and grab a bite to eat at the **Union Inn,** built in 1880 by four wandering French-Canadian adventurers.

- **Murphys:** Murphys's main street wouldn't feel out of place in Napa or Sonoma, but the rustic Wild West vibe is quintessential Gold Country. Check into **Dunbar House, 1880** to enjoy cozy claw-foot tubs and crackling gas stoves.

- **Twain Harte:** Enjoy the fresh mountain air in tiny Twain Harte, east of Sonora. Find romance at **McCaffrey House Bed and Breakfast,** where you can sign up for a luxurious couples massage right in your room.

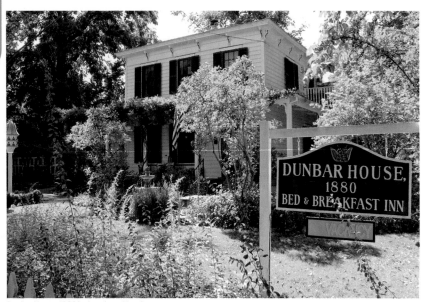

Dunbar House, 1880 in downtown Murphys

Shenandoah Valley

Amador County's Shenandoah Valley is the Gold Country's answer to Napa and Sonoma. Some of California's oldest vineyards are here, but the glory belongs to newcomers producing top-notch wines from small lots of estate-grown grapes.

Begin your tour in Plymouth, with stops at C.G. Di Arie Vineyard and Winery, Borjon, and Terre Rouge Wines. More wineries line the English-style countryside between County Route E16 and Fiddletown Road. Wrap up the day with dinner at the outstanding Restaurant Taste in Plymouth. At night, meander farther south to Amador City and stay at the grandly historic Imperial Hotel. In the morning, look forward to mouthwatering pastries made from scratch at Andrae's Bakery.

Murphys

Try something new by skipping over to Calaveras County and exploring Murphys. This rugged burg is the Gold Country's St. Helena, with a long drag peppered with tasting rooms, haunted buildings, rustic bistros, and a smattering of cheeky saloons. Visit some of the tasting rooms around the outskirts of town—Ironstone Vineyards, Val du Vino Winery, and Twisted Oak Winery—before strolling Main Street to try varietals from Chiarella Wines.

Wrap up a day of wine-tasting with dinner at Grounds or gourmet veggie cuisine at Mineral Restaurant. At night, join the packed throng at the 1856 Saloon in the Murphys Historic Hotel and party like a bandit. Stay at the Dunbar House, 1880 and collapse into homespun luxury.

SACRAMENTO

Forget what you know about Sacramento. Once dismissed as a cow town, California's state capital has blossomed into a hip, thriving metropolis with renowned museums, an evolving nightlife scene, and an exploding lineup of innovative eateries. With seemingly endless sunshine and a unique setting on two rivers, the city has become the gateway to Northern California's endless bounty of outdoor recreation.

Sacramento has always been the linchpin to California's evolution into the economic dynamo of the American West. A sleepy 19th-century outpost in California's vast Central Valley, Sacramento exploded almost overnight in 1848 when James W. Marshall discovered gold only 50 miles to the east. Paddle-wheeled riverboats clogged the Sacramento River carrying decks of eager prospectors hoping to strike it rich. These gold-mad denizens of the Gold Rush passed through Sacramento, filling the saloons and boardinghouses to bursting. The outpost became a boomtown and then a city, the place where Pony Express riders ended their frenetic route and Wells Fargo stagecoaches clattered down mud-splattered streets. Flinty industrialists eventually followed the scruffy prospectors, and they decided California needed a railroad to bring capital for a new Gold Rush: one that extracted precious metals from deep mine shafts in the foothills. From their smoky back rooms and offices in Sacramento, the city's

HIGHLIGHTS

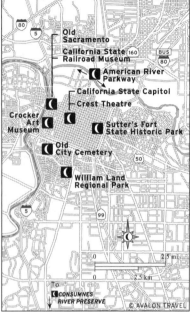

LOOK FOR **(** TO FIND RECOMMENDED SIGHTS, ACTIVITIES, DINING, AND LODGING.

(**California State Capitol:** Sacramento's iconic State Capitol building is the epicenter for the city's political history—past and present. Be sure to check out the museum's impressive collection of art and antiques (page 30).

(**Old Sacramento:** Take a tour of Old Sacramento for a new sense of how the state cap-

ital grew up over its 160-year existence (page 34).

(**California State Railroad Museum:** Visit 21 restored locomotives while exploring Sacramento's connection to the First Transcontinental Railroad (page 35).

(**Crocker Art Museum:** Check out the Golden State's premier collection of Californian artwork in this surprisingly cosmopolitan museum (page 37).

(**Sutter's Fort State Historic Park:** Long before Sacramento became California's capital, it was just this adobe outpost guarding John Sutter's sprawling rancho (page 41).

(**Old City Cemetery:** Pay your respects to the city's founding fathers and mothers at this decadent Victorian graveyard (page 44).

(**American River Parkway:** One of Sacramento's secrets hidden in plain sight is this 23-mile-long urban park on the American River (page 44).

(**The Crest Theatre:** Catch an indie flick, a film festival, or performing arts at one of Sacramento's last grand movie houses, easily recognizable by the old-fashioned marquee glowing over K Street (page 57).

(**William Land Regional Park:** Come spend a lazy day enjoying Sacramento's largest developed park, with a zoo, a fishing pond, a golf course, and two children's theme parks (page 73).

(**Cosumnes River Preserve:** This protected area was once North America's largest riparian wilderness. During annual bird migrations, hundreds of species choke the waterways for one of nature's most spectacular rituals (page 126).

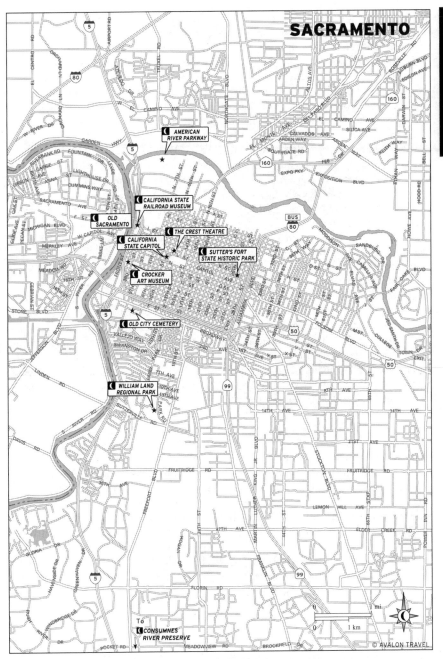

SACRAMENTO

AMERICAN RIVER PARKWAY

CALIFORNIA STATE RAILROAD MUSEUM

OLD SACRAMENTO

THE CREST THEATRE

CALIFORNIA STATE CAPITOL

SUTTER'S FORT STATE HISTORIC PARK

CROCKER ART MUSEUM

OLD CITY CEMETERY

WILLIAM LAND REGIONAL PARK

To CONSUMNES RIVER PRESERVE

0   mi
0   1 km

© AVALON TRAVEL

newly minted elite guided the construction of the First Transcontinental Railroad that linked California to the rest of the United States.

Today the city proudly shows off its Gold Rush credentials, but modern life hums around new things: politics, agriculture, food, and recreation. Sacramento plays a prominent role in the Golden State's political economy. The Capitol's gleaming dome is a beacon for suited lobbyists and lawmakers who represent California's 37 million citizens and the world's ninth largest economy. And all those people have to eat, right? As a steel island rising amidst the Central Valley's sea of cornfields, vineyards, almond orchards, and cattle pastures (yes, they still have cows in Sacramento), the city is squarely in the hub of California's important agricultural community. So close, in fact, that Sacramento has welcomed yet another Gold Rush. This one is led by culinary prospectors—farm-to-table chefs who mine the city's farmers markets for sustainable, local, and organic produce. That's why Sacramento became the self-proclaimed Farm-to-Fork Capital of America in 2012. Foodies are taking notice: Sacramento's restaurants have been ranked among the country's best eateries by critics and reviewers.

And finally, the city has become a mecca for outdoor fanatics drawn to the miles of running and biking trails that crisscross the gently rolling landscape, rivers teeming with fish, and months of pristine blue sky. It's a great place to stay on the move, which is one reason Sacramento was named one of the country's healthiest and fittest cities in 2012 by the American College of Sports Medicine.

This dynamic brew of politics, agriculture, food, and recreation has created a city that's distinctively Californian and yet stubbornly different. Sacramento stands between the coast and the Sierra Nevada, a true Western capital shaped by gold and iron and soil, salted by the earth's bounty in extraordinary ways. For all of these reasons, this city is bristling with energy. A visit to Sacramento is like riding a powerful locomotive. Everything seems to be moving forward while staying rooted to the past.

PLANNING YOUR TIME

Sacramento is a flat city with a grid layout that's easy to navigate on foot or with a bike. Most attractions can be found in downtown Sacramento near the **California State Capitol** along J, K, and L Streets, known as the JKL Corridor, which is lined with restaurants and nightclubs. Plan on spending several hours strolling through **Capitol Park,** or peek inside the California State Legislature from the galleries. From downtown, it's only a few blocks west to **Old Sacramento** and the riverfront, where you can ride a steam-powered train at the **California State Railroad Museum,** explore the city's secret underground passageways with **Old Sacramento Underground Tours.** Make sure to spend at least one evening in Old Sacramento walking down the cobblestones by the ancient loading docks while enjoying a sunset over the river.

East Sacramento is a green oasis of sprawling parks, mellow pubs, and early 20th-century Arts and Craft bungalows. The **American River Parkway** is just a few blocks north, a meandering 23-mile-long urban wilderness where cyclists, runners and families can easily spend their entire day along the water. To the south, **William Land Regional Park** deserves at least a full day: the Sacramento Zoo, Fairytale Town, and Funderland are all packed into this enormous urban park.

Sights

Think of Sacramento as both the starting gate and the finish line for one of the greatest migrations in history. During the frenetic early days of the Gold Rush, Sacramento was an important staging point for 19th-century prospectors toting their pans and picks to the Gold Country. The Pony Express and the First Transcontinental Railroad ended their cross-country routes here, and numerous Wells Fargo stagecoach lines also passed through on their way to San Francisco. Landmarks from that era form the backbone of modern-day Sacramento and many attractions remain, especially around Old Sacramento and the Capitol District. But even though Sacramento is steeped in Gold Rush lore, it's also a bustling

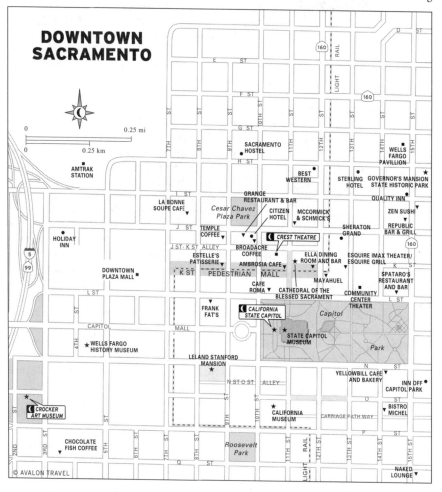

commercial and political hub for the ninth largest economy in the world, and so it has all the museums, urban parks, historical landmarks, and stately architecture you'd expect from a prominent state capital.

Don't forget to check out Sacramento's neighborhoods. Many were built at the height of the Gilded Age and into the early 20th century. In some places, beech and maple trees reach high over the street to form a shaded tunnel. It's a fantastic place to see restored Victorian townhomes, American Craftsman bungalows, and Neocolonial mansions, all making for an excellent afternoon bike ride.

DOWNTOWN AND OLD TOWN

Until the Gold Rush began in 1848, Sacramento was just a small trading post on a river wharf called the Embarcadero. California was still a loose confederation of ranchos ruled by Mexican landlords. Only 1,000 European settlers lived in the territory. In 1839, a Swiss immigrant named John Sutter arrived and received a land grant for 50,000 acres from Mexico. He founded a tiny camp called Sutterville and constructed an adobe fort near the Sacramento River. Sutterville never took off, but Sutter's son (John Sutter Jr.) learned from his old man's mistakes and built another city closer to where the Sacramento and American Rivers forked. The son's gamble paid off when gold-hungry prospectors flooded the new city on their way to the Sierra Nevada.

John Sutter Jr.'s city can still be explored between Old Sacramento and downtown. There's a dramatic contrast between the modern skyscrapers around the State Capitol and the brick storefronts along the restored embarcadero. Walking between these two districts is almost like traveling in time.

Downtown is bordered by I-5 on the west, the old Southern Pacific Railyards to the north, and U.S. 50 to the south. Downtown revolves around the **Capitol District,** an area roughly

bounded by J, N, 9th, and 16th Streets. Most of the city's nightclubs and attractions lie within this square. Anything west of 10th hasn't really caught up with Sacramento's urban renaissance. Farther south there's the **R Street Historic District,** the city's old warehouse district that's turning into a 27-block-long strip of bars and upscale eateries. Just north of downtown in **Alkali and Mansion Flats,** visitors will find edgy districts still lagging behind the rest of Sacramento's rebirth.

Downtown can be reached from Old Sacramento by crossing I-5 on Capitol Mall (on bike, on foot, or by car) or by taking byways underneath the massive freeway. If you're walking from Old Sacramento, take the K Street pedestrian tunnel into downtown.

◖ California State Capitol

The jewel of Sacramento's skyline is the California State Capitol (10th and L Sts., 916/324-0333, www.parks.ca.gov, 8 A.M.–5 P.M. Mon.–Fri., 9 A.M.–5 P.M. Sat.–Sun., free). Surrounded by a halo of steel skyscrapers, the building's white Neoclassical dome was modeled after the U.S. Capitol in Washington DC and completed in 1874. It's a busy place. On any given day, you might stumble across demonstrators protesting on the West Steps or politicians giving a press conference. Before heading inside, take a moment to check out the golden ball atop the dome. Back when the building was finished, some folks wanted a replica of Lady Freedom (the statue crowning the U.S. Capitol) instead, but planners were looking for something that would uniquely represent California. They choose the gilded ball to represent the Gold Rush.

Inside you'll find the governor's office and the two chambers of the California State Legislature. Along the brightly lit corridors are 58 informative exhibits, one for each county. Walk upstairs to reach the Legislature's upper galleries, and note the large oil paintings of

© CHRISTOPHER ARNS

the west portico of the State Capitol

each governor hanging in the landings; Jerry Brown's first portrait is the most controversial work of the bunch because of its quasi-abstract (and sort of random) style. If the 80 assembly members or the 40 state senators are in session, watch from either the Senate or Assembly gallery as they feverishly debate policy. Go back downstairs to the black-and-white checkerboard floor of the Capitol's dazzling Rotunda and check out the controversial statue of Christopher Columbus. Native American and Latino groups protested when the statue was returned to this spot after restoration work in the 1970s, and the Native Sons of the Golden West pointed out that Columbus never came close to visiting California. Yet Columbus remains— for now, anyway. Above the statue, you can see the gilded inner dome glowing 128 feet overhead. Stop here and listen to the echo chamber created by this majestic space. All around you'll hear the dull roar of tourists, reporters, politicians, and staff members going about their

day. Note that cameras, cell phones, and backpacks will pass through a security scanner as you enter the building, and no pets are allowed except for service animals. Public tours are offered for free 9 A.M.–4 P.M. daily.

Capitol Park

Capitol Park (15th and L Sts., www.parks. ca.gov) was first created in 1870 when the grounds were planted with 800 trees and 200 varieties of plants. Today the park spans 40 acres and 12 city blocks of verdant lawns, beautiful flower gardens, and 155 memorials. Nearly 1,200 trees from around the world grow in the park, including California redwoods, Norwegian firs, and cedars from the Himalayas. A stocked fishpond teems with rainbow trout near the Civil War Memorial Grove, which has saplings taken from several famous Civil War battlefields. Explore the 650 roses in the Victorian-style World Peace Rose Garden along 15th Street. Some of the most notable monuments include the Vietnam Veterans Memorial inscribed with the names of 5,822 Californians who died or went missing in that war. Other memorials include the Camellia Grove, which honors Sacramento's official flower and the pioneers who brought it to the state more than 160 years ago, and the California Firefighter Memorial honoring 900 men and women who died in the line of duty. The park is a great place to lie on the thick grass or take a stroll around the magnificent gardens. Whatever you do, just don't throw a Frisbee or a kick a soccer ball because those activities (along with biking, inline skating, football, baseball, or pretty much any other kind of game) are banned. Sounds strict, but the memorials here make Capitol Park sacred ground for many people, and the rules are meant to encourage respect.

State Capitol Museum

Peek into California's political past at the State Capitol Museum (10th and L Sts., State Capitol Building, Room B-27, 916/324-0333, http:// capitolmuseum.ca.gov, 8 A.M.–5 P.M. Mon.– Fri., 9 A.M.–5 P.M. Sat.–Sun., free). The museum is the curator of the domed building's history. Exhibits include portraits depicting past governors and 12 jaw-dropping murals that once graced the Capitol Rotunda. Visitors can also check out several historic rooms from the building's past that are no longer used by state officials and have been restored to their turn-of-the-20th-century glory. These suites include the Governor's Private Office with its swanky leather chair, box of cigars, and old papers strewn across the desk. There's also the Secretary of State's old office with its stack of law books and a vintage Diebold safe. Maybe the most fascinating rooms are the two Treasury Offices from 1906 and 1933. Each contains a vault, ornate wooden desks where technocrats sweated over tax receipts, and old registers for keeping track of the state's income.

A tour is the best way to explore the Capitol's historic treasures, and the museum offers hourly guided trips between 9 A.M. and 4 P.M. daily from the museum office.

California Museum

As the outbreak of World War II sparked the nation into action, one decision still haunts Californians. President Franklin D. Roosevelt signed Executive Order 9066 in February 1942 and ordered Japanese Americans into internment camps. One of the most moving exhibits at the California Museum (1020 O St., 916/653-7524, www.californiamuseum.org, 10 A.M.–5 P.M. Tues.–Sat., noon–5 P.M. Sun., adults $8.50, students and seniors $7, youth $6, children free) wrestles with Franklin's order and the effect it had on California's Japanese citizens. This fascinating museum does an excellent job of teasing out California's triumphs while also exploring the challenges faced by the state's women, Native Americans, Latinos, African American, and Asian Americans. One of the most illuminating exhibits is the story of Ishi, the state's "last wild Indian," and the media hype that surrounded his assimilation into white culture. The museum is also home to the California Hall of Fame, a living exhibit that inducts new members every year. Past inductees include Clint Eastwood, Steve Jobs, Willie Mays, Ronald Reagan, and Cesar Chavez.

Leland Stanford Mansion

While named for one of the Golden State's most famous statesmen, the Leland Stanford Mansion (800 N St., 916/324-0575, www.stanfordmansion.org, 10 A.M.–5 P.M. Wed.–Sun., adults $5, children $3) actually served as headquarters for three California chief executives. The palatial Renaissance Revival–style mansion offers a perfect look back at California's rise from muddy backwater to sophisticated statehood. It was built in 1856, long before the

the Leland Stanford Mansion in downtown Sacramento

© CHRISTOPHER ARNS

(1526 H St., 916/323-3047, www.parks.ca.gov, 10 A.M.–5 P.M. Wed.–Sun., adults $5, children $3) was the residence of California's chief executives. Walking inside past Italian marble fireplaces, gilded French mirrors, Persian rugs, and Victorian-era fixtures, it's hard to believe that Nancy Reagan thought the place too shabby to live in (she claimed it was a "firetrap"). Exploring the mansion really feels like walking in on California's first families. The rooms and exhibits have been painstakingly arranged with artifacts left behind by the previous inhabitants. You can check out the clothing of first ladies (including a display of evening gowns), a long dining table set with exquisite chinaware, an outdoor pool installed by Jerry Brown's father, Governor Pat Brown, and a bathroom that for some reason has an easy chair in the corner. These exhibits (along with several other restored rooms) give the mansion—and its

Capitol was completed, and served as a residence and then the governor's office until 1869. Leland Stanford made his dough as a merchant in the Gold Rush and became president of the "Big Four" industrialists who funded the First Transcontinental Railroad. When he decided to run for office in 1861, Stanford decided a future governor needed a swanky pad. He purchased the mansion for $8,000 and eventually expanded it, adding 17-foot ceilings, gilded mirrors, and elaborate woodwork and furnishings that you can still see today. The Park Service recently completed a $22 million restoration of the 19,000-square-foot building and its detailing now resembles Stanford's Gilded Age.

Governor's Mansion State Historic Park

From 1877 until Ronald Reagan's state administration in the 1960s, the Governor's Mansion

Many of California's former gubernatorial leaders lived in the historic Governor's Mansion.

© CHRISTOPHER ARNS

governors—a human touch, making the state's first families seem more real and accessible.

⟨ Old Sacramento

Old Sacramento (http://oldsacramento.com) is the heart and soul of the city's long journey from disaster-prone outpost to stately capital of California. Both a flood and a cholera epidemic killed thousands of people in 1850, and several fires repeatedly destroyed the town later that same decade. To cap it all off, another flood drowned the city in 1862. The city's dreadful luck was headline news around the world, and newspapers speculated that John Sutter Jr.'s city wouldn't last. But city leaders had a plan: Using powerful hydraulic jacks, they raised Sacramento's brick buildings by one full story in what's now Old Town. They also built

a levee between Sacramento and the river. I guess it worked. The star-crossed river town became a thriving commercial port as prospectors and investors poured into Sacramento seeking riches in the Gold Country. Those old brick buildings are now Old Sacramento's pride and joy, and visitors pack the wooden boardwalks as they browse gift shops, art galleries, clothing boutiques, and sports bars. Take a ride on the cobblestoned streets in a horse-drawn carriage ($10) and check out the *Delta King* riverboat docked at the restored wooden docks; the old steamer's sailing days are long gone, and it now serves primarily as a restaurant and hotel.

Old Sacramento has loads of offbeat stores that play off the city's Gold Rush history. Honestly, many are tourist traps selling "Governator" T-shirts dating back to Arnold Schwarzenegger's gubernatorial stint. The best way to feel connected to Sacramento's old-timey essence is on a tour. Among the best are the **Old Sacramento Underground Tours** (916/808-7059, www.historicoldsac.org), which explores the hidden passageways buried underneath the city's streets, and the **Hysterical Walks** (916/441-2527, http://hystericalwalks. com), which offer comedy and ghost tours through Old Town's cobbled streets.

Huntington, Hopkins and Company Hardware Store

After exploring Old Sacramento's riverfront, check out the Huntington, Hopkins and Company Hardware Store (113 I St., 916/323-7234, www.csrmf.org, 11 A.M.–4 P.M. daily, free), next to the California State Railroad Museum. The hardware store re-creates the mercantile owned by Collis P. Huntington and Mark Hopkins. These two merchants eventually became part of Sacramento's "Big Four" industrialists. Along with Leland Stanford and Charles Crocker, they masterminded the First Transcontinental Railroad. Inside the hardware store you'll find lanterns hanging from

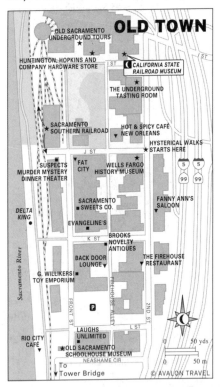

a replica of the Huntington, Hopkins and Company Hardware Store in Old Town

the ceiling, vintage toys, dry goods like cast iron cookware and 19th-century tools covering the far wall.

◖ California State Railroad Museum

It's been said that Sacramento is a cow town. No way. Sacramento will always be a railroad town, and if you don't believe me, check out the California State Railroad Museum (111 I St., 916/445-6645, www.csrmf.org, 10 A.M.–5 P.M. daily, adults $10, children $5). Few other museums pack the emotional punch you'll feel when gazing at 21 restored locomotives and railroad cars from different eras. The Virginia and Truckee 13 *Empire* steam engine is the most stunning of all. Mirrors surround the black, red and gold-trimmed Baldwin "iron horse" to give a 360-degree view of the locomotive's powerful pistons and wheels. You can also climb inside gleaming 1940s-era Santa Fe Railroad dining car No. 1474 and walk past

place settings of silver utensils and Mimbreno-patterned chinaware. Other exhibits tell the story of Sacramento's contribution to railroad history. When the city became wealthy during the Gold Rush, four local industrialists plotted a steel ribbon that would tie California to the country's East Coast factories and banks. This First Transcontinental Railroad eventually became the Central Pacific. You can explore the Big Four's vision at the museum and see how the undertaking was the most daunting engineering project of its day.

Staring at trains is great. Riding them is even better. The park grounds include Old Sacramento's restored railroad tracks and turnstile outside the museum's vast building. During the summer, book a ride on the **Sacramento Southern Railroad** (first class $15, regular adults $10, youths $5, children free) on tracks alongside the Sacramento River. It doesn't get better than this. A restored diesel locomotive pulls several closed coach cars and

© CHRISTOPHER ARNS

an old steam locomotive at the California State Railroad Museum

open-air gondolas through Old Sacramento. You'll pass the *Delta King*, the Tower Bridge spanning the river, and six miles of levees. Lemonade and cookies are served, but upgrade to first class in the 1920s El Dorado observation lounge for air-conditioning. Tickets are first-come, first-served starting at 10:30 A.M. at the office on Front Street.

Wells Fargo History Museum

Before the railroad came to the West, stagecoach routes ferried passengers and cargo between cities and far-flung outposts. You can explore the story of the stagecoach at the Wells Fargo Museum (1000 2nd St., 916/440-4263, www.wellsfargohistory.com, 10 A.M.–5 P.M. daily, free). The museum has two locations; the second is a short walk away in the downtown Wells Fargo History Museum (400 Capitol Mall, 916/440-4161, www.wellsfargo. com, 9 A.M.–5 P.M. Mon.–Sat., free). The

Old Town museum, housed in the Hastings building, first opened in 1852 as Wells Fargo's second office after its headquarters in San Francisco. As the Gold Rush brought more people and more business to Sacramento, the bank needed a faster way to transport things across the frontier. The Wells Fargo stagecoach and later the Pony Express, also used by the bank, became the fastest shipping routes in the country. A stagecoach could also transport up to 18 people and was usually pulled by teams of four to six horses. The Hastings building in Old Sacramento was the last stop on the Pony Express. Today the museum has been restored to resemble a 19th-century Wells Fargo agency with gold scales, a scaled stagecoach replica, and an interactive Pony Express exhibit. Over in the downtown museum is the star of the bank's collection: a fully restored 1866 Abbot-Downing stagecoach displayed beneath a five-story atrium. It's one of 11 stagecoaches owned by Wells Fargo in the entire country. The downtown museum also exhibits a working telegraph line, real gold nuggets, stagecoach harnesses for the horses, authentic postal covers used to protect the mail, and other artifacts.

Old Sacramento Schoolhouse Museum

The one-room Old Sacramento Schoolhouse Museum (1200 Front St., 916/483-8818, www. scoe.net/oldsacschoolhouse, 10 A.M.–4 P.M. Mon.–Sat., noon–4 P.M. Sun., free) is a throwback to the days of stern schoolmarms wielding chalk in one hand and a paddle in the other. No, really—costumed "marms" and "masters" are on hand to talk about 19th-century California school life. For one, it was cold; a grim-looking woodstove dominates the center of the museum. Desks looked like small wooden sleds all bolted in rows. And judging from the voluminous bookcase, students read

© CHRISTOPHER ARNS

the Old Sacramento Schoolhouse Museum

their eyeballs out. The schoolhouse usually has a fun schedule of family-oriented events lined up for holidays, such as making arts and crafts on St. Patrick's Day and pasting gooey gingerbread houses together before Christmas. The museum is an easy visit lasting no more than 30 minutes but is a great place to learn more about early California education.

Tower Bridge

Sacramento's most scenic river crossing is the gilded Tower Bridge (Capitol Mall crossing over the Sacramento River). Twin steel towers rise 160 feet above the Sacramento River within sight of Old Town. The bridge's Streamline Moderne design was conceived during the 1930s when Art Deco architecture was the rage. The most impressive feature of the 52-foot-long bridge is the vertical lift component that raises the middle span when riverboats pass beneath. The Tower Bridge is quite

a sight as evening falls and soft orange lighting makes the steel glow like a copper penny. The best vantage spots are from Raley Field, where you can spot Old Sacramento's embarcadero behind the bridge, or looking down river from the dock alongside the *Delta King*.

◖ Crocker Art Museum

One of the most underrated attractions is the Crocker Art Museum (216 O St., 916/808-7000, www.crockerartmuseum.org, 10 A.M.–5 P.M. Tues.–Sun., until 9 P.M. Thurs., on certain holiday 10 A.M.–5 P.M. Mon., adults $10, seniors and students $8, youth $5). Donated to the city in 1885 by Margaret Crocker, sister-in-law of Big Four railroad magnate Charles Crocker, this museum hosts an incredible collection of Californian art. When you arrive, stand outside and appreciate the contrast between the museum's stately Victorian mansion (and former

Crocker Art Museum

Crocker residence) and the brilliant contemporary Teel Family Pavilion that opened next door in 2010. The new wing added 125,000 square feet of exhibition space and tripled the Crocker's size. Inside, the collection spans 150 years of Impressionism, Abstract Impressionism, Modernism, Surrealism, and Pop Art. Notable Californian artists include Thomas Hill, Joan Brown, and Guy Rose; the museum also boasts quite a few works by former Sacramento State student Wayne Thiebaud. The Crocker's rising profile in the art world has attracted prestigious traveling exhibits, which means visitors might see works by Western painter Edgar Payne, pop artist Andy Warhol, realist Georgia O'Keeffe, or illustrator Norman Rockwell. The Crocker also has enormous amounts of international art, including 16th- and 17-century Dutch and Flemish masters, African and Oceanic art, and Asian artifacts that include Japanese armor and Chinese ceramics.

Cathedral of the Blessed Sacrament

Even if you're not religious, the Cathedral of the Blessed Sacrament (1017 11th St., 916/444-3071, www.cathedralsacramento.org, 10 A.M.–5:45 P.M. Mon.–Thurs., 10 A.M.–4 P.M. Fri., 10 A.M.–6 P.M. Sat., 10 A.M.–8 P.M. Sun.) is an awesome building. First dedicated in 1889, the cathedral is a stunning Victorian interpretation of French Renaissance architecture. Inside, it's hard not to gasp at the combination of frescoed arches, gleaming wooden sanctuary, and polished marble floor that makes this place positively glow. It's the home of Sacramento's Catholic diocese and also one of the largest cathedrals west of the Mississippi. A two-year restoration in 2005 did wonders for the interior's spectacular artwork (which includes works inspired by Giotto and Perugino, and a reproduction of Raphael's Sistine Madonna), but one of the most spectacular attractions is the hanging 13-foot crucifix suspended above the altar.

THEODORE JUDAH AND SACRAMENTO'S BIG FOUR

Thanks to a handful of ambitious and eventually wealthy men, Sacramento will always be a railroad town. The Big Four (known among themselves as "The Associates") were Leland Stanford, Mark Hopkins, Charles Crocker, and Collis P. Huntington, a group of Sacramento merchants who funded the western leg of the First Transcontinental Railroad.

The Big Four had no experience in building rail lines before they met Theodore Judah, an engineer who had built the Sacramento Valley Railroad from Folsom to the future capital in 1852. Judah dreamed of laying rails through the Sierra Nevada to link California with the East Coast. Most people thought he was crazy. However, after trekking through much of the Gold Country in the 1850s, Judah was positive the railroad could be built. He met with the four Associates and sold them on the idea. With investors firmly behind him, Judah went to Washington DC and lobbied Congress to pass the 1862 Pacific Railroad Act, which authorized and helped fund the Central and Union Pacific lines that would eventually link up at Promontory, Utah in 1869. Judah never got to savor his contribution to this mighty achievement. The Big Four cut him out of the company, and he never earned the wealth and power that Stanford and friends would reap over the years. The engineer eventually caught yellow fever and died crossing the Isthmus of Panama in 1863. He was only 37 years old. There's a small monument and plaque dedicated to Judah in Old Sacramento at the intersection of 2nd and L Streets.

The Big Four became railway tycoons through their investment in the deal. They eventually purchased the Southern Pacific Railroad in 1868 and merged it with the Central Pacific. Stanford, who started out as a Sacramento grocer before investing in Judah's project, eventually became governor of California in 1861 and later founded Stanford University near Palo Alto. Collis P. Huntington used his Central Pacific profits to form the Chesapeake and Ohio Railway in 1869. Mark Hopkins, who had operated a Sacramento hardware store with Huntington prior to investing in the Central Pacific, became the company's treasurer and is buried in the **Old City Cemetery** (1000 Broadway). Charles Crocker, who managed the railroad's construction after the Associates demoted Judah, became president of Wells Fargo and purchased Woolworth National Bank, which later became Crocker-Citizens Bank. Crocker was worth approximately $300-400 million when he died in 1888. To this day, the Big Four loom over Sacramento history like the snowcapped Sierra Nevada they eventually conquered.

For more info about the Big Four, check out the **California State Railroad Museum** (111 I St.) in Old Sacramento or pick up *The Associates: Four Capitalists Who Created California*, a fascinating tome by Richard Rayner.

To really appreciate the cathedral, take a tour (10 A.M. and noon Sun., 12:40 P.M. Wed., free), or buy the self-guided tour booklet for $5.

California Automobile Museum

Yes, Sacramento loves its railroads. But while trains helped win the West, the mighty automobile ushered in a new era of drive-ins, hot rods, and of course, the spacious backseat. Visitors can explore that legacy at the California Automobile Museum (2200 Front St., 916/442-6802, http://calautomuseum.org, 10 A.M.–6 P.M. daily, until 9 P.M. some Thurs.,

adults $8, seniors $7, students $4, children free). The exhibits include 160 classic cars mostly owned by private collectors, which means the autos here constantly change. Make sure to check out Jerry Brown's blue Plymouth Satellite from his first term as governor and Malcolm Forbes's 1984 Lamborghini Countach. Other cars you might see include two different Shelby Cobras, a 1923 Studebaker, a 1909 Ford Model T, and my favorite, a 1954 Chevrolet Corvette. The Going Green exhibit is also cool and includes information about building energy-efficient automobiles.

SACRAMENTO

MIDTOWN AND EAST SACRAMENTO

Sacramento's bucolic neighborhoods never seem to get much credit from outsiders—many were built before World War I when the "suburb" was still a strange concept. Today these beautiful neighborhoods form part of Sacramento's famous urban forest. Redwoods, camphor trees, beech, and maples make an emerald green canopy over rows of Craftsman bungalows, Italianate townhomes, and Neoclassical manors.

The city's most vibrant neighborhood is Midtown, a throbbing hive of boutiques, bars, cafés, and restaurants. The area lies roughly between 16th Street and the Capital City Freeway to the east, with U.S. 50 making the southern boundary. Just as in downtown, the JKL Corridor is the place to be. There's also the **Handle District,** a two-block area of upscale eateries centered around L and 18th Streets. Midtown's **Sutter District**—between 24th, P, and I Streets, and the Capital City Freeway—is

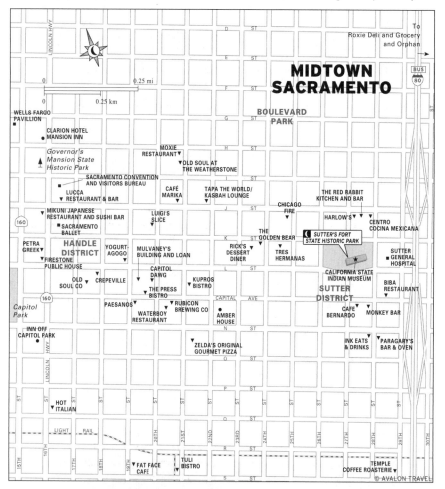

© AVALON TRAVEL

famous for the old fort constructed there in the 1840s, making this neighborhood one of Sacramento's oldest. The area also is chock-full of posh lounges.

A little farther north is **Boulevard Park,** a neighborhood built in 1905 on top of the Union Race Track. Boulevard Park is the place to ride a bike past two-story bungalow homes listed on the National Register of Historic Places or chill at the handful of coffee shops in this area. The American River flows along Midtown's northern limits; there's access to the American River Parkway at C and 20th Streets in **New Era Park.**

East Sacramento is dominated by **McKinley Park,** which spans more than six city blocks, and the swanky mansions and bungalows in the Fabulous Forties residential area where Ronald Reagan lived during his two terms as California's governor. This is one of the best places in Sacramento for a leisurely bike ride or a stroll at twilight. The neighborhood

bumps up against **California State University, Sacramento** along J Street and **Fair Oaks Boulevard.** Overall, East Sacramento is much more laid-back than Midtown but there's a fair amount of bars and restaurants along J and H Streets and **Folsom Boulevard** to the south.

◖ Sutter's Fort State Historic Park

It's easy to see why Sacramento's iconic adobe fortress has endured for 170 years. But Sutter's Fort State Historic Park (2701 L St., 916/445-4422, www.suttersfort.org, 10 A.M.–5 P.M. Tues.–Sun., adults $5, youth $3) wasn't always in such sparkling shape. Swiss immigrant and Sacramento founding father John Sutter Sr. built the fort in 1839 and planned to rule his 50,000-acre rancho from there. For almost 10 years, that's exactly what he did. Sutter's Fort was an important commercial post during the 1840s when the land baron exported crops, furs, liquor, and wool from

© CHRISTOPHER ARNS

Sutter's Fort was an important outpost during Sacramento's early days.

his colony. In 147 when the Donner Party got trapped in a terrible snowstorm, Sutter sent riders from the fort to rescue the starving pioneers. Ironically, it was another Sutter property that led to the fort's downfall. The place became a ghost town in 1848 when James W. Marshall (one of the land baron's employees) discovered gold at Sutter's logging outpost in Coloma. After years of decay, the fort was partially rebuilt in the 1890s by Native Sons of the Golden West, and the Park Service took it over in 1947. It's been restored to pre–Gold Rush condition and is an awesome place to take children. From the outside, a wide belt of grass surrounds the impassive white fortress; once inside the gates, you'll discover costumed docents spinning wool, pounding iron at the **Blacksmith Shop,** or perhaps cooking bread in a beehive adobe oven in the courtyard. Take a good look at Sutter's grim-looking cannons: They've actually never been fired to defend the fort. Kids will enjoy shopping for a memorable keepsake such as a handmade toy, some old-fashioned candy, or a harmonica at the **Trade Store** (10 A.M.–5 P.M. daily), and adults will like the handmade ceramics, books, and DVDs that explore Sutter's mark on California history. Docents are always on hand for lessons about the fort's past, and there's also self-guided tour.

California State Indian Museum

The story of California's native people is often forgotten when folks celebrate the Gold Rush. The California State Indian Museum (2618 K St., 916/324-0971, www.parks. ca.gov, 10 A.M.–5 P.M. Wed.–Sun., adults $3, youth $2) presents the layered and sometimes tragic history of the Native Americans who were slowly displaced by prospectors and European settlers. The museum's nondescript appearance (it looks like an extension of Sutter's Fort) sometimes flies under the radar for travelers. That would be a mistake. This museum does an admirable job of exploring California's 150 separate tribal groups and 64 distinct languages. The state's prehistoric population was one of the largest and most diverse in the Western hemisphere before Franciscan missionaries arrived. Sacramento tribal groups included thousands of Miwok, Nisenan, Patwin, and Northern Valley Yokut Indians. By the 20th century, disease had wiped out 90 percent of California's tribes, and the survivors struggled in poverty for many years. You can celebrate their memory and culture by viewing the museum's exhaustive collection of baskets, a redwood dugout canoe, hunting and fishing tools at least 2,400 years old, and beautiful ceremonial regalia. There's also a hands-on area where visitors can practice using native tools such as a mortar and pestle.

Fabulous Forties

The Fabulous Forties neighborhood (roughly 38–49th Sts. between H St. and Folsom Blvd.) was built during the first four decades of the 20th century. It was the golden age for American suburbia, and the Fab Forties certainly reflect a different, more bucolic time. Expect to see some of Sacramento's finest homes: a collection of custom-built manors, Tudor-style mansions, and Craftsman bungalows. When the Reagans refused to live in the Governor's Mansion during the late 1960s and early 1970s, they rented a Mediterranean-style villa on 45th Street. The expansive streets are some of the widest in Sacramento; the city's old streetcar line used to end here and needed the space to turn around. Simply put, the beautiful homes, towering trees, and old-money vibe makes the Fab Forties feel like an elite East Coast university campus. A bike route runs down M Street through the neighborhood's leafy heart and makes a perfect evening ride in East Sacramento.

BROADWAY AND LAND PARK

Among Sacramento's neighborhoods, this one holds the most promise. The long drag known as Broadway is a bit scruffier than polished Midtown. Expansion of U.S. 50 in the early 1960s created a giant concrete causeway that cut off Broadway from the Capitol area. Things are finally starting to improve, especially in the **Tower District** between Riverside Boulevard, 21st Street, W Street, and 1st Avenue, as new restaurants and coffee shops have started opening here.

Land Park is both a neighborhood and a sprawling expanse of greenery between Freeport Boulevard, Sutterville Road, Broadway, and I-5. This is Sacramento's largest developed park and the most family-friendly district. Two children's theme parks and the city zoo are located off **Land Park Drive.** Most of the shops and restaurants in this area are situated on **Freeport Boulevard** near 21st Street, and near **Sacramento City College** at the intersection with Sutterville Road. Many locals simply call this area "South Sacramento," but they may also refer to specific neighborhoods such as Curtis Park and South Land Park, which are in the general vicinity.

Sacramento Zoo

The Sacramento Zoo (Sutterville Rd. and Land Park Dr., 916/808-5888, www.sac-zoo.org, 9 A.M.–4 P.M. daily Feb.–Oct., 10 A.M.–4 P.M. daily Nov.–Jan., adults $11.25, seniors $10.50, children $7.25) opened in 1927 with just 40 animals. Back then, it was known as the William Land Park Zoo and displayed monkeys, raccoons, birds, and some deer. Things have definitely changed. Now you can visit 600 animals from 140 different species, including lemurs, lions, grizzly bears, reptiles, giraffes, and other creatures. No matter how you feel about zoos, it's hard to explain the sensation of locking eyes with a Sumatran tiger for the first time. For just $3, visit the new **Giraffe Encounter** (11:45 A.M. and 2 P.M. daily) to feed a small tree branch to the long-necked animals. It's some of the most fun you can have. To mix things up, download the zoo's **Art Tour** map from their website and keep an eye out for sculptures depicting different animal species throughout the facility.

Fairytale Town

Younger kids will fall in love with Fairytale Town (3901 Land Park Dr., 916/808-7462, www.fairytaletown.org, 9 A.M.–4 P.M. daily Mar.–Oct.; 10 A.M.–4 P.M. Thurs.–Sun. Nov.–Feb., adults $4, children $4, admission $5 on weekends). Inside the merry walls of this cheerful 2.5-acre theme park are miniature re-creations of notable children's fables and nursery rhymes. The **Storybook Park** has the Old Woman's Shoe, Mother Goose, Sherwood Forest, and many scenes from other fairy tales. There's also a little herd of farm animals that include fuzzy lambs living in Mary's schoolhouse, a brick house with three little pigs, several goats with a bridge in their pen, and Eeyore the miniature donkey.

Funderland Amusement Park

Funderland Amusement Park (1350 17th Ave., 916/456-0131, http://funderlandpark. com, 11 A.M.–5 P.M. Fri., 10 A.M.–5 P.M. Sat.–Sun. Feb.–mid-Mar. and Nov.; 11 A.M.–5 P.M. Wed.–Fri., 10 A.M.–6 P.M. Sat.–Sun. mid-Mar.–Apr. and Sept.–Oct.; 11 A.M.–5 P.M. Mon.–Fri., 10 A.M.–6 P.M. Sat.–Sun. Apr. 1–15; 11 A.M.–5 P.M. Mon.–Fri., 10 A.M.–6 P.M. Sat.–Sun. May–Labor Day, $1.75–1.95) is popping with kid-size rides. The most iconic attraction might be the **Funderland Train** that gives children (and parents) a leisurely tour around the park. That's just the beginning. Funderland has a bunch of carnival-style rides like the whirling **Tea Cups** or the **Dragon Coaster.** They might sound scary, but these rides are pretty toned down and shouldn't freak out your little ones. For something that everyone will enjoy, take a spin on the classic **Carousel,** which has been giving rides to Sacramento's kids for more than 60 years.

◖ Old City Cemetery

Ancient headstones at the delightfully creepy Old City Cemetery (1000 Broadway, 916/448-0811, www.oldcitycemetery.com, 7 A.M.–7 P.M. Fri.–Mon. in summer, 8 A.M.–5 P.M. Mon.–Tues. and Fri., 7 A.M.–5 P.M. Sat.–Sun. in winter) read like a who's who of Sacramento's 19th-century elite. The graveyard was established in 1849 with a 10-acre land grant and has some of California's oldest memorial plots. Since the Gold Rush, 25,000 pioneers and their families have been laid to rest in the Old City Cemetery; among the first were 600 victims of the city's 1950 cholera epidemic. John Sutter Jr., the founder of modern Sacramento, lies here, along with railroad tycoon Mark Hopkins, museum founder Edwin Crocker, and a rogues gallery of legislators, Civil War veterans, and three California governors. The cemetery is more than an old boneyard. Inside these hallowed grounds you'll find beautiful Victorian-era gardens, including the **California Native Plant Demonstration Garden.** The prosaic title doesn't do justice to the 125 species of native flowers and plants, including California poppies, fuchsias, buckwheat, and goldenrods. Across the cemetery is the **Sacramento Historic Rose Garden,** a plot filled with antique roses planted more than 100 years ago. The best time to visit the cemetery is before Halloween when you can take a guided **lantern tour** (weekends in mid and late October). If you go, remember this place is still a working cemetery and families do come in mourning. Make sure to respect the burial sites and ask for permission before taking rubbings of the headstones.

GREATER SACRAMENTO

Greater Sacramento is everything that's left over—the city's outer reaches beyond the urban grid. It's not really a scenic area, but you can find a surprising number of top-notch restaurants here, especially along **Fair Oaks Boulevard** just beyond East Sacramento. From Fair Oaks, take **Fulton Avenue** north to explore the city's best Middle Eastern restaurants. Continuing north, Fulton crosses **Arden Way;** head west to find the Arden Fair Mall and link up with the Capital City Freeway.

Heading north from Midtown, you'll follow 16th Street when it turns into **Del Paso Boulevard** and drive through the newly buffed brick facades of **Old North Sacramento,** another historic area shaking off decades of blight to open new eateries and shops. Farther north is **Natomas,** a neighborhood with a weird mix of aging suburban homes, ultramodern townhomes and apartments, and slick Mediterranean-style strip malls. Keep heading north on I-5 and eventually you'll find **Sacramento International Airport** amidst a sea of rice fields and river levees.

◖ American River Parkway

A trip to Sacramento wouldn't be complete without a hike along the American River Parkway (www.msa2.saccounty.net, 23 miles, easy/moderate). It's actually a series of paved trails that run through wetlands, oak woodlands, and several regional parks along the American River. The trails start at **Discovery Park,** a grassy 302-acre park at the confluence of the Sacramento and American Rivers and ends 23 miles near the city of Folsom. Along the way, you'll pass cyclists pedaling along river levees, families pushing strollers by the water, and plenty of dog lovers taking their pets for a walk. If you're hiking on the trail near Folsom, stop by the **Nimbus Fish Hatchery**

© CHRISTOPHER ARNS

The American River Parkway is a 23-mile-long playground for outdoor fun.

(2001 Nimbus Rd., Gold River, 916/358-2820, www.dfg.ca.gov) to check out dozens of tanks where the hatchery raises fingerling steelhead trout and salmon. The parkway has more than just hiking and biking trails; anglers will find plenty of fishing opportunities along the river, and boating enthusiasts can launch from various points along the river.

One of the more popular Sacramento-area parks actually runs through the separate town of West Sacramento. **River Walk Park** (651 2nd St., www.cityofwestsacramento.org, 0.5 mile, easy) features a paved pathway that runs along the river. As you walk the path, read the interpretive plaques to learn about the flora and fauna that inhabit this part of the Sacramento River ecosystem. Bring a cooler and have a picnic at one of the various picnic areas along the path, or bring your rod and tackle and walk out onto the fishing dock. A major boat dock lets private boaters moor at the park. River Walk Park also encourages visitors to jump out into the water for a refreshing swim in the river.

Discovery Museum Science and Space Center

The Discovery Museum (3615 Auburn Blvd., 916/575-3942, www.thediscovery.org, noon–4:30 P.M. Tues.–Fri., 10 A.M.–4:30 P.M. Sat.–Sun., adults $6–8, seniors and teens $5–7, children $4–6) is a kids' favorite. Future astronauts will enjoy exploring the starry skies at the **planetarium** (20 minutes, 1 and 3 P.M., Sat.–Sun.). In the **Nature Discovery Room,** you can check out birds, mammals, reptiles, fish, and amphibians that live in the exhibits, while the **Challenger Learning Center** teaches visitors about space exploration.

Entertainment and Events

Sacramento has a surprising amount of entertainment for a former railroad town. From bars and clubs to comedy and old-fashioned cinema to Broadway and ballet, the River City boasts attractions worthy of a much larger burg. That tradition goes back to the Gold Rush when prospectors and merchants demanded entertainment. The first performances were bawdy minstrel shows performed by semiprofessional vaudeville acts, and many often went bankrupt after a few shows. Things have come a long way since then. Today Tony Award–winning shows arrive just weeks after closing in New York, and critics routinely applaud boffo performances by local drama companies.

This city definitely knows how to party. Every second Saturday of the month, Midtown throws open its art galleries and hosts live bands for a rocking street fair. The capital's renowned jazz festival has received a much-needed facelift to include blues, country, and R&B. And don't forget the biggest event of them all—the California State Fair happens just up the street at Cal Expo every July.

NIGHTLIFE

Things have changed in Sacramento. Downtown and Midtown, once seedy pockets of urban decay, have rebounded over the past decade to become bustling hives of nightlife. More new bars and clubs seem to open every month. That means visitors have a wide array of choices. Downtown tends to skew more toward clubs and sleek lounges, while Midtown tends toward pubs and bistros that stay open late.

Bars and Clubs

Before the city's Midtown district began its current renaissance, Sacramento's hottest lounge was **Harlow's** (2708 J St., 916/441-4693, www.harlows.com, 5:30 P.M.–close

daily, tickets $10–30, shows 21 and over). Time has passed and Sacramento's nightlife has grown up, but Harlow's is better than ever. The sleek, urbane interior has a big-city feel that might remind visitors of New York or Los Angeles. No T-shirts and flip-flops here; make sure to spiff up before rubbing elbows with the swanky crowd at this joint. Despite the moneyed vibe here, the live acts aren't pretentious, ranging from local favorites like Bay Area cover band Tainted Love and Irish rockers Young Dubliners to hot new DJs at the city's Electronic Music Festival, usually hosted by Harlow's in May. Harlow's often draws a line, especially if there's a show, so arrive early if you don't want to wait.

Just steps from the Capitol, **Mix Downtown** (1525 L St., 916/442-8899, www.mixdowntown.net, 4 P.M.–midnight Tues., 4 P.M. –2 A.M. Wed. –Fri., 6 P.M. –2 A.M. Sat. –Sun.) is a great place to rub elbows with Sacramento's power elite. Lobbyists and lawmakers alike come here after hours to let loose or haggle over state business—and it's also a great spot to meet friends for a night on the town. Inside, the polished wooden ceilings and wall panels give the decor a minimalist, European vibe with a Californian flair. On the rooftop patio, you'll find fire pits and comfy chairs for relaxing with a glass of wine or a beer; perfect after a long day of strolling around Sacramento's sidewalks. While Mix occupies a cavernous building, there are still plenty of nooks and intimate crannies perfect for group outings or date night for two. Mix is popular on weekends, and there will definitely be a line if you arrive later in the evening.

There's no secret password, but the **Shady Lady Saloon** (1409 R St., #101, 916/231-9121, http://shadyladybar.com, 11 A.M.–2 A.M. Mon.–Fri., 9 A.M.–2 A.M. Sat.–Sun.), feels like a speakeasy with a Gold Rush vibe. Inside,

inside the Shady Lady Saloon

bartenders wear vests and garters on their sleeves while serving up libations with names like White Linen or Horse Neck. There's a stylish decadence to this bar's decor; ornate wallpaper glows red behind muted old-fashioned lights while silver chandeliers gleam overhead. There's also live music every day of the week, and you can catch a variety of local acts, from country to reggae to trip-hop. If the redbrick exterior looks like a refurbished warehouse, you're not far off; it's right in the heart of downtown's up-and-coming R Street Historic District, Sacramento's old industrial district. Shady Lady also serves dinner, and the Southern-themed menu is delicious; get there a little earlier because service can lag once the cocktail crowd arrives.

A great place to rack 'em up is **Blue Cue** (1004 28th St., 916/441-6810, www.bluecue. com, 4 P.M.–2 A.M. daily). It's part lounge and part sports bar. They have pool tables and big screens playing a couple of sporting events.

Weekends get busy with a DJ on Friday and Saturday, and the place turns more into a meat market, while weekdays are more chill and better for just knocking some billiards around.

Can't wait to throw down some dance moves? **The Park Ultra Lounge** (1116 15th St., 916/442-7222, www.theparkdowntown.com, 9 P.M.–1:30 A.M. Fri.–Sat.) is a swanky hot spot for the city's power elite to rub elbows and grind it out on the floor. The place has three bars, an outdoor patio, and a two-way mirror in the bathroom that usually inspires double-takes. It's definitely not cheap fun and be ready to pay at least $15 to get in. Once inside, the drinks are usually between $10–15. The music tends to be Top 40 hits or DJs.

With sleek faux marble bars, modernist furniture, and Surrealist art on the wall, **District 30** (1016 K St., 916/737-5770, http://district-30sacramento.com, 9:30 P.M.–3 A.M. Wed.–Sat.) wouldn't be out of place in either Vegas or Manhattan. Whoever built this place didn't spare any expense, down to the three-foot disco ball over the spacious dance floor. They play copious amounts of Euro-style electronica here, so it's a good place to get your Oakenfold or Paul Van Dyk fix on. They have live DJs every weekend, and D30 (as some locals have started calling it) stays open later than other places.

For a faux grungy watering hole there's **KBAR** (1000 K St., 916/446-9800, www.paragarys.com, 11 A.M.–midnight Mon.–Wed., 11 A.M.–2 A.M. Thurs.–Fri., 9 A.M.–2 A.M. Sat., 9 A.M.–midnight Sun.), which strives for a neo-Seattle hipster vibe. I think they pull it off, right down to the Pop Art murals plastered all over the wall. For a true urban experience, grab a cocktail and sit outside as the light-rail train rattles by. KBar can get a little busy—it's right in the middle of downtown near the Sacramento Convention Center and the Capitol—so get there early for a table.

Parlare Euro Lounge (1009 10th St., 916/448-8960, www.parlaresac.com, 9 P.M.–2 A.M. Wed.–Sat.) looks like an Ikea with a bar. That's not a dig; this place is hip, modern, and sleek. Prepare to spiff up and don't wear tennis shoes or the bouncers might keep you out. There are two floors and sometimes there's a DJ playing, but the default tunes seem to be Top 40 hits and remixes. Yes, it's fancy, and the drinks aren't cheap, but Parlare is definitely one of the nicer spots for cocktails.

For a clubby sports bar vibe and youthful crowd there's **Barwest** (2724 J St., 916/476-4550, 11 A.M.–2 A.M. Mon.–Fri., 9 A.M.–2 A.M. Sat.–Sun.). With 15 flat-screen TVs hooked up with NFL Ticket and a digital jukebox, this place rocks on football Sundays. You'll find two floors with bars on both bottom and top levels, 14 beers on tap, leather booths, and a trendy slew of sleek touches to the decor. Some locals call this place "Bro West" because the place sometimes feels like a frat party and there can

be a line on weekends. What can I say—don't be a party pooper and get inside.

Need more hops in your life? Head to **Pyramid Alehouse** (1029 K St., 916/498-9800, www.pyramidbrew.com, 11:30 A.M.–9 P.M. Mon.–Thurs., 11:30 A.M.–11 P.M. Fri., noon–10 P.M. Sat., noon–7 P.M. Sun.), which serves up 15 brews on tap like their popular Apricot Ale and Hefeweizen. It makes a great pit stop after checking out the State Capitol just a block away. If you make it by 4 P.M., take the free brewery tour to sample different Pyramid beers straight from the stainless steel vats. This place also serves pub grub like burgers, sandwiches and pizzas.

A good spot for beers after a long day is **Monkey Bar** (2730 Capitol Ave., 916/442-8490, www.monkeybarmidtown.com, 11 A.M.–midnight Sun.–Thurs., 11 A.M.–2 A.M. Fri.–Sat.). It's another mellow dive bar that's embraced pseudo-grungy decor. Most people come here after work, but it's really better later at night when you can drink pints on the outside patio during a warm summer's night or shoot pool in the back room. The bar has 12 beers on tap and reasonably priced well drinks during happy hour.

For shooting pool or catching a big game there's **R15** (1431 R St., 916/930-9191, www.paragarys.com, noon–2 A.M. Mon.–Fri., 9 A.M.–2 A.M. Sat.–Sun.). They've got four pool tables, and the bar area is bristling with flat-screen TVs. It gets loud as the night goes on, so arrive early if you don't feel like shouting. Pool tables go quickly on weekends.

For late-night grub and drinks, **Ink Eats and Drinks** (2730 N St., 916/456-2800, http://inkeats.com, 11:30 A.M.–1 A.M. Mon.–Tues., 11:30 A.M.–3 A.M. Wed.–Thurs., 11:30 A.M.–4 A.M. Fri., 9 A.M.–4 A.M. Sat., 9 A.M.–1 A.M. Sun.) will fill your belly. Most folks head to Ink once other bars close because it stays open later and serves food until closing time on weekends. Yep, you read that right; they serve food until 4 A.M. Isn't it really breakfast at that point? Late happy hours (starting at 10 P.M.) are another reason to dig this joint.

From outside, **The Golden Bear** (2326 K St., 916/441-2242, www.goldenbear916.com, 11:30 A.M.–2 A.M. Mon.–Fri., 10 A.M.–2 A.M. Sat.–Sun.) looks like someone's front porch. That's about right because the vibe here is friendly and chill, and visitors sometimes feel like they're right at home. That can be a bad thing, of course (see late Friday and Saturday nights), but the Golden Bear never takes itself too seriously. It's a flip-flops and shorts kind of place, a joint where you can spend a lazy afternoon studying the carbonation rise in a pint of Blue Moon. Nights get crowded and the music is pretty loud so it's not the greatest spot for a conversation, but better for letting loose with a couple of cocktails. If you get hungry, try the diabolically delicious sausage and slaw pizza served until 9 P.M.

If a Seattle coffeehouse married a Vegas lounge, their baby would look like **Capitol Garage** (1500 K St., 916/444-3633, www.capitolgarage.com, 6 A.M.–midnight Mon.–Thurs., 6 A.M.–2 A.M. Fri., 8 A.M.–2 A.M. Sat.–Sun.). This espresso bar-nightclub serves coffee and cocktails all day long. Stop by for karaoke every Thursday and Sunday.

You're not hallucinating; those are mermaids swimming at **Dive Bar** (1016 K St., 916/737-5999, http://divebarsacramento.com, 4 P.M.–2 A.M. daily). Once bar-hoppers get past the random weirdness of mermaids cavorting above their heads (they usually show up between 8 and 9 P.M.), this place is just another sweaty watering hole with expensive drinks.

Another novelty watering hole is **Bull's Restaurant and Bar** (1330 H St., 916/235-8674, www.sacramentobulls.com, 11 A.M.–2 A.M. Mon.–Fri., 9 A.M.–2 A.M. Sat.–Sun.), where visitors can ride a mechanical bull. You'd think this kind of thing is right

The mermaids are real at Dive Bar.

© CHRISTOPHER ARNS

up Sacramento's alley (hello, cow town?), although the faux cowboy vibe does seem a little contrived after a while. Take a shot at the bull and then head somewhere else for the rest of your night.

DIVE BARS

An oldie but goodie, **Pre-Flite Lounge** (513 L St., #9, 916/441-7963, www.preflitelounge.com, 11:30 A.M.–9 P.M. Mon.–Wed., 11:30 A.M.–11:30 P.M. Thurs.–Fri., 2–10 P.M. Sun.) goes way back to a different era. During the 1970s and 1980s, airlines like Pan Am and Eastern (remember them?) had ticketing offices downtown. The Pre-Flite was next door. You could show up, punch your boarding pass, and knock back a cocktail before catching a taxi out to the airport. I suppose you could still do that, and this divey, retro watering hole still has a swinger-ish '70s vibe (right down to the weird fake fireplace) that makes it fun.

The **Townhouse Lounge** (1517 21st St.,

NIGHTLIFE TIPS

Sacramento is fairly safe after dark, and you'll have a great time enjoying the city's nightlife. However, before hitting the town, there are a few things to keep in mind. **Always keep your ID handy.** Try to keep a driver's license rather than a passport; a few bars won't accept them. Either way, bouncers at Sacramento's bars and nightclubs always check for ID so make sure to remember it. If you don't have a valid ID, it's nearly impossible to get in everywhere.

Have enough cash before arriving at bars and nightclubs. Most places accept credit cards for drink tabs, but you'll need to pay cover charges at some places and dive bars often only take greenbacks. If you can't find an ATM and need cash like it's yesterday, swing over to the **Golden 1 Credit Union** (1109 L St.) or **SAFE Credit Union** (2901 K St., Ste. 100) branches for slightly lower ATM charges for noncustomers.

Drink plenty of water, especially during warmer months or during festivals and concerts. Don't be afraid to ask bartenders for cups or bottles of water; it's important to stay hydrated and alert during your visit to the region. Sacramento summers often become hotter than the doors of Hades; thus, it's best to keep the liquids flowing.

If you're under 21, it's best to stay home. Like St. Peter at the pearly gates, bouncers won't admit anyone before their time. Restaurant servers and bartenders are equally strict; in other words, don't count on doing any underage drinking in Sacramento.

"Dram shop" liability rules have been defanged over the past few years, which means businesses are now rarely at fault if they oversell to a customer. Despite the weaker laws, bartenders will still cut you off in Sacramento if you're acting extremely drunk. They don't want the hassle of cleaning up after someone who went overboard.

Don't drink and drive! This advice should be obvious because of the serious implications, but I'll just say it again; don't get behind the wheel if you've been drinking. Taxis are everywhere in Sacramento, and cab rides won't set you back too much. A DUI usually costs around $6,000; a taxi should only cost $20. The Sacramento Police Department often runs sobriety checkpoints at strategic points around Midtown, so it's not worth trying to sneak home.

916/837-3374, 9 P.M.–1:30 A.M. daily) is a jack-of-all-trades. From outside, the neon facade looks like an old-school casino, the kind of place where Sammy Davis might headline. But this dive mixes things up. One night might showcase local DJs, and the next evening might host '80s Goth. There's often a cover, but it's not too spendy (usually $5–10). Sometimes they won't charge anything at all.

You haven't lived without visiting the Dirty Bird. That's what locals call **Club Raven** (3246 J St., 916/447-8142, 10 A.M.–2 A.M. daily), a proud East Sacramento dive that's shabby but cool all at the same time. I doubt much as changed here since the 1970s, and I mean that in a sincerely complimentary way. Drinks are cheap, and the service is usually friendly. Try to grab one of the mini-booths along the wall, and then fire up some Mellencamp on the jukebox.

Like a crusty East Coast bar, **Socal's Tavern** (5200 Folsom Blvd., 916/455-1646, 6 A.M.–2 A.M. daily) is a great place for a few pints, debating Super Bowl contenders, and the Holy Trinity of bar games: shuffleboard, darts, and pool. What else could you need? The vibe here is laid-back but friendly, and the East Sacramento location means it's more of a neighborhood bar so it doesn't get too crowded.

For cheap beer and awesome jukebox oldies there's **Back Door Lounge** (1112 Firehouse Alley, 916/442-5751, 9 A.M.–2 A.M. Mon.–Sat., 9 A.M.–8 P.M. Sun.). The location is

© CHRISTOPHER ARNS

Socal's Tavern

maybe the best thing about this place. It's tucked down an alleyway in Old Sacramento and feels like an old-fashioned hole-in-the-wall. If you're lucky, some codger will be playing tunes on the bar piano—just like a classic Western saloon. To be clear, this spot is definitely a dive, but in a secret speakeasy kind of way; the vintage mirrors and colorful paisley wallpaper behind the bar have Victorian flair, although the overstuffed leather booths probably date back to the '70s.

Flame Club (2130 16th St., 916/442-9622, 6 A.M.–2 A.M. daily) has cheap drinks, friendly bartenders, and a genuinely decrepit dive atmosphere. Drop by for some shuffleboard or plunk a few quarters into the jukebox. One downside: they only accept cash.

Club 2 Me (4738 J St., 916/451-6834, 7 A.M.–2 A.M. daily) serves stiff drinks and a lively atmosphere over in East Sacramento. You could say it's a "classy" kind of dive bar, if such a thing exists.

PUBS

At **de Vere's Irish Pub** (1521 L St., 916/231-9947, http://deverespub.com, 11 A.M.–2 A.M. Mon.–Fri., 9 A.M.–2 A.M. Sat., 9 A.M.–midnight Sun.), the walls practically breathe Irish history and for good reason: Most of the vintage photographs and mementos you'll see belong to the owners. If that's not authentic enough, all of the furniture and fixtures were designed and imported from Ireland, including the towering wooden bar that spans two rooms. The pub serves 20-ounce pints of Guinness, but you can also order from a sizable cocktail list. There's a full menu of Irish and British cuisine; the stew tastes like Dublin in every bite. One word of caution—de Vere's is one of the busier stops on Sacramento's singles scene, so be prepared for a meat market on weekends; otherwise, you'll enjoy unwinding here or watching sports from the array of flat-screen TVs on either side of the bar. To properly experience de Vere's pub culture, come for a whiskey dinner or a seasonal event like Bourbon Month; check the website for more information.

For pints at a true neighborhood pub there's the **Bonn Lair** (3651 J St., 916/455-7155, 11:30 A.M.–1 A.M. daily). Most East Sacramentans think of this place as their "local," and quite a few have their own personalized mugs hanging over the bar. They have several English and Belgian-style ales on tap, along with wine and Magners Irish Cider. They serve traditional English pub food (shepherd's pie, anyone?) and usually have English Premier League soccer (I mean, football) matches or rugby games on the big screen. If you feel like tossing some Bullseye, there's a decent-size area in back for darts.

Streets of London (1804 J St., 916/498-1388, www.streetsoflondon.net, 11 A.M.–2 A.M. daily) is another popular English-style pub. This one gets busier on weekends and the crowds skews a little younger; there's usually a line by 10 P.M. or so. You'll find a large patio out back, a fireplace inside with easy chairs, and two dart boards up front. Thirsty visitors should be satisfied with the vast brew selection of 16 different draughts on tap.

WINE BARS

Sacramento's wine bars are a study in contrasts—and heights. You can drink wine like it's 1860 again at **The Underground Tasting Room** (900 2nd St., 916/444-2349, http://theundergroundtastingroom.com, 11 A.M.–6 P.M. Wed.–Sun.). It's one of Old Sacramento's few shops that's on the city's original level, one story below street level, which makes for a memorable setting. You can either enter ancient brick archways into the tasting room or sit outside at wooden bistro tables on the Victorian-style patio. The wine comes from El Dorado producers Twisted Twig and Fenton Herriott Vineyards, but the best part of coming here is still the location.

After visiting Sacramento's underground, check out its rooftops. **Rail Bridge Cellars Penthouse Lounge** (921 11th St., 916/492-2530, http://railbridgecellars.net/penthouse, by appointment noon–5 P.M. Sat., noon–8 P.M. second Sat. of the month, noon–4 P.M. Sun., $10–20) is 14 floors above downtown in the Elks Tower, a towering Renaissance-style brick edifice built in 1926. From up here you can look out over the State Capitol and downtown's steel skyline. There's some backstory to the space; it was a private nightclub called Top of the Town during the 1940s and 1950s. Inside, the room is dominated by a huge chandelier and several ceiling-high windows. The Penthouse is operated much like a modern speakeasy. They only admit visitors with reservations, although it's easy to call ahead and book your spot. Rail Bridge produces its wines (cabernet sauvignon, pinot noir, zinfandel, and merlot are on the list) in an urban production facility in downtown Sacramento, and they are decent. But the view is spectacular, and you should make an effort to visit.

Feeling a little more epicurean in your evening pursuits? Head over to **58 Degrees and Holding** (1217 18th St., 916/442-5858, www.58degrees.com, 11 A.M.–10 P.M. Mon. and Wed.–Thurs., 10 A.M.–11 P.M. Sat., 10 A.M.–9 P.M. Sun.), an upscale eatery and wine bar in Midtown's Handle District. The wine list is stacked with European and Californian wines, including a few from Amador County, and the waitstaff is generous with dispensing knowledge about the vino. I think there's a good balance here between busy and chill; there's a plush seating area with mid-size flat-screens for watching big games, but you can also sit at the bar or bistro tables. It's a great place for couples and small groups.

GAY AND LESBIAN

Sacramento has a thriving gay and lesbian scene that revolves around Midtown. These places are all within a block of each other, so there's no need to go far. Midtown seems to be a tolerant place with few safety issues involving the gay and lesbian community.

The most established joint is **Faces** (2000 K St., 916/448-7798, www.faces.net, 4 P.M.–1:45 A.M. Mon.–Fri., 3 P.M.–1:45 A.M. Sat., 2 P.M.–1:45 A.M. Sun.). While it's definitely a gay club (they have male go-go dancers), it's actually really popular with the straight crowd. They have two floors, 15 bar stations, and a pool. Faces is notorious for their quirky theme nights, like Twilight Halloween, and accomplished DJs. They also have beer pong. A modestly strict dress code is enforced (no sagging or baggy clothes).

Badlands (2003 K St., 916/448-8790, www.sacbadlands.com, 6 P.M.–2 A.M. Mon.–Thurs., 5 P.M.–2 A.M. Fri.–Sat., 4 P.M.–2 A.M. Sun.) appears to have an urban grunge theme going on. If you're looking for a traditional gay club, this one is the place. This place has go-go dancers, a three-foot mirror ball, four bars, and an outdoor patio. They also hold a popular drag show every third Friday.

Mercantile Saloon (1928 L St., 916/447-0792, 10 A.M.–1:45 A.M. daily) has an outdoor patio, pool tables, a unisex bathroom, and a reputation for friendly confines. The Merc, as it's known around town, also pours some of the stiffest drinks. Straight locals seem to feel comfortable hanging out here.

The Depot (2001 K St., 916/441-6823, www.thedepot.net, 4 P.M.–2 A.M. Mon.–Thurs., 4 P.M.–4 A.M. Fri., 2 P.M.–4 A.M. Sat., 2 P.M.–2 A.M. Sun.) is a laid-back bar with fun theme parties, big-screen TVs, and pool tables. Note this bar is cash only.

Live Music

Sacramento's music scene has experienced a reboot in recent years. The River City has a long-held reputation for incubating badass Dixieland jazz bands at the old Jazz Jubilee Festival (now the Sacramento Music Festival), but rock and punk groups also once flourished in the capital. Sacramento's venerable grunge-punk scene

may be long dead, along with the clubs that promoted that era, but live shows are everywhere—from suburban parks to small clothing boutiques and art galleries during the Second Saturday street fair.

Sacramento is a regular stop for big-name tours swinging down the West Coast, and the city boasts several large concert halls and auditoriums. The most common venue for mainstream acts is **Power Balance Pavilion** (One Sports Pkwy., 916/928-6900, www.powerbalancepavilion.com). It's usually the place where Eminem, The Black Keys, Elton John, and Carrie Underwood will play when they come to town. Sacramento's NBA team (Kings) also plays here. Some folks claim the place is dated and it's often hit-and-miss for music, but most of the time Power Balance usually hosts damn good shows.

Try to get tickets for **Sacramento Memorial Auditorium** (1515 J St., 916/808-5291, www.sacramentoconventioncenter.com) when

© CHRISTOPHER ARNS

Sacramento Memorial Auditorium

LOCAL MUSICIANS

Sacramento may not be a huge music town like Austin or Nashville, but a few major bands and some hot up-and-comers first hung out their shingle here.

- **Cake:** Cake is an alternative band known for songs like "The Distance" and their cover of "I Will Survive." Founding member John McCrae grew up in Sacramento and started the band after a short stint playing music in Los Angeles. Since 1991 when McCrae formed the band, Cake has released six albums, including two platinums and one gold.

- **The Deftones:** The title of "most famous" Sacramento band is up for debate, but The Deftones have to be somewhere near the top of the list. Three of this alt-metal rock band's founding members went to Sacramento's McClatchy High School together, but eventually cut their teeth playing on the road around Sacramento. The band formed in 1988 and has released seven albums.

- **The Golden Cadillacs:** A kick-ass local act, they've got a bouncy country sound that evokes early Johnny Cash. Their debut album dropped in 2009, and since then Golden Cadillacs often play around Sacramento.

- **Jackie Greene:** Known for bluesy Americana rock with a slight resemblance to Bob Dylan, Greene grew up and went to high school in Cameron Park, a sleepy community about 30 minutes east of Sacramento. His songs have played on network TV shows and the Oscar-winning soundtrack to *Brokeback Mountain*.

- **Oleander:** This post-grunge band had roots in the 1990s alternative wave. Founding members Thomas Flowers and Doug Eldridge met while working at Fat City Bar and Café in Old Sacramento before putting together a band. They eventually released four studio albums, played at Woodstock '99, and had one song airing on popular TV show *Dawson's Creek*.

- **Papa Roach:** Many people think the platinum-selling rock band hails from the capital, but they don't. The band members actually grew up in and went to school in Vacaville, about 32 miles southwest of Sacramento.

- **Sea of Bees:** Bees is another band of the moment with a debut album released in 2009. They play regularly at Austin's SXSW Music Festival. Every few months, you can catch their smoky indie sound at Bows and Arrows Collective or joints around town.

- **Sister Crayon:** This newish indie band released its first album in 2010. Lead singer Terra Lopez croons with a haunting, almost mournful voice; imagine a hybrid love child spawned by Portishead and Sarah McLachlan.

- **Steel Breeze:** This anthem rock band had 15 minutes of fame in 1982 when their single "You Don't Want Me Anymore" peaked at number 16 on the *Billboard* 100.

- **Tesla:** Formed in 1984, this is Sacramento's reigning godfather of heavy metal bands. The group has toured with David Lee Roth, Alice Cooper, and Def Leppard; they've also produced eight albums of which they have sold 14 million copies.

headliners play this classic Art Deco concert hall. The Memorial first opened in 1927 and has hosted acts like the Beach Boys, the Rolling Stones, Michael Buble, and Death Cab for Cutie. Governors have hosted inauguration balls under the glowing gilded columns and archways, and the acoustics aren't bad for an 80-year-old building.

A fantastic outdoor music venue is **Raley Field** (400 Ballpark Dr., West Sacramento, 916/371-4487, www.raleyfield.com). Home of Sacramento's AAA baseball team, it's a fairly new stadium with a view of Old Town. Headliners hit this place often; past acts include Dave Matthews Band, The Black Eyed Peas, Journey, Zac Brown Band, and Lady Gaga.

It's been hard to keep track of Sacramento's small music venues as more seem to operate at nontraditional places like bistros, art galleries, and bars. **Marilyn's on K** (908 K St., 916/446-4361, www.marilynsonk.com, 4:30 P.M.–1:30 A.M. Tues.–Fri., 6 P.M.–1:30 A.M. Sat.,) is a hole-in-the-wall where local bands play Wednesdays and Fridays; it's where perennial Sacramento favorites like Jackie Greene, Mother Hips, Kate Gaffney, and The Pinder Brothers perform. The bar is pretty good about letting newcomers play here, but that also means it's hit-and-miss.

Fox and Goose Pub and Restaurant (1001 R St., 916/443-8825, www.foxandgoose.com, 6:30 A.M.–10 P.M. Mon.–Tues., 6:30 A.M.–11 P.M. Wed.–Thurs., 6:30 A.M.–midnight Fri.–Sat., 6:30 A.M.–3 P.M. Sun.) usually has a random lineup of indie rock bands, electro folk acts, and, once a month, traditional Irish jam sessions. The setting (English-style pub) attracts an unpretentious crowd.

Bows and Arrows Collective (1815 19th St., 916/822-5668, http://bowscollective.com, 11 A.M.–11 P.M. Tues.–Sat.) is one of Sacramento's newest venues to emerge from the post-grunge apocalypse, and it's leading the trend among Midtown venues that are half gallery or clothing boutique, half café or bar. Walls are plastered with artwork from local Pop Art and modernist painters, and the back patio is practically an urban jungle decked out with vintage patio furniture. Sea of Bees, Golden Cadillacs, and Autumn Sky often perform here.

Blue Lamp (1400 Alhambra Blvd., 916/455-3400, 7 P.M.–2 A.M. Thurs.–Sat.) has a stripped down, edgy kind of vibe with local artwork on the wall. The music is fairly eclectic; bands include hard-core punk like Battalion of Saints and Kill the Precedent, cover bands like Cash Prophets, and singer/songwriter types like Mercies.

Press Club (2030 P St., 916/444-7914, 10 A.M.–2 A.M. daily), just off 21st Street, stays versatile with electronica, folk, rock-anthem bands, and hip hop. Come here for the tunes and stay for cheap tallboys of Pabst Blue Ribbon.

The Old Ironsides (1901 10th St., 916/443-9751, www.theoldironsides.com, 8 A.M.–midnight Mon., 8 A.M.–2 A.M. Tues.–Sat.) is a no-frills dive bar on the outskirts of downtown. This space first opened in 1934 (nabbing Sacramento's first liquor license after Prohibition), and the dark-wood ceiling beams evoke a cave-like vibe that still feels cozy. It's a great place to sit at the bar and catch local bands like Ghost River and Armed Forces Radio.

If Bob Dylan traveled back in time and opened a speakeasy, it would look like the **Torch Club** (904 15th St., 916/443-2797, www.torchclub.net, 2 P.M.–2 A.M. Tues.–Sun.), another old-school dive bar from 1934 cranking out local music. It's possible to catch live acts on the small retro stage almost every day.

Comedy

Is it surprising that Sacramento has three major comedy clubs? It shouldn't be. The city draws well-known comedians, especially at **Punchline** (2100 Arden Way, 916/925-5500, www.punchlinesac.com, shows Wed.–Sun., tickets $15–35). Guys and gals you've probably seen on late-night TV will perform here. Expect to find funny people like Christopher Titus, Margaret Cho, Chris Rock, and Dana Carvey making jokes in front of that quirky Capitol mural onstage. Make sure to book tickets early online or by calling ahead, and arrive early to grab a table close to the stage.

Old Sacramento's funny bone is at **Laughs Unlimited** (1207 Front St., 916/446-8128, www.laughsunlimited.com, shows Wed.–Sun., tickets $3–24), a classic comedy dive close to the waterfront. Comedy heavyweights such as Jerry Seinfeld, Jay Leno, Bob Saget, Dennis

Miller, and Paul Reiser have made stops here. Local comedian Jack Gallagher also regularly performs. Note that there's a two-drink minimum, which is actually perfect because it helps wash down the greasy appetizers they serve here.

If you're a sucker for improv comedy, head to the **Sacramento Comedy Spot** (1050 20th St., 916/444-3137, http://saccomedyspot.com, shows Wed.–Sun., tickets $10). Attend an improv class to sharpen your comedic skills or watch the mostly local and occasionally national acts run through their skits. It's open to all ages, but note that shows can get a little salty sometimes for kids.

Casinos

The closest place for Vegas-style fun is **Thunder Valley** (1200 Athens Ave., Lincoln, 916/408-7777, www.thundervalleyresort.com). Is it Swingers? I'm not sure it's even Sinatra. California's Indian casino culture (maybe just the casino culture in general?) usually panders to older folks on RV trips, and you'll see plenty of that crowd here. On the other hand, Thunder Valley does an admirable job of drawing weekend warriors away from Sacramento's downtown. The floor has 2,800 slot machines and 150 table games, and the casino claims the largest jackpot payout ($12 million) in California happened here. If winning makes you hungry, hit the three different restaurants, the buffet, or the food court. If you need a drink after betting on red instead of black (hey, it happens), the casino also has six different bars on the floor.

Can you spot the difference between a trotter and a pacer? If so, lay down a trifecta for **Cal Expo Harness Racing** (1600 Exposition Blvd., Lot D, 916/263-3279, www.calxharness. com). The sport might be an acquired taste for some who aren't used to horses pulling jockeys in little carts. But watching wheels bump and

horses strain for the finish line is pretty damn exciting. Drinks and food are typical stadium fare (hot dogs and light beer), but prices are reasonable compared to major sporting events. You can place bets on horses in every race, and when harness racing is over for the year, Cal Expo basically turns into an offtrack betting facility with a satellite feed. Sure, tracks have reputations as being somewhat seedy (thanks HBO), but I've often found harness races to be family-oriented at Cal Expo.

Limelight (1014 Alhambra Blvd., 916/446-2208, www.limelightcardroom.com, 9 A.M.–2 A.M. daily) is a fun little dive bar in East Sacramento with an adjoining 24-hour card room. Games include hold 'em, lo ball, and blackjack.

CINEMA

During the late 1940s, catching a flick in Sacramento used to be a big deal. Dozens of theaters, each with at least 1,000 seats, once lined downtown's J and K Streets. Now, only a handful of those grand movie palaces remain. But you don't have to head for the multiplex; Sacramento still has several great movie houses, including a couple of vintage theaters.

Movie purists still grimace when talking about **The Tower** (2508 Land Park Dr., 916/442-0985, www.thetowertheatre.com, adults $9.50, matinee $6.50, student $6.50, seniors $6, youth $5.50). You see, classic movie palaces only had (and have, in the Crest's case) one screen. But multiplexes make more money (more screens, more eyeballs, more tickets—you get the idea). By the 1980s, Tower management decided to revamp the 1938 theater with three smaller screens. Thankfully, they left the iconic Art Deco spire intact on the exterior. Despite the Tower's "demise," it's definitely the best place to catch indie flicks in Sacramento and often plays movies that don't show at the Crest.

If watching pro wrestling inside a vintage movie house sounds fun, check out **The Colonial** (3522 Stockton Blvd., 916/456-7099, www.colonialtheatre.biz). I assume wrestling pays the bills, but man, this joint could be something. Neon glows from the sideways-facing Art Deco marquee, casting a greenish glow onto the sidewalk. Inside, it's not large like the Crest or as flashy, but there's a single screen and elegant red velvet chairs. They occasionally have live music and horror film festivals, but mostly host live wrestling. For now, the owners also rent out this classy 1940s theater for corporate events and private parties. It's rare that something noteworthy happens here, but occasionally they'll surprise you. Check the website for upcoming events and ticket prices.

Sometimes, movies just look better when everyone on-screen is 50 feet tall. Or better yet, they're in 3D. The **Esquire IMAX Theater** (1211 K St., 916/443-4629, www.imax.com/sacramento, $8–17.50) is usually showing at least one blockbuster on their Godzilla-sized screen, although I also get thrills from watching animal documentaries like *March of the Penguins* and *Born to Be Wild* here. Generally, 3D movies are a few bucks extra than the standard ticket price, and of course, you have to wear the funny glasses. Visitors might look at a map and say "huh?" when trying to find this place. It's actually in the Sacramento Convention Center complex; the 1200 block of K Street becomes a pedestrian walkway and that's where you'll find the Esquire. Look for the neon marquee. I suggest getting there a little earlier to park and find your way.

Big screens: check. Popcorn: yep, got that too. Reclining in the front seat (or back, I'm not judging) of your car? That's the best part about **West Wind Sacramento 6 Drive-In** (9616 Oates Dr., 916/363-6572, www.westwinddriveins.com, adults $5–7.00, kids $1). Come park and watch new releases from the parking lot of this local favorite. You'll need to drive about 10 minutes east of downtown to get here, but it's worth it to see the latest hits. For some reason, there's a persistent rumor going around town that West Wind is about to close—don't believe it. Folks have been saying so for at least 10 years (in desperation, the owner finally hung up a sign that said, "Yes! We're Still Open!"), so keep that in mind if someone tries to convince you otherwise.

How about watching movies in the park? **Screen on the Green** (http://sacscreenonthegreen.com, weekends, July and Aug., free) shows classics a few times every summer at select parks in East Sacramento, Midtown, and Natomas. This annual string of events is great for bringing little ones to see films like *The Wizard of Oz* or newer favorites like *Madagascar*. Sometimes they also show R-rated flicks; check the website in early July when they post the new schedule.

◖ The Crest Theatre

The Crest (1013 K St., 916/442-7378, www.thecrest.com, adults $9.50, children $6) first opened in 1913, when it was known as the Empress. In 1918, the name changed again when a new company took over the theater and called it the Hippodrome; it wasn't renamed again until the late 1940s when the marquee crashed to the sidewalk, killing a pedestrian. Under new management, the Hippodrome was revamped and renamed the Crest. A century later, the Crest is still a beautiful place to watch the silver screen or see a play. At night, you can see the multistory neon facade from several blocks away; inside, the glittering interior still looks like a 1940s movie house decked out in gold leaf Art Deco trim. Shows include indie films on the Crest's single screen, French and Jewish film festivals, concerts with legends like Dave Brubeck and B. B. King, and live comedy acts from top-notch comics like Paula

© CHRISTOPHER ARNS

A light-rail train passes The Crest Theatre downtown.

Poundstone, Joe Rogan, Carrot Top, and Lisa Lampanelli.

THE ARTS

Sacramento's first playhouse was a canvas tent called the Eagle Theatre. Built in 1849, it went bankrupt four times and eventually shut down (in mid-performance, no less) during the Great Flood of 1850—three months after opening. Sacramento's theater scene was a little more resilient. At least 23 other playhouses opened over the next 60 years after the Eagle's untimely end, and the capital still has a lively theater tradition today.

Some of the most intriguing cultural events go down at **Sacramento State** (6000 J St., 916/278-4323, www.csus.edu/sfsc/ticketoffice, $8–20), the capital's only four-year institution and part of the California State University system. Here the University Union hosts everything from cultural events like African dance

troupes, string quartets, and jazz ensembles to random performances by men juggling chainsaws. Usually there's a monthly film screening where they show recent big-screen releases. Events at Sac State (as it's known locally) get overshadowed because the Union isn't a glamorous venue like the Mondavi Center at UC Davis, but the variety here is astounding.

Theater

The **California Musical Theater** (916/557-1999, www.calmt.com, $19–73) brings the Big White Way to Sacramento every year. Shows have included Broadway favorites like *Billy Elliot, Les Misérables, Phantom of the Opera, Wicked,* and many more. These productions boast professional Broadway actors who can belt out tunes with the best of them. The company uses the Wells Fargo Pavilion (1419 H St.), the Cosmopolitan Cabaret (1000 K St.), and the Community Center Theater (1301 L St.) for shows. Each venue is drastically different. The Cosmopolitan produces dinner theater where patrons sit at small bistro tables to watch small-ensemble comedies and solo acts. The Community Center Theater traditionally has the big Broadway productions. And the Pavilion is my favorite when the music circus is in town. Never heard of a music circus? It's Sacramento's take on theater-in-the-round. Shows include family favorites like *Peter Pan, Spamalot,* and *Annie.* Even though many folks outside of Sacramento haven't heard of CMT, the tickets go fast every season. Check the website in advance if you're planning on visiting.

For off-Broadway plays, check out **Capital Stage** (2215 J St., 916/995-5464, http://capstage.org, $18–32). Shows are critically acclaimed; the *Sacramento News and Review* has named Capital the best professional theater in the region, and the performances here are usually crisp and inspired. Each season is filled with award-winning shows such as *American Buffalo, Boy Gets Girl,* and *Jesus Hopped the 'A'*

Train. For more than 10 years, the company performed on the *Delta King* before moving into Midtown's Old Armory building in 2011. Expect to watch productions fresh from New York performed by some of Sacramento's best local actors. Among the shows, drama nerds will recognize playwrights like David Mamet, Sam Shepard, Neil LaBute, and Rebecca Gilman. Shows sell out quickly so skim the website before coming to town.

B Street Theatre (2711 B St., 916/448-9707, www.bstreettheatre.org, $27–35) is a great place to catch Tony Award–winning plays with edgy plotlines. Shows range from comedic farces to complex dramas. Past productions have included *God of Carnage, Red,* Arthur Miller's *The Price;* if you enjoy the heavy stuff, check out the company's B3 series for more serious themes. B Street is planning a move soon to a new venue on Capitol Avenue in Midtown; check the website or call to pin down its current location.

For something a bit lighter there's **Suspects Murder Mystery Dinner Theater** (1000 Front St., 916/443-3600, www.suspectstheater.com, $39.50–43.20). Everyone is involved during these who-done-its. Actors and guests mingle unknowingly (for the guests at least) as mysterious events unfold. Your waiter? He might get whacked. The charming gentleman at your elbow? He suddenly becomes a detective. And anyone else might be the killer. A prize is awarded for solving the crime. The shows take place aboard the *Delta King* on Old Sacramento's embarcadero and seating begins promptly at 7:30 P.M. For an extra treat, book an overnight package and stay in the riverboat's hotel.

Classical Music and Opera

Sacramento has Broadway, ballet, a world-renowned orchestra, and even an opera at the **Sacramento Community Center Theater** (1301 L St., 916/808-5181, www.

sacramentoconventioncenter.com). This modern concert hall is the home of the **Sacramento Philharmonic Orchestra** (916/732-9045, http://sacphil.org, $21–117), which performs works by Beethoven, Mozart, Mendelssohn, and Sibelius here almost every month. Directed by conductor Michael Morgan, the orchestra often accompanies visiting musicians like Rachel Barton Pine and Jeffrey Kahane. The Philharmonic also performs jointly with the **Sacramento Opera** (916/737-1000, www.sacopera.org, $19–79). The Opera performs here sporadically throughout the year, along with doing a few shows at the Crest and Folsom's Three Stages Theater. It's what you'd expect; arias, duets, and ensembles from all-star composers like Rossini, Puccini, and Verdi.

Can't get enough classical music in Sacramento? The **Camellia Symphony Orchestra** (Sacramento City College Performing Arts Center, 3835 Freeport Blvd., 916/929-6655, www.camelliasymphony.org, adults $28, seniors $24, student $15, children $8) has played strains of Tchaikovsky, Debussy, Gershwin, and Mozart since 1961. It doesn't get enough credit, frankly, as the other orchestra in town. Don't make the same mistake, because the Camellia's performances are legendary among locals. The 75-member volunteer symphony (named for Sacramento's official flower) performs at least four times a year during the fall, winter, and spring months and often mixes it up by playing jazz or blues arrangements. Special family concerts are free; check the website for an updated schedule.

Ballet

The capital's crown jewel of performing arts might be the **Sacramento Ballet** (1631 K St., 916/552-5800, www.sacballet.org, performances Thurs.–Sun., adults $15–68, children $9–32.50). This company's outstanding choreography stands toe-to-toe with San Francisco's ballet productions and stacks up amazingly

The Sacramento Convention Center can throw one heck of a party.

well. Each holiday season, they perform a rousing interpretation of Tchaikovsky's *Nutcracker* with a slew of young dancers from local schools. Other performances have included *Romeo and Juliet* and *Where the Wild Things Are.*

FESTIVALS AND EVENTS

Thanks to Sacramento's central location and predictable weather, people flock to the capital city for events and festivals. It seems something is happening every month, and many celebrate Sacramento's ethnic diversity with food and film festivals. On any given day, you might stumble across a beer festival at Raley Field, one of America's oldest dog shows at Cal Expo, a Shakespeare festival in the park, or a wine festival featuring offerings from hundreds of vineyards. Many events are also geared toward families, like children's book festivals and model train expos.

In keeping with Sacramento's stature as California's capital, every kind of celebration has a place in the River City. Midtown has several gay and lesbian events that welcome all participants. Every February or March, there's a Jewish Film Festival at the Crest. And in January, residents from every faith, age, and race take to the streets to March for the Dream, which commemorates Martin Luther King Jr.'s birthday.

For a complete guide to upcoming events in Sacramento check out www.sacramento365. com; click on Events before searching by date for what's happening in the River City. It's also not a bad idea to contact the **Sacramento Convention Center** (1400 J St., 916/808-5291, www.sacramentoconventioncenter.com). The Convention Center is the city's second largest venue for events behind Cal Expo, and there's usually something going on every week. Their website has a calendar with upcoming festivals and shows.

Year-Round Events

Food trucks band together for **SacToMoFo** (www.sactomofo.com), also known as the Sacramento Mobile Food Festival. You take one park, add a few dozen food trucks, and voila—that's the concept. It's pure awesomeness. In addition to many different kinds of chow, beer is served, and there's usually live music. The key is to check the website for the location, which changes whenever the festival happens every three or four months.

What began as a coordinated effort between a few art galleries has become a full-fledged street fair at the **Second Saturday Art Walk** (Midtown and downtown Sacramento, http://sacramento.downtowngrid.com, second Sat. of the month). It happens rain or shine, throughout downtown and Midtown. Bands play on the street, street vendors sell wares and food, and the general atmosphere is lively and fun. Most people now show up just for the street fair element, but art galleries are still very much engaged, and many of them have special showings of local artists for the event. Most of the action happens around a block at J and 20th Streets, which has a few hip bars, live blues and rock bands playing back to back, and a handful of boutique clothing stores that stay open later. The event lasts roughly 6–10 P.M. Unfortunately, the Art Walk has attracted some late-night crime in recent years. Bars become extremely crowded around Midtown on Second Saturday, and fights tend to break out between groups. Stay aware of your surroundings during this event and especially afterward.

They're robbing the train! "Desperados" frequently hold up the **Sacramento RiverTrain** (400 North Harbor Blvd., West Sacramento, 800/866-1690, www.sacramentorivertrain.com, adults $53–92, children $28–40), but it's just for fun. The rolling dinner theater stages mock train robberies and murder mysteries while guests ride through the Central Valley between West Sacramento and Woodland.

Most trips last about three hours round-trip as the train chugs leisurely along between 10 and 20 mph through rice fields and wetlands. The open-air cars give great views of costumed "bandits" that attack the train on **Great Train Robbery** trips, and two dining cars offer beer and wine during the ride. Live music plays in the Club Car, which has a laid-back beach theme.

Sacramento's premier venue for festivals is the **California Exposition & State Fair Center** (1600 Exposition Blvd., 916/263-3000, www.calexpo.com). When the gun show is in town, you'll find it at Cal Expo. It's also the place for evangelical concerts, RV and home shows, and hobby expositions. The site spans 350 landscaped acres, four large buildings, and eight smaller buildings surrounding a lagoon at the **Expo Center.** The **Miller Lite Grandstand** often hosts motorcycle races and monster truck shows. Cal Expo's website has a calendar of all upcoming events if you're interested in swinging by. If you make it out here, do check out the somber **September 11th Memorial Plaza,** featuring a large sculpted granite ball inscribed with the names of victims who perished on that terrible day. Debris from the World Trade Center also forms part of the memorial.

January

Every fall and winter, millions of birds visit the Central Valley during their yearly migration through the Pacific Flyway. Sandhill cranes, Canada geese, rails, thrushes, and starlings, just to name a few, land at the Cosumnes River Preserve south of the capital. Check them off your list at the **Winter Bird Festival** (209/366-7115, www.ci.galt.ca.us). They offer several birding tours ($15–75) into the preserve, along with food, art, educational displays, and guest speakers. Photographers will dig the **Wetlands Dawn Photo Tour,** which includes lessons on how to capture wildlife images with different ISOs, shutter speeds, and aperture lengths. If you enjoy spending time outdoors, and especially if stalking the valley's 250 bird species seems exciting, make sure to check out this festival.

For more than 30 years, **March for the Dream** has celebrated the legacy of Martin Luther King Jr. with a six-mile walk to the Sacramento Convention Center. Participation has swelled every year, and 20,000 people usually attend, filling the streets of downtown Sacramento. The march starts from three different places (Oak Park, Sacramento City College, and North Sacramento) before heading toward the Convention Center. Dress warmly; the march begins at 8:15 A.M., and January mornings are definitely brisk in Sacramento.

Great Train Expo (www.greattrainexpo. com, adults $7, children under 12 free) chugs into Cal Expo on tiny tracks. This traveling model train exhibit is the largest of its kind. Hundreds of vendors set up six different scales of Lionel, Atlas, Kato, Bluford, and Bachmann model railroads. Beginners and advanced modelers can take workshops in building better layouts.

February

Oh, the joy of chrome. The **Sacramento Autorama** (877/763-7469, www.rodshows. com/sa, adults $18, youth $10, children under 6 free, parking $10) is three full days of choppers, white-walled tires, and gleaming fenders at one of the oldest custom car shows around. Founded over 60 years ago, the Autorama features more than 450 custom cars, motorcycles, hot rods, and specialty vehicles from around the country. The event's organizers claim Sacramento is the Custom Car Capital of the World. There's no way to prove it, but visiting the Autorama might be enough to convince you.

There are more than 20 craft breweries within an hour of Sacramento and every year,

the city celebrates with **Sacramento Beerweek** (http://sacramentobeerweek.com, late Feb.). Roughly 300 brew-themed events take place over the course of 10 days at various restaurants and pubs. Sign up for beer tastings, special dinners with ale pairings (bacon with IPA, anyone?), brew classes, and brewery bus tours. The week wraps up with a huge craft beer festival at Cal Expo with more than 80 local and California brews.

The **Sweet Potato Festival** (www.svsncnw. org/spf.html, free) is just what it sounds like: an ode to the humble orange and yellow tuber. It's an entertaining event. Crowds of vendors are usually on hand to sell jewelry, skin products, and boutique clothing. There's also a puppet show, a choir, and sweet potato ice cream. But the festival's true mission aims to settle a burning question: Who makes the best sweet potato pie in town? The festival's yearly contest awards that very title—but only after everyone is fully stuffed with delicious, mouthwatering pie.

March

Schlep over to the Crest for the annual **Sacramento Jewish Film Festival** (1013 K St., 916/346-6467, www.sacjff.org). They usually play a good mix of documentaries, shorts and feature-length movies with ample coverage of the American Jewish experience and also themes involving Israel. Past films have included *Holy Land Hardball, This is Sodom,* and *Inside Hannah's Suitcase.* The festival has also taken place in February; check the website to confirm the schedule.

Listen to thunder fill the air at the **California Capital Airshow** (Mather Airport, 10510 Superfortress Ave., 916/876-7568, http://californiacapitalairshow.com, adults $20, youth $10, children under 6 free). Dozens of aircraft perform aeronautic and gravity-defying maneuvers over your head. Watch U.S. Air Force F-16 Thunderbirds almost touch wings as they fly in formation, massive C-17 and C-5 transport planes lumber down the runway, and a once top secret U-2 spy plane make an appearance. Paratroopers and several WWII fighters also make flybys. Interactive displays let once and future pilots crawl underneath cargo planes and sit in real cockpits. And the stunt pilots make an extra effort to meet with kids and give autographs.

Old Sacramento turns green during the **St. Patrick's Day Parade** (http://oldsacramento. com). More than 1,000 marchers participate, including Irish dancers, pipers, firefighters, police, and school bands, all striding across the ancient streets of the River City. The parade starts promptly at 1 P.M., but you should arrive earlier to find parking.

Every bookshelf needs at least one musty leather-bound tome to truly be respectable. The **Sacramento Antiquarian Book Fair** (Scottish Rite Temple, 6151 H St., 916/849-9248, www. sacbookfair.com, general admission $5) will hook you up. More than 60 vendors sell thousands of rare and out-of-print books, maps, and photos. They also offer free appraisals, *Antiques Roadshow*–style, if you've got an old book to sell. Dealing books makes a person hungry, so the fair has food vendors on hand. Parking in the Scottish Rite Temple lot is free.

Here's a fun fact: Sacramento's official flower has been the camellia since 1941 and is known as Camellia Capital of the World. The **Sacramento Camellia Show** (Memorial Auditorium, 15th and J Sts., www.camelliasocietyofsacramento.org, free) celebrates the city's flower power. One of the show's highlights has to be the gardening contest. Entrants can claim prizes for Best Seeding, Best Arrangement, and Best Fragrant Bloom, along with 49 other awards. It's more dramatic than the Oscars.

April

For Earth Day, help the environment and sign up for **Creek Week** (www.creekweek.net). The Sacramento Area Creeks Council started this fun event to clean up more than 20 of Sacramento's urban waterways, and it's turned into a celebration of green values. Volunteers get a free lunch and T-shirt to help remove debris, trash, and other detritus from the city's creeks. Once the work is over, there's a concert with green exhibits, activities, and contests.

Vegans, unite at the **Sacramento Earth Day** (Southside Park, www.sacramentoearthday.net) for some tempeh tacos and vendors waxing eloquently about methane digesters. Food, live music, and dozens of informational exhibits line the park in the name of raising awareness about sustainability. The grub is mostly from local farmers, and yes, it's 100 percent vegan.

Fiesta de la Familia (Cal Expo, http://festivaldelafamilia.org, adults $10, seniors $7, children under 13 free) celebrates Sacramento's Latin communities with an explosion of dancing, art, music, and food. This multicultural event highlights culture from the Caribbean, Central America, South America, Mexico, and Spain. You can watch salsa and even learn Spanish at the fiesta's Casa de Espanol.

Sacramento International Film Festival (www.californiafilm.net, $10–12 per show, festival passes $50–100) has lofty goals. For 20 years, the organizers have sought to make Sacramento the capital of California's indie film scene. They're on the right track. The films are a mash-up of documentaries focusing on global issues, minorities, and California history, plus a healthy amount of time devoted to local up-and-comers. Showing flicks at the Crocker Art Museum (216 O St.) also doesn't hurt. Past films have included *The Legacy of Pat Brown, Being Elmo,* and *Silver Tongues.* In addition to the Crocker, showings happen at the Artisan (1901 Del Paso Rd., 916/929-9900, www.artisansacramento.com) in North Sacramento.

Run by one of the oldest kennel clubs in the country, the **Sacramento Kennel Club Dog Show** (www.calexpodogshow.com, adults $10, seniors and youth $8.50, children free, parking $10) is a weekend dedicated to the most well-behaved canines in the country. Blow-dried, brushed, and peppy breeds from poodles to Irish setters trot around Cal Expo for a long weekend to showcase their talents. The show first started judging Fidos in the 1920s and now attracts hundreds of entries. Whatever you do, this dog show is for competitors only, so you must leave pets at home.

If you dig a forward roll and playing up the neck, the **Banjo-Rama** (www.banjo-rama.com, $25–55) is the place to be. It's three days of jams, shows, and workshops for folks looking to finally learn clawhammer style or perfect their bluegrass picking. World-class banjo players such as Dick Martin and Bill Lowrey have headlined, including a few local and West Coast banjo bands. Tickets can be purchased online, and proceeds benefit Sacramento charities.

May

Something about May means drinking beer for Sacramentans. Two different brew festivals take place. The larger of the two events is the **Raley Field Brewfest** (www.raleyfield.com, $30–50). At least 50 breweries set up tents on the green outfield at Sacramento's minor league baseball stadium, pouring ales, lagers, bocks, and porters. Expect to taste beer from local breweries such as Lagunitas, Sudwerk, River City Brewing, Rubicon, and the Auburn Alehouse, along with interlopers like North Coast and Anderson Valley from Mendocino County. There's also live music and for a few extra bucks you get food.

Only craft beers from California, Oregon, and Washington get poured at the **West Coast Field Brewfest** (Miller Park, 916/924-3836, www.matsonian.com/wcbf/home.html, $35–95, designated drivers $5). Grab a glass, catch some sun, and enjoy tasting hundreds of entries

in the fest's Commercial Craft Competition. Food is served and there's live music. Try to arrive early; the beer starts to run out by mid-afternoon.

Founded by local food impresario Frank Fat, the **Sacramento Pacific Rim Festival** (Old Sacramento and Downtown Plaza, www.pacificrimstreetfest.com, late May, free) is an explosion of colorful costumes, music, and food from a dozen Asian Pacific countries. Performers include beautiful lion dancers, Korean drum squads, Filipino martial artists, and Indian fusion musicians. The food is pretty damn good, maybe the best you'll find at a Sacramento street fair.

The city's other yearly (and often forgotten) carnival is the **Sacramento County Fair** (Cal Expo, 1600 Exposition Blvd., 916/263-2975, www.sacfair.com, adults $5, children under 13 free). Locals love this event because it's a cheaper and less hectic version of the State Fair. It's more like something you'd find out in the Gold Country, and because it happens over Memorial Day weekend, there's a festive patriotic vibe in the air. Just because it's small doesn't mean there's less fun to be had. The fair has more than 50 rides, a junior livestock auction, bull riding, and a demolition derby. Leave the smokes outside the gates; there's no smoking allowed at the fair.

For one long weekend every year, **Sacramento Music Festival** (Old Sacramento, www.sacjazz.com, end of May, adults $20–100, youth $15–50) turns Old Town into one giant party. Bands play everywhere from the wooden boardwalks to train cars at the California State Railroad Museum. Formerly known as the Sacramento Dixieland Jazz Jubilee and the Sacramento Jazz Festival, you can still find every style of jazz imaginable—including classic, zydeco, big band, western, skiffle, funk, and so much more. Festival organizers have also added bands playing blues, bluegrass, rock, country, and R&B, giving the event an inclusive feel that all music lovers will appreciate. Some old-timers think the name change (and new kinds of music) is sort of lame, but it really just shows that Sacramento's music scene no longer needs to rely on jazz.

Another sign of progress: the city's electronica scene has come of age with the **Sacramento Electronic Music Festival** (Harlow's and Momo Lounge, 2708 J St., http://sacelectronicmusicfest.com, early May, $13–30), which has only been around since 2010 but already kicks ass. If you're in town, it's a must for beatniks. Held at swanky Harlow's and Momo Lounge, the music gets better every year and most of the acts (Little Foxes, Dusty Brown, Tel Cairo) are local.

You can't really call Sacramento's **Concerts in the Park** (Cesar Chavez Plaza, 10th and J Sts., 916/442-8575, http://downtownsac.org, 5–9 P.M. every Fri., early May–late July, free) a music festival, but it is freshly brewed live music. One entire city block shuts down and turns into several acres of booze and beats. These weekly music-thons are a summer rite of passage for Sacramento locals, who mark the turning of the seasons by the thump-thump tha-thump ricocheting off downtown's highrise buildings. For most local bands like ZuhG, Mumbo Gumbo, and Walking Spanish, playing the park concerts helped launch them into Sacramento's music scene. Parking is usually terrible, which is why most people ride their bikes (there's a secure bicycle corral if you're pedaling there).

June

For those who can't make it to Amador or El Dorado's wine country, **Raley's Grape Escape** (Cesar Chavez Park, 10th and J Sts., www.raleysgrapeescape.com, 4–7 P.M. first Sat. in June, $40–50) brings local vino to you. Best described as urban wine-tasting amidst a sea of steel high-rise buildings, this event has the boozy friendliness of a cocktail party. Wineries have included foothill favorites such as Madroña Vineyards, Ironstone Vineyards, and Boeger, along with a grip of Lodi producers such as Macchia and d'Art. Parking is typically terrible because it's downtown and you'll most likely get buried deep in some parking garage if arriving late.

The **French Film Festival** (www.sacramentofrenchfilmfestival.org, single tickets $10–16, festival passes $35–90) has been voted Best Film Festival several times by locals, and it delivers that mysterious je ne sais quoi that all French cinema seems to embody. By this time of year, being outside in Sacramento feels hot and sticky, making it easy to duck inside The Crest (1013 K St.) and overdose on newer flicks like *Polisse,* a film about cops in Paris, and classics like *Children of Paradise.* Films typically include a mix of mainstream filmmakers like Mathieu Kassovitz, Maïwenn, and Nicole Garcia with less heralded auteurs like Jennifer Devoldère.

Four parks in East Sacramento turn into concert venues for **Pops in the Park** (http://eastsacpopsinthepark.com, free). Although it's only been around for a few years, people flock to see classic rock and Beatles cover bands, Spanish flamenco fusion (for lack of a better term), and country. The crowd is heavy on families so kids kind of run amok, but the event also draws 20-somethings with stocked beer coolers.

"Cowboy Heaven" might be a better name for the **Western States Horse Expo** (Cal Expo, 1600 Exposition Blvd., www.horsexpo.com, adults $15–45, youth $5, parking $10). There's barrel racing and equestrian events, plus a horse sale. Workshops dispense horse sense about feeding older animals, how to tame bucking and biting, trail riding tips, and esoterically minded seminars on "Understanding the

Horse's Mind" and "The Secret Lives of Horse Trailers." Kids can mosey over to the young rider park for games and a petting zoo.

The **Women's Fitness Festival** (www.womensfitnessfestival.com, early June) kicks off with a 5K run through Midtown and downtown, passing iconic Sacramento landmarks like Sutter's Fort before finishing at the State Capitol. The event includes breakfast, free health screenings, and rows of booths. Sorry guys, no men allowed; just so you don't feel too badly, they also put the kibosh on strollers and pets. Check the website for entry costs when registration opens early in the year.

Come celebrate diversity at **Sacramento Pride** (Capitol Mall, 916/442-0185, www.sacramentopride.org, early June). There's a short parade down N Street that wraps up near the State Capitol where the festival happens. For $10, come watch live music onstage and browse the food vendors. You can also visit souvenir and artisan booths and learn more about HIV testing. Check the website for updates and schedules.

July

The granddaddy of all events is the **California State Fair** (Cal Expo, 1600 Exposition Blvd., www.bigfun.org, adults $12, seniors $10, youth $8). It's best described as an over-the-top beauty pageant for everything and anything Californian. It takes place for more than two weeks at Cal Expo, Sacramento's main venue for large events. You wouldn't believe what goes on here. Ever chowed down on deep-fried Twinkies? What about deep-fried Coke? You can at the State Fair, which first started nearly 160 years ago as meet-up between farmers to swap trade secrets and seeds. There's actually a small farm inside Cal Expo growing rows of waist-high squash, tomatoes, pumpkins, lettuce, soy, and cotton—all crops that flourish in California's $43 billion agriculture industry. The farm also boasts a cutting-edge aquaponics system in the greenhouse that turns fish poop into fertilizer for plants, which then filter water for the fish. Pretty cool stuff, and that's usually what the fair shows off: random exhibits that make visitors go "Wow!" You can learn about green building with recycled wood, watch the birth of baby piglets and lambs, and pet a nine-foot-long sturgeon that produces the world's finest caviar.

Every one of California's 58 counties hosts a 3D booth at the fair. Maybe the weirdest (and most creative) is Humboldt's Bigfoot display, celebrating the mythical forest dweller from the North Coast; other displays have included scenes from 19th-century Amador County and Placer County's outdoor recreation. Out on the midway, the fair boasts roughly 70 different heart-in-stomach rides with names like Turbo Force, Techno Jump, and Remix II, along with the iconic Sky Flyer swing ride. Back on the ground, head to the grandstand for thoroughbred horse racing, or check out live concerts on three different stages. The only bummer? Gang violence in the parking lot is a concern at night. It's rare, but just keep your eyes and ears open, and immediately walk away if you see crowds start gathering.

Men (and women) in tights perform the Bard's classics at the **Sacramento Shakespeare Festival** (William Carroll Amphitheatre, William Land Park, www.sacramentoshakespeare.net, adults $18, students and seniors $15). You get to chill out at the capital's largest developed park and watch classics like *Taming of the Shrew, Romeo and Juliet, Macbeth,* and *A Midsummer Night's Dream.* Every once in a while, they also slip in something different; *Count of Monte Cristo* and *Robin Hood* are two plays the company has performed in past years. Bring short lawn chairs for the grassy area and a light blanket in case the evening cools down.

Sacramento 4th of July Celebration (Cal Expo) is the largest fireworks display in the capital. Things kick off around 6 P.M. or so with live music (usually pop rock and country patriotic tunes) in the Miller Lite Grandstand. The sky finally lights up around 9:30 P.M. and continues until a blowout grand finale.

It's a zombie apocalypse! Nope, just the **Trash Film Orgy** (1013 K St., http://trashfilmorgy.com, $9–10, all shows are age 18 and over), a campy movie festival dedicated to cheesy horror flicks. Get decked out in fake blood and gore for the Orgy's opening night zombie walk from Midtown to the Crest. Flicks have included *Army of Darkness, The Terminator,* and *Planet of the Vampire Women.*

August

Take a vintage movie house, add the city's most promising indie directors, and what do you get? The **Sacramento Film and Music Festival** (1013 K St., www.sacfilm.com, $2–15, festival pass $60), which has committed itself to encouraging local and student filmmakers. The flicks run a gamut of short dramas, documentaries, and a few longer dramas, and everything plays at the Crest downtown. Soundtracks are heavy on tunes from Sacramento bands.

Ah, the versatile banana. Celebrate this fruit's a-peel at the **Sacramento Banana Festival** (William Land Park, http://banana-festival.sojoarts.net, adults $5, children under 8 free). Basically, this is your chance to test culinary frontiers. Get those taste buds fired up for banana hamburgers, banana cobbler, and banana salsa, along with sweeter fare such as banana pudding and banana pancakes. You can also check out live music and dance performances (banana hula, anyone?).

Who needs Doc Brown and a DeLorean? Old Sacramento goes back to the past with **Time Travel Weekends** (www.historicoldsac.org). Costumed actors perform skits and live music jams straight from the Gold Rush. Meet the Big Four, Sam Brannan, and other luminaries from Sacramento's formative years. The time traveling actually starts in early July and

runs through August; check the website for updated schedules.

September

Bring Yia Yia and Papou to the **Sacramento Greek Food Festival** (Sacramento Convention Center, http://annunciation.ca.goarch.org, early Sept., adults $5, seniors $4) for some baklava, a few cups of Greek (don't call it Turkish!) coffee, and a bit of folk dancing. If there's one thing Greeks do well, it's food, and this festival stays true to form. Honestly, it's one of the most welcoming events in town, and you'll probably make a friend telling you to "Eat! Eat!" as you nosh on plates of moussaka and dolmathes.

Saddle up your steed and ride into Old Sacramento's dusty streets for **Gold Rush Days** (Old Sacramento, Labor Day weekend, 916/808-7777, www.sacramentogoldrushdays.com). For this long weekend, the city covers Old Town's cobblestones with 200 tons of dirt to re-create an 1850s boomtown. A few hundred costumed actors suit up in bonnets, bustles, top hats, and frock coats (among other things) to play Sacramento's 19th-century celebrities like Theodore Judah and Leland Stanford. Bluegrass musicians and folk bands jam away on wooden boardwalks as you pass by. Gold panning, wagon rides, storytelling, craft-making, and a re-created Tent City are just a few other attractions.

CalBrewFest (http://calbrewfest.com) shows just how barley, hops, and some yeast can yield frothy goodness. More than 60 breweries and distributors pour their beer at this event. Venerable labels from the likes of Guinness, Sierra Nevada, and Kloster Reutberg to upstarts like New Belgium and 21st Amendment are usually represented.

A priest, a rabbi, and a minister walk into the **Sacramento Comedy Festival** (1050 20th Street, Ste. 130, www.saccomedyfest.com, $8–12, passes $12–55). The punch line? I'm working on it, but the jokes are much better at this weeklong laughfest. Performers include improv groups, stand-up comedians, musical comedy acts, and much more. Most of the acts are local, like the Anti-Cooperation League and Lady Business, but a few entries hail from Southern California and across the country. Tickets can range from $5 to $12, but the wrap party is free. **ScholarShare Children's Book Festival** (3901 Land Park Dr., 916/808-7462, www.fairytaletown.org) is a free event featuring author and illustrator performances encouraging literacy for young kids.

October

Sacramento's first German immigrants arrived in 1854. No doubt they brought a few beers with them. **Turn Verein's Oktoberfest** (3349 J St., 916/442-7360, http://sacramentoturnverein.com) keeps the party going every year at this large brick hall in East Sacramento. It's become really popular, even at $10 just to get in the door. Inside, it's everything you'd expect: dancing, beer, German food, and folks dressed in lederhosen and dirndls. You can bet they fit several renditions of the Beer Barrel Polka into the evening. The only downside is the line stretching out to the sidewalk; come as early as you can.

Run for the cure at the **Sacramento Valley AIDS Run/Walk** (www.sacvalleyaidsrunwalk.org, mid-Oct.). The event raises awareness for HIV/AIDS prevention, and entry fees help support more than a dozen AIDS charities around the Sacramento area. There are two courses; the run is a 5K race around Capitol Park, while the family walk has a separate route. Check the website for exact times and schedules.

For slasher fans there's the **Sacramento Horror Film Festival** (Colonial Theatre, 3522 Stockton Blvd., www.sachorrorfilmfest.com, $10–15 per show, passes $30–50). Future Wes Cravens from across the globe submit their

work here. The Art Deco architecture of the Colonial Theatre makes a great setting, and live music is also featured.

November

Come celebrate the turning of the seasons at the **Harvest Festival** (Cal Expo, www.harvestfestival.com, adults $9, seniors $7, youth $4), an annual handicraft fair with roughly 300 vendors. While you're at it, knock out some Christmas shopping while wandering past artisans selling wood crafts like a handmade telescope or a beautiful ceramic wall hanging shaped like the moon. Before browsing for stocking stuffers, drop off little ones at the Kidzone, an interactive play area with nontoxic and ecofriendly art activities. Visitors get $2 off admission if you bring a nonperishable food donation to the fair.

More than 225 artisans show off their talents at the **Sacramento Arts Festival** (Sacramento Convention Center, www.sacartsfest.com, adults $8, seniors $7, children under 12 free). Every kind of medium is represented, from watercolors, ceramics, jewelry, and glass to wood, stone, and sculpture. Musicians perform jazz and blues to help set the mood.

December

A popular tradition in Sacramento is the **Christkindlmarkt** (Turn Verein, 3349 J St., 916/442-7360, http://sacramentoturnverein.com), a German-style children's market with Christmas shopping booths, food, and live music. Make sure to try glühwein, a mulled wine that's a typical German Christmas drink, with a handful of lebkuchen gingerbread cookies. Santa Claus always makes an appearance around the same time as the Christkind (Christ child). There's no charge if you donate a child's coat for a local Christmas clothes drive, but it's only $2 for empty-handed visitors.

Christmas doesn't start in Sacramento until Santa shows up—obviously. The Jolly

Elf himself makes an early appearance for the **Santa Parade** (Midtown and downtown, www.sacholidays.com). In past years, the parade started in front of City Hall, drifted toward Midtown, and then swung back, passing the Capitol, the Downtown Ice Rink, and finally ended at the Downtown Plaza. Check the website for an updated parade route. The parade is for a good cause: Entry fees for the floats help support children's arts programs.

Shopping

Sacramento's urban renaissance has brought a flood of new shops, and visitors will find it easier than ever to find them. The leafy streets of **Midtown** (16th–28th Sts., www.exploremidtown.org) are the best place to start. Shopping here is easier than anywhere else because street parking is decent and you can leisurely browse the boutiques, art galleries, and various small shops in courtyards set back from the street, without feeling the big city crushing in. The only downside? Well, Midtown is a large area with long stretches of houses, restaurants, and parks. Shops are sort of clustered into a few areas; J and K Streets make up the heart of Midtown's shopping district.

On the other hand, **Old Sacramento** (http://oldsacramento.com) is bristling with gift shops, clothing stores, and just random different businesses, all within six small blocks. It's definitely the best place for souvenir shopping if you're looking for postcards, mugs, or clothing with a California or Sacramento theme. Downside: tourists. Old Sacramento becomes a busy hive of out-of-towners during summers, especially on weekends, which means searching for parking. I recommend the **Tower Bridge Garage** ($1.50 each half hour, $15 daily) at Capitol Mall and Front Street; seems like there's always a space waiting there.

If there's something you just can't find in Midtown or Old Sacramento, head for a mall. The capital has two malls with several large department stores and hundreds of small shops.

ANTIQUES

57th Street Antiques Mall (855 57th St., 916/451-3110, www.57thstreetantiquerow.com, 10 A.M.–5 P.M. Tues.–Sun.) is a long row of seven smaller antiques shops in East Sacramento. If you can't find it here, it might not exist. Expect to see racks of knickknacks like Hummel dolls, beautifully restored furniture, chinaware, vintage lamps and chandeliers, plus books and estate jewelry.

The **Sacramento Antique Faire** (W and 21st Sts., 916/600-9770, www.sacantiquefaire.com, 6:30 A.M.–3 P.M., second Sun. during fall, adults $3, youth free) is held every second Saturday. For collectors, this event is like striking the mother lode. The possibilities are endless. Hundreds of vendors sell wares from their booths, dealing in vintage clothing, furniture, old cameras, ceramics, and pretty much anything you'd imagine would show up at an antiques flea market like this one.

Remember going to your grandparents' house and playing with the old toys they kept in the garage? Then swing by **Brooks Novelty Antiques** (1107 Firehouse Alley, 916/443-0783, www.brooksnovelty.com, 11 A.M.–6 P.M. daily). This amazing shop has vintage slot and pinball machines with shiny chrome trim, toy cars and trucks, neon signs, and priceless old vending machines.

If you thought antiquing was only appropriate for retired folks, guess again. Browsing stock at **Scout Living** (1215 18th St., 916/594-7971, www.scoutliving.com, 11 A.M.–7 P.M.

Tues.–Thurs., 11 A.M.–8 P.M. Fri.–Sat., noon–5:30 P.M. Sun.) confers hipster points on anyone who shops here. Maybe it's how organized everything is; there's none of the frenetic clutter usually found in dusty antiques barns. Much of the merchandise dates to the 1950s, '60s and '70s. Retro clothing, furniture, shoes, home decor, knickknacks: you name it, this vintage heaven has it.

ART GALLERIES

Spanglish Arte (905 23rd St., #2, 916/436-6079, www.shopspanglish.com, 11 A.M.–7 P.M. Tues.–Sat., 11 A.M.–9 P.M. second Sat. of month) showcases local Latino and Chicano artists who produce handcrafted jewelry, beautiful murals, photographs, and sometimes even tattoos. If you can, make it to their Pinata Parties and learn how to decorate your own.

Artworks 21 (1812 J St., 916/440-1210, 11 A.M.–6 P.M. Tues.–Fri., 10 A.M.–4 P.M. Sat.) has an eclectic supply of Mexican-themed kitsch, including Día de los Muertos skulls, Our Lady of Guadalupe prints, and painted crucifixes.

At the **Sacramento Art Complex** (2110 K St., 916/444-4224, www.sacramentoartcomplex.com, 11 A.M.–6 P.M. Wed.–Fri., 11 A.M.–5 P.M. Sat.), expect to find two floors of ever-changing exhibits featuring more than 20 local and California artists. Mediums include metal and ceramic sculptures, photography, paintings and tapestries, and handmade jewelry.

MAIYA Gallery (2220 J St., Ste. 1, 916/476-3964, 1–7 P.M. Wed.–Sat.) has a simple and welcoming theme: My art is your art (hence the acronym). The works in this cozy space are reasonably priced, and the gallery staff will spend plenty of time talking about the pieces with you. Expect a fantastic experience whether visitors are aficionados or beginning art collectors.

ARTS AND CRAFTS

For artists and budding writers, **University Art** (2601 J St., 916/443-5721, www.universityart.com, 9:30 A.M.–5:30 P.M. Mon.–Wed. and Fri.–Sat., 9:30 A.M.–7 P.M. Thurs., noon–4 P.M. Sun.) has any kind of supplies you need. They stock paints, canvas, Moleskine notebooks, reams of different art papers, boards, adhesives, frames, and more. Need a gift for somebody artsy in your life? You've come to the right place, especially if that artsy person likes journal writing with a sweet fountain pen.

If Indiana Jones could open a store, it would look like **Zanzibar** (1731 L St., 916/443-2057, www.zanzibartribalart.com, 11 A.M.–6 P.M. Mon.–Sat., 11 A.M.–3 P.M. Sun.). Treasures sold here include Tibetan singing bowls, sterling silver jewelry from India and Nepal, Turkish silk scarves, and wooden tribal artifacts from Africa, South America, and Asia.

BOOKS AND MUSIC

The neatly organized stacks of used tomes at **Time Tested Books** (1114 21st St., 916/447-5696, http://timetestedbooks.blogspot.com, 11 A.M.–7 P.M. Mon.–Sat., 11 A.M.–3 P.M. Sun., until 9 P.M. second Sat. of the month) rarely disappoint. The vast literature section never seems to end. They also sell books on history, psychology, religion, politics, and numerous other nonfiction categories. Check the display case at the cash register for the current supply of rare and out-of-print books. If it has been printed, you'll probably have a shot at finding it here. The store itself is another attraction: It's brightly lit with high ceilings, rough brick walls, and an open area where Time Tested hosts author readings and film viewings.

The Book Collector (1008 24th St., 916/442-9295, 10 A.M.–6 P.M. Mon.–Sat., 11 A.M.–4 P.M. Sun.) is a smaller shop that still manages to impress with the amount of used books crammed into the space. Every genre is represented; fiction gets a large section to itself, but otherwise you can expect to find almost anything here. One fun thing about this store: the owner's daughter likes to drop handwritten snippets of poetry in the books, so don't be surprised if you find a well-turned limerick or phrase inside a purchase.

The largest used bookstore in Sacramento is **Beers Books** (915 S St., 916/442-9475, www.beersbooks.com, 10 A.M.–6 P.M. Mon.–Wed., 10 A.M.–8 P.M. Thurs.–Sat., 11 A.M.–5 P.M. Sun.). This sprawling space has thousands of paperbacks from every genre. The store has moved a few times, but it first opened downtown in 1936. Beers offers reasonable buy-back rates for used books and boasts a considerable selection of history books about Sacramento. Raffles, the fluffy bookstore cat, will help you browse.

In the age of iPods and iTunes, **The Beat** (1700 J St., 916/446-4406, www.thebeatsacramento.com, 10 A.M.–9 P.M. Mon.–Sat., 11 A.M.–8 P.M. Sun.) is a 45-speed throwback. Get used CDs, records, and DVDs at this awesome warehouse. Just in case someone you know still yearns for that smell of new CDs wrapped in cellophane, The Beat has a vast department filled with new music.

CLOTHING AND SHOES

Need more hipster chic in your closet? **Cuffs** (2523 J St., 916/443-2881, www.shopcuffs.com, 11 A.M.–7 P.M. daily) stocks vintage and newish clothing, shoes, and accessories. If you know someone who loves printed T-shirts, this is the place. Over on the ladies' side, there's a vast assortment of rompers, maxi dresses, sweaters, and blazers.

Cotton Club (2331 J St., 916/442-2990, 10 A.M.–6 P.M. Mon.–Sat., 11 A.M.–4 P.M. Sun.) is for ladies with slightly more mature tastes. They have purses, sweaters, and beautiful flowered dresses. The return policy is strict, so make sure you really, truly love it before finalizing that sale.

Like a page from an Allen Ginsberg poem, **Bows and Arrows Collective** (1815 19th St., 916/822-5668, http://bowscollective.com, 11 A.M.–11 P.M. Tues.–Sat.) boasts a howling mash-up of vintage artifacts and thrift clothing. The assortment is best described as hipster vintage chic, and you'll never see the same thing twice. Boots, jackets, shirts, and blouses fill the racks, and there's a display case of antique-inspired jewelry.

For thrifty and ecoconscious shoppers there's **French Cuff Consignment** (2527 J St., 916/442-3724, www.frenchcuffbtq.com, 10 A.M.–7 P.M. daily). If you've soured on buying new clothing at ridiculous prices, this shop sells used vintage and slightly used designer clothing, jewelry, and handbags. Top designers and brands are represented including J.Crew, Jones New York, Coach, and Prada.

A peek inside Don Draper's closet would probably reveal **Ed's Threads** (1125 21st St., 916/446-8138, 10 A.M.–4:45 P.M. Tues.–Wed.

© CHRISTOPHER ARNS

Ed's Threads stocks vintage men's clothing.

and Fri.–Sun.). Ed Castro sells vintage men's clothing from this tiny hole-in-the-wall. The vibe and the merchandise are pure 1960s cool. There's usually some bebop or Sinatra playing in the background, and racks are filled with jackets, silk shirts, leisure suits, and '70s Hawaiian shirts. **FTC** (1006 J St., 916/444-4494, http://ftcsf.com, 11 A.M.–7 P.M. Mon. and Wed.–Sat., 11 A.M.–5 P.M. Sun.) is the place for designer skatewear. Urban to the core, it's the place for puffy down vests and camouflage parkas.

Looking for a new pair of running kicks? The helpful staff at **Fleet Feet Sports** (2311 J St., 916/442-3338, 10 A.M.–7 P.M. Mon.–Fri., 10 A.M.–6 P.M. Sat., 11 A.M.–5 P.M. Sun.) will help you try on different brands to match your size, gait, and preferred activity. For women, they'll help pick out sports bras that don't pinch or rub. Racks of runner's apparel will help keep you dry and comfy on the trail or on the street. They're also the keepers of Sacramento's running culture.

DEPARTMENT STORES AND MALLS

For department store brands and 165 shops, **Arden Fair** (1689 Arden Way, 916/920-1273, www.ardenfair.com, 10 A.M.–9 P.M. Mon.–Sat., 11 A.M.–7 P.M. Sun.) is the largest and cleanest mall within Sacramento. Here you'll find Nordstrom, Macy's, JC Penney and Sears; smaller stores include J.Crew, Apple, Abercrombie and Fitch, Banana Republic, and dozens of others. If you need to keep youngsters entertained, head for the shiny carousel on the second floor or get them a bite to eat at the 12 different restaurants in the food court.

Downtown Plaza (5th and L Sts., 916/442-4000, 10:30 A.M.–8 P.M. Mon.–Fri., 10 A.M.–8 P.M. Sat., 11 A.M.–6 P.M. Sun.) has everything going for it: location, an open-air setting, and a vast underground parking garage. It's on the way to Old Sacramento if you're walking, and a 24 Hour Fitness is next door. Stores include Express, Bath and Body Works, Lids, Brookstone, Gymboree, and Victoria's Secret.

TOYS AND GIFTS

Perhaps the most beloved store in Sacramento is **Evangeline's** (113 K St., Old Sacramento, 916/448-2594, www.evangelines.com, 10 A.M.–9 P.M. daily, until 7 P.M. Sun. in Jan.). It's your resident purveyor of joke gifts, greeting cards, toys, and irreverent humor. Housed in the Lady Adams Building, a stately gem from 1852 and one of Sacramento's most treasured buildings, Evangeline's shouldn't be missed during any tour of Old Town. The place becomes a madhouse during Halloween as folks browse the costume shop upstairs and look for props.

Say it out loud: **G. Willikers! Toy Emporium** (1113 Front St., Old Sacramento, www.stagenine.com, 916/447-1091, 10 A.M.–8 P.M., Mon.–Thurs., 10 A.M.–9 P.M. Fri.–Sat., 10 A.M.–7 P.M. Sun.). Fun to say and fun to visit, this place, frankly, is amazing. Someone spent hours building a model Train Mountain, which resembles Lord of the Rings if dinosaurs invaded Mordor, and a rack filled with Route 66 collectibles. Expect to find Thomas the Tank Engine and Lionel trains, Schleich action figures, novelty and gag toys, and vintage board games. There's also a Robot Room and a "vault" filled with movie posters and paintings.

Sports and Recreation

Get used to seeing the sun in Sacramento, where it shines 78 percent of the time and for 265 days a year. Having such predictable and warm weather is a boon for outdoor fun. The landscape also helps. Being in a valley makes Sacramento flat as a tabletop, perfect for pedaling beach cruisers, going for a run, or just walking along the river. And don't forget the rivers. The Sacramento and American converge just north of downtown, and the water is peppered with red and orange rafts during summer. Fishing is popular, especially for salmon and chrome-colored striped bass longer than your arm. You can't beat the climate for golfing, and Sacramento has several beautiful courses within a long 3-wood of downtown.

There's something different happening every day. As a major city, Sacramento has two professional sports teams. Locals love their bikes, and there are plenty of trails to ride; the city has received a "silver" ranking for bike friendliness from the American League of Bicyclists. Other sporty activities are also popular. Yoginis have taken over the city in droves, opening new studios almost every month, and you can always find impromptu (and free) sessions at local parks.

PARKS

Sacramento is practically glowing with green spaces. Already known for being the City of Trees (the capital claims more trees per capita than anywhere in the world), Sacramento has the second best park system (916/808-6060, www.cityofsacramento.org) in the country according to the Trust for Public Land. The city mows them on a regular basis while keeping tennis courts freshly paved, softball diamonds free of weeds, and pools sparkling clean. The parks usually stay open from sunrise to sunset every day.

◖ William Land Regional Park

William Land Regional Park (3800 Land Park Dr., Freeport Blvd. and Sutterville Rd., www.cityofsacramento.org) is the largest developed park in Sacramento with 166 acres of sports fields, theme parks, and rolling greenery. Not only that, but the park sits in the capital's bucolic community of Land Park, a *Leave it to Beaver* kind of neighborhood filled with bungalows and Eichler homes, which are modern ranchero-style residences unique to California. Old-growth shaded maples and beech trees crowd the sky overhead, blocking out that steaming Sacramento heat during the summer. Bring a bat or a soccer ball for the three soccer fields and five ball fields (three baseball, two softball). Two tennis courts are lighted for evening play, and there's also a volleyball court. The park is also home to the city zoo, two children's theme parks, and a nine-hole golf course (www.williamlandgc.com). Bring a picnic, or bring a fishing rod; the park has three ponds just teeming with trout. Land Park sits about three miles south of downtown and makes a great stop on a bike ride.

Cesar Chavez Plaza

Cesar Chavez Plaza (910 I St.) is right smack in the middle of downtown across the street from Sacramento's City Hall. This 2.5-acre urban park is named for the famed community organizer who fought to secure equal rights for California's migrant agricultural workers. State workers often take their lunch here during breaks from the Capitol, and food trucks often park nearby so come hungry if it's midday. There's not much to do other than picnic, relax in the shade, or attend an event; but you can take some great photos of Sacramento's tallest buildings or start a walking tour from here. The plaza hosts concerts every Friday during

SACRAMENTO'S BARRIO

The unofficial heart of Sacramento's Chicano population is the area around **Southside Park.** The term Chicano usually refers to a person of Mexican American descent born in the United States (although some people associate the term with the migrant farmworkers' movement from the 1960s).

To explore the area, walk around the park by T Street and check out the vibrant **murals** painted on the amphitheater. Look across T Street for the rising steeple and beautiful mural at **Our Lady of Guadalupe Catholic Church.** Civil rights leader Cesar Chavez stopped at Our Lady of Guadalupe during his famous 1966 protest march from Delano in the Central Valley to the Capitol in Sacramento. Every year, local unions and progressive activist groups hold a **Cesar Chavez March** from Southside Park to downtown Sacramento.

For more information about Sacramento's Chicanos, read *Barrio Boy*, a memoir by activist and Sacramento native Ernest Galarza.

© CHRISTOPHER ARNS

Our Lady of Guadalupe looks down over Southside Park.

the summer with a beer garden, bike corral, and local bands; the city's downtown association lists upcoming events on their website (http://downtownsac.org). The plaza has a public restroom open during the day.

East Portal Park

Play some bocce ball or toss the pigskin around at East Portal Park (1120 Rodeo Way). This bowl-shaped oasis has a rustic feel to it; hulking evergreens diffuse mountain-scented air throughout the park's seven acres and carpet picnic areas with pine needles. Located in mellow East Sacramento, East Portal also has a bocce ball court, playground, and softball field. Restrooms are available and there's on-street parking around the park's perimeter.

McKinley Park

In East Sacramento, head to McKinley Park (601 Alhambra Blvd.). Locals love coming here for the **McKinley Park Loop** (one mile, flat) dirt running track that winds past tennis courts, an Olympic-size pool, a trout pond, softball fields, and a soccer pitch. If you're looking for a romantic picnic spot, pack a basket and bring a blanket to the **McKinley Park Rose Garden** (1.5 acres, near H and 33rd Sts.), which has more than 1,000 rosebushes, rose trees, and other blooming annuals. Sadly, the park once had a fortress-like playground for kids, but it burned down in 2012; call the park service if you'd like updates on whether the playground has been rebuilt. There are public restrooms in the middle of the park between the pool and the tennis courts.

Miller Park

Put in your boat at Miller Park (2710 Ramp Way) on the banks of the Sacramento River. It's next to the city marina a couple of miles from downtown. Beneath canopies of oak trees there are 57 acres of picnic areas overlooking the water where you can grill some barbecue or watch boats sail by. Bring a rod and tackle in the fall for salmon fishing and cast your line right from the grass. Park facilities include drinking fountains and public toilets, and there's also a snack shop.

Southside Park

One of the city's most underrated green spaces is Southside Park (2115 6th St.). Many folks skip this place in favor of Land Park, which is just on the other side of U.S. 50, but Southside is actually a rad place to spend an afternoon. There's a lake stocked with trout and catfish, and anglers can set up shop on the short pier

jutting out into the water. Athletes train on the fitness course, which includes four stations, each with pull-up bars, balance beams, parallel bars, and other equipment. Runners come for the 0.75-mile trail around the park, which is 20 acres in size and also includes a swimming pool, a wading pool, and an enormous sandy playground stocked with digging toys. Finally, take a moment and check out the amphitheater's beautiful mural painted by local Chicano artists in honor of Cesar Chavez's 1966 march from Delano that ended here.

28th and B Street Skate Park

Drop in at 28th and B Street Skate Park (20 28th St., 916/808-5611, www.cityofsacramento.org, 4–9 P.M. Mon.–Fri, noon–9 P.M. Sat.–Sun. early Sept.–early June; 2–9 P.M. Mon.–Fri., noon–9 P.M. Sat.–Sun. mid-June–early Sept., $3). It's inside a cavernous old warehouse, and shredders will find quarter and half pipes, boxes and ten-stair rails for busting tricks. There's also a new pool-size bowl. Instruction camps for young skaters are a hit for kids aged 5 to 18; youngsters get a T-shirt, a snack, and lessons on sharpening their skills.

AMUSEMENT PARKS

Everyone gets butterflies on the slides at **Raging Waters** (1600 Exposition Blvd., 916/924-3747, www.rwsac.com, $22–31). Once school is out, kids flock to this water park all summer to scream down rides named Shark Attack, Hook's Lagoon, Hurricane, and Cliffhanger. Anyone with adrenaline left over can float down the Calypso Cooler Lazy River or body surf waves at Breaker Beach, or just hang by the volleyball courts until someone starts a pickup game. Bring a packed lunch or order food from the five different snack shacks. Packed isn't the right word to describe summer crowds; think of something busier and you'll be close. Get

© CHRISTOPHER ARNS

Have a picnic at McKinley Park Rose Garden in East Sacramento.

there early on mercury-melting July days to be first in line.

Anyone with a short attention span will enjoy **Scandia Family Fun Center** (5070 Hillsdale Blvd., 916/331-5757, www.scandiasports.com). You can go miniature golfing, take some cuts in the batting cages, blow fistfuls of quarters in the video game arcade, or rub wheels at the go-kart track. Thrill seekers, don't fret; there's stuff for you, too. At 165 feet above the ground, the Scandia Screamer is an airborne seesaw that spins at 65 mph. Back on terra firma, head over to the snack bar for pizza, hot dogs, smoothies, or hot chocolate.

BIKING

Sacramento is very much about the bike. For starters, the city was named California's best bike commuter state in 2010 by *American Bicyclist* magazine. And the League of American Bicyclists have given Sacramento's city government a "silver" rating for efforts to make the capital more bike-friendly.

The capital's topography is picture-perfect for riding bikes. Sacramento claims to have more trees per capita than any other city in the world, a distinction that's obvious when driving through neighborhoods like Land Park, Midtown, and East Sacramento. The city's flat terrain, 265 days of sunshine, and venerable park system (ranked second in the United States by the Trust for Public Land) just beg visitors to peddle around town. Cyclists can also hop on the paved **Jedediah Smith Bike Trail** (32 miles, moderate) that leads into the American River Parkway (23 miles).

For wheels, try either **City Bike Works** (2419 K St., 916/447-2453, http://citybicycleworks.com, 10 A.M.–7 P.M. Mon.–Fri., 10 A.M.–6 P.M. Sat., 10 A.M.–5 P.M. Sun., bikes $10–40) or **Practical Cycle** (114 J St., 916/706-0077, www.practicalcycle.com, 10 A.M.–7 P.M. daily in spring and summer, 10 A.M.–6 P.M. daily in

fall and winter, bikes $5–40) to rent a ride for the day or just a few hours.

FISHING

Some of California's best fishing can be found on the American and Sacramento Rivers. More than 750,000 chinook salmon, striped bass, steelhead, sturgeon, and American shad swim through the Sacramento watershed—and they're all just waiting to bite your hook. Well, it's not really that easy. Knowing the best spots, tackle, and time periods is at least half the battle. Prime fishing season starts in late September when salmon began their fall run from the ocean back to spawning grounds at higher elevations.

If salmon is a go (the fishery was closed in 2008 and 2009), grab a handful of spinners and post up along the Sacramento River anywhere between **Miller Park** and **Discovery Park.** Steelhead, an ocean-going species of rainbow trout, flood both the American and the Sacramento Rivers from fall to early spring; start at Discovery Park and work your way up the American. Night crawlers, salmon roe, spinners, and spoons should get some bites. If you like really, really big fish, white sturgeon move up through the California Delta in late fall before peaking in late winter and early spring; try pile worms, ghost shrimp, or salmon roe. Keepers are between 46 and 66 inches, and you can only keep one per day, not that you could carry more of these monsters anyway. These behemoths can reach 100 years old and make great fishing for beginners. Finally, both rivers teem with striped bass and American shad, which fight like crazy.

If you're near Folsom, stop by the **Nimbus Fish Hatchery** (2001 Nimbus Rd., Gold River, 916/358-2820, www.dfg.ca.gov) to check out the dozens of tanks where the hatchery raises fingerling steelhead trout and salmon. The parkway has more than just hiking and biking trails; anglers will find plenty of fishing

SACRAMENTO BIKE TOUR

This easy ride around Sacramento takes visitors through some of the capital's historic neighborhoods.

Time: 1.5 hours
Distance: 11 miles round-trip

Blend in with the hipster crowd by renting a cruiser at **Practical Cycle** (114 J St., 916/706-0077, www.practicalcycle.com) in Old Sacramento. After cruising the cobblestoned streets, ride east up Capitol Mall before veering right up N Street. Follow this one-way street toward the **California State Capitol** (10th and L Sts.) to check out the 12 square blocks of leafy urban park, or head inside to view a live session of the California State Legislature. You might need to troll L Street for a bike rack if there are none available here.

From the Capitol, walk your bike one block north up 11th Street for a quick detour to the **Cathedral of the Blessed Sacrament** (1017 11th St.) and gaze up at the 215-foot-high spire that towers over downtown Sacramento. Ride east on K Street to 13th Street and turn into **Capitol Park** (15th and L Sts.). Walk your bike east through the park to the flagpoles on 15th Street and continue riding on Capitol Avenue. For the next dozen blocks or so, you'll pedal through Midtown's **Victorian Row,** a green tunnel of elm and palm trees, while passing dozens of restored 19th-century homes dating back to the Gilded Age.

Keep heading east and hang a left at 28th Street to reach **Sutter's Fort State Historic Park** (2701 L St.) and the **California State Indian Museum** (2618 K St.). Enter the fort's whitewashed adobe walls and watch costumed docents reenact 19th-century life, or view relics in the Indian Museum.

From Sutter's Fort, head north on 28th Street, then turn right at G Street to reach **McKinley Park** (601 Alhambra Blvd.), where you can feed the ducks, watch a softball game, or enjoy a picnic in the rose garden.

Take H Street from the park, turning right on 36th Street to J Street where you'll walk the bike east to **Juno's Kitchen and Delicatessen** (3675 J St., 916/456-4522, http://junoskitchen.com, 11:30 A.M.-3 P.M. and 5-8:30 P.M. Mon.-Fri, 11:30 A.M.-8:30 P.M. Sat.) for a sandwich. Or grab a pint of craft brew at **Bonn Lair** (3651 J St., 916/455-7155, 11:30 A.M.-1 A.M. daily).

Now that you're feeling refreshed, head across J Street and turn right on 37th Street heading south. Hang a left at M Street to pedal through the **Fabulous Forties** (38-49th Sts. between H St. and Folsom Blvd.), a stately residential neighborhood filled with palatial mansions. Make sure to check out Ronald Reagan's old house on 45th Street. Keep heading up M Street to 51st Street at **East Portal Park** (1120 Rodeo Way) and the end of the tour. Stop here for a breather or a game of bocce ball before heading back to Old Sacramento the way you came.

---

opportunities along the river, and boating enthusiasts can launch from various points. If you're going to fish here, it's best to know the rules. Every angler needs a license (residents $44.85, nonresidents $120.14 for one year; one- and two-day licenses also available) from the California Department of Fish and Wildlife (www.dfg.ca.gov). Check the website for updated info on fishery closings and when seasons open. A treasure trove of angling information from maps to bait tips is **Fish Sniffer** (www.

fishsniffer.com), which also gives out hot reads on local guides and boat services.

Whether it's prince nymphs or tying a tippet, **American Fly Fishing** (3523 Fair Oaks Blvd., 916/483-1222, www.americanflyfishing. com, 9 A.M.–6 P.M. Mon.–Fri., 7:30 A.M.–5 P.M. Sat., 9 A.M.–3 P.M. Sun.) has the friendliest staff around. The store is loaded with fly-fishing gear and offers exhaustive workshops on casting, reading the water, and choosing the correct rod. They'll also hook you up with clothing, boots, a huge selection of flies, and info for local guides.

GOLF

When most weekend duffers hit the links in Sacramento, they're usually teeing off at **Haggin Oaks** (3645 Fulton Ave., 916/481-4653, www.hagginoaks.com, $14.50–57). Golfing magic lurks under the 100-year-old heritage oaks on these fairways. Famed course architect Alistair MacKenzie (the brains behind Augusta National) designed the 18-hole championship layout here, and golfing legends like Sam Snead and Walter Hagen have putted the greens. The ambience suffers from the nearby freeways, which zoom by on either side, but the course is extremely playable; no elevation change (it's Sacramento, remember), but trees and several water hazards makes this track a challenging round. Haggin is actually two golf courses: There's the more esteemed MacKenzie course (18 holes, 6,991 yards) for low handicappers and the neighboring **Arcade Creek Golf Course** (18 holes, 6,552 yards) for beginners. Get warmed up at the driving range, named by *Range Magazine* as one of the top 100 in the country; it stays open almost all night (closed from 3–5 A.M. for maintenance) and boasts 100 stalls.

Bing Maloney Golf Course (6801 Freeport Blvd., 916/808-2283, www.bingmaloney.com, $11–46) is Sacramento's other urban playground for hacks and handicappers. I actually find this course more challenging than Haggin Oaks. Massive trees really seem to crowd the narrow fairways and punish you for errant drives. Water runs throughout the course in streams and small ponds, greens are like putting on tortoiseshells, and quite a few holes border a junglelike pasture where Titleists go to die. If the 18-hole championship course (a relatively short 6,569 yards) sounds too tough, try the nine-hole executive course (1,357 yards).

Cherry Island Golf Course (2360 Elverta Rd., 916/991-7293, www.golfcherryisland.com, $16–37) seems to fly under the radar for most Sacramento golfers. It's probably the location, just beyond the northern city limits, but you should head out there anyway. The course is beautiful and damn tough. The layout is 18 holes, a modest 6,494 yards, and looks like a typical California course shaded by towering heritage oak trees. But it's the water that gets you; almost every hole has some kind of watery grave lurking. My advice: bring an extra sleeve of balls. At the right time of day you can golf more cheaply here than at most other Sacramento courses and without giving up course quality. Walking the course at twilight is usually only $19 if you book tee times online.

Out by the airport you'll find **Teal Bend Golf Club** (7200 Garden Hwy., 916/604-8563, www.tealbendgolf.com, $20–65), one of Sacramento's newest courses. This layout is a beauty. It's long (18 holes, 7,061 yards), peppered with bunkers on every hole, and features undulating greens that take your Slazenger for a ride back into the rough. For a course tucked alongside the Sacramento River, the layout has few water hazards—although who wants to complain about that, right? Teal Bend's skinny fairways are as well-maintained as you'd expect from a young course, and though expensive, most golfers will enjoy their rounds here.

HIKING

A trip to Sacramento wouldn't be complete without a hike along the **American River Parkway** (www.msa2.saccounty.net). It's actually a series of paved trails that run through wetlands, oak woodlands, and several regional parks along the American River. The trails start at **Discovery Park,** a grassy 302-acre park at the confluence of the Sacramento and American Rivers, and ends 23 miles away in the city of Folsom. Along the way, you'll pass cyclists pedaling along river levees on the Jedediah Smith Bike Trail, families pushing strollers by the water, and plenty of dog lovers taking their pets for a walk.

One of the more popular Sacramento-area parks actually runs through the separate town of West Sacramento. **River Walk Park** (651 2nd St., www.cityofwestsacramento.org, 0.5 mile, easy) features a paved pathway that runs along the river. As you walk the path, read the interpretive plaques to learn about the flora and fauna that inhabit this part of the Sacramento River ecosystem. Bring a cooler and have a picnic at one of the various picnic areas along the path, or bring your rod and tackle and walk out onto the fishing dock. A major boat dock lets private boaters moor at the park. River Walk Park also encourages visitors to jump out into the water for a refreshing swim in the river.

RAFTING AND KAYAKING

Rapids on the lower American River are no widow makers. They're more like riffles—mostly lazy Class I–II drops to keep you awake. Rafting this water is a leisurely float through the American River Parkway. Trips begin near Fair Oaks, a suburb 14 miles east of Sacramento off U.S. 50, and float for roughly three to four hours through swimming holes, past parks, and along scrubby islands before ending in Rancho Cordova, another local suburb. Rafting companies offer return shuttle service back to Fair Oaks for a few extra bucks, and you'll be finished by supper time. Expect to pay a launch fee of $2.50.

One necessary word of caution: during summer holidays such as July 4th or Labor Day, the lower American River becomes clogged with rafters between Fair Oaks and Discovery Park. Not to be a prude, but it's really not safe. Alcohol is usually banned on the river during holidays although many rafters ignore the rules, creating a boozy party scene that often leads to drunken fights and deaths when people fall into the water. Law enforcement and park rangers will cite folks if they bring booze and will definitely arrest anyone starting fisticuffs.

American River Raft Rentals (11257 South Bridge St., Rancho Cordova, 916/635-6400, http://raftrentals.com, Apr.–Sept., rafts $60–165, kayaks $35) will rent several different raft sizes, from 4-person to 12-person rafts. Kayaks are also available. They usually rent until early afternoon and expect rafts back by 6 P.M.

River Rat Raft and Bike (4053 Pennsylvania Ave., Fair Oaks, 916/966-6777, www.river-rat.com, Apr.–Sept., rafts $55–160, kayaks $40–59) rents out equipment until 11:30 A.M. They offer several sizes from 4-person rafts to 12-person behemoths.

SWIMMING

When the mercury rises during Sacramento's notorious summer heat waves, head to **Discovery Park** (Garden Hwy. and I-5, www.msa2.saccounty.net, sunrise–sunset, vehicles $5). This 302-acre oasis cradles the American and Sacramento Rivers where they converge. A sandy beach and calm water make this spot one of Sacramento's go-to swimming holes. It's no local's secret by any means; the water is roiling with people by sweltering July. Keep an eye on kids (and yourself!) at all times for safety reasons because the park doesn't have lifeguards. The park calms down during cooler times of the year. Other amenities at this park include an archery range, picnic area, and boat ramp for small watercraft ($3 launch fee).

Sand Cove Park (2005 Garden Hwy.) has 10.3 acres of grassy park space on the American River with a sandy beach area and a nature area for walks.

YOGA

Sacramento's yoga studios will get you feeling limber. Most places offer variants of vinyasa although Bikram-style (hot yoga) is becoming more popular. The place most Sacramento yoginis talk about is **Zuda Yoga** (1515 19th St.,

916/441-1267, http://zudayoga.com, adults $16, students $12). They practice vinyasa flow yoga in large classes where the room temperature climbs into the 90s. This is yoga as social experience—people chat with one another before and after practice, and you'll often see three or four people arrive together. Most hard-core yoginis sniff that Zuda is just too trendy for them, and it does seem more casual. Imagine if someone held a tattoo convention in a lululemon store and you've got the idea. Classes are packed (the room holds five rows of students), and beginners may stumble here as less attention is given to each yogini. New students can pay $10 to try the studio for 10 days. Try to bring your own mat and arrive early to nab a coveted spot away from the wall.

On the other hand, **Asha Yoga** (1050 20th St., #110, 916/443-6535, http://ashayoga. com, $16) seems to cater toward new yoginis. Instructors focus on helping students hold balance and form instead of just powering through the postures. Trendy might not be the word to describe Asha. The studio seems more focused on building a serene environment in their medium-size space and encouraging healthy practice through vinyasa, yin-yang, and restorative yoga techniques. Newbies can check the website before their first class for a list of helpful tips about practicing here. Asha also has a second location in East Sacramento (3610 McKinley Blvd., 916/443-6535).

It's All Yoga (2405 21st St., 916/501-4692, www.itsallyoga.com, $15) is another friendly, welcoming studio with helpful teachers. Finally, a vinyasa studio where you don't need the newest yoga pants and won't feel self-conscious for being just a tad bit out of shape. The owner, Michelle Marlahan, goes out of her way to make all students feel comfortable with their bodies. They're committed to healing "hackerback"—the poor posture we all get from

pounding the keyboard at work. Newbies can sign up for $20 and come for a week to try it.

Ask yoginis who know about Bikram yoga and watch their eyes widen. Also known as hot yoga practiced at 105 degrees and 35 percent humidity, it's a form of torture in 86 different countries. (Not really, but you'll think so around minute 75.) The only "official" Bikram studio is **Sacramento Bikram Yoga** (6350 Folsom Blvd., 916/456-9642, www.sacramentobikramyoga.com, $16). Their yoga room is spacious and covered in newish gray carpet that doesn't smell (a common complaint in Bikram studios). There's a large parking lot next door and each bathroom has several showers. Cubbies are provided for handbags and car keys.

Yoga Loka (4820 Folsom Blvd., 916/454-4100, www.yogaloka.net, $16) offers Bikram-style hot yoga. One thing that's nice about this place is the bamboo floor, which keeps the temperature down slightly and doesn't smell after a long day of classes. There are limited bathroom and parking facilities, two small changing rooms, and showers are shared outside. For the price, this studio could offer more amenities. Arrive early to grab a spot during evening classes.

The best deal in town is **Yoga in the Park** (McKinley Park, 916/501-3069, free). Free vinyasa classes are held behind the McKinley Park Rose Garden at 9 A.M. every Saturday.

SPECTATOR SPORTS

Once upon a time, Sacramento's NBA basketball team sold out every game. Even when times were rough and the team only won a handful of games, the city had some of the most passionate fans in the league. While times have changed, loyal fans still worship the **Sacramento Kings** (One Sports Pkwy., 916/928-6900, www.nba.com/kings,

© CHRISTOPHER ARNS

Sacramento's Triple A baseball team, the RiverCats, plays at Raley Field.

$22.50–140, parking $10). The team plays at **Power Balance Pavilion,** one of the loudest venues in the league, although Kings' management has been seeking a new arena for several years. Note that as this book went to press, the Kings remained in Sacramento but were in talks to move.

The crack of wooden bats and umpires hollering "safe!" If you love baseball, get tickets to see the **Sacramento RiverCats** (Raley Field, 400 Ballpark Dr., West Sacramento, 916/371-4487, www.rivercats.com, $8–37, parking $8–10). Rosters of major league players have done stints with this Triple A farm affiliate for the Oakland A's. Here families will enjoy bringing a blanket to spread out in the grassy lawn area behind the outfield. An evening here can be ridiculously cheap. Lawn tickets are $8, and the team sells $1 hot dogs and desserts on Fridays. To catch a game, you can either walk over the Tower Bridge from Old Sacramento or park closer to the field.

There's pain, and then there's pain on skates. The **Sac City Rollers** (http://saccityrollers. com, $6–15) doles out both. Sacramento's first all-women flat-track roller derby league has more than 100 skaters who throw down between March and December. Rules are simple: Teams skate around a track and keep the other team from lapping them. Pushing, shoving, and other physical contact ensue. Expect to watch the Sweaty Betties, Rude Girls, Folsom Prison Bruisers, and other local teams go at it. There are various venues, but the most consistent one is The Rink (2900 Bradshaw Rd., 916/363-2643, www.therinksacramento.com).

Accommodations

Sleeping in Sacramento used to be an adventure for folks. Early Gold Rush pioneers usually sought some shut-eye in tents by the Sacramento River where they were plagued with mosquitoes from the marshy delta. If they didn't catch yellow fever from the bugs, there was still a good chance floods might sweep away their tent in the night. Things swung the other way during Prohibition when Sacramento became California's speakeasy capital. The city's lax stance on illegal drinking attracted Hollywood stars who flocked here on weekends. But the Depression hit the city hard, especially for farmworkers and immigrants who lived in downtown and on Sacramento's riverfront. The area, known as the West End, became a fetid skid row of bordellos, gambling houses, and bars. Until Old Sacramento was fixed up in the 1970s, the West End was the worst slum west of Chicago. But even after Old Sacramento received a face-lift, the city's accommodations could still shock you. (During the 1980s, authorities caught an older woman burying guests at her downtown boardinghouse after stealing their Social Security checks.)

Yes, Sacramento might have a sordid past in the hospitality industry, but those days are long past. A newer, trendier burg has emerged instead. Gone are the dodgy West End flophouses and motels that charge by the hour; instead, you'll find penthouse lofts and plush suites with spas. You can still find cheap motor court dives out off I-5 heading toward the airport, but Sacramento's urban lodgings are catching up to luxe destinations like San Francisco or Napa. Hitting the sack is certainly better near downtown. Lobbyists and corporate flacks need swanky places to crash before sauntering over to the Capitol or the Sacramento Convention Center. Downtown hotels have figured that out, so they cater to deep-pocketed out-of-towners who expect comfortable rooms with few hassles. Sure, you'll pay more for location and better digs, but it's so worth it.

Choosing to stay downtown is a great option, but remember to make reservations well in advance. The Golden State's capital is a busy place. Gatherings, conventions, and trade shows happen year-round at the city's convention center. Foreign delegations visit California's lawmakers on goodwill trips. On a really busy week, Sacramento's hotels will sell out. To make sure you lock down top hotels, I would recommend booking rooms at least 2–3 months ahead of time.

DOWNTOWN AND OLD TOWN
Under $100
Built in 1885, the **Sacramento Hostel** (925 H St., 916/443-1691, www.norcalhostels.org/sac, $29–92) attracts budget travelers with a taste for Gilded Age surroundings. The restored Italianate mansion is a beauty. Inside you'll find vaulted ceilings, a wrap-around veranda, restored wood paneling, old-fashioned fireplace grates, chandeliers, and a restored grand entryway. For a hostel, the dorm rooms aren't bad and accommodate 8–10 people per room. But most folks prefer private rooms decked out with stenciled wood flooring, brightly painted walls, wrought-iron bed frames, and comfy beds. If you get bored, walk down to the recreation room and watch a DVD, grab a book from the small library, or stroll outside into the gardened patio area. Honestly, this place does have downsides. It's part of Hostelling International, so the atmosphere sometimes comes off as somewhat cold and lacking personality. Moreover, guests often mutter that hostel staff members need better manners. It is, however, the most reasonably priced lodging in town, and you can't beat the old building's charm.

If you need a home base during a quick trip to Sacramento, the **Quality Inn Downtown** (818 15th St., 916/444-3980, www.quality-inn.com, $50–80) is an option. I'll just say for the price, folks get what they pay for here. It's a budget motel with free wireless Internet, free parking, a continental breakfast, outdoor pool, and a short walk to the Capitol. Expect nothing fancy in the rooms other than coffeemakers, hair dryers, and ironing boards; some have refrigerators. Nonsmoking rooms are available by request.

$100-150

For the best view in town, there's the ℂ **Citizen Hotel** (926 J St., 916/447-2700, www.jdvhotels.com, $135–225). This majestic Beaux Arts masterpiece is one of downtown's most recognizable landmarks. Newlyweds often take their wedding photos on upper story patios that look out over the Capitol. The Citizen describes itself as a "luxury

© CHRISTOPHER ARNS

Citizen Hotel

boutique hotel"; I say the retro decor has a 1960s *Mad Men* vibe. Inside the lobby you'll find a stunning color scheme of cherry red and gold trim on dark wood paneling, designed to match the glowing wall of law books inside a two-story library. The framed *Sacramento Bee* political cartoons spaced around the lobby are another nice touch. It's hard to really do proper justice to this grand space, which feels like an oil magnate's private study. After checking in, walk down the marble foyer to the elevators and ride up to your room. The retro theme continues with vintage pinstriped wallpaper, upholstered headboards, and tasteful early '60s colors. Amenities include a mini-bar, flat-screen TV, Italian down bedcovers, complimentary bathrobes, coffeemakers, and ironing board. Other services include same-day laundry, a fitness center, and valet parking ($25 per day).

If railroad tycoons still ran Sacramento, they'd stay at the **Sterling Hotel** (1300 H St., 916/448-1300, http://sterlinghotelsacramento.com, $100–230), a perfect example of the capital's 19th-century Victorian architecture. From the gleaming white portico and wide front porch to the immaculate gardens out back, the Sterling evokes pure decadence. Sixteen rooms are decked out with antique four-poster beds, down comforters, flat-screen TVs, and double-size marble spas (bathrobes included). In the morning, fill up on the continental breakfast and check your email on the free wireless Internet. Not every vintage building has an elevator, but the Sterling does have a lift so you don't have to lug your bags up the staircase. Other room amenities include individual climate control in each room, ironing boards, and hair dryers.

A useful home base for business travelers is the **Inn off Capitol Park** (1530 N St., 916/447-8100, www.innoffcapitolpark.com, $115–145). This modern, contemporary hotel packs convenient amenities into a sleek package. Rooms

The Sterling Hotel adds a dash of class to downtown's urban scene.

are stocked with flat-screen TVs, refrigerators, microwaves, medium-size desk, and sofa. Consider this place a step up from dull corporate chains; rooms open out onto a brightly lit atrium with a pool and recessed spa. For business tasks, there's free wireless Internet along with fax and copying services. Parking is free on-site, and continental breakfast is served in the morning.

"Convenient" is the best word to describe the **Holiday Inn Capitol Plaza** (300 J St., 916/446-0100, www.holidayinn.com, $110–180). This towering corporate behemoth is right off I-5 between Old Sacramento and downtown, and the airport is only 15 minutes away. As a brand-name chain hotel, it does lack some charm, and freeway noise can be a problem, although business travelers or active sightseers probably won't notice. Rooms are usually spotless and comfortable with flat-screen TVs, premium cable and pay-per-view channels, free

wireless Internet, and closets stuffed with standard hotel-type appliances (hair dryer, ironing board, and iron). Parking is meager unless visitors spring for valet service or the garage down the street.

Best Western Plus Sutter House (1100 H St., 916/441-1314, www.thesutterhouse.com, $100–150) is one of the better deals for downtown Sacramento. It's perfect for active sightseers who still want that happy feeling when they slide the key card in the door. For my money, Sutter House is surprisingly homey for the normally bland Best Western chain. Whoever decided that plants would really tie the rooms together at this hotel, I salute you. Your sleeping quarters are better for it, and the comfy beds, spacious bathrooms, and nonsmoking environment are also commendable. Outside you'll find a pool for cooling off on sizzling-hot Sacramento days. Breakfast is slightly heartier than run-of-the-mill continental spreads, with waffles, hard-boiled eggs, biscuits and gravy, and cereal along with juice and coffee. There's also free on-site parking.

To travel in a style that Mark Twain would have enjoyed, there's the **Delta King** (1000 Front St., 916/444-5464, www.deltaking.com, $120–220). Guests can stay overnight on this 285-foot riverboat that once ferried passengers between San Francisco and Sacramento through the California Delta. The steamer first sailed during Prohibition and quickly earned a rep as a booze cruiser, hosting gambling, drinking, jazz bands, and fine dining. Sadly, the *King*'s sailing days are behind him, and the grand riverboat remains permanently moored to Old Sacramento's restored embarcadero. Reserving a room is the closet you'll get to re-creating the ship's glory days. Staterooms are decorated with darkly finished desks and armoires, brass or wooden bed frames, antique-style lamps, and flat-screen TVs. The soft beds will have you dreaming in no time. Other amenities include free wireless Internet and free breakfast in the Pilot House restaurant on the boat. For an evening cocktail before hitting the sack, head upstairs to the fully restored bar looking upriver toward the I Street Bridge. If I had a choice, the best accommodations are the river-facing quarters or the captain's suite, which has a sitting room and beautiful wood paneling covering the walls. One tip: call ahead and make sure valets are waiting to park your car.

$150-250

From the outside, the **Inn and Spa at Parkside** (2116 6th St., 916/658-1818, www.innatparkside.com, $170–240) looks like a stately Mediterranean villa overlooking Southside Park. So it probably comes as a shock when you step inside and find contemporary suburban decor with hints of esoteric Asian influences. Most of the 11 rooms have different themes, from the Tranquility room with a "British plantation–style" vibe, as the inn describes it, to the Buddhist-inspired Passion room. Some suites have four-poster beds, flat-screen TVs with cable and DVD players, iPod clocks, whirlpool tubs, marble showers, and a fireplace. Slow down by slipping on the provided robe and slippers, lighting a candle left in the room, and turning on the spa jets. More relaxation is available with Parkside's spa treatments, which include massage, facials, waxing, and body polishing. Parking and free wireless Internet are also part of the deal.

The **Sheraton Grand** (1230 J St., 800/325-3535, www.starwoodhotels.com, $165–300) is a mixed bag. This sleek hotel is situated in the old Sacramento Public Market building designed by famed architect Julia Morgan. The exterior brick facade has been restored and looks striking among the glass and steel of downtown's high-rises. Guests are treated to fast and friendly service, and the Sheraton is next door to the Sacramento Convention Center. You'll find a heated outdoor pool, a

sprawling lounge area in the lobby, and rooms that are simple and luxurious with outstanding views of the city. There's also Morgan's Restaurant on the first floor if you don't feel like eating out. But this place obviously caters to high-flying business travelers or Sheraton members, otherwise guests pay $16 to use wireless Internet (it's free in the 24-hour business center). They also don't provide complimentary continental breakfast. Expect to pay $18 per day for parking while fighting the valet line out front. And for a pricey hotel, there's no airport shuttle. You'll pay for convenience and a short walk to the Capitol, but don't expect anything else.

Embassy Suites Sacramento (100 Capitol Mall, 916/326-5000, http://embassysuites.com, $140–190) is right next to Old Sacramento and the waterfront. This place doesn't hold back on making folks feel comfortable. The two-room suites open out into an atrium spanning up to the roof. Each room boasts chic decor that seems comfortably modern without that bloodless chain vibe apparent at so many other corporate hotels. Expect comfy beds, dark wood furniture, flat-screen TVs, minibar, pull-out sofa, microwave, and fridge. Guests get spoiled here with free breakfasts that include omelettes and waffles, a free cocktail hour, and free airport shuttles. After settling in, slip on your swimwear and head down to the heated indoor pool or spa, or make a stop at the fitness center for some exercise. The amenities are reasonable for the price, and guests won't find a better location for hanging out in Old Sacramento.

The **C Hyatt Regency** (1209 L St., 916/443-1234, http://sacramento.hyatt.com, $150–350) looks out over the State Capitol across the street. Arnold Schwarzenegger regularly stayed here during his two terms as California's chief executive in a special penthouse far above the city. The Hyatt is probably Sacramento's classiest chain hotel, and all rooms have a sleek Euro design with hip

The Hyatt Regency is adjacent to the State Capitol.

ultramodern linens and furniture. Amenities include HD TVs, windows that open and let fresh breezes into the room, minibars, individual climate control, and free wireless Internet in the lobby ($10 upstairs). Downstairs, you'll find an indoor-outdoor lounge and 24-hour business center services such as printing, copying and PC workstations ($7.50 per 15 minutes). Bring your swimwear and grab a book for the sparkling outdoor pool area which is lined with awnings and comfortable lounge chairs. One thing the Hyatt doesn't offer? Airport shuttles. You'll have to take taxis or book through local shuttle services.

MIDTOWN AND EAST SACRAMENTO
Under $100

There's a funny story about the **Clarion Hotel Mansion Inn** (700 16th St., 916/444-8000, www.clarion-mansion-inn.pacificahost.com,

$80–90). Oscar-winning screenwriter Aaron Sorkin spent four months here in 1992 while he penned a play for the B Street Theatre. Sorkin also starred in the play, which I guess means he didn't mind staying at the Clarion for a little longer. And it's a fairly comfortable place. The inside courtyard has a woodsy outdoor pool area shaded by a couple of pine trees. Inside, the rooms are tidy, and amenities include a TV, desk area, free wireless Internet, coffeemakers, and refrigerators by request. Downsides? Well, the Clarion could use a makeover; both the rooms and the lobby seem a little shabby. Yes, it's worth a look for visitors trying to stretch their dollars, but you may want to first browse other budget options in downtown. They do allow pets but only for an extra $50 per stay.

For a cheap getaway near Sutter's Fort there's **Motel 6 Sacramento Downtown** (1415 30th St., 916/454-4400, $45–55). Expect nothing fancy. The motel is right by Highway 99, about five minutes from Cal Expo on the fringes of Midtown and East Sacramento. McKinley Park is just six blocks away. Rooms are decent and tidy, and there's an outdoor pool. You can order wireless Internet for $3. Just a heads-up: the area does attract a fair bit of homeless folks and has a rep for car break-ins, so bring everything into the rooms. East Sacramento is a bucolic residential neighborhood just waiting for someone to open a bed-and-breakfast, but until then you'll only find chain hotels like this one near the freeway.

Another budget option is **Econo Lodge** (711 16th St., 916/443-6631, www.econolodge.com, $50–90), on the border of Midtown and downtown just a few blocks from the Governor's Mansion and the Wells Fargo Pavilion. Amenities are basic: free continental breakfast in the morning; simple rooms with clean beds, refrigerators, and ironing boards; free coffee offered all day. Note that Econo Lodge does offer smoking rooms so make sure you state

© CHRISTOPHER ARNS

Vizcaya Pavilion in Midtown

which kind is preferred. Pets are welcome with an extra surcharge per night.

Victorian-style accommodation is available at **Vizcaya Pavilion** (2019 21st St., 916/594-9285, www.vizcayapavilion.com, $80–90). This 1899 Colonial Revival mansion has a gleaming white tower and beautiful gardens out back. Inside, you'll find eight tidy rooms with Italian marble bathrooms, soaking tubs, antique furnishings, fireplaces, and crown molding fringing the ceiling. Amenities are basic: free wireless Internet, ironing boards, and hair dryers round out the hotel's offerings, although guests do get complimentary bathrobes. One quibble you might have with the rooms is that they seem a little bland; maybe it's the Crayola-colored carpet or the wicker furniture, but these sleeping quarters could use a makeover.

$150-250

Folks who walk by ◖ **Amber House** (1315 22nd St., 916/444-8085, www.amberhouse.

com, $170–280) would never know this gem existed. It just looks like two Victorian homes situated on adjacent lots. Just wait until you head inside either the 1895 Colonial Revival or 1905 Craftsman bungalow. From the looks of things, Theodore Roosevelt and Frank Lloyd Wright collaborated on designing the common room: elegant stained-glass fixtures, wooden easy chairs with leather cushions, a roaring brick fireplace, and shiny plank floor. Friendly staff members lead you to one of 10 rooms, each named after a famous composer or poet. Some of these luxurious chambers are decked out with a flat-screen TV, antique soaking tub, four-poster bed, and gas fireplace. Wake up feeling like a million bucks after a night sleeping on pillow-top mattresses covered in goose feather down comforters. Amber House even spoils you in the bathroom with microfiber towels, bathrobes, and L'Occitane toiletries. After a relaxing night in those plush beds, take breakfast in your room or mosey down to the main dining area for gourmet French toast or eggs Benedict. Should you need to connect to the real world, there's also free wireless Internet.

BROADWAY AND LAND PARK $100-150

If you need to stay by UC Davis Medical Center for any reason, the **Best Western Med Park Inn** (2356 Stockton Blvd., 916/455-4000, www.bestwesterncalifornia.com, $100–155) takes good care of their guests. The rooms are comfortable and modern, and amenities include refrigerator, microwave, hair dryer, personal safe, and free wireless Internet. In the morning, the hotel provides a free mini breakfast, and there's also a fitness center. Parking is limited, but guests can make arrangements in the nearby medical center garage.

For the price, **Courtyard Sacramento Midtown** (4422 Y St., 916/455-6800, www.marriott.com, $110–170) is a hip, modern hotel with decent amenities. It's also near the medical center, but business travelers and anyone looking for a quiet stay will enjoy this place. Rooms are cheerfully designed, with tasteful bright colors, large windows, and comfortable beds. Amenities are pretty typical for a large chain hotel; expect to find handy electronic stuff in the closet like irons and hair dryers. Studios include a full kitchen with stovetops, ovens, sinks, microwaves, and large refrigerators. Outside there's a pool if you need to cool off during summer. For other recreation, there's a whirlpool and small fitness center.

GREATER SACRAMENTO

You'll find a gaggle of budget lodgings clustered just north of downtown, off I-5 and on the way to Sacramento International Airport. Many of these lodgings are corporate chains, and they're all pretty similar. Still, it's worth giving you a quick lowdown to spell out differences between some of them.

Under $100

Among the best of the bunch is **Days Inn** (228 Jibboom St., 916/443-4811, www.daysinnsacramentodowntown.com, $60–120), which is dog-friendly and boasts very tidy and spacious rooms that seem almost new. Amenities include refrigerators, microwaves, free wireless Internet, whirlpool baths in some rooms, and cable TV. Outside, the pool looks spotless with clean, sparkling water and a well-swept patio area. Don't worry about parking because there are plenty of spaces.

Don't let the blah exterior fool you— **Governors Inn** (210 Richards Blvd., 916/448-7224, www.governorsinnhotel.com, $90–145) is a step-up from an everyday motel. Walking into the lobby is a breath of fresh air: local artwork on the walls, faux antique chairs, newish sofas, and spotless carpets. The rooms are also sweet. Comfy beds are wrapped in cotton linens with high thread counts and soft bedspreads (not the thin scratchy kind you'll find elsewhere). The rooms are larger than average with enough space for a long sofa and stuffed easy chair. Amenities include free wireless Internet, air-conditioned rooms, coffeemaker, and cable TV. Outside, there's a pool and spa area where guests can relax after a long day in Sacramento's notorious summer heat. Breakfast isn't a big thing here, just a continental spread with cereal, yogurt, juice, and coffee, but it's enough to get you started. The hotel also offers free airport shuttles to and from Sacramento International.

Between Cal Expo and downtown, you'll find **Woodlake Hotel** (500 Leisure Ln., 916/922-2020, www.woodlakehotel.com, $90–110). There are many things to like about this place. The hotel's Mission-style architecture and vast inner courtyard with grassy lawns and man-made lagoon give the place an exotic feeling, almost like a coastal resort in Monterey or Santa Barbara. Rooms are spacious and comfortable. Amenities include flat-screen HD

TVs, free high-speed Internet, cable TV, and ironing boards; outside, you'll find a lakeside pool and spa. There are a few quibbles about the Woodlake. For one thing, it's noticeably a bit old. The hotel often has concerts in the vast inner courtyard, which is either a fantastic way to hear free music or an incredible annoyance. But the Woodlake is just two minutes away from Cal Expo and less than 10 from the State Capitol, and the free parking is also nice.

Just north of downtown off I-5, there's the **Hilton Garden Inn** (2540 Venture Oaks Way, 916/568-5400, www.hiltongardeninn.com, $80–190). This place is just oozing with good stuff. Yeah, it's a corporate chain, but the area is quiet and surrounded by tended lawns, giving off an office park vibe. Business travelers and even couples will dig the bland serenity. Rooms are modestly decorated with comfy beds and large flat-screen TVs. The business center is open all day if you need to run any copies or fax the office. Wireless Internet is free. There's also a pool outside for hot summer days. The Hilton Garden has a small market inside with microwavable meals that you can heat up in the room, so guests don't need to go shopping in the city.

Doubletree Sacramento Hotel (2001 Point West Way, 916/929-8855, www.doubletree. com, $80–160) is close to Cal Expo and the Arden Fair Mall. Rooms are clean and decked out with amenities you'd expect from chain lodgings; there's also a lounge, bar, and café on-site. The greatest thing about this hotel is the shuttle with takes guests anywhere within a three-mile radius, which unfortunately stops just short of Midtown and downtown. Work out at the fitness center or dip into the pool for some exercise. One sour note: the hotel charges $8 for overnight parking.

$100-150

If Austin Powers designed hotels, they'd look like **The Greens** (1700 Del Paso Blvd.,

916/921-1736, www.thegreenshotel.com, $100–120). Expect über-hip '70s color schemes (pea-green and black), leather upholstered headboards, and artwork by Californian artists hanging on the walls. And it's nice to fall asleep beneath down comforters while having control over the room's heating and air-conditioning. To round out the swinging '70s vibe, for a few extra bucks the hotel provides bathrobes and a minibar. Wireless Internet is free. A word to the wise: the neighborhood around The Greens is undergoing a face-lift, but it's still kind of a rough area. There's gated parking available if needed.

The **Courtyard Sacramento Cal Expo** (1782 Tribute Rd., 916/929-7900, www.marriott.com, $110–150) is on the other side of the Capital City Freeway from Cal Expo and just four miles from downtown. Rooms are reasonably priced and decked out with semi-upscale furnishings. You'll feel comfortable staying here; the area is safe, parking is ample, and while the hotel itself is nothing fancy, it has everything you need. Just a quick heads-up: there's no smoking in this hotel, so make sure to light up outside only. The **Fairfield Inn Sacramento Cal Expo** (1780 Tribute Rd., 916/920-5300, www.marriott.com, $95–125) is part of the Courtyard complex but seems a step below its Marriott cousin. The furniture is less fancy (think generic Ikea and you'll have the idea), but otherwise most amenities are the same as the Courtyard.

$150-250

Land your seaplane at the ◖ **Le Rivage** (1020 Captains Table Rd., 916/706-3384, www.le-rivagehotel.com, $175–230) and taxi right into their private marina. Okay, maybe that's a little far-fetched, but this ultra-swanky river palace does have its own boat parking. Best described as a neo-Mediterranean villa built on a levee, Le Rivage claims to provide "boutique European luxury." They must be referring to the marble bathrooms, claw-foot soaking tubs, goose down pillows and comforters, expensive mattresses swaddled in Italian linens, and dark leather furniture—and don't forget the bocce ball courts! Other amenities include a day spa offering massages and skincare treatments, a fitness center, outdoor pool, and whirlpool tubs, and access to trails on the Sacramento River. Some of the rooms look out over the water; make sure to request and confirm these reservations so you don't get moved at check in.

Food

There's no better time for foodies to visit Sacramento. Few restaurants in the country have the natural bounty found in the fields and orchards surrounding the capital. Sacramento's prime location in Central Valley farm country means freshly picked produce arrives by the truckload every day, while ranchers raise grass-fed and organic meat within view of the capital's skyline. California's best ocean fisheries are only two hours away, so seafood comes in straight from the nets. With these resources, Sacramento's executive chefs have turned kitchens into culinary labs for the food-to-table movement, dreaming up new grub that competes with anything you'll eat in San Francisco or Los Angeles. On occasion you'll find that some restaurants are still catching up to the rest. That's becoming rarer every month. Eateries in Sacramento are known for serving amazing Mexican food, California fusion, fine cuisine, and Italian dishes. Keep an eye open for the food trucks that park around town. These mobile chefs can grill with the best, and their food is cheaper than most restaurants. Coffee house culture is also big; many cafés roast their own beans and brew up creative drinks.

It's become so easy to eat well in Sacramento, but keep an eye on your wallet. Eating out in the capital can be expensive. Even if you stay away from fine-dining joints, an average meal will run $10–20 per diner. On the other hand, there's no problem finding a bite all day long. Most places have pretty typical hours, serving breakfast from 7 A.M. until 11 A.M., lunch from 11 A.M. until 2 P.M., and dinner from 5 until 9 or 10 P.M. Some places serve grub until the wee hours of the morning, although they're still rare. Whatever you're craving, most likely these restaurants below serve it.

FARMERS MARKETS

If you're looking for fresh produce from local growers, there's no better place than Sacramento's farmers markets (www.california-grown.com). Dozens of vendors sell produce, artisanal honey, wild-caught fish, grass-fed beef and lamb, free-range chicken, organic rice, dips, cheese, and truckloads of other homemade, farmstead products. The largest market happens underneath the U.S. 50 overpass near 8th and W Streets (8 A.M.–noon Sun.). If you miss that one, there's another market at Cesar Chavez Plaza on Wednesdays, but only during warmer months (10th and J Sts., 10 A.M.–1:30 P.M. Wed. May–Oct.).

DOWNTOWN AND OLD TOWN

You'll find eateries strung out along J and K Streets in downtown, while the best places in Old Sacramento often hide down cobblestoned alleyways. The established joints are near the Capitol, but make sure check out the **Historic R Street District** in the city's former warehouse district, which has arguably become the capital's trendiest place to grab food and drinks. These areas will blow holes in your travel budget after a few rounds. Still, both

FOLLOW THAT FOOD TRUCK!

© CHRISTOPHER ARNS

Food truck madness has arrived in Sacramento.

The capital's food truck scene has exploded over the past few years. During weekdays at lunch, you might find trucks stacked along Cesar Chavez Plaza or idling by the Capitol. If you don't feel like searching for a food truck, check out the Twitter pages or websites for the mobile kitchens listed below for their upcoming locations. Or check out Sacramento's unofficial mobile food site at **www.sactomofo.com** for upcoming events and festivals.

- **Davepops** (www.davepops.com): Creamy popsicles with flavors such as cantaloupe, root beer, apple-pie oat crust, lemon-lime, vanilla chocolate toffee chip, Red Bull, and mango mandarin orange.

- **Drewski's Hot Rod Kitchen** (916/502-0474, http://drewskis.com): Menu items include pulled pork, mac n' cheese, Korean beef with kimchi, and grilled cheese and hot dogs; noteworthy sides are garlic and rosemary tots, sweet potato fries, and deep fried mac n' cheese balls.

- **It's Corn Cake** (916/517-9123, @itscorncake): Southern-style corn bread

served alongside barbecue and other Dixieland grub.

- **Krush Burger** (916/790-0025, www. krushburger.com, @krushburger): Gourmet sliders with toppings like bacon, gouda cheese, crimini and shiitake mushrooms, and provolone cheese.

- **Mama Kim Cooks** (916/515-9971, www. mamakimcooks.com, @mamakimcooks): Falafel sandwiches, salads, turkey and ham sandwiches, and pasta salad.

- **Smoothie Patrol** (916/792-7285): Offers blended flavors like OrangeTwister, Tropical Lemonade, Mookachino, and Monster's Revenge.

- **Volks Waffle California** (916/213-6363, @volkswaffleca): Belgian-inspired waffles coated in sugary caramelized goodness.

- **Wicked'wich** (916/365-3775, @wichonwheels): Awesome sandwiches with homemade bread and some vegan ingredients.

The Historic R Street District is becoming popular with foodies and bar-hoppers.

© CHRISTOPHER ARNS

Old Sacramento and downtown have budget options if you look closely enough.

American

In Old Sacramento, everybody loves **Fanny Ann's Saloon** (1023 Second St., 916/441-0505, http://fannyannsaloon.com, 11:30 A.M.–midnight Sun.–Wed., 11 A.M.–2 A.M. Thurs.–Sat., $8–20). The place is named for one of Sacramento's first paddle-wheeled steamboats. Sadly, the first *Fanny Ann* burned in 1869, but relics from the boat now hang from this saloon's quirky walls. Fanny's has four floors of cozy booths and vintage Americana decor where you can eat greasy diner food; the hamburgers are awesome with an order of curly fries, and you can't go wrong with the sandwiches.

A culinary institution in Old Sacramento is **Fat City Bar and Cafe** (1001 Front St., 916/446-6768, www.fatsrestaurants.com, 11:30 A.M.–2:30 P.M. and 4–9 P.M. Mon.–Fri., 11:30 A.M.–2:30 P.M. and 5–9 P.M. Sat.–Sun.,

$9–33). Best described as a family-friendly saloon, this place has the brick arches and huge wooden bar of a typical Wild West watering hole. Folks come here for the burgers (the Bourbon Barbecue Burger kicks ass), the Sunday brunch, and mostly for the novelty of chowing down in "authentic" Gold Rush surroundings.

Magpie Café (1409 R St., #102, www.magpiecaterers.com, 10:30 A.M.–9 P.M. Mon.–Sat., $10–29) only serves what's in season on local farms, so the menu changes all the time. Veggie fans should dig this place for the gourmet meat-free options like baked polenta squares or the caprese sandwich. It's one of the newish joints in the up-and-coming R Street District, and locals flock here on weekend evenings; get in early because they don't take reservations. Don't be surprised if the service lags even on slower nights.

An old standby for locals is **Café Bernardo's** (1431 R St., 916/930-9191, www.paragarys.

com, 7 A.M.–9 P.M. Mon.–Wed., 7 A.M.–10 P.M. Thurs.–Fri., 8 A.M.–10 P.M. Sat., 8 A.M.–9 P.M. Sun., $8–15). This place is like a trusty wingman who's always down to hang out and makes good conversation. Grab one of the wicker chairs and chill here for a while. Best described as a European café serving old favorites with a healthy twist: plates like hanger steak and griddled ham and cheese sandwiches. Bernardo's has sworn off trans fat oils and only grills free-range chicken, Niman Ranch beef, local cheese, and dairy raised without hormones.

Channeling the spirit of an Old English pub, **Burgers and Brew** (1409 R St., 916/442-0900, http://burgersbrew.com, 11 A.M.–midnight Sun.–Wed., 11 A.M.–3 A.M. Thurs.–Sat., $9) serves food all day long in this old brick building. It's another R Street location that's buzzing with trendy foodies, especially late-nighters who can eat here until 2:45 A.M. on weekends. As the name says, they do burgers and beer; both are outstanding. My favorite is the lamb burger (marinated in olive oil and topped with feta cheese, roasted garlic, and yogurt sauce). And even though it's bar food, don't feel too guilty about eating here; they serve all natural Niman Ranch meat, so hey, it can't be too bad for you. Guzzle one of 17 beers on tap, like Arrogant Bastard Ale or Scrimshaw Pilsner, or pick something from their huge selection of bottled brews. The place gets packed so come early.

A great place for drinks and grub is **Shady Lady Saloon** (1409 R St., #101, 916/231-9121, www.shadyladybar.com, 11 A.M.–midnight Mon.–Fri., 9 A.M.–midnight Sat.–Sun., $10–13). Most people come here for the bar's faux-speakeasy decadence and neo-Victorian decor, but the chow is actually pretty damn good. The menu is small—it's basically a bar menu—so don't come here to satisfy gnawing hunger. Typical plates include portobello sliders, hanger steak salads, and fried green tomatoes.

It's official: food trucks are invading

Sacramento's restaurants. **Republic Bar and Grill** (908 15th St., 916/822-5152, www.republicsac.com, 4 P.M.–2 A.M. Mon. and Wed.–Fri., 9 A.M.–2 A.M. Sat.–Sun., $8) serves up grill grub from Drewski's Hot Rod Kitchen, a popular mobile food vendor among locals. The menu is a creative mash-up of bar chow and American diner food. Typical plates include deep-fried macaroni cheese balls, the Magnum burger with gruyère cheese and garlic sauce, and a whole spread of breakfast options smothered in cheese, meat, and eggs. But this place is more than just food, it's like a playground for adults. They have board games, darts, pool tables, video games, and Skeeball. Yes, really. Football fans pack this place on weekends for NFL matchups on satellite TV or UFC fights.

Esquire Grill (1213 K St., 916/448-8900, www.paragarys.com, 11 A.M.–9 P.M. Mon.–Thurs., 11 A.M.–10 P.M. Fri., 4:30–10 P.M. Sat., $13–32) serves traditional American fare. Apparently it was good enough for Arnold Schwarzenegger, who was spotted here frequently when he was governor. He was probably chowing down on the wild king salmon, served with yellow wax beans, or the chicken potpie. Hard-core politicos will recognize other big-name California lawmakers eating here at midday; Esquire is right across from the Capitol and gets packed for lunch. Call for a reservation so you can grab a table.

While I was growing up, my mother would always make potpie with creamy gravy and a golden-brown crust. To this day, potpie feels like comfort food. **Pronto** (1501 16th St., 916/444-5850, www.prontogo.com, 11:30 A.M.–9 P.M. Mon.–Fri., 9 A.M.–9 P.M. Sat., 9 A.M.–8:30 P.M. Sun., $10) comes close to replicating Mom's perfect chicken potpie. The menu is stacked with hearty Midwestern hits like bacon meatloaf, chicken parmesan, and five-cheese lasagna. They top it off with a generous hunk of garlic bread for mopping up the finger-licking sauce. Folks with a gluten-intolerance can feel comfortable eating here because Pronto has a special menu for those with food allergies. No need to dress up for this eatery's casual diner-slash-lunch counter format. The only thing you need is an appetite.

◖ Fox and Goose Pub and Restaurant (1001 R St., 916/443-8825, www.foxandgoose.com, 6:30 A.M.–10 P.M. Mon.–Tues., 6:30 A.M.–11 P.M. Wed.–Thurs., 6:30 A.M.–midnight Fri.–Sat., 6:30 A.M.–3 P.M. Sun., $10) might just dish up Sacramento's best breakfast. Whether you're jonesing for fresh pastries, delicious pancakes, or kick-ass omelettes, make sure to come here. And do show up early; a line starts forming around 9:30–10 A.M. on weekends.

Asian

Lotus Restaurant (425 J St., 916/448-5568, 11 A.M.–3 P.M. and 5–9 P.M. Mon.–Fri., noon–9 P.M. Sat., $5–10) dishes up authentic Thai and Vietnamese food in Sacramento's Chinatown district. Not many folks know about this hole-in-the-wall, and they're certainly missing out. Try the spring rolls, the pad Thai, or the pho ga Vietnamese soup with large chicken chunks and delicious noodles swimming in broth.

For more than 70 years, **◖ Frank Fat's** (806 L St., 916/442-7092, www.fatsrestaurants.com, 11 A.M.–10 P.M. Mon.–Fri., 5–10 P.M. Sat.–Sun., $9–27) has been the godfather of Sacramento's food scene. It was founded by the restaurant's namesake in 1939 and is still going strong. I crack up when driving by this place because the sketchy exterior looks like a members-only joint from the 1970s. That's actually not far from the truth. For years, Frank's has been a favorite among local politicos who practice "napkin diplomacy" as they debate policy over lunch here. But the interior doesn't give off that smoky backroom vibe. The interior has a hip, cosmopolitan flavor with classy

leather booths, a long shiny bar, and modern furniture. The food is best described as upscale Chinese fare and it's tasty; typical plates include mango ginger chicken, chow mein, and pineapple sweet and sour pork.

If you enjoy a club environment, **Zen Sushi** (900 15th St., 916/446-9628, www.zen-sushi.com, 11:30 A.M.–10 P.M. Sun.–Thurs., 11:30 A.M.–10:30 P.M. Fri.–Sat., $5–15) is the spot for you. Best described as "swanky," word on the street seems to say this place focused too much on recent renovations and not so much on the service. The food is still good, and you can get awesome rolls and top-notch fish at this place, which stays open for the late-night crew on weekends.

Harry's Café (2026 16th St., 916/448-0088, 7 A.M.–9 P.M. Tues.–Sat., 7 A.M.–5 P.M. Sun., $6–20) is downtown's best kept secret. Harry's serves Pacific Rim cuisine from Hawaii, Vietnam, and China. But the biggest surprise is the American-style breakfasts, which include omelettes and pancakes. If you're feeling a travel bug coming on (sore throat, sniffles, that achy feeling), Harry's "cold or flu" chicken veggie soup is a bowl of germ-fighting goodness.

Bakeries and Cafés

Starbucks who? Sacramento's bean scene moved past trendy chains long ago. Most cafés roast their own coffee or buy from other roasters in town. Pour-over bars have also become a new thing, where baristas brew a single cup of your chosen coffee in a French press. One of the capital's caffeinated pioneers is **◖ Temple Coffee** (1010 9th St., 916/443-4960, www.templecoffee.com, 6 A.M.–11 P.M. daily, $4). All beans are roasted every day at their S Street location. Grab a Mexican mocha or pick your own beans and watch the barista brew up a single cup just for you at the pour-over bar. The vibe here is quasi-social; Temple attracts both students cramming for finals and friends commiserating about their love lives. Both seem to coexist at the 13-foot handmade tables where people sit family-style and imbibe their steaming cups of joe.

The godfather of Sacramento caffeine might be ⓒ **Naked Lounge** (1500 Q St., 916/442-0174, www.nakedcoffee.net, 6 A.M.–11 P.M. daily, $4). This café brews up a neo-grungy vibe that's manifested in edgy artwork on the wall and overstuffed couches where folks sip drinks like the Bowl of Soul (chamomile tea served with steamed condensed milk and honey) and the Kerouac, billed as the "martini of coffee drinks." At four shots of caffeine, the "heart attack of coffee drinks" sounds more like it. This place feels more social than Temple or other cafés. It's a perfect place to take a date or catch up with friends; maybe not so much for quietly reading or studying. There's another Naked Lounge on downtown's northern frontier (1111 H St., 916/443-1927, www.nakedcoffee.net, 6:30 A.M.–7 P.M. Mon.–Fri., 8 A.M.–7 P.M. Sat.–Sun., $4) purveying the same kind of social slacker vibe.

Temple and the Naked Lounge threw down the caffeine gauntlet nearly a decade ago for Sacramento's coffee houses. Another café following their lead is **Broadacre** (1014 10th St., 916/442-1085, http://broadacrecoffee.com, 6 A.M.–11 P.M. daily, $4), down the street from the State Capitol. This café actually occupies Temple's old location but feels like a stripped down version. The decor is minimal, almost bleak. On the other hand, their coffee drinks are pretty innovative. Try either the lavender or the honey lattes.

Insight Coffee Roasters (1901 8th St., 916/642-9555, http://insightcoffee.com, 7 A.M.–8 P.M. daily, $4) keeps things simple. No fancy coffee drinks; just the basics like lattes, mochas, Americanos, and house coffee. They've got a beautiful copper espresso machine and postmodern grungy decor, and the brew is among the best in town. They also have

a pour-over bar where baristas will brew a single cup with beans of your choosing.

Chocolate Fish Coffee Roasters (400 P St., #1203, 916/400-4204, www.chocolate-fishcoffee.com, 6:30 A.M.–4 P.M. Mon.–Fri., 8 A.M.–3 P.M. Sat., 9 A.M.–4 P.M. Sun., $4) also roasts their own beans. So far, this place has flown under the radar. If you're visiting the Crocker Art Museum, walk over and try a New Zealand–style latte or a mocha.

Yellowbill Café and Bakery (1425 14th St., 916/668-7514, 6:30 A.M.–6 P.M. Mon.–Sat., $5–10) is twins with Magpie Café up the R Street District. The concept is basically the same: local, seasonal grub that skews heavily toward vegetarian. Yellowbill is the coffeehouse version serving pastries and freshly brewed coffee from Chocolate Fish Coffee Roasters. You can get a carrot cake cookie, a scone, or a quick sandwich on focaccia bread to go.

Imagine a futuristic cyborg whose only mission is to sell the best doughnuts around. Except for the whole cyborg thing, that's exactly the concept behind **Doughbot** (2226 10th St., 916/444-5157, www.doughbotdonuts.com, 7 A.M.–2 P.M. Tues.–Sun., $2). Their motto? "Resistance is futile," so just go ahead and order one. The most popular doughnuts have hipster names like The Dude, The Picard, and Mr. Manager. To be honest, they're smaller than you'd expect; but with diet-busting flavors like raspberry, pink lemonade, vanilla bean, and s'mores, you won't mind a bit.

For French-style goodies, **Estelle's Patisserie** (901 K St., 916/551-1500, www.estellespatisserie.com, 7 A.M.–6 P.M. Mon.–Fri., 8 A.M.–5 P.M. Sat., $4) feels like a true Euro bakery. The menu reads like an elegant poem to the art of baking. Sugary almond tarts, fluffy pistachio financiers, danishes, several flavors of flaky croissants, muffins, and cookies fill the display cases in this charming little joint. Everything is made fresh daily as state workers are hurrying by on their way to sky-high office buildings. Pack a few pastries to go and enjoy them on a bench in Capitol Park, or drop by for lunch sandwiches.

Ambrosia Cafe (1030 K St., 916/444-8129, www.ambrosiacafesacramento.com, 6:30 A.M.–5 P.M. Mon.–Fri., 8 A.M.–3 P.M. Sat.–Sun., $7) serves coffee, pastries, and paninis inside this cozy Parisian-style spot. Sit outside on K Street and watch the light-rail train whoosh by.

Don't let your dentist catch you at **The Sacramento Sweets Co.** (1035 Front St., 916/446-0590, www.sacsweets.com, 10:30 A.M.–8 P.M. Mon.–Thurs., 10 A.M.–10 P.M. Fri.–Sat., 10 A.M.–9 P.M. Sun., $5). Every kid has probably dreamed of scarfing down fistfuls of peanut brittle and saltwater taffy. You can do both inside this candy store and ice cream parlor. Handmade brittles come in at least eight different varieties, including macadamia-almond-coconut and cashew. Tubs of saltwater taffy rise from the floor. They also have sugar-free brittles and fudge on hand. If candy isn't your thing, try a chocolate-covered banana or a soft-serve ice cream cone instead. As you walk outside, cross-eyed from staring down at your ice cream, make sure you don't trip off the wooden boardwalk; it's been known to happen.

Cajun

Pack the Tums if you stop by **Hot & Spicy Café New Orleans** (117 J St., 916/443-5051, 11 A.M.–9 P.M. Sun.–Thurs., 11 A.M.–10 P.M. Fri.–Sat., $10–17), which serves up spicy bayou food straight from Louisiana. Alligator skewers, turtle soup, jambalaya, and hearty gumbo round out the menu. Your gutty works may reel after eating here, but your taste buds will approve.

Californian

You could flag down a steamboat from **Rio City Cafe** (1110 Front St., 916/442-8226, www.

riocitycafe.com, 11 A.M.–10 P.M. Mon.–Fri., 10 A.M.–10 P.M. Sat.–Sun., $12–27), which is right on the Sacramento River. Folks come here for drinks and dinner (or sometimes just drinks), but the brunch might be Sacramento's best. Food is typical Californian cuisine; grilled salmon smothered with lentils and fennel, roasted chicken breast slathered with sweet pea pesto, and Pacific pasta teeming with mussels and fresh fish. Good food requires damn good wine, and Rio's wine list reads like a who's who of the best vintners. Change it up after dinner and order a cocktail from the full bar and watch the sun set behind the Tower Bridge.

Fine Dining

Without a doubt, **C Ella Dining Room and Bar** (1131 K St., 916/443-3772, www.elladiningroomandbar.com, 11:30 A.M.–9 P.M. Mon.–Thurs., 11:30 A.M.–10 P.M. Fri., 5:30–10 P.M. Sun., $10–28) is downtown's culinary superstar. Created by local food impresario Randall Selland, this upscale eatery dishes up local, sustainably farmed fare from farmers markets. There's sort of a neo-retro vibe to this place: high ceilings with long white drapes, minimalist wooden furnishes, and '60s-style lighting. You be almost positive that Don Draper is showing up later. But don't forget the food. Plates include Scottish salmon with succotash, vegetarian nut burger and wood-fired flatbread. Good luck dropping in without a reservation unless it's earlier in the week. I'd call ahead of time on weekends to secure a table.

There's no other way to say this: **C The Firehouse** (1112 2nd St., 916/442-4772, www.firehouseoldsac.com, 11:30 A.M.–2:30 P.M. and 5–9:30 P.M. Mon.–Thurs., 11:30 A.M.–2:30 P.M. and 5–10 P.M. Fri., 5–10 P.M. Sat., 5–9:30 P.M. Sun., $12–56) is a classic old-school steak house oozing Gilded Age glamour. The gnarly brick building once housed California's first paid fire department and dates

Ella Dining Room and Bar

back to 1853. Ronald Reagan held both of his inaugural dinners here when he was governor just a few years after Old Sacramento was raised from the dead. Sit outside in the Victorian-style courtyard under a huge mulberry tree or head inside to the handsome dining room, where crystal chandeliers gleam over white table-cloths. If that doesn't sell it, just wait for the food. Plates are served in courses although you can order à la carte. Elderflower almond duck, Moroccan lamb with tomato-apricot chutney, and Mediterranean game hen are just a few hits from the menu. You're probably already thinking this, but I'll say it anyway: Call ahead for reservations because tables go fast every night of the week.

Grange (926 J St., 916/492-4450, www.grangesacramento.com, 6:30–10:30 A.M. and 11:30 A.M.–2:30 P.M. Mon.–Fri., 5:30–10 P.M. Mon.–Thurs., 5:30–11 P.M. Fri.–Sat., 5:30–9 P.M. Sun., $20–40) has a superb location on the bottom floor of the Citizen Hotel.

The cuisine is American farmstead; most of their food comes from local ranches like Capay Organics, Full Belly Farms, and Soil Born Farms just outside of Sacramento.

McCormick and Schmick's (1111 J St., 916/442-8200, www.mccormickandschmicks.com, 11:30 A.M.–10 P.M. Mon.–Thurs., 11:30 A.M.–11 P.M. Fri., 4–10 P.M. Sat., 4–9 P.M. Sun., $18–40) is an upscale steak house with an East Coast vibe. The location couldn't be better—spread out over the bottom floor of Sacramento's Elks Tower, a redbrick Art Deco behemoth evoking the capital's Prohibition past.

French

You'll find the world's best French onion soup at ◖ **La Bonne Soupe Café** (920 8th St., 916/492-9506, 11 A.M.–3 P.M. Mon.–Sat., $4–8). That's not just coming from me; venerable reviewers from Zagat made that call in 2009. Order a smoked salmon sandwich (with prosciutto, goat cheese, and balsamic dressing) along with some of that famous soup and dunk away. It's a little hard to find, especially when the RT light-rail passes by and blocks the painted sign on the window. Just park in the garage across the street and look for the neon bail bonds sign next door.

For some unknowable reason, the French were blessed with the magic culinary touch. One of Sacramento's most authentic places to eat la cuisine française is **Bistro Michel** (1501 14th St., 916/346-4012, www.bistromichel.com, 11:30 A.M.–2:30 P.M. and 5–9 P.M. Tues.–Wed., 11:30 A.M.–2:30 P.M. and 5–10 P.M. Thurs.–Sat., 10:30 A.M.–2:30 P.M. and 5–8 P.M. Sun., $10–27). It's an urbane, upscale kind of place. Come here after watching California's Senate debate budget cuts at the Capitol down the street. You can discuss Golden State politics over *sous vide* and a bottle of French wine as streetlights flicker on down by Capitol Park. By closing time, you'll be ready to run for office.

Italian

As any Italian will tell you, it's all in the sauce. Downtown Sacramento has a handful of places with amazing pasta, lasagna, and sauce like Mama used to make. For starters, **Café Roma** (1013 L St., 916/594-7292, http://caferomaonline.com, 8 A.M.–7 P.M. Mon.–Fri., $7–19) is a family-owned joint dishing up homemade pasta. Locals seem to like the paninis best, like the mozzarella tomato pesto sandwich or the turkey and havarti on focaccia bread. Make sure to save room for one of the eight different flavors of gelato and sorbetto.

If you're trying to impress a date, there's **Spataro's Restaurant and Bar** (1415 L St., 916/440-8888, www.spatarorestaurant.com, 11:30 A.M.–2:30 P.M. Mon.–Fri. and 5–9 P.M. Mon.–Sat., $13–23). It's sort of dressy; jeans and flip-flops won't get you kicked out but the decor is fancy and the food is borderline

fine cuisine. Plates range from cannelloni (Florentine crepes stuffed with a fistful of meats, herbs, and sauce) to tagliata (sounds like a Mafia family, but it's really flat iron steak with arugula, trumpet mushrooms, and parmesan).

Mexican

Tequila Museo Mayahuel (1200 K St., 916/441-7200, http://tequilamuseo.com, 11 A.M.–10 P.M. Mon.–Wed., 11 A.M.–midnight Thurs.–Fri., 5 P.M.–midnight Sat., $8–23) is an ultra-trendy eatery with its own tequila room. Inside, this place is pretty modern—not your typical dive serving chips and salsa in plastic cups. The menu is best described as gourmet Cali-Mex food, so it's heavier on veggies like olives and avocado, herbs such as cilantro, and leaner meats like chicken and fish. Locals rave about the earthy-red mole sauce (chocolate, tomatoes, chiles, and spices) served on chicken or enchiladas.

MIDTOWN AND EAST SACRAMENTO

Restaurants in these neighborhoods are mostly found in small clusters along the same streets. Streets like H, J, K, and Capitol Avenue plow a racing stripe of über-hip eateries and bistros from Midtown to the far bounds of East Sacramento. This area is vast; more than 40 blocks separate trendy restaurants on 16th Street from the tiny diners and family-owned restaurants along quiet Folsom Boulevard. You'll find that eating out in Midtown is more of a scene. Hipsters in pegged jeans riding fixed-gear bikes might sit down next to wannabe cage fighters with sleeves of tattoos. East Sacramento caters more to families. You'll probably see moms and dads toting babies on their beach cruisers as they all ride to their favorite hot spot. But everywhere you go, eateries serve creative plates with long lists of California wines and craft brews.

American

Eateries in Sacramento and the Gold Country are starting to follow a simple recipe: Take an old building, strip it down to the bricks and plank flooring, add some neo-retro furniture, and bam, you've got a hip new bistro. In Midtown, that's the formula at **Red Rabbit Kitchen and Bar** (2718 J St., 916/706-2275, www.theredrabbit.net, 11:30 A.M.–midnight Mon.–Wed., 11:30 A.M.–2 A.M. Thurs.–Fri., 10:30 A.M.–2 A.M. Sat., 10:30 A.M.–midnight Sun., $8–20), an East Coast–style place with an upscale urban theme. Bowing to the farm-to-table craze, most entrées come from sustainable farms and fisheries. Hits on the menu include the Shorty Melt stuffed with rib meat, cheddar, and chipotle sauce on ciabatta, and the Loco Moco with rich spinach, free-range beef patty, mushrooms, and an egg. If you're not hungry, order cocktails with handmade syrup from the bar menu; the Krakow Salt Mine is a favorite. It never hurts to have a reservation before coming here, especially on weekends.

With stained glass and stately woodwork, **Kupros Bistro** (1217 21st St., 916/440-0401, www.kuprosbistro.com, 11 A.M.–midnight Mon.–Thurs., 11 A.M.–2 A.M. Fri.–Sat., 10 A.M.–midnight Sun., $12–23) is a culinary cathedral inside a 1910 Craftsman. The building actually used to be a costume shop, but has been restored to resemble the original home. Plates are classy updates on American favorites. White truffle mac and cheese, organic chicken, and pappardelle are just a few. But it's the bar menu that gets props. You can pick three items for $10 everyday; things like fried pickles, sweet potato fries, and chicken satay. Most locals rave about the Kobe beef burger smothered with a mess of grilled veggies, cheese, and sauce. The late hours are another nice thing about this place, but I'd still recommend a reservation for a larger party on weekends.

What could be simpler: a doughy bun, juicy franks, and heaping toppings. At **Capitol Dawg** (1226 20th St., 916/444-1226, www.capitoldawg.com, 11 A.M.–3:30 P.M. Mon., 11 A.M.–8 P.M. Tues.–Sat., until 11 P.M. second Sat. of the month, $4), they've turned a basic American favorite into perfection. Walls are covered with old baseball pennants, football posters, and vintage photos from Sacramento's sporting yesteryears. It's got that classic East Coast hole-in-the-wall feel. They prepare dogs with 30 different combos of toppings, sauces, and bread. Consider something like the Sutter's Fort Dawg (taco style with salsa, cheddar cheese, guacamole, and sour cream) or the Land Park Dawg (Italian style), and order one of the 19 bottled beers on hand to wash it down.

Skating the margins of fine dining while still keeping a down-home vibe, ◼ **Mulvaney's B&L** (1215 19th St., 916/441-6022, www.mulvaneysbl.com, 11:30 A.M.–2:30 P.M. and 5–10 P.M. Tues.–Fri., 5–10 P.M. Sat., $15–34) has become one of Midtown's most respected restaurants. Folks around the country have also taken notice; OpenTable tapped this place for a Diners' Choice Award in 2011 and it's not hard to see why. Inside this 1893 firehouse building, owner and head chef Patrick Mulvaney serves "handcrafted new American cuisine," like griddled arctic char smothered in chocolate chile sauce and braised lamb shoulder paired with creamy polenta. Staying sustainable is Mulvaney's mantra; the food is harvested from Central Valley and most waste is recycled. If you're coming with a group, ask for the 10-person "snug" room for cozy and private dining. I'm not sure why, but some folks have a hard time finding this place; just look for two white firehouse doors in a red brick building.

An old standby is **Café Bernardo** (2726 Capitol Ave., 916/443-1180, www.cafebernardo.com, 7 A.M.–9 P.M. Mon.–Thurs., 7 A.M.–10 P.M. Fri., 8 A.M.–10 P.M. Sat., 8 A.M.–9 P.M. Sun., $8–14). Locals usually come here for lunch and sandwiches, although

Sunday brunch is an underrated experience. No surprises on the menu; just classic American fare like tri-tip, roasted turkey sandwiches, griddled ham and cheese, and pan-seared chicken breast.

Grandma would approve of **Evan's Kitchen** (855 57th St., 916/452-3896, www.chefevan. com, 8 A.M.–9 P.M. Tues.–Sat., 8 A.M.–3 P.M. Sun., $8–27) because no one goes home hungry. Expect hearty portions of surf and turf, and Italian-inspired plates. The '80s-style oak furniture and booths almost look vintage at this point, a nice change from ultra-slick bistros aping the industrial look. As a result, this place feels like someone's dining room. Evan's serves food all day, but breakfast beats everything: heaping piles of hash browns, pancakes, and omelettes the size of catchers' mitts.

Moxie Restaurant (2028 H St., 916/443-7585, www.moxierestaurant.com, 5–10 P.M. Tues.–Sat., $16–34) is a good old-fashioned Manhattan steak house buried on Midtown's sleepy fringe. For that reason, it gets lost on Sacramento's foodie radar. Look for the mysterious red door on the corner of H and 20th Streets. Inside, the walls are covered in classy black-and-white photos of ballplayers, starlets, New York's skylines, and random shots of people making out. Plates are familiar variations of traditional American surf and turf; Chilean sea bass, lamb, beef, scallops; and more. It's not a very big place so call ahead for reservations.

◖ **The Golden Bear** (2326 K St., 916/441-2242, www.goldenbear916.com, 11:30 A.M.–2 A.M. Mon.–Fri., 10 A.M.–2 A.M. Sat.–Sun., $11) is like that slacker friend who made millions in the stock market: casual and laid-back but worth every penny. Locals usually choose Golden Bear for drinks, but the food demands respect. There's nothing fancy about it, just pub grub with the Bear's special touches. Try the Juicy Lucy sandwich (Niman Ranch beef stuffed with jack, bacon, cheddar,

homemade pickles, and a grip of other toppings) or the butternut calzone. Dinner is good here, but brunch stands on its own with other local breakfast joints.

After a night on the town, stop by **Ink Eats and Drinks** (2730 N St., 916/456-2800, http://inkeats.com, 11:30 A.M.–1 A.M. Mon.–Tues., 11:30 A.M.–3 A.M. Wed.–Thurs., 11:30 A.M.–4 A.M. Fri., 9 A.M.–4 A.M. Sat., 9 A.M.–1 A.M. Sun., $8–14) for late-night sandwiches and finger food. Ink also serves a vast amount of dinner and breakfast entrées; mostly surf and turf fare.

The Shack (5201 Folsom Blvd., 916/457-5667, http://eastsacshack.com, 11 A.M.–3 P.M. Mon., 11 A.M.–9 P.M. Tues.–Fri., 8 A.M.–3 P.M. Sat.–Sun., $10) draws the local bike crowd for pub trivia and mouthwatering burgers like the Cajun bacon blue burger with blue cheese, grilled onions, Cajun seasoning, and blue cheese dressing. If only they'd break off the smoking patio away from the burger-eating patio, the Shack would rock. Another downer: it takes about 45 minutes for grub to come out of the kitchen. If you've got an afternoon to kill, the burgers are the best in East Sacramento.

Breakfast is king at ◖ **Orphan** (3440 C St., 916/442-7370, http://orphanbreakfast. com, breakfast 7 A.M.–2 P.M. daily, lunch 11 A.M.–2 P.M. Mon.–Fri, $5–12), where they serve the best pancakes in town. You have two choices: buttermilk "Naked cakes" (the owner also runs Naked Lounge coffee houses in downtown and Midtown) or cornmeal flapjacks. If you're really lucky, daily specials might include peach griddle jacks or banana-walnut-Nutella pancakes. There's certainly more to love. Overall, the fare seems like a Californian take on Latin-Mediterranean fusion; heavy on soy products (tofu, soy chorizo), rosemary, pesto, avocado, and black beans. Judging by what most people like here, the soy chorizo scramble is the top vote-getter on the menu.

Before you go, here's a friendly heads-up: They only take cash. There's an ATM by the cash register if your wallet is empty.

Asian

Shanghai Garden (800 Alhambra Blvd., 916/446-6358, http://shanghaigardenca.com, 11 A.M.–9:30 P.M. Mon.–Thurs., 11 A.M.–10 P.M. Fri., noon–9:30 P.M. Sat.–Sun., $7) dishes up authentic Chinese food with rich, savory sauces that aren't too greasy. After a long day at McKinley Park, you'll find this place just down the block on a low-key street corner. They'll deliver orders over $15 within three miles.

For American-style sushi and an upbeat atmosphere, there's █ **Mikuni Japanese Restaurant and Sushi Bar** (1530 J St., 916/447-2112, www.mikunisushi.com, 11:30 A.M.–10 P.M. Mon.–Thurs., 11:30 A.M.–midnight Fri., noon–midnight Sat., noon–9 P.M. Sun., $5–17). The crowd skews toward the young side on weekends, when Midtown bar-hoppers start their evenings here with sake bombs. It's also a popular place to celebrate birthdays; the man or woman of the hour spins a party wheel for free prizes. Expect to wait on busier evenings unless you have a reservation, but make the extra effort to eat here on your trip. Most locals would agree the sushi is better than average and they're known for spicy sushi rolls packed with stuff like fried tempura, seared ahi, and salmon roe.

There's an ongoing debate about Midtown's best sushi. Some say Mikuni for the atmosphere, but others vote for **Kru** (2516 J St., 916/551-1559, www.krurestaurant.com, 11:30 A.M.–9:30 P.M. Mon., 11:30 A.M.–10 P.M. Tues.–Thurs., 11:30 A.M.–11 P.M. Fri., noon–11 P.M. Sat., 5–9:30 P.M. Sun., $15) because they wrap a mean roll with top-notch fish. Do yourself a favor and grab a bar seat for quicker service. The vibe here is best described as chill lounge meets California-style sushi. Rolls are

slightly more expensive than average, but they use organic rice in everything, which probably bumps up the cost a bit.

For a different take on Japanese food, head **Shabu Japanese Fondue** (1730 16th St., 916/444-6688, www.shabujapanesefondue.com, 5–9:30 P.M. Sun.–Thurs, 5–10 P.M. Fri.–Sat., $15). If you're not familiar with hot pot cuisine, it's actually a blast. You get a meat platter, veggies, a couple of sauces, some rice, and a boiling water pot. Dunk the meat and veggies into the pot until cooked, pull out with chopsticks, and mix with rice and sauce. The result is somewhere between a stew and a rice bowl. It's a great idea for dates or couples in the mood for something new. One thing that could be better here is the atmosphere. It's located on the first floor of a bland-looking office building. Inside, there's nothing very Japanese about the decor and Muzak or Top 40 hits usually play in the background. The food, however, is darn good.

Bakeries and Cafés

Do not, I repeat, do not engage in staring contests with the display case at █ **Rick's Dessert Diner** (2322 K St., 916/444-0969, http://ricksdessertdiner.com, 10 A.M.–midnight Tues.–Thurs., 10 A.M.–1 A.M. Fri.–Sat., noon–11 P.M. Sun., 10 A.M.–11 P.M. Mon., $6). Those cakes staring back at you? They win every time. Diets be damned, this retro diner serves more than 285 kinds of American and Euro-themed goodies like pies, tarts and tortes, pastries, and yeah, those sinfully yummy cakes. I'm talking about sweet potato pecan pie, apple cranberry walnut pie, apricot white chocolate cheesecake, and red velvet cakes. Should I go on? The desserts are only half the fun. Rick's is decorated like a 1950s diner with murals of James Dean and Humphrey Bogart staring down from the walls. Grab a seat in the old-fashioned leather booths and gobble down that cake. They also serve espresso drinks and ice cream.

Seems like fancy coffee drinks have taken over the coffee house genre. But for a great cup of gourmet joe, head to **Old Soul** (1716 L St., 916/443-7685, www.oldsoulco.com, 6 A.M.–7 P.M. daily, $2–5). They advertise themselves as a "boutique coffee roaster and baker" tucked down a Midtown alley. Locals debate it, but Old Soul might be the purest Seattle-style coffee house in town. Choices are simple here; just tea, house coffee, and basic lattes and mochas. They also have another Midtown location, **Old Soul at the Weatherstone** (812 21st St., 916/443-6340, www.oldsoulco.com, 6 A.M.–11 P.M. daily, $2–5), a few blocks away in the Boulevard Park neighborhood. At both places, you'll find a stripped down urban grunge vibe with weathered plank tables, retro leather chairs, and occasional live jazz.

A Sacramento institution for locally roasted beans, **Temple Coffee** (2829 S St., 916/454-1272, www.templecoffee.com, 6 A.M.–11 P.M. daily, $4) revived a crumbling urban building into a hip coffee joint. They also serve two dozen blends of herbal, white, green, oolong, and black teas. If you want a simple cup of house blend or a fancy espresso steamer, they'll do either one.

Tupelo Coffee House (5700 Elvas Ave., 916/538-6124, www.nakedcoffee.net, 6 A.M.–11 P.M. daily, $4) is a boutique beanery serving Naked Coffee. Their specialty drinks are famous, especially the Bowl of Soul (chamomile tea, steamed condensed milk, honey, and spices). The atmosphere is low-key, mostly students holding quiet study groups or typing on laptops. Like most Sacramento coffee shops, the decor is stripped down warehouse chic with modernistic tables and chairs.

Hands down the best place for froyo is **Yogurtagogo** (1801 L St., 916/346-4649, http://yogurtagogo.com, 11 A.M.–11 P.M. Sun.–Thurs., 11 A.M.–2 A.M. Fri.–Sat., $5). This bouncy little shop serves homemade flavors like red velvet, Eurotart, raspberry pomegranate tart, and other yummy concoctions.

Brewpub

Rubicon Brewing Company (2004 Capitol Ave., 916/448-7032, www.rubiconbrewing.com, 11 A.M.–11:30 P.M. Mon.–Thurs., 11 A.M.–12:30 A.M. Fri.–Sat., 11 A.M.–10 P.M. Sun., $10) pours awesome beer produced by men with stupendous facial hair. Stop by and check if you don't believe me. Every pilser, ale, and lager is brewed right here at this mellow pub. And the food is darn good. I recommend starting with a sausage sampler and a pint of Monkey Knife Ale. For something more substantial, Rubicon's thick, juicy burgers and delicious sandwiches are slathered in generous toppings.

Firestone Public House (1132 16th St., 916/446-0888, www.firestonepublichouse.com, 11 A.M.–midnight Mon.–Tues., 11 A.M.–2 A.M. Wed.–Fri., 9 A.M.–2 A.M. Sat., 9 A.M.–midnight Sun., $10–17) serves up traditional American favorites in an upscale sports bar environment. The fare is pretty basic: burgers, pizza, sandwiches, and surf/turf. Large tables mean families can bring the whole clan and groups of coworkers can pop in to watch Monday Night Football. Beer flows freely from the four-sided bar with more than 30 brews available.

Hoppy Brewing Company (6300 Folsom Blvd., 916/451-4677, www.hoppy.com, 11 A.M.–midnight Mon.–Wed., 11 A.M.–1 A.M. Thurs.–Fri., 10 A.M.–1 A.M. Sat., 10 A.M.–midnight Sun., $10–15) produces beer straight from their taproom. Come here for big games and order a flatbread spread (falafel, tzatziki, hummus, and flatbread) with your brew, or double down with an eclectic dinner menu. Burgers, ribs, spicy prawns, salmon, and enchiladas are just a few things served up here.

Californian

Barely noticeable from the street, **Tuli Bistro** (2031 S St., 916/451-8854, www.tulibistro.com, 11 A.M.–9 P.M., Mon.–Wed., 11 A.M.–10 P.M. Thurs.–Fri., 5–10 P.M. Sat., 9:30 A.M.–2 P.M. and 5–9 P.M. Sun., $15–26) is a pearl hidden in Midtown's leafy depths. Local wunderkind Adam Pechal grew up in Sacramento and graduated top of his class from the venerable Culinary Institute of America. Working behind his long granite "chef's bar," Pechal whips up internationally inspired plates that lean heavily on seasonal influences. Veal sweetbreads, squid ink pasta, Southwestern-style pork tenderloin, and pizza fill the menu. The only quibble: the service can be hit-and-miss, and table waiting becomes an hour-long game on weekends (only drop-ins accepted).

If the capital's trendier bistros are the new hipsters on the block, **Paragary's Bar and Oven** (1401 28th St., 916/457-5737, www. paragarysmidtown.com, 5–9 P.M. Mon.–Thurs., 5–10 P.M. Fri., 4:30–10 P.M. Sat.–Sun., $11–22) is the older gentleman wearing slacks and a blazer. Consider Paragary's the don of Sacramento's Midtown foodie revolution. Back when Midtown was struggling through blight and decay in the 1980s, dining magnate Randy Paragary boldly opened this joint a few blocks from Sutter's Fort. It's now the heart of Midtown's culinary revival. They serve food inspired by Italian and French influences paired with a long list of California wines. Inside, the atmosphere is classy and laid-back, but the patio's gnarled oak trees and weathered fireplace make Paragary's stand out. You definitely need a reservation here, so make sure to call ahead especially on weekend evenings.

The Press Bistro (1809 Capitol Ave., 916/444-2566, http://thepressbistro.com, 4–9 P.M. Sun. and Tues.–Wed., 4–10 P.M. Thurs.–Sat., $9–23) has a Californian take on Mediterranean influences from Italy and France. The highlights here are the tapas; bite-size finger food with marinated olives, hummus with grilled pita, and grilled fig paired with prosciutto. Plates are pretty straightforward; entrées include chicken parmesan and swordfish, along with pasta dishes like ricotta ravioli and cannelloni. The wine list and cocktails are the stars of the show at this eatery, although don't expect many local varietals. It's mostly Italian, French, and some Californian vino. The cocktails, on the other hand, are all handmade here.

For a healthy take on breakfast, there's **Crepeville** (1730 L St., 916/444-1100, www. crepeville.com, 7 A.M.–11 P.M. daily, $8). No greasy platters here. This place serves up a dozen different kinds of homemade crepes. First things first: let your eyes wander over the menu scrawled on chalkboards over the cash register. The crepes tend more toward Mediterranean/Californian tastes (with the notable—and amazingly good—exception of the Hawaiian crepe); lots of pesto, chicken, and avocado are stuffed inside these doughy little goodies. The banana Nutella crepes are so good you'll think they're illegal. Sometimes crepes are an acquired taste. Instead, order an omelette at breakfast or one of the sandwiches. Anyone familiar with Squat and Gobble in San Francisco will notice similarities between these two creperies—they're owned by the same people.

East Sacramento's most intriguing restaurant is **33rd Street Bistro** (3301 Folsom Blvd., 916/455-2233, http://33rdstreetbistro.com, 8 A.M.–10 P.M. Sun.–Thurs., 8 A.M.–11 P.M. Fri.–Sat., $7–29). The food is advertised as Pacific Northwest cuisine. Entrées have names like the Tillamook Cheddar Cheeseburger or the Mount St. Helens Panini. If we're being frank, the food is essentially Californian cuisine with a few new wrinkles. Some locals adore this place, although frankly you might not. Yes, the food is above average, but the service lags and sometimes seems a little sullen.

Czech

Imagine sitting down with a nice Czech-Hungarian couple inside their kitchen for a feast. That's what you'll find at ⟨ **Café Marika** (2011 J St., 916/442-0405, 11 A.M.–3 P.M. Mon.–Wed., 11 A.M.–9 P.M. Thurs.–Sat., $12). The owners, a husband and wife, run this place by themselves. You'll find only five tables waiting. The owners kept the numbers down so they could focus on cooking up homemade old-world fare such as chicken paprikash and goulash. All meals come with a small salad and a warm piece of strudel for dessert. You'll definitely need a reservation here or be prepared to get there early.

For goulash and pizza, there's **La Trattoria Bohemia** (3649 J St., 916/455-7803, http://latrattoriabohemia.com, 11:30 A.M.–9 P.M. Tues.–Thurs. and Sun., 11:30 A.M.–10 P.M. Fri.–Sat., $12–27). No doubt it's a strange combination to most diners, but the blend of Czech-Italian cuisine is perfectly married together. Most folks come for Czech beer and hearty helpings of chicken paprikash pizza or schnitzel, but the breakfasts are a secret weapon. You'll wait an hour for a table without a reservation, so phone ahead.

Delis

⟨ **Selland's Market-Cafe** (5340 H St., 916/736-3333, www.sellands. com, 10:30 A.M.–8 P.M. Mon.–Tues., 10:30 A.M.–9 P.M. Wed.–Sat., 9:30 A.M.–8 P.M. Sun., $5–15) is a Euro-style deli where your meals are served from display cases. But this grub is gourmet. Selland's is owned by the same culinary brain trust that runs Ella's in downtown. You start off by ordering a meat—something like grilled salmon, meatloaf with gravy, or Mediterranean chicken—and add fruit, maybe some quinoa salad, or garlic green beans. Order a sandwich if the deli case isn't your style, and pair a glass (or a bottle—why not?) of El Dorado wine to go with it. Things

© CHRISTOPHER ARNS

Selland's Market-Cafe in East Sacramento

stay cool on the patio during summer when cooling misters spritz folks who eat outside. No reservations needed; drop-ins only.

Corti Brothers (5810 Folsom Blvd., 916/736-3800, www.cortibros.biz, 9 A.M.–7 P.M. Mon.–Sat., 10 A.M.–6 P.M. Sun., $5–8) creates Italian sandwiches and picnic lunches to go. This European-specialty store also has the most global liquor aisle I've ever seen, just in case your booze cabinet needs an absinthe or rakia refill.

Serving what could possibly be Sacramento's best lunch menu, **Juno's Kitchen and Delicatessen** (3675 J St., 916/456-4522, http://junoskitchen.com, 11:30 A.M.–3 P.M. and 5–8:30 P.M. Mon.–Fri, 11:30 A.M.–8:30 P.M. Sat., $10) serves internationally themed sandwiches and entrées, like the phenomenal halloumi cheese sando and the rock shrimp mac-n-cheese. This East Sacramento deli is a tight squeeze with few tables, so just order to go and walk a few blocks to McKinley Park for a picnic. The care going into this food is mind-blowing. Juno's (named for the chef's dog) bakes their own handmade sourdough and uses antique kitchen tools to whip up smoked trout sandwiches, chicken pasta, and burgers with manchego cheese.

Like a traditional New York sandwich joint, **Roxie Deli** (3340 C St., 916/443-5402, 7 A.M.–7 P.M. Mon.–Fri., 8 A.M.–7 P.M. Sat., 8 A.M.–5 P.M. Sun., $7–12) is part convenience store and part lunch counter. Walk past the huge smoker barbecue wafting savory smells outside, and step right up to the deli. In true New Yawker style, you'll have to speak up; don't be shy or the dudes behind the counter might take someone else's order instead! Frankly, sometimes the sandwiches here are mostly bread; they don't really skimp on toppings, but the rolls are too hefty and drown out the meat. Don't be afraid to pipe up if you feel shorted.

Name three things that don't go together and you might mention popsicles, vintage boutiques, and gourmet sandwiches. Those are actually three things **Fat Face Café** (1815 19th St., 916/822-5668, 11 A.M.–9 P.M. Tues.–Sat., 11 A.M.–3 P.M. Sun., $10) does exceedingly well. Located in the Bows and Arrows Collective—which often hosts live singer-songwriter acts alongside racks of hipsteresque vintage clothing, Fat Face serves up delicious grub and handmade popsicles. The sandwiches defy convention, with combos like cola-braised pork or peach BLT (a PLT?) with feta. And it's fun to eat out back on the patio, which feels like an urban jungle with dozens of vines and plants, salvaged 1960s lawn furniture, and an outsize fountain sending gentle spritzes your way. Popsicle flavors change all the time, but look for the Thai iced tea or the kaffir limeade.

By far the healthiest deli in town is **Sacramento Natural Foods Co-op** (1900 Alhambra Blvd., 916/455-2667, www.sacfoodcoop.com, 7 A.M.–10 P.M. daily, $5–10). This place rocks for several reasons. For starters, it's a full-size organic foods store with a butcher, fish department, kick-ass wine and beer department, and vast produce section. You'll also find natural grocery items, dry goods, frozen foods, vitamins, and herbs. Every item is either organic or all-natural; produce and meats come from sustainable, local sources. All that healthy goodness sounds great, but there's also a deli counter inside. They serve wraps, smoothies, salads, casseroles, and vegan bakery products. Ingredients for these meals come from those same local farms and ranches you'll find in the grocery department. Finally, two things: it gets crazy in there during lunch, and parking is limited.

Fine Dining

There was a time when **Biba Restaurant** (2801 Capitol Ave., 916/455-2422, www.biba-restaurant.com, 5:30–9 P.M. Mon., 11:30 A.M.–2 P.M. and 5:30–9 P.M.

2801

© CHRISTOPHER ARNS

Biba Restaurant is the place for fine cuisine.

Tues.–Thurs., 11:30 A.M.–2 P.M. and 5:30–10 P.M. Fri., 5:30–10 P.M. Sat., $16–23) was the only fancy place in town. Owned since 1986 by celebrity food guru Biba Caggiano, who once hosted cooking shows on TLC and the Discovery Channel, this elegant Italian-themed eatery still dominates Sacramento's dining scene. Biba still hangs out every day and usually sweeps around to greet restaurant guests. If we're talking about the food, it's ultra-upscale Bolognese fare served both prix fixe and à la carte in a country club atmosphere. Valet parking is offered outside because of ongoing construction at the medical center next door.

For some old-fashioned pizzazz, head to **The Waterboy Restaurant** (2000 Capitol Ave., 916/498-9891, www.waterboyrestaurant. com, 11:30 A.M.–2:30 P.M. and 5–9 P.M. Mon., 11:30 A.M.–2:30 P.M and 5–9:30 P.M. Tues.–Thurs., 11:30 A.M.–2:30 P.M and 5–10:30 P.M. Fri., 5–10:30 P.M. Sat., 5–9 P.M. Sun., $10–27). Picture a high-flying 1940s salon with

miniature palm trees, stylish wicker chairs, and French and Italian-inspired cuisine that earns Best of Sacramento awards every year from local magazines. If we're discussing specific plates, the pan-roasted duck breast with gnocchi is worth every penny, along with the bouillabaisse and the seared scallops. Wine lovers will be excited by the dozens of international and regional choices. It goes without saying at a place like this, but make sure you lock down a reservation.

French

Café Rolle (5357 H St., 916/455-9140, www.caferolle.com, 11 A.M.–3 P.M. Tues.–Sat., 5:30–7:30 P.M. Wed.–Fri., $5.50–16) is about as French as they come. The owners greet visitors with a "bonjour!" every time the door opens. Choices range from gourmet sandwiches, salads, and finger food to salmon or chicken plates for dinner.

Italian

The food at **Lucca Restaurant and Bar** (1615 J St., 916/669-5300, www.luccarestaurant.com, 11:30 A.M.–10 P.M. Mon.–Thurs., 11:30 A.M.–11:30 P.M. Fri., noon–11:30 P.M. Sat., 4–9 P.M. Sun., $10–20) is simply darn good Italian grub. The "Californian" influence comes from fresh veggies lurking in your pasta; squash, baby artichokes, green beans, and olives are just a few byproducts of the Golden State's farms that Lucca weaves into their food. Do yourself a favor and order zucchini chips for an appetizer. You'll kick yourself for skipping them. Most locals come here for special occasions, like birthday parties or dates, because the vibe is casual but elegant. During warmer months, the most popular tables are on the covered patio. Call ahead; you'll definitely need reservations at this fashionable eatery.

OneSpeed Pizza (4818 Folsom Blvd., 916/706-1748, http://onespeedpizza.com, 11:30 A.M.–10 P.M. Tues.–Sat., 9 A.M.–9 P.M.

Sun., $10–16) uses local ingredients to remix classic Italian fare into something distinctively Californian. Expect mostly wood-fired pizza and pasta dishes here. Typical plates include margherita pizza, fish and shellfish stew in a tomato-saffron sauce, and calzones.

Tucked away like some buried treasure, **Zelda's Original Gourmet Pizza** (1415 21st St., 916/447-1400, www.zeldasgourmetpizza.com, 11:30 A.M.–10 P.M. Mon.–Thurs., 11:30 A.M.–11 P.M. Fri., 5–11 P.M. Sat., 5–9 P.M. Sun., $10–22) serves Chicago-style pan pizza with a thick doughy crust. Some people think this place can do no wrong; Zelda's earned "best pizza" honors in 2011 in the *Sacramento News and Review* annual readers' poll. It's true the pies are legendary and delicious. Ordering is a challenge. Pizzas take at least 30 minutes to bake. And service resembles gruff Brooklyn more than friendly Chicago, an attitude seemingly out of place in sunny Sacramento. My advice: call ahead and take your pie to go.

Sometimes a long night of bar-hopping leaves a gnawing hunger in your belly. **Luigi's Slice** (1050 20th St., #150, 916/447-1255, 11 A.M.–11 P.M. Sun.–Wed., 11 A.M.–midnight Thurs., 11 A.M.–2:30 A.M. Fri.–Sat., $5) will slay that hunger like the growling beast it is. Frankly, it may not compete with Zelda's. Think back to your college days and the pizza you inhaled during late-night study sessions, and Luigi's pies will suddenly trigger long-lost memories. Bands often play out front on the concrete patio during the Second Saturday Art Walk.

Chicago Fire (2416 J St., 916/443-0440, www.chicagofire.com, 4–10 P.M. Mon.–Wed., 11:30 A.M.–10 P.M. Thurs. and Sun., 11:30 A.M.–11 P.M. Fri.–Sat., $9–27) is a snazzy upgrade on mom-and-pop pizza parlors. Expect deep-dish Chicago-style pies served in iron pans drowned in sauce, cheese, and other toppings.

Hot Italian (1627 16th St., 916/444-3000, www.hotitalian.net, 11:30 A.M.–9:30 P.M.

Sun.–Thurs., 11:30 A.M.–10:30 P.M. Fri.–Sat., $15) is sleek and yet somehow still unpretentious. This place feels like a traditional urban deli similar to anything you'd see in Milan and Rome. The interior's simple black-and-white decor is spare yet trendy. They're known for pizza and paninis made with seasonal ingredients, but the pasta is also pretty darn good.

Paesano's (1806 Capitol Ave., 916/447-8646, www.paesanos.biz, 11:30 A.M.–9:30 P.M. Mon.–Wed., 11:30 A.M.–10 P.M. Thurs., 11:30 A.M.–10:30 P.M. Fri., noon–10:30 P.M. Sat., noon–9:30 P.M. Sun., $9–13) blends California cool with retro Euro style. You'll find a very social environment, from the bar to the large groups of families eating here. I especially dig the Vespas and old-fashioned liquor advertisements decking out the walls. Foodies will enjoy the traditional yet innovative menu, with favorites like fusilli with ginger-braised pork. Diners with gluten-intolerance will breathe sighs of relief when they see the special menu created just for them. Come hungry, don't worry about coming too casual, but be ready for a wait on weekends.

Mediterranean

A choice for modern Greek food is **Opa Opa** (5644 J St., #A, 916/451-4000, www.eatatopa.com, 10:30 A.M.–9:30 P.M. Sun.–Wed., 10:30 A.M.–10 P.M. Thurs.–Sat., $10). Anyone who knows anything about moussaka and pastitsio would agree that sauce is a crucial component. This place passes with flying colors. Students from nearby Sacramento State usually queue up at lunchtime, but dinner is quieter and more relaxed. There's a youthful buzz in the air from college-aged staff in the kitchen; expect a smile and some friendly banter when you order some of that rockin' moussaka.

Zeus himself would eat at **Petra Greek** (1122 16th St., 916/443-1993, www.petragreek.com, 11 A.M.–11 P.M. Mon.–Tues., 11 A.M.–3 A.M. Wed.–Fri., 2 P.M.–3 A.M. Sat.,

the dining room at Tapa the World

© CHRISTOPHER ARNS

$7–13) for the gyros. The owners hail from Crete, and it's clear they brought the secret to authentic Greek fare with them. Warning: a real gyro is stuffed with french fries, sauce, and shaved meat. Healthy, no; delicious, yes. And they even stay open after the bars close. Ask for a pint of Olympia beer and gobble down a lamb or chicken gyro, then finish it off with real baklava.

It's a shame that **Vanilla Bean Bistro** (3260 J St., 916/457-1155, www.vanillabean-bistro.com, 11 A.M.–2 P.M. and 5–9 P.M. Mon.–Thurs., 11 A.M.–2 P.M. and 5–10 P.M. Fri.–Sat., 10 A.M.–2 P.M. and 5–9 P.M. Sun., $14–25) bears such a generic name. Stumbling into this joint off the street wouldn't prepare you for the outstanding Turkish-inspired fare on the menu. Don't be scared off; Turkish food is very similar to Greek food, and this charming little eatery adds a Californian flair. For the record, the owner grew up in Turkey with a family in the spice business. Somehow, that bit of trivia is a comforting thought when you're considering the moussaka or the stuffed poblano chiles. Wine enthusiasts will enjoy the extensive vino list, and I recommend trying a glass of sangiovese from the Shenandoah Valley with a plate of Turkish meatloaf. Not to be a downer, but they can be kind of lax about observing their posted business hours. Call ahead if you're in doubt.

For tapas, you must try **◖ Tapa the World** (2115 J St., 916/442-4353, www.tapatheworld.com, 11:30 A.M.–midnight daily, $5–22). Partly for the boisterous ambience and mostly for the food, Tapa's (as locals call it) is a hit. Eating here feels like hanging out on La Rambla in Barcelona. With hazy mood lighting, live Spanish guitar, and a wine list full of cavas and tempranillos, this lively bistro is the next best thing. Tapas originated in Spain about a hundred years ago when a Spanish café owner put bread slices over glasses of wine to protect the vino from dust and flying things. The trend caught on, and other Spanish eateries began putting bits of food on the bread cover (*tapa* literally means "lid" in Spanish) to draw more customers. Unlike some places that serve only a half dozen tapas, expect between 16 and 20 small Spanish-inspired plates on the menu here. I recommend the Kobe beef with blue cheese butter and crispy onions. Contrary to some reports, the sangria is fantastic. Expect a wait if you come between Thursday and Saturday evenings.

Mexican

Anyone who speaks Spanish will recognize that **C Tres Hermanas** (2416 K St., 916/443-6919, www.treshermanasonk.com, 11 A.M.–9 P.M. Mon.–Thurs., 11 A.M.–10 P.M. Fri., 7 A.M.– 10 P.M. Sat., 7 A.M.–8 P.M. Sun., $9–14) means "three sisters." Well, here's why. Three siblings named Sonia, Dora, and Norma came from Chihuahua to start this restaurant. In this casual but lively eatery, the sisters dish up the best mole sauce in Sacramento. Food is influenced by northern Mexican cuisine, so expect quesadillas, tacos, and enchiladas heavy on herbs and veggies, lots of pork and fish, and enchiladas smothered in one of three amazing sauces, each one wildly different. Like most Midtown eateries, this one gets busy, maybe even busier than most. If you're walking up between 7 and 9 P.M., figure on waiting 30 minutes. No worries. Just grab a spot at the small bar and order a Mexican lager or a Blue Cadillac margarita as you keep an ear open for your table.

Centro Cocina Mexicana (2730 J St., 916/442-2552, www.centrococina.com, 11:30 A.M.–9 P.M. Mon.–Tues., 11:30 A.M.– 10 P.M. Wed.–Thurs., 11:30 A.M.–11 P.M. Fri., noon–11 P.M. Sat., 4–9 P.M. Sun., $9– 18) serves up trendy Cali-Mex cuisine. Don't expect a traditional beans-and-rice kind of place. In fact, without 100 tequila brands behind the bar and some Mission-style crucifixes on the wall, you'd be hard-pressed to guess the cuisine without a menu. While it's neither cheap nor very traditional food, you'll still enjoy it. Regional influences come from every *estado* south of the border. The enchiladas Oaxaqueñas are my top pick.

Ernesto's Mexican Food (1901 16th St., 916/441-5850, www.ernestosmexicanfood. com, 11 A.M.–10 P.M. Mon.–Wed., 11 A.M.– 11 P.M. Thurs., 11 A.M.–midnight Fri., 9 A.M.– midnight Sat., 9 A.M.–10 P.M. Sun., $10–15) is another upscale Mexican bistro that's been Americanized. The difference between traditional *comida* and the Cali-Mex fusion served at places like Ernesto's is all in the veggies. Here the plates brim with sautéed zucchini, carrots, garlic, cilantro, and avocados, mixed in with meats like shrimp, pork, and carne asada. I've got to be honest; my favorite thing about coming in here is the mariachi band that frequently stops by. Sit on the patio to soak in the pure awesomeness of men wearing huge sombreros while they strum humpbacked *guitarróns* and blast away on shiny trumpets.

Here's a secret: in my experience, the most authentic Mexican food comes from shiny trucks or tiny taco stands. **Midtown Taqueria** (3754 J St., 916/452-7551, 8:30 A.M.–11 P.M. daily, $3–8) is neither, but makes basic burritos and tacos like you'd expect from a roadside stand. They even serve breakfast. On a balmy evening it's fun to sit on the patio and watch locals ride cruisers down J Street, unless your favorite Mexican futbol team is playing on the inside TV. **La Fiesta Taqueria** (1105 Alhambra Blvd., 916/454-5616, www.lafiestataqueria.com, 9 A.M.–10 P.M. daily, $4–10) is another Mexican joint serving traditional burritos alongside beans and rice. Here the vibe is more urban, like a lunch counter, but the horchata and seam-bursting burritos definitely give La Fiesta a dose of street cred.

Middle Eastern

If Berber tents featured a bar, they'd be just

like ◖ **Kasbah Lounge** (2115 J St., 916/442-4388, http://kasbahlounge.com, 5 P.M.–1 A.M. Sun.–Wed., 5 P.M.–2 A.M. Thurs., 5 P.M.–3 A.M. Fri.–Sat. in summer; 5 P.M.–midnight Sun.–Wed., 5 P.M.–1 A.M. Thurs., 5 P.M.–3 A.M. Fri.–Sat. in winter, $10–18). As the name suggests, Kasbah serves up mostly North African fare and Middle Eastern flavors. That means choices include tagine (Moroccan slow-cooker stew), plus kabobs, falafel, and shawarma. Just like at authentic Moroccan restaurants, guests can recline on plush cushions around the walls or sit at small bistro tables. I say go for the pillows to get the full effect as if you're camping in the Sahara. Dessert consists of baklava or banana beignets; try ordering a pot of Moroccan mint tea or Turkish coffee along with the sweets. Did I mention the belly dancers? They jingle into the restaurant every night around 9 P.M. Finally, bar-hoppers love this place for the unique cocktails and for smoking waterpipe hookahs on the patio late into the early morning.

BROADWAY AND LAND PARK

Unlike the diffusion of eateries throughout neighborhoods in Midtown and East Sacramento, most restaurants in Broadway and Land Park are clustered in just a few spots. Out here on the outskirts of the capital's urban core, the dining scene feels decidedly less trendy. The farm-to-table movement seems miles away at established chophouses like Tower Café and Jamie's Bar and Grill. Nor has the Broadway district caught up to Midtown's urban rebirth; businesses here have a scrappy edge to them after surviving the neighborhood's decay. That doesn't mean you should stay away. In fact, Broadway's eating scene is showing green shoots as a new brewery and several upscale eateries prepare to open in 2013. There's no better time to visit while the district retains its grungy authenticity and flexes a newfound vitality.

American

Jamie's Bar and Grill (427 Broadway, 916/442-4044, www.jamiesbroadwaygrille.com, 11 A.M.–9 P.M. Mon.–Fri., $8–30) is a cubby off Broadway serving the city's best clam chowder according to the *Sacramento Bee*. According to local legend, Jamie's back room bar was salvaged from the 1906 San Francisco earthquake. Overall, this place oozes rustic Midwestern kitsch, right down to the stuffed elk and deer heads staring impassively from the wall. What you'll find on the menu is classic American comfort food. Hearty plates range from the pork chops made with homemade applesauce to the veal parmesan. But the steak sandwiches might just top them all.

Maybe it's the jukebox belting out hits from Johnny Cash and the Rolling Stones. Maybe it's the black bar stools and spartan redbrick walls. But for whatever reason, the grub at **Hideaway Bar and Grill** (2565 Franklin Blvd., 916/455-1331, 4 P.M.–2 A.M. Mon.–Fri., noon–2 A.M. Sat., 10 A.M.–2 A.M. Sun., $10) just tastes better than ordinary dive bar fare. To be specific, the fried zucchini sandwich does wonders to slay your hunger. Service can be a little gruff, but it is a dive bar after all.

Taylor's Kitchen (2924 Freeport Blvd., 916/443-5154, www.taylorskitchen.com, 5–9:30 P.M. Wed.–Sat., 9 A.M.–1 P.M. Sun., $14–28) is a gourmet grocery store, but they serve dinner several nights a week and brunch on Sunday. As you might expect from a specialty grocer, the cuisine is toward the classy end of the scale and runs pricy. Locals will tell you it's worth it. To keep the bill down but still try out Taylor's cuisine, opt for the half-pound burger grilled with local grass-fed and all-natural beef.

Holy blue cheese and bacon! You have to try the burgers at ◖ **Dad's Kitchen** (2968 Freeport Blvd., 916/447-3237, http://ilovedadskitchen.com, 11 A.M.–9 P.M. Tues.–Fri., 9 A.M.–9 P.M. Sat., 9 A.M.–8 P.M. Sun., $10–14). As seen on the Food Network's *Diners, Drive-Ins and Dives,* Dad's is a tiny hole-in-the-wall next to Freeport Bakery. The "Dad's Burger" is legendary: bacon and blue cheese seared onto a grass-fed beef patty with house-made garlic and paprika oil. Make sure to start with an order of deep-fried garbanzo beans. Take my advice and sit outside on the patio, which looks and feels like someone's backyard.

Right next to the renowned Tower Theatre, **Tower Café** (1518 Broadway, 916/441-0222, 8 A.M.–11 P.M. Sun.–Thurs., 8 A.M.–midnight Fri.–Sat., $10–18) has become one of the city's most venerable breakfast joints. International themes pop up on the menu in items like the Thai steak or the Jamaican jerk chicken. You'll also get that global vibe from the art, colorful masks and profusion of knickknacks hanging on the wall. The patio is by far the best place to eat, under the gnarled trees and surrounded by an explosion of plants.

Asian

Just to be clear: this place does *not* serve the kind of ramen sold in Styrofoam cups. At **Shoki Ramen House** (2675 24th St., 916/454-2411, www.shokiramenhouse.com, 5:30–9 P.M. Mon., 11 A.M.–2 P.M and 5:30–9 P.M. Tues.–Fri., noon–3 P.M. and 5–9 P.M. Sat., $5–10), you can order six different kinds of broth served in three sizes. Toppings include beef, corn, spinach, bamboo, seaweed, and other veggies. Their ramen is free of MSG, preservatives, and they make it from scratch.

Heat Shabu Baru (2416 18th St., Ste. E, 916/930-9888, www.heatshabu. com, 3:30 P.M.–midnight Tues.–Thurs., 3:30 P.M.–1 A.M. Fri.–Sat., 5 P.M.–midnight Sun., $10–20) serves Japanese fondue in a ultra-hip setting. What's different about this place is that they offer three broths to choose from. Meats include American-raised Kobe beef and New Zealand grass-fed lamb.

Bakeries and Cafés

Sacramento's caffeine revolution has just begun creeping beyond Midtown and downtown's boundaries. The best local beanery in south Sacramento is **Old Soul @ 40 Acres** (3434 Broadway, 916/453-8540, www.oldsoulco. com, 6 A.M.–10 P.M. daily, $2–5), in a scruffy neighborhood known as Oak Park that's beginning a long-awaited turnaround. Coffee is roasted fresh up in Midtown and delivered to this sparsely furnished yet cheerful coffee shop on the corner of Broadway and 3rd Avenue. The drinks are fairly simple—no fancy blended beverages here, just house coffee, tea, lattes, and mochas.

It might seem sometimes that the American bakery, a bedrock of Main Street cuisine, has been replaced by supermarket chop shops and Betty Crocker. Not so fast, my friend. **Freeport Bakery** (2966 Freeport Blvd., 916/442-4256, http://freeportbakery.com, 7 A.M.–6:30 P.M. Mon.–Fri., 7 A.M.–5:30 P.M. Sat., 8 A.M.–3 P.M. Sun., $5) is keeping the flame alive. Owned by a third-generation German baker with a flair for cakes, this small but cute pastry shop and espresso bar in Land Park always has a line out the door. Carrot cake, raspberry cream torte, tiramisu, or fudge cake: these are just a few choices lurking in the display case. Cakes aren't the only thing here. They also bake tarts, pizza bagels, croissants, cookies, and most of what you'd expect from a neighborhood bakery.

Brewpub

Geography nerds will perk up over ◖**Pangaea Two Brews Café** (2743 Franklin Blvd., 916/454-4942, http://pangaeatwobrews.com, 11 A.M.–10 P.M. Tues.–Sun., $8). Pangaea was a prehistoric supercontinent that existed 200 million years ago. The brewpub sits on the boundary of two Sacramento zip codes, forming a meeting of the neighborhoods. Beer choices go far beyond just two brews. Owner Rob Archie spent several years playing

Gunther's Ice Cream

professional basketball in Europe and fell in love with the café scene. Along the way, he also discovered Belgian ales. Now Archie pours around 20 Belgian or Belgian-style beers in this hip little eatery. But hey, let's not forget the food. The sandwiches are as good as anything you'll find in Midtown. If I had to recommend one, I'd advise trying the Aprihopped Chicken with apricot marmalade, cream cheese, and pepper jack.

Californian

Café Dantorels (2700 24th St., 916/451-2200, 7 A.M.–11 P.M. daily, $8) has a huge colorful chalkboard hanging over the cash register. A vast selection of crepes, omelettes, and sandwiches are handwritten on the board. The menu mimics Crepeville's in Midtown because the ownership used to be the same. This place is located in Curtis Park and is usually more accessible and laid-back than its cousin uptown.

Dessert

☾Gunther's Ice Cream (2801 Franklin Blvd., 916/457-6646, www.gunthersicecream.com, 10 A.M.–10 P.M. daily, $2–5) is right across from Pangaea Two Brews. Gunther's handmade ice cream has been mixed, whipped, frozen, and served on-site since 1949. And man, is it good. They use a slow, hand-controlled process with extra butterfat to make the stuff, taking after old-fashioned ice cream from the early 1900s. More than 40 flavors fill the vintage black-and-white menu board on the wall, including two with no sugar added and four choices each for sherbet and frozen yogurt. Order any size from a cone all the way up to a three-gallon tub. If you can't find the place, look for Jugglin' Joe on Gunther's neon sign. During the day, Jugglin' Joe looks like a four-armed Vishnu slinging ice cream from hand to hand. At night the neon lights up, and Joe appears with only two arms, just as he's been doing all these years.

For some reason, south Sacramento

dominates the dessert category when it comes to sweet creamy goodness. **Vic's Ice Cream** (3199 Riverside Blvd., 916/448-0892, www.vicsicecream.com, 10 A.M.–8 P.M. Mon.–Thurs., 10 A.M.–9 P.M. Fri.–Sat., 11 A.M.–8 P.M. Sun.; 10 A.M.–10 P.M. Mon.–Sat., 11 A.M.–11 P.M. Sun. in summer, $2–5) has been around since 1947 and boasts the round swivel stools and checkered floor that proves it. What they lack in sheer volume of flavors (roughly two dozen depending on the time of year), they compensate for with a *Happy Days* ambience that remains elusive anywhere else. You can also get a sandwich or soup although it's clearly not in their wheelhouse. Stick to ice cream here, and you won't regret it.

Italian

For starters, **Masullo Pizza** (2711 Riverside Blvd., 916/443-8929, www.masullopizza.com, 11:30 A.M.–9 P.M. Mon.–Thurs., 11:30 A.M.–9:30 P.M. Fri., 5–9:30 P.M. Sat., $11–15) doesn't seem like a typical pizza parlor when you walk in. The whitewashed brick walls and tiled facade on the pizza oven are the first hint, setting up sleek contemporary surroundings more suitable for a hip lounge or retro bistro theme. Once the steaming-hot pizza arrives on your table, everything clicks. Masullo's 800°F wood-fired oven bakes Neapolitan-style pies with toppings like chorizo, all-natural bacon, prosciutto, and mozzarella.

Mexican

I'm still waiting for someone to open a "not very Mexican" restaurant. Until then, there's **Oscar's Very Mexican Food** (3061 Freeport Blvd., 916/443-8310, 7 A.M.–10 P.M. daily, $2–8). You guessed it; Oscar's serves traditional fare inspired by our neighbors south of the border. I'd describe it as fast food but that wouldn't be quite right. It's basically a taco and burrito stand housed in a small shop, the kind you'd find on every corner in southern

California. You can't go wrong with the breakfast burritos here, but locals also swear by the California burrito. Stuffed with steak, fried potatoes, cheese, and sauce, it's a beast.

GREATER SACRAMENTO

Beyond the capital's urban districts you'll actually find quite a few amazing bistros and upscale eateries. Most of these can be found in the neighborhood known as Arden-Arcade just northeast of the American River. A few more lie scattered in different directions. If you're already downtown, there's no need to go searching in the weeds for something new; Midtown's cuisine scene offers more choices in a smaller area. It's not that Greater Sacramento lacks great restaurants; they just don't offer much that's different or new. There are some exceptions listed below.

American

You wouldn't wear it around town, but the cheese skirt at ◖ **Squeeze Inn** (5301 Power Inn Rd., 916/386-8599, 10 A.M.–7 P.M. Mon.–Fri., 10 A.M.–6 P.M. Sat., $5–10) stops traffic on weekends as folks converge on this little joint in southern Sacramento. So what's a cheese skirt? Picture a juicy beef patty buried with a mountain of cheese and grilled under a hood. What comes out is a burger wearing a seared cheesy blanket that extends far beyond the bun. In case you were wondering, they can do this with veggie burgers by request. As no doubt goes without saying, cheese skirts won't earn diet points for anyone. Ever since Squeeze Inn was featured on the Food Network, this place gets packed every weekend and waits can take upwards of an hour or more. Try to arrive before 11:30 A.M. or after 1:30 P.M. to miss the rush.

Bandera (2232 Fair Oaks Blvd., 916/922-3524, 5–11 P.M. Fri.–Sun., 5–10 P.M. Mon.–Thurs., $14–33) sits in Sacramento's Gourmet Gulch, a nickname for a row of upscale restaurants along Fair Oaks Boulevard in the

Arden-Arcade district. Bandera takes the neighborhood bar and grill category and injects a dose of upscale cool. Exposed wooden beams loom overhead as you walk into the dining room. Take a seat at the bar or slide into the red leather booths. Across the room, the exposed kitchen buzzes with activity as cooks prepare skillet cornbread, Scottish salmon, grilled lamb, and other delectable updates on classic American favorites. Don't sweat the wine list. More than 50 West Coast wines and a few from Europe are here, including C. G. Di Arie from the Shenandoah Valley near Plymouth. The food here beats expectations, but figure on one thing: Dinner at Bandera will probably take a bite out of your wallet.

Go on food safari at **Flaming Grill Café** (2319 El Camino Ave., 916/359-0840, www.flaminggrillcafe.com, 11 A.M.–4 P.M. Mon., 11 A.M.–9 P.M. Tues.–Wed., 11 A.M.–10 P.M. Thurs.–Fri., noon–8:30 P.M. Sat., 11 A.M.–5 P.M. Sun., $8–12). This small but immaculate roadside joint grills ostrich, buffalo, elk, venison, salmon, and other exotic burgers. Few locals actually seem to know about this place. You can find out what they've been missing.

Pocket Bistro (6401 Riverside Blvd., 916/391-7990, http://pocketbistro.net, 11:30 A.M.–9:30 P.M. Tues.–Thurs., 11:30 A.M.–10 P.M. Fri.–Sat., 10 A.M.–8:30 P.M. Sun., $7–20) does a cosmopolitan take on the neighborhood bar. It's named for the Pocket neighborhood in southern Sacramento where the Sacramento River makes a wide, bulging turn in the valley. Plates include meatloaf, skirt steak, burgers, and more. The wine list is distinguished and boasts quite a few names from El Dorado and the California Delta. There's also a full bar mixing top-shelf cocktails.

For hubcap-size plates of breakfast, you have to try **Uptown Cafe** (1121 Del Paso Blvd., 916/649-2233, 6 A.M.–2:30 P.M. Tues.–Fri., 6 A.M.–1:30 P.M. Sat.–Sun., $5–10). It's a rustic diner in North Sacramento, a district on the rise after decades of sleaze. Get the biscuits and gravy on the side with an omelette, or try the eggs Benedict.

Asian

The menu at **Noble Vegetarian** (5049 College Oak Dr., 916/334-6060, www.nobleveg.com, 11 A.M.–8:30 P.M. Mon.–Sat., $5–10) is a home run for non-meat eaters and vegans. Dishes are chock-full of plant-based meat items with names like the Peaceful Ginger Vegeken. The cuisine is mostly Vietnamese-inspired, although you can also pick up hints of Chinese, Thai, and Mongolian influences.

Thai Chef's House (2851 Fulton Ave., 916/481-9500, www.thaichefshouse.com, 11 A.M.–3 P.M. and 5–9:30 P.M. Mon.–Fri., noon–9:30 P.M. Sat.–Sun., $5–10) has a loyal following among locals. The atmosphere has few frills; it's sort of a work in progress, but the food is fantastic.

Taro's by Mikuni (1735 Arden Way, 916/564-2114, www.mikunisushi.com, 11:30 A.M.–9:30 P.M. Mon.–Thurs., 11:30 A.M.–10:30 P.M. Fri., noon–10:30 P.M. Sat., 4–9 P.M. Sun., $5–17) is an offshoot of the sushi juggernaut in Midtown. Taro's is more of a sushi lounge than a restaurant. The vibe is decidedly urban sleek. Imagine chowing down on spicy tuna rolls in the middle of an Ikea store, and you'll get what this place is like. That's not a knock on Taro's. With an upbeat energy, creations like the Incredible and Train Wreck rolls, and attentive chefs, it sets a festive tone for a bar-hopper's evening.

Bakeries and Coffee Shops

The food at **Ettore's European Bakery and Restaurant** (2376 Fair Oaks Blvd., 916/482-0708, www.ettores.com, 6 A.M.–9 P.M. Mon.–Thurs., 6 A.M.–10 P.M. Fri.–Sat., 7 A.M.–4 P.M. Sun., $8–20) looks almost too pretty to eat. But it's not just a bakery with frosted cookies, fruitcakes with piles of berries and pineapple, cinnamon rolls, and pastries. Ettore's also dishes up mouthwatering burgers and sandwiches for lunch, and a gourmet dinner menu consisting of classic American fare such as rotisserie chicken and pork chops. This place sits on Gourmet Gulch, a fancy dining district in Sacramento's Arden-Arcade neighborhood, and holds its own against formidable company.

Californian

If you don't feel like braving the hectic downtown scene for gourmet grub, **Ravenous Cafe** (7600 Greenhaven Dr., 916/399-9309, www. ravenouscafe.com, 11 A.M.–2 P.M. Tues.–Fri., 5–9 P.M. Tues.–Sun., $5–23) is an excellent alternative. This family-owned bistro sits amidst unassuming surroundings in a strip mall right next to a 24 Hour Fitness. Don't hold the location against them. Owner Wade Sawaya helped run the venerable Penrose Room restaurant in Colorado Springs and has deftly used his magic touch on this place. Start with a plate of grilled halloumi cheese before asking about the risotto of the day. Make sure to book reservations.

The new boss of Gourmet Gulch might just be ◖ **Roxy Restaurant and Bar** (2381 Fair Oaks Blvd., 916/489-2000, www.roxyrestaurantandbar.com, 11 A.M.–9 P.M. Mon.–Wed., 11 A.M.– 10 P.M. Thurs.–Fri., 9 A.M.–10 P.M. Sat., 9 A.M.–9 P.M. Sun., $10–29). The same folks who own this place also own Lucky Dog Ranch in Dixon, which hooks up most of Sacramento's dining scene with all-natural Angus beef. Their goal: a marriage of Parisian glamour and down-home ranch style. A huge chandelier sparkles over rawhide booths arranged in a horseshoe pattern. Some menu items seem inspired by chuck wagon fare, like the piquillo peppers, chipotle cheddar mashed potatoes, and the buffalo burger. Others seem pretty far removed from the range—pan-seared salmon, free-range roasted chicken, and Southwest cioppino. Usually I don't go out of

my way to recommend a happy hour; Roxy's, however, is one you shouldn't miss, with a modified bar menu for everything under $5, including cocktails. If you enjoyed Lucca Restaurant in Midtown, the owners here run that place as well.

Fine Dining

Sacramento's answer to Napa's venerable French Laundry is ◖ **The Kitchen Restaurant** (2225 Hurley Way, 916/568-7171, www.thekitchenrestaurant.com, 6:30 P.M.–close Wed.–Thurs., 7 P.M.–close Fri.–Sat., 5 P.M.–close Sun., $135). Without a doubt, the Kitchen is the capital's finest place to eat. Imagine it this way: Combine *Top Chef* with Shakespearean stagecraft, all while allowing guests to wander into the open kitchen and observe, and that's the concept. Only you and about 50 other people are admitted each night for a six-course gourmet extravaganza that lasts 3–4 hours. And the show begins: Chef Noah Zonca fires up the room with a warm greeting before drawing cheers as he explains the rules: everything goes. The menu is prix fixe, but Zonca and his kitchen crew make every and any request come true (especially if you have dietary concerns or allergies). Most items on your plate came from a local farmers market that morning. The menu changes monthly, but courses might include lobster potpie, wedge salad, sushi and sashimi, crayfish thermidor, rack of lamb, and chocolate mousse for dessert. Eating at The Kitchen is like gaining entry to a private club, and reservations sell out far in advance. You'll need to call or book online at their website to secure a place. There's a 20 percent gratuity charge added to the bill.

Italian

An upscale joint in Gourmet Gulch is **Zinfandel Grille** (2384 Fair Oaks Blvd., 916/485-7100, http://zinfandelgrille.com, 11 A.M.–3 P.M. Mon.–Fri., 4–9 P.M. Sun.–Mon., 4–10 P.M.

Tues.–Thurs., 4–11 P.M. Fri.–Sat., $10–32). Jazz and amazing patio ambience combine for one of Sacramento's most sophisticated dining experiences. The food is a dash of Italian-inspired cuisine with a whole lot of surf and turf. Their wine list is substantial, but they could have included more local vino from Amador and Lodi—both areas that produce amazing zinfandel—especially for a place named after the varietal.

Mediterranean

Finding truly authentic Greek food can be like scaling Mt. Olympus. The gods themselves would approve of the **Greek Village Inn** (65 University Ave., 916/922-6334, 11 A.M.–9 P.M. daily, $11–29). A meal with Greeks is truly an experience in hospitality and sure enough, you'll feel like an honored guest at this homey little restaurant. This, my friends, is truly authentic Greek cuisine. Most folks might be familiar with moussaka or gyros, which are both traditional Hellenic favorites. But Greeks will tell you that avgolemono—lemon and rice soup—is just as important. I'm happy to say it's made it perfectly here. Start with the soup and move on to the pastitsio, a baked pasta dish stuffed with ground beef and coated in béchamel sauce. While there's a patio for outside dining, I recommend staying in and grabbing one of the large and comfy booths.

If someone ever invented a World Cup of falafel, **Pita Kitchen** (2989 Arden Way, 916/480-0560, 11 A.M.–9 P.M. Mon.–Sat., 11 A.M.–8 P.M. Sun., $10–19) would take the title every time. How they do it I don't know, but these perfectly-browned chickpea nuggets are outstanding: not charred or rubbery, just seared delicately with olive oil to a light crisp. True to its name, Pita Kitchen makes light, spongy fresh bread. Ask for some hummus and a plate of sliced pita before ordering either the famous falafel or a meaty shawarma. The menu is helpfully notated with vegan and gluten-free options for guests with food allergies.

Since 1981 **Café Europa** (1537 Howe Ave., 916/779-0737, http://cafeeuropasacramento. wordpress.com, 11 A.M.–8:30 P.M. Mon.–Sat., $8) has been churning out some of Sacramento's best gyros. It's best described as a collision of American and Eastern Mediterranean cuisine because they serve hamburgers along with kabobs, gyros, and little side plates (called "meze" in Greek) like tzatziki, dolmades, and spanakopita spinach squares. Tucked away in a strip mall facing away from the street, you'll have to search for it.

The Kabob House (1726 Fulton Ave., 916/485-0163, www.kabobhousefulton.com, 11 A.M.–9 P.M. Mon.–Sat., $9–19) serves authentic Greek plates, including salad, gyros, and chicken kabob skewers. You'll find it smack-dab in the middle of a bland strip mall, although the food is anything but bland. Try the moussaka and wash it down with a cold bottle of Mythos beer.

Mexican

You'll see the crowded sidewalk before you actually see ◖ **Chando's Tacos** (863 Arden Way, 916/641-8226, http://chandostacos.com, 10 A.M.–9 P.M. Sun.–Thurs., 10 A.M.–10 P.M. Fri.–Sat., $1–5). Without a doubt, the tacos from this tiny eatery are the best in town. Anyone familiar with Southern California's profusion of corner Mexican food stands will recognize Chando's for what it is: a purveyor of silky soft corn tortillas wrapped around juicy carne asada. Don't bother coming during peak lunch hours when the line stretches onto the sidewalk. Try to arrive before 11:30 A.M. if you can, or visit during the evening when it's less busy. There are plenty of picnic benches and tables if you want to eat there.

Middle Eastern

For the most authentic Lebanese food in

town, there's 🌙 **Maalouf's** (1433 Fulton Ave., 916/972-8768, http://maaloufs.com, 11 A.M.–9 P.M. Tues.–Sat., $7–20). The owner, Abdul Maalouf, is one of the great characters of Sacramento's dining scene. After you order, Abdul usually comes around with a joke or a quick hello. The restaurant itself is a small hole-in-the-wall, but it's worth squeezing in here for the food. Immediately after you walk inside, the smell of sizzling paprika, garlic, lemon, and olive oil wafts past your nose. I recommend any of the shawarmas and especially the kabobs. On some nights they have belly dancing, so be prepared; the dancers like to drag people out of their chairs to participate.

For Persian cuisine, there's **Famous Kabob** (1290 Fulton Ave., 916/483-1700, www.famouskabob.com, 11 A.M.–10 P.M. daily, $12). The specialty is probably obvious: skewers of marinated lamb, chicken, or steak barbecued with pieces of bell peppers and onions. Try the khoresht, a type of stew usually packed with braised meats, beans, scallions, and saffron. If you dare, try some "doog," a homemade yogurt drink along with the meal, although be warned: it's an acquired taste.

Seafood

Between Land Park and the Pocket area you'll find **Scott's Seafood on the River** (4800 Riverside Blvd., 916/379-5959, 6:30 A.M.– 10 P.M. daily, $11–30), which claims to serve the best seafood in Sacramento, and several local TV surveys have backed them up. You can also order filet mignon and pasta dishes like capellini Provencal and wild prawn fettucine. Plates are kind of pricy, but the place does have amazing views of the Sacramento River.

Information and Services

TOURIST INFORMATION

The **Sacramento Convention and Visitors Bureau** (800/292-2334, www.discovergold. org) has copious amounts of information for tourists and business travelers to the capital. From their website, you can book hotels, check upcoming events, find deals from local restaurants and hotels, or just browse through photo galleries to get pumped up before visiting. Frequent visitors to Sacramento can look into the **Sacramento Gold Card** when they book hotels; at certain places, the card hooks you up with free food and two-for-one admission to museums and attractions.

For advice from a real, honest to goodness live person, swing by the **Sacramento Visitors Center** (1002 2nd St., 916/442-7644, 10 A.M.–5 P.M. daily) in Old Sacramento. The friendly and knowledgeable attendants will help make last-minute travel arrangements with local hotels and also give you the lowdown on any special events happening that week.

Gay and lesbian visitors to Sacramento can find more info at **Sacramento Gay and Lesbian Center** (1927 L St., 916/422-0185, http://saccenter.org, noon–9 P.M. Mon.–Fri.). Another wealth of knowledge for GLBT news, politics, and events is *Outword Magazine* (www.outwordmagazine.com), published twice a month on second and fourth Thursdays.

MEDIA AND COMMUNICATIONS

The city's newspaper is the *Sacramento Bee,* a typical medium-size metro daily covering state and city politics, sports, and entertainment. Despite recent cutbacks, the *Bee* does an outstanding job following high school athletics and breaking news at the Capitol. Every week there's a special entertainment insert called The Ticket with upcoming events. The *Bee* can be found all over town.

A smart, edgy town needs a hard-hitting newspaper, and that's where the **Sacramento News and Review** fits in. The *SN&R,* as it's known around town, is the capital's second largest paper and top alternative weekly. It has a take-no-prisoners reputation for digging deep into city scandals with thoughtful, irreverent reporting. Pick up a free copy for investigative pieces on local issues like the environment, civil rights, and scandals at city hall, or the latest coverage on local bands. Every week, the *SN&R* publishes a list of shows at the city's clubs so you can stay plugged into Sacramento's busy music scene. The *SN&R* can be found anywhere in Sacramento and all over the Gold Country at funky little newsstands.

It seems like every major city has a stylish monthly magazine with breezy restaurant reviews, photos from glamorous parties, and some pithy commentary on local culture. *Sactown* magazine covers all that and more inside its glossy pages, along with features on local celebrities and entertainment big shots. *Sactown* is sold at supermarkets and convenience stores all over town.

The city's original glossy monthly is **Sacramento Magazine,** known for its annual "Best of Sacramento" issue ranking the capital's top eateries, shops, and bars. It can be purchased at most grocery stores and corner stores and provides an additional perspective on Sacramento culture.

There are several post offices located in Sacramento's central district. Start with **Fort Sutter** (1618 Alhambra Blvd., 916/227-6503) in East Sacramento by the Capital City Freeway. Closer to Sacramento State, look for another office at (4750 J St.). In south Sacramento there's **Broadway** (2121 Broadway, 916/227-6503), and anyone can mail a letter at the **Downtown Plaza** (560 J St., Ste. 165).

MEDICAL SERVICES AND EMERGENCIES

In the event of an emergency, call **911.** Nonemergency numbers include the following contacts: **Sacramento Police Department** (916/264-5471, www.sacpd.org), **Sacramento County Sheriff's Department** (916/874-5115, www.sacsheriff.com), **Sutter General Hospital** (2801 L St., 916/733-8900, www.suttermedicalcenter.org) located in Midtown near the Capital City Freeway/Highway 99, **Sutter Memorial Hospital** (5151 F St., 916/733-1000, www.suttermedicalcenter.org) in East Sacramento, **UC Davis Medical Center** (4150 V St., 916/734-5010, www.ucdmc.ucdavis.edu) in south Sacramento, **Sutter Children's Center** (5151 F St., 916/454-3333) in East Sacramento, and **UC Davis Children's Hospital** (2315 Stockton Blvd., 800/282-3284) located in south Sacramento near U.S. 50. To reach the city of Sacramento from a landline within the capital, call **311.**

Getting There and Around

Sacramento is fairly easy to navigate either with or without a car. Veins of massive gray freeways pump traffic in and out of the capital like a beating concrete heart—unless it's early morning or late afternoon when state workers begin their daily commute from the Capitol. Getting around by foot or bike is also a snap, especially downtown on the city's checkerboard grid layout. If you're going deep, as in beyond the city limits to eastern Sacramento County or beyond, the Sacramento Regional Transit network has decent coverage with light-rail and bus routes. On the other hand, trips to check out Nevada City or Amador's wine country usually require a rental car.

BY AIR

The **Sacramento International Airport** (SMF, 6900 Airport Blvd., 916/929-5411, www.sacramento.aero/smf) handles all commercial flights to and from the capital. As airports go, it's actually not too bad. While SMF might be small, you'll find it extremely modern and easy to navigate. A recent expansion added a brand spanking new $1 billion terminal with über-modern conveniences like a monorail, four-story terminal, and double-decker roads for arrivals and departures. No longer will visitors arrive in Sacramento to a shabby barn that smells like cigarette butts and mothballs.

Despite the name, SMF's only direct international flight goes to Guadalajara, Mexico. However, making international connections is a snap since Sacramento's 11 airlines fly to San Francisco, Los Angeles, Seattle, Phoenix, Dallas, Chicago, and New York City. Major passenger airlines include the following: Aeromexico (800/237-6639), Alaska Airlines (800/426-0333), American Airlines (800/433-7300), Delta (800/221-1212), Frontier Airlines (800/432-1359),

Hawaiian Airlines (800/367-5320), Horizon Air (800/547-9308), JetBlue (800/538-2583), Southwest (800/435-9792), United/United Express (800/241-6522), and US Airways (800/428-4322).

During the airport makeover, local restaurants asked for a slice of the pie. So instead of blowing money at cheap food courts in the new Terminal B, now you can sample plates from Sacramento's Esquire Grill, grab coffee roasted at Old Soul, and chow down on juicy beef patties from Burgers and Brew. In another sign that progress has arrived, you can order food from the freeway and have it waiting at your gate. An app called **B4 You Board** hooks up air passengers with takeaway orders or gate deliveries so rushed travelers don't have to stand around waiting for their food while the plane is boarding. All these cool upgrades mean one thing: more time for buying souvenirs. The best shop for loading up on trinkets is definitely **Capitol Marketplace** over in Terminal A, where they hawk cheap T-shirts, ball caps, mugs, and stuffed RiverCats toys.

The lamest thing about Sacramento's airport is simply the extra flying it takes to reach other cities. Sacramento only has 28 nonstop destinations. That means one or two connections to reach cities in the American South or the Great Plains. At least getting to and from the airport is a breeze. Since the airport's face-lift in 2011, extra hourly and daily parking means one less hassle at SMF. Hourly parking costs $2 for every 30 minutes, but there's a **free waiting area** for early-bird drivers waiting to make pickups. In daily parking count on shelling out $17 to leave your car for the entire day, although Economy lots offer $10 daily rates for travelers on longer trips. Call the airport for current parking info at 916/874-0670 if you have a question.

Airport Shuttles

Someday in the distant future, Sacramento's light-rail system will link downtown with the airport. Until then, **SuperShuttle** (916/929-5411, www.supershuttle.com, $13–16) is the quickest and most convenient ride to SMF. Otherwise you can take a cab for roughly $35–55 depending on starting point or ride the #42B **Yolobus** (530/666-2877, www.yolobus.com) for $2 from the Capitol, a journey that takes about 25 minutes.

BY TRAIN

You can bet on catching a train to and from Sacramento, the former terminus for the First Transcontinental Railroad. In fact, in downtown there's a beautifully restored Art Deco station with gnarly wooden benches and a huge chandelier hanging inside the waiting area. The **Sacramento Valley Station** (401 I St., 800/872-7245, www.amtrakcalifornia.com) links the capital with the Bay Area, the Central Valley, the Pacific Northwest, and the great Midwest with four dedicated Amtrak routes. For local travel between the Gold Country and the Bay take the Amtrak *Capitol Corridor,* which runs between Auburn and San Jose or Oakland nearly a dozen times daily.

Amtrak's *Capitol Corridor* rolls through Davis, but you can also ride **Yolobus** (530/666-2877, www.yolobus.com, $2) on either bus 42A or 42B to reach UC Davis and other destinations in Yolo County. Amtrak also runs three bus routes to a smattering of Northern California destinations including the upper Central Valley and Siskiyou Mountain range, the Gold Country and Sierra Nevada, and south to Stockton and the San Joaquin Valley.

BY BUS AND LIGHT-RAIL

Sacramento doesn't have a subway system or extensive streetcar network. There's talk of adding a streetcar line in the next decade, but until that happens, there's **Sacramento Regional Transit** (916/321-2877, www.sacrt.com), which operates the city's light-rail and bus system. The light-rail is mostly for commuters heading into downtown from the north, south, and east. The Gold Line connects downtown with Sacramento Valley Station and Amtrak service, while the Blue Line loops through Broadway, downtown, and out through Alkali Flat toward North Sacramento. Taking the light-rail can be quite, ahem, memorable during certain times of the day and even a little dangerous after dark. Most of the passengers are students, state workers, and other commuters, but off-peak riders are a different crowd, often causing fights with light-rail security officers and each other. Stay alert and leave the train if you don't feel safe. Bikes are allowed on board if placed in the awkward and unwieldy racks in each car; otherwise you might get a rather gruff reminder from ticket conductors to follow the rules.

Taking the bus is a different story. The routes are much more extensive and will carry you almost anywhere throughout the city. For newcomers trying to figure out a journey, make sure to check out Sacramento's online route planner (www.sacrt.com), which usually spits out a trip combining bus routes with light-rail lines to help you reach a destination. Whether taking a bus or riding the rails, a one-way ticket costs $2.50. Do yourself a favor and buy a daily pass ($6) if you plan on taking more than two trips on public transit. Buy tickets at the Sacramento Natural Foods Co-op or any Save Mart supermarket; each light-rail station has electronic ticket kiosks that accept credit cards.

Greyhound (420 Richards Blvd., 916/444-6858) also has a station in Sacramento just a mile north of downtown. Take the Sacramento Regional Transit bus 15 from J and 6th to reach the bus station.

Commuter Shuttles

Most of the Gold Country towns run commuter shuttles to Sacramento and back during the week. From the Southern Gold Country there's **Amador Transit** (209/267-9395, www.amador-transit.com, $5.50), making twice daily trips on the Sacramento Express between Monday and Friday. Auburn's **Placer Commuter Express** (530/885-2877 or 916/784-6177, www.placer.ca.gov, $4.75) connects smaller foothill towns like Colfax, Clipper Gap, Penryn, and Loomis with the capital while also making stops in Auburn, Rocklin, and Roseville. And from Placerville you can take the big blue **El Dorado Transit** (530/642-5383, www.eldoradotransit.com, $5) during the week; the bus makes 11 return trips from downtown Sacramento and includes stops in Shingle Springs, Diamond Springs, Cameron Park, and El Dorado Hills.

BY CAR

California cities have a love-hate relationship with their highways, and Sacramento is no different. Four major thoroughfares plough through the city's urban neighborhoods: U.S. 50, I-5, I-80, and State Route 99. Traffic is a problem, especially on a stretch of road northeast of downtown known as the Capital City Freeway. Avoid it if you can during morning and late afternoon. To the west and south, concrete causeways like I-5 and U.S. 50 have divided and bisected the city into districts, but that doesn't mean it's easy to get around. Driving in Sacramento can feel like navigating a tangled spaghetti bowl of merging freeways. Don't fret; once off the highway, it becomes much easier to manage the city's urban grid of straight one-way streets.

Car Rental

Planning any kind of day trip or journey to the Gold Country is another matter. In that case, you'll need wheels. Rental companies will rent cars at the airport and at several locations downtown. Those companies include: **Alamo** (800/327-9633), **Avis** (916/922-5601), **Budget** (800/763-2999), **Dollar** (916/569-2885),

Enterprise (800/736-8227), **Hertz** (800/654-3131), **National** (800/227-7366), **Advance Rent a Car** (916/442-1362), and **Payless Car Rental** (800/729-5377).

Parking

The chance of finding an open, on-street parking spot in downtown Sacramento on weekdays is fairly dismal; remember, you're fighting for street parking with government workers downtown. Old Sacramento also has very little on-street parking. Things open up in Midtown and East Sacramento, where it's easier to find two-hour non-metered spots on the street. Sacramento has special meters that accept most major credit cards; the rates are $1.25 for one hour. If parking seems nonexistent, pay garages near the Capitol will usually have some available spaces.

TAXI

Cabs are available in Sacramento, but they're not cheap. A typical taxi ride across town from the Capitol to East Sacramento runs about $16. Calling for a cab on busy evenings like Friday or Saturday can involve waiting on hold for 10–15 minutes. It's easier to book online. Both **Yellow Cab** (916/444-2222, www.yellowcabsacramento.com) and **California Co-Op Cab** (916/444-7777, http://californiacoopcab.com) offer both phone and Internet reservations. There's also **Taxi Dave** (916/862-0445, 8 P.M.–4 A.M.), an independent cabbie contracted with Yellow Cab who operates every day except for Sunday.

BICYCLE

Sacramento is a terrific place to ride bikes. Everywhere it seems folks are riding beach cruisers around Midtown and downtown. The American League of Bicyclists gives the capital a "silver" rating for creating 371 miles of bicycle lanes throughout the city. Unfortunately those lanes have gaps in some places. Recently the city of Sacramento has been trying to plug these holes with some success, but beware when riding through downtown. Ride defensively and don't assume that drivers can see you. The **Sacramento Area Bicycle Advocates** (www. sacbike.org/sacbiking) is the best resource for cyclists and casual bike riders. They cover everything from safety tips to rules for sidewalk riding. Check their website for a list of local bike maps in Sacramento and surrounding areas.

It's a great idea to rent a bike during your stay in Sacramento. For rentals in Old Sacramento there's **Practical Cycle** (114 J St., 916/706-0077, http://practicalcycle.com), which rents cruisers for $5 an hour and $25 per day, and multispeed bikes for $8 per hour and $40 for the whole day. They'll also set you up with electric bikes ($10/$50) and tandem bicycles ($12/$60). In Midtown there's **City Bike Works** (2419 K St., 916/447-2453, http://citybicycleworks.com). Rentals include road bikes for $10 per hour ($40 for a day) and hybrids ($5/$20).

If you'd rather let someone else pedal for a change, there's **Velocab** (916/498-9980, http://ridevelocab.com), which offers pedicab service in Midtown and downtown between noon and 8 P.M. Rides cost $2 for the first block and $0.50 for every block thereafter.

TOURS
Bike Tours

Sacramento has perfect topography for a bike ride. It's a flat city with wide streets and decent infrastructure; there's currently 288 miles of on-street bikeways and 83 more miles off-street. Sacramento's grid layout makes it hard to get lost, but if you're thinking about taking a guided ride, look into **Fast Eddie Bike Tours** (Midtown Sacramento, 916/812-2712, www. fasteddiebiketours.com, Mar.–Oct. by reservation, $20–25). For about $20, they'll take you on a five-mile swing through Midtown. Fast Eddie offers two different themed trips—a

historical ride (focusing on vintage architecture and Sacramento's notable historical figures) and an urban art trip (a jaunt past public art and graphics). Rides are about 90 minutes and don't run on set schedules; Fast Eddie takes riders by demand. A Raleigh rental bike costs an extra $5.

Culinary Tours

Sacramento's organic and sustainable farms have boomed in the past few years. Foodies can learn more about the Capital City's culinary Gold Rush on the **Local Roots Food Tours** (800/407-8918, http://local-food-tours.com, adults $45–58, seniors $48, kids $45, veterans $50). These four trips take visitors to graze at farmers markets and nosh at fine restaurants, all while explaining the city's local food culture. If you enjoy history on the side, take the **Origins of Sacramento Walking Food and Cultural Tour** (2.75 miles, 10:15 A.M. Wed. and Fri.–Sat.) through Midtown's Sutter District and the Fabulous Forties in East Sacramento. This tour is a walking excursion through the city's oldest neighborhoods and into local bistros. You'll sample dishes such as pork carnitas on homemade tortillas, Dungeness crab cakes, stuffed dates with goat cheese, and wash it down with a Czech pilsner.

River Cruises

Elegant paddle-wheeled steamboats were the main form of transportation between Sacramento and San Francisco during the Gold Rush. Re-create that journey and book passage with **Hornblower Historic River Cruises** (Old Sacramento embarcadero, 916/446-1185, www. hornblower.com, 1:30 P.M. and 3 P.M. Thurs.–Sun., $20). For one hour, you'll steam up and down the Sacramento River, passing underneath the Tower Bridge and along historic waterfront. It's also a chance to learn a bit more about Sacramento's history. The narrated cruise offers fascinating insight into the River City's

© CHRISTOPHER ARNS

Sail the Sacramento River on the *Empress Hornblower*.

past. Snacks and refreshments are provided. For something a little different, book a **happy hour cruise** (5:30 P.M. Fri.) and take in the experience with a cocktail.

Walking Tours

Sometimes it's easy to miss the littlest things when visiting a new place. Luckily, Sacramento has a whole list of great walking tours that show multiple shades of California's capital. You can roam beneath the city's cobbled streets with the **Old Sacramento Underground Tours** (916/808-7059, www.historicoldsac.org, adults $15, children $10). Back in the 1860s, Sacramento was repeatedly inundated with catastrophic floods, so officials decided to raise the city by one story to escape the ravaging waters of the Sacramento River. The Underground Tours show you the hidden corridors and passageways that were entombed after the city was elevated. You can see the city's underground from March to November

and the schedule frequently changes during those months, so check the website for current times. Tours start at the **Sacramento History Museum** (101 I St., 916/808-7059, www.historicoldsac.org, 10 A.M.–5 P.M. daily, adults $6, children $4), which has a glass floor looking down into the city's buried past. It's worth coming here maybe 15 minutes early to walk around and get up to speed on Sacramento's tortured history before taking the tour.

One fun trip is the **Historic Old Sacramento Walking Tours** (101 I St., 916/808-7059, www.historicoldsac.org, early June–late Aug. 11 A.M. and 1 P.M. Sat.–Sun., $5). Costumed tour guides act like they're actually guiding you through the 19th century. Actors reenact scenes from Sacramento's Gold Rush days, and you might witness a gunfight, the arrival of Pony Express riders, or perhaps press flesh with a Gilded Age politician. Along with re-creating the sense that visitors are stepping back in time, guides will also explain Old Sacramento's

A staircase leads down to Sacramento's buried past.

brick architecture and discuss the original uses of many buildings.

Let's face it, we all need a laugh sometimes. **Hysterical Comedy Tours** (J and 2nd Sts., Old Sacramento, 916/441-2527, http://hystericalwalks.com, 6 P.M. Fri.–Sat., adults $20, youth $15) take visitors on a side-splitting walk around Old Sacramento while pointing out interesting (and funny, of course) tidbits about the city. The costumed guides are friendly and extremely informative. If you liked the comedic waltz around Sacramento, sign up for the **Hysterical Walk of the Dead** (7:30 P.M. Fri.–Sat. Oct. 1–Mar. 31, 8:30 P.M. Fri.–Sat. Apr. 1–Sept. 30, adults $20, youth $15). It's a lighthearted take on Old Town's ghouls and goblins that seem to lurk more closely as Halloween approaches.

There's another spooky option if you enjoy stalking the undead. **Historic Old Sacramento Ghost Tours** (101 I St., 916/808-7059, www.

historicoldsac.org, weekends mid to late Oct., 6:30–9 P.M., adults $15, children $10) don't deploy the comedy quite like Hysterical Walks, but these creepy walking trips include "real" ghosts (as in costumed actors) who lament their untimely end dating to the Gold Rush. Some of these "ghouls" play the role of real murder victims from Sacramento history. This tour sells out fast, so buy tickets ahead of time.

Finally, the **Old Speakeasy Tour** (River City Saloon, 916 2nd St., http://downtownsac.org, 5:30 P.M. every third Sat., $10) goes back underground to explore Old Sacramento's banned watering holes dating back to Prohibition. On one hand, that time period "dried out" Sacramento's economy; the city's Buffalo Brewery (largest beer producer west of the Mississippi at the time) was crippled after passage of the 18th Amendment banned alcohol. But Sacramento's underground party scene took off. The *Delta King* became a floating vessel of vice with jazz bands, gambling, and illegal booze. This walk makes several stops along Sacramento's speakeasy trail, and yes, it's definitely "wet"; feel free to order a Prohibition-era cocktail along the way.

Old Sacramento isn't the only fun place for walking tours. **Downtown Sacramento Tours** (916/442-8575, http://downtownsac.org, $10) have a slew of guided and self-guided trips around the Capitol District. Music lovers will dig the **Rock and Roll History Tour and Pub Crawl** (Torch Club, 904 15th St., 6:30 P.M. Thurs. May–July). This tour connects the head-banging dots between downtown and bands like Nirvana, the Beach Boys, and the Rolling Stones. As the name says, it's a pub crawl, so grab a cocktail and get ready to make new friends. If beer goggles don't appeal to you, sign up instead for the **Public Art Tour** (Downtown Plaza at 3rd and K Sts., 9 A.M. Mon.–Fri.), which shows you around downtown's urban artwork collection created by both local and nationally acclaimed artists.

Lastly, tie it all together with the **Tales of the Central City Tour** (Cesar Chavez Plaza at 9th and J Sts., 11 A.M. Mon.–Fri.). Nothing is off limits on this trip. Explore more about the State Capitol, find out about Leland Stanford's ghostly progeny and who built the city's most famous landmarks.

If having a guide sounds like a drag, opt instead for the **Sacramento Heritage self-guided tours** (www.sacramentoheritage.org). There are at least 10 tours that focus on various themes and neighborhoods. Some of the best include the **Bungalow Tour,** which passes almost 100 of Sacramento's Midtown and East Sacramento bungalow homes. The **Boulevard Park Tour** loops through one of the city's first suburbs; it's also the former site of the California State Fairgrounds and Union Park Race Course where Leland Stanford owned a harness racing team. These walks are free, really easy to complete, and can definitely be transformed into self-guided biking tours.

Vicinity of Sacramento

Two vastly different frontiers sandwich California's capital between a fertile checkerboard of farmland and a maze of twisting waterways. Imagine if Louisiana's bayous were just a stone's throw away from the Great Plains. That's the diverse landscape surrounding Sacramento, which hugs the immense California Delta to the west and embraces the Central Valley to the north and south. True to Sacramento's tendency to defy expectations, there are a few surprises lurking between the endless sloughs and cattle ranches. Some of California's most diverse wildlife can be found just south of Sacramento in the Cosumnes River Preserve. And you can't miss the wineries in the delta, which produce head-turning zinfandel and chardonnay.

CALIFORNIA DELTA

Seven rivers wander across the Central Valley to converge southwest of Sacramento, forming the watery expanse known as the California Delta. At least 1,000 miles of waterways snake through this vast estuary, creating islands, sloughs, and pockets of small farms where pears and grapes are produced. Things definitely move much slower in the sleepy delta. Towns crouch behind tall levees, shrouded by tall valley oak trees, and visitors can easily miss the beautiful mansions hidden behind overgrown thickets by the road. An afternoon drive is an excellent idea in these parts. I recommend taking Highway 160 south from Freeport to follow the Sacramento River past towns like **Walnut Grove, Isleton, Locke,** and **Clarksburg.** You can find some darn good wineries in these parts, and it's worth stopping to check them out.

Wineries

Your first stop should be the imposing brick fortress of the **Old Sugar Mill** (35265 Willow Ave., Clarksburg, 916/744-1615, www.oldsugarmill.com, 11 A.M.–5 P.M. daily). Visitors from the East Coast will be stunned at the similarity between this monolithic compound and the crumbling factories of New York's Rust Belt. The mill opened in 1935 and operated until the early 1990s when it was shut down. Now the building has been renovated into a custom crush facility and a home for eight tasting rooms. Some of the notable wineries include **Carvalho Family Winery** (916/744-1625 www.carvalhofamilywinery.com, 11 A.M.–5 P.M., Wed.–Sun., $5) and **Heringer Estates** (916/744-1094, www.heringerestates.com, 11 A.M.–5 P.M. Thurs.–Sun., tasting fee $5). These small family outfits have been farming the delta for decades in the Clarksburg area,

© CHRISTOPHER ARNS

Highway 160 winds through the California Delta.

and their pride clearly shows in the chenin blancs and tempranillos. The hours seem to change frequently at the Old Sugar Mill; tasting rooms may have different posted hours than the facility itself, so call ahead if you're not sure.

If name recognition is what you're after, there's **Bogle Vineyards** (37783 County Road 144, Clarksburg, 916/744-1139, www.boglewinery.com, 10 A.M.–5 P.M. Mon.–Fri., 11 A.M.–5 P.M. Sat.–Sun., tasting $5). California earned its stripes producing world-class chardonnay and that's what Bogle does better than anyone, winning gold and double-gold awards every year at the California State Fair and the *San Francisco Chronicle* Wine Competition. When pouring a dash of this liquid gold, take a moment to savor the perfectly layered hints of green apples, pears, toasty oak, and finishes with subtle notes of lemon meringue. I also recommend the refreshing sauvignon blanc, built on notes of lively

citrus and lemongrass, and the Phantom port, a full-bodied blend of zinfandel, petite syrah, and mourvèdre. Better yet, wine lovers with a "green" palate will embrace Bogle's move to mostly certified sustainable vineyards.

Miner's Leap (54250 South River Rd., Clarksburg, 916/813-6909, www.minersleap.com, 1–6 P.M. Fri., 11 A.M.–5 P.M. Sat.–Sun., $5) also produces vino from grapes grown in the delta. They have a brand-new garden area by an old-timey barn right off the highway. Make sure to try the reds; the pinot noir and the grenache are standouts.

◖ Cosumnes River Preserve

North America's largest expanse of oak savanna and river wetlands once blanketed the valley south of Sacramento. Only a small chunk remains at the Cosumnes River Preserve (13501 Franklin Blvd., 916/684-2816, www.cosumnes.org, visitor center 9 A.M.–4 P.M. daily), located south of Sacramento on the delta's eastern rim.

the Old Sugar Mill in Clarksburg

Some 1,500 acres of valley oaks, California's largest and oldest species of oak trees, are clustered along the lower Cosumnes River in small groves now protected from development. The river preserve is also a sprawling haven for 250 bird species like the greater sandhill crane, the Swainson hawk, and tricolored blackbird. From late fall through early spring, thousands of winged creatures descend onto the preserve as they travel through the Pacific Flyway, the West Coast's major north-south migration route. Watching this yearly invasion of feathers and beaks is something you'll never forget. Check out the action on the **Cosumnes River Walk Trail** (three miles round-trip, moderate) where it starts north of the visitor center. The walk curves along raised levees through buttonbush thickets, groves of valley oak by the river, cottonwoods, willow trees, and several wetland restoration projects. Another great hike is **Rancho Seco Howard Ranch Trail** (seven miles round-trip, moderate), a long jaunt past vernal pools, seasonal wetlands, and oak woodlands. Remember to stay on the trails during these hikes and leave pets at home; more than 230 delicate and threatened plant species grow in the preserve, and any disturbance can harm them. Make sure to bring insect repellent for the bugs and binoculars for the birds.

Travel deeper into the delta's murky depths by **kayaking** or taking a **boat tour.** A great place to start paddling is just east of the visitor center at the Cosumnes River Preserve. Believe it or not, the Pacific Ocean pulls on the Cosumnes way up here, exposing sandbars and shoals at different times of day. Keep an eye out for 40 species of fish in these waters like brown trout and white catfish. If you're around in October and November, the chinook salmon runs upriver during fall spawning season. If only some enterprising soul would offer kayak rentals closer to the preserve. For visitors without their own canoe or kayak, you'll have to rent in Sacramento. These shops will hook you up: **Sport Chalet** (2401 Butano Dr., 916/977-1731, www.sportchalet.com, 10 A.M.–9 P.M. Mon.–Sat., 11 A.M.–6 P.M. Sun., canoes and sea kayaks $40), **California Canoe and Kayak** (11349 Folsom Blvd., Ste. C, 916/851-3600, www.calkayak.com, 10 A.M.–6 P.M. Mon. and Wed.–Sat., 11 A.M.–6 P.M. Sun., kayaks $60–150, canoes $80–150).

Entertainments and Events

Did you know California produces more Bartlett pears than any other state? Some 130,000 tons are picked near the tiny river town of Courtland. Every year, the town throws a Bartlett harvest bash at the **Delta Pear Fair** (Courtland, http://pearfair.org, 916/775-2000, late July, free, parking $10). What better place to stuff yourself with pear bread, pear ice cream, pear pies, and pear fries. Soon you'll have a pear coma! To avoid getting flurpy on Bartletts, the fair also has a proper food court hawking grilled corn, hot dogs, and other kinds of carnival food. Loosen up by knocking back a pear martini or a pear mimosa, and then catch a live blues band before they crown the Pear Fair Queen. No pets are allowed, and please, no picking pears off nearby trees! The fair has bags of fresh pears for sale.

Grab a plate of spicy crawdads at the **Isleton Cajun Festival** (Isleton, 916/777-4800, http://isletoncajunfestival.net, June, $6) and listen to Cajun music all weekend. That's basically the format, and Isleton—a crumbling river burg that bears an uncanny resemblance to the Mississippi bayou—is really the ideal place for it. People start mobbing the beer trucks toward late afternoon and things get a little rowdy, so you really should take the kids home by that point.

The **Wine Cheese and Bread Faire** (35265 Willow Ave., Clarksburg, 916/744-1615, www.oldsugarmill.com, July, $25–30) takes place over a weekend at the venerable Old Sugar Mill on the banks of the Sacramento River. All eight wineries hold tastings. Local artisan vendors sell locally made chocolate, cheeses, olive oil, sausage, nut products, teas and coffee, and lavender honey.

Sports and Recreation

Squeeze in a round at **Bartley Cavanagh Golf Course** (8301 Freeport Blvd., Sacramento, 916/665-2020, www.bartleycavanaugh.com, $26–46). Sandwiched between the Sacramento River and I-5, duffers might decide the location could be better, but the greens and fairways are carefully tended. Watch the water hazard on the 400-yard No. 9, considered the toughest hole on the course.

Accommodations

Staying overnight in the California Delta can be a peaceful and memorable trip if you don't mind a step down in quality. The sad fact is that no one has stepped up and opened a top-notch bed-and-breakfast in the area. Maybe that will change soon. For now, check out the places listed below.

For pure comfort, there's **New Moon River Inn** (8201 Freeport Blvd., Sacramento, 916/665-2293, www.newmoonriverinn.com, $100–150), although don't expect fireworks from the decor. From the highway it looks like a clubhouse at a golf course. Ten rooms boast simple, modern furnishings, private bathrooms, down comforters, free wireless Internet, and whirlpool bathtubs. No breakfast is served in the morning although they do offer a beverage service with beer and wine.

Rogelio's Dine and Sleep Inn (34 Main St., Isleton, 916/777-5878, www.rogelios.net, $90–100) harks back to old roadside inns from the early 20th century. For around $100, you'll get a decently sized room and dinner for two people. Each of the 10 rooms has basic amenities, including heating and air-conditioning, private bathrooms with shower, and access to second-story balconies overlooking downtown

Isleton. Everything looks clean and spotless even though the furniture probably hasn't changed since the late 1970s.

Food

You'll find a few memorable roadside joints during trips to the California Delta. After dining at Sacramento's trendy bistros, restaurants in Isleton or Walnut Grove probably lack glamour. Figure on grabbing lunch or a quick dinner, but don't judge these places by big-city standards. You should be mindful of the delta's sleepy influence on local businesses, which often shut down early if they think it's a slow day. As always, call ahead to be sure.

Moon River Café (8201 Freeport Blvd., Sacramento, 916/665-2293, www.newmoonriverinn.com, 8–11 A.M. and noon–3 P.M. Tues.–Fri., $4–16) serves American-style breakfast and lunch. Plates include chicken sandwiches, burgers, quesadillas, and grilled seafood. In the morning, make sure to try the sweet potato waffle or the custard French toast. The café is attached to the lodgings at Water's Edge Retreat.

Peter's Steak House (203 2nd St., Isleton, 916/777-6004, www.peterssteakhouse.net, 11 A.M.–9 P.M. daily, $10–28) grills the best steak sandwiches in the delta. The menu is basic American surf and turf; other than the steak sandwich, I'd recommend the crawdad melt or the fish-and-chips.

Rogelio's Dine and Sleep Inn (34 Main St., Isleton, 916/777-5878, www.rogelios.net, 4–8 P.M. Tues.–Wed., 11 A.M.–2 P.M. and 4–8 P.M. Thurs., 11 A.M.–9 P.M. Fri.–Sat., 11 A.M.–8 P.M. Sun., $16) has a somewhat puzzling menu of Chinese, Mexican, and American grub, so you can either order chow mein or ribs. The food is actually pretty good, although with nearly 100 choices it should be. Folks staying at the inn automatically get a free dinner coupon.

For burgers and steaks, there's **Al the**

Wop's (13936 Main St., Locke, 916/776-1800, 11:30 A.M.–9 P.M. Mon.–Fri., 3–9 P.M. Sat.–Sun., $10–20), a quirky restaurant in the tiny town of Locke. The restaurant's namesake was actually Italian, which explains why he picked such an irreverent moniker for the place. Between 1934 and 1961, Al didn't have a menu; he grilled steaks and that was it. Well, I take that back: He made sure every table had jars of peanut butter and jelly. They still do, and the restaurant will toast you a mean piece of bread upon request.

For just a few precious hours every Sunday, **◖ Grand Island Mansion** (13415 Grand Island Rd., Walnut Grove, 916/775-1705, www.grandislandmansion.com, 10:30 A.M.–2 P.M. Sun., $22–27) serves a champagne brunch at this plantation-style location, the largest private estate in Northern California. Visitors to this gleaming white Italianate palace have included Franklin D. Roosevelt and Ronald Reagan. Ideally the best way to experience this place is by boat; the villa has a marina right on the Sacramento River and approaching from the water is a *Gone With the Wind* kind of moment. Brunch consists of entrées like eggs Benedict, maple glazed salmon, Italian toast (a sweeter take on French toast), and chicken crepe. Notice that it's not cheap, although I think it's worth it.

Giusti's (14743 Walnut Grove-Thornton Rd., Walnut Grove, 916/776-1808, www.giustis.com, 11:30 A.M.–1:30 P.M. and 5–10 P.M. Tues.–Fri., 11:30 A.M.–2 P.M. and 5–11 P.M. Sat., 11:30 A.M.–2 P.M. and 4–10 P.M. Sun., $12–25) claims to be the oldest bar and restaurant in the delta. Four generations of Giustis have worked the hospitality business in Walnut Grove since shortly after 1900s. Combine an archaic dive bar with an old-school Italian joint, and you'll have the right idea about this place. Locals mob it on weekends and especially for the champagne Sunday brunch, consisting of eggs Benedict, fresh salmon, ribs, huevos rancheros, and a few other plates. Dinner is traditional Italian food with linguine, ravioli, and lasagna. Hats off to their choice of local vino for the page-long wine list, which includes notables from Clarksburg and Lodi. Thanks to the marina out back, you can arrive by boat if needed.

Busaba on the Delta (15476 Hwy. 160, Isleton, 916/777-6655, 11 A.M.–8:30 P.M. Wed.–Fri., 8 A.M.–8:30 P.M. Sat., 8 A.M.–8 P.M. Sun., $13–19) does American and Thai cuisine. If you ask locals, they'll say the fish-and-chips are kick-ass and the American-style breakfasts top anything else in town. There's nothing special about the surroundings, but the service is fast and friendly.

Almost any time of day, you can get a sandwich, espresso, and a cone of Gunther's Ice Cream at **Mel's Mocha and Ice Cream** (14131 River Rd., Walnut Grove, 916/776-4333, 6 A.M.–7 P.M. Mon.–Thurs., 6 A.M.–8 P.M. Fri.–Sat., 7 A.M.–7 P.M. Sun., $7). Expect to wait in line during lunch on weekends.

Information and Services

The California Delta is a chain of 58 islands strung together by a system of aging steel bridges and levees. Towns have few of the major conveniences that you'd find in Sacramento or even larger towns in the Gold Country. At most there are a handful of gas stations, banks, and supermarkets. In Walnut Grove, you'll find an ATM at the **Bank of Rio Vista** (14211 River Rd., 916/776-1755, www.bankofriovista.com). There's also an ATM in Isleton (212 2nd St.).

There's a **post office** in Isleton (103 C St., 9:30–11:30 A.M. and 12:30–4:30 P.M. Mon.–Fri.) and Walnut Grove (14165 River Rd., 9:30 A.M.–5 P.M. Mon.–Fri., 9:30 A.M.–noon Sat.) if you need to buy stamps or mail something.

The **California Delta Chambers and Visitor's Bureau** (169 W. Brannan Island Rd., Isleton, 916/777-4041, www.californiadelta.org) is a loose confederation of local chambers of commerce and visitor centers; their website is bristling with good travel tips and advice about the delta. They don't have a brick-and-mortar location, but the **Delta Farmers Market** (2510 Hwy. 12, Isleton, 916/777-4000, 9 A.M.–7 P.M. Mon.–Sat., 9 A.M.–6 P.M. Sun. in summer; 10 A.M.–6 P.M. Thurs.–Sun. in fall and winter) has maps and brochures.

The only delta newspaper is the weekly *River News-Herald and Isleton Journal* (http://rivernewsherald.org), which mostly covers Isleton's dysfunctional city politics.

If you have a major medical emergency in Isleton or Walnut Grove, the closest hospitals are **Sutter Delta Medical Center** (3901 Lone Tree Way, Antioch, 925/779-7200, www.sutterdelta.org) or **Lodi Memorial Hospital Urgent-Care Clinic** (1235 W. Vine St., Ste. 20, Lodi, 209/339-7600, www.lodihealth.org). Each facility is about 20 miles away.

For medical treatment in Clarksburg or the northern delta, head to **Sacramento Urgent Care** (7200 South Land Park, #100, Sacramento, 916/422-9110, www.sacurgentcare.com) or **Elk Grove Urgent Care** (9045 Bruceville Rd., Elk Grove, 916/479-9110, www.elkgrove-urgentcare.com).

Getting There and Around

Like a modern-day Indiana Jones, tourists can see the California Delta by air, land, or water, and getting around does become an adventure. Few people realize how enormous this freshwater estuary really is, but it's huge: More than 1,000 miles of waterways create a patchwork quilt of 58 large islands and countless hundreds of smaller ones. If you have the time, I suggest seeing this natural wonder by boat; most restaurants and businesses have marinas where you can dock for a few hours without charge.

© CHRISTOPHER ARNS

a drawbridge in the California Delta

BY BOAT

An archaic drawbridge system stitches together the California Delta's roads and waterways. Each steel overpass is tended by a bridge tender during certain operating hours. If you're traveling through the delta by boat, it's *absolutely critical* to know where these bridges might be. Not all of them are drawbridges and certain vessels won't be able to pass. A great resource for boaters is **BoatHarbors.com** (www.boatharborslocator.com), which has phone numbers for each drawbridge in California along with clearance heights. If the channel becomes blocked or a bridge is malfunctioning, contact the **U.S. Coast Guard 11th District Bridge Section** (office 510/437-3514, mobile 510/219-4366, 6:30 A.M.–4 P.M. Mon.–Fri.).

Maritime vessels must worry about a plethora of other things. Besides the drawbridge system, the delta is peppered with control gates, canals, and temporary barriers meant to manage water flow and block out saltwater. And don't forget the tides; the Pacific Ocean's pull adds another wrinkle into navigating this watery spiderweb. For updated water levels, check the **California Data Exchange Center** (http://cdec.water.ca.gov/river/deltaStages. html) or the **California Delta Chambers and Visitor's Bureau**'s website (www.californiadelta.org/deltatides.htm).

Once you figure out the rules of the watery road, boating through the delta becomes a leisurely way to visit restaurants and see local attractions. For the most part, local marinas won't charge to use their slips for a few hours unless you plan on staying overnight. To find out where to launch, the California Delta Chambers and Visitor's Bureau sells a map ($8), or you can check out this website (www. boatrampslocator.com) to find different spots along the Sacramento and San Joaquin Rivers.

One last note: conditions can change quickly

during certain seasons. If local officials close waterways or issue restrictions, they'll broadcast that info over Marine Band Radio channel 16. For emergencies, contact the U.S. Coast Guard Station in Rio Vista (707/374-2655), or the Sacramento County Sheriff's Department (916/874-5111). If something doesn't feel right or you get lost, don't risk the boat, your life, or your passengers' lives by taking a chance. Always observe proper maritime regulations and boat safety rules, and avoid boating under the influence of alcohol.

BY CAR

If you are driving, the delta's drawbridge system can become a minor nuisance when a boat needs to cross. Count on waiting for about 10–20 minutes as the drawbridge is raised or swings on a turntable, the boat passes underneath, and then finally the bridge lowers or swings back around.

There's limited access into the delta. The roads are narrow, winding highways that twist and turn with the rivers. Take your time and don't hurry. If you are coming from Sacramento, take Highway 160 south to Freeport. From here, cross over the river to the west bank and continue down Highway 160 for 4.3 miles to Clarksburg, or continue on the east bank for 12.6 miles to reach Courtland. If you are starting from Davis, take I-80 to West Sacramento and head south on Jefferson Boulevard; turn left on either Clarksburg Road or Courtland Road and head east toward those towns.

To reach Walnut Grove, continue driving south on Highway 160. From Clarksburg, it's about 17 miles to Walnut Grove. If your destination is Isleton, it's another 10 miles southwest from Walnut Grove.

If you're headed into the delta from the Central Valley, there are a few options. To reach Isleton, take Highway 12 west from Lodi for 20 miles before turning right on Jackson Slough Road; the town is two miles north. The quickest way to Walnut Grove is on Twin Cities Road or W. Walnut Grove Road/County Road J11 from I-5; from the freeway, it's about six miles west to Walnut Grove.

BY BUS

There is limited local bus service in the eastern California Delta. If you're headed west toward the bay, there's the **Rio Vista Delta Breeze** (100 2nd St., 707/374-2878, Isleton, www.riovistacity.com, $1.75), which operates between Isleton and Rio Vista.

The **South County Transit Delta Route** (209/745-3052, www.sctlink.com, four times daily Mon.–Fri., local $1, to Lodi $4) travels between Isleton and Lodi, and will make stops in between.

Amtrak (www.amtrak.com) and **Greyhound** (www.greyhound.com) will make pickups and drop-offs in Isleton at the Delta Breeze stop. Call the Delta Breeze office to arrange tickets.

BY AIR

The only true airfield in the California Delta is the **Rio Vista Municipal Airport/Jack Baumann Field** (3000 Baumann Rd., 707/374-2176, www.riovistacity.com), just over the river from Isleton.

DAVIS

More than just a college burg, Davis is a bustling town with a lively nightlife and restaurant scene. It's also home to the region's agricultural brainpower at the University of California, Davis—home of the Aggies. The town sits among rice fields and orchards in the fertile valley between Sacramento and California's coastal mountain ranges. Most of the region's organic and community-supported farms lie just northwest of Davis, which spreads this bounty twice a week at the town's renowned farmers market.

Known for its progressive vibe and left-leaning politics, Davis also consistently earns national recognition as a top-notch bicycle town with some of the country's most expansive and well-maintained bike paths. Downtown, you'll find plenty of arty boutiques and antiques stores scattered throughout the shady streets, a perfect place for avoiding the hot valley sun. Whether you're visiting the college campus or scouting local organic farms, Davis is worth a stop if you're heading east toward Sacramento or going west toward the Bay Area.

University of California, Davis

One of the country's most esteemed educational institutions is the University of California, Davis (Old Davis Rd., www.ucdavis.edu). Students at UC Davis are known as Aggies in a nod to the school's storied agricultural background. First opened in 1905 as a farm school, the expansive campus (California's largest at 7,156 acres) has an on-site dairy and a working farm. These days, UC Davis is also renowned for its biology and political science programs, along with one of the nation's biggest engineering schools. Sports are also an important part of Aggie life, and the UC Davis athletic program has rivalries with other NCAA Division I schools like Stanford, UC Berkeley, and nearby Sacramento State. If you visit Davis, make sure to go to the beautiful campus for at least a stroll or to catch an Aggies game.

How many universities teach students to brew their own beer? At the **Robert Mondavi Institute for Wine and Food Science** (392 Old Davis Rd., 530/754-6349, http://robertmondaviinstitute.ucdavis.edu, tours $3–25), the on-campus brewery is just one of the world-class research facilities dedicated to food and

beverage-making at UC Davis. Completed in 2008 and named for the famed Napa winemaker who donated $25 million to build it, the sprawling agricultural complex also boasts a green-certified winery and an organic vegetable garden on-site. Many of the cutting-edge techniques developed here have been applied at California's top wineries. Foodies will love hearing about the institute's olive oil center, which offers courses in how to produce artisan olive oils. Stop by for a student-led tour, or pay a little more for a faculty member to lead you around the institute.

If you love bugs, than check out the **Bohart Museum of Entomology** (1124 Academic Surge, 530/752-0493, http://bohart.ucdavis.edu, 9 A.M.–noon and 1–5 P.M. Mon.–Thurs., parking $7). With more than seven million insects, the museum has one of the largest collections in North America, and 50,000 new specimens get added every year. Kids will especially love checking out the museum's trove of wasps, bees, and native California insects. If you're coming with a group, call ahead and reserve a special guided tour around the facility.

Entertainment and Events

Some of the world's greatest performers have dazzled audiences at the beautiful **Mondavi Center For the Performing Arts** (1 Shields Ave., 866/754-2787, www.mondaviarts.org, $10–89). Musicians from Joshua Bell and Anoushka Shankar to more mainstream acts like Florence and the Machine and Wilco have played here. If you love classical music, the center regularly hosts quartets and traveling symphonies, along with occasional concerts performed by the UC Davis Symphony Orchestra. Besides music, you can also catch dramatic performances, documentaries, indie films, and headliners from the center's guest speaker series—including big names like Apple

© CHRISTOPHER ARNS

Mondavi Center For the Performing Arts, at UC Davis

cofounder Steve Wozniak and *This American Life* host Ira Glass. The center's architecture alone is worth the trip: Built of glass and bricks of cream-colored sandstone, the building is a stunning spectacle when lit up at night.

Accommodations

Located smack-dab between the university and downtown Davis, the **Aggie Inn** (245 1st St., 530/756-0352, www.aggieinn.com, $110–165) has a range of cozy, stylish accommodation options including two-bedroom cottages. Every bed has pillow-top mattresses, so you'll sleep like a baby; if that's not relaxing enough, book a room with a Jacuzzi and soak away your aches and pains from a full day of traveling. All the rooms come with microwaves, mini-refrigerator, coffeemaker, air-conditioning, and free wireless Internet. Some rooms also boast kitchenettes, and if you're traveling on business, the convenient work area with a sizable desk will come in handy. The Aggie is a perfect place to

stay if you dig the "boutique" inn experience instead of crashing at a big-name motel.

The most convenient option for visiting UC Davis is the **Hyatt Place UC Davis** (173 Old Davis Road Extension, 530/756-9500, http:// ucdavis.place.hyatt.com, $140–180). Right on the university's campus, the Hyatt is also just a five-minute walk from the city's downtown district. Upscale, modern, and one of the more luxurious accommodations in Davis, the large rooms have a large flat-screen TV, a mini-refrigerator, coffeemaker, hair dryer, and complimentary wireless Internet. In the morning, grab breakfast at the free continental buffet in the lobby; if you're still hungry, order a full meal or pick up some muffins at the hotel's café. On the downside, the train runs behind the hotel, so light-sleepers might want to inquire about rooms farther away from the tracks.

The renovated **Hallmark Inn** (110 F St., 530/758-8623, www.hallmarkinn.com, $125–155) is a homey, laid-back option near downtown Davis. With plush beds and leather furniture, you'll certainly feel pampered. The simple, tasteful room layout with ivory-colored bedding and with artwork on the walls might feel refreshing after staying at other corporate hotel chains. You'll find all the basic hotel amenities in your room here: free wireless Internet, microwave, mini-refrigerator, coffeemaker, and hair dryer, plus a few extras like a flat-screen TV, breakfast buffet, and marble bathroom. There's also an outdoor pool and complimentary bicycles for cruising around Davis, although everything is within walking distance if the two-wheeled option isn't for you. After a long, hot day trekking around town, come back to the hotel for the free cocktail hour and wander out to the pool area to gaze at the hotel's giant wall mural that depicts scenes from the Sacramento Valley.

The **Best Western Plus Palm Court Hotel** (234 D St., 530/753-7100, www.bestwestern-california.com, $140–180) is on a leafy street corner in downtown Davis. Close to just about everything in Davis, this smaller hotel is a quiet, comfortable spot for business travelers or students looking to visit the university. The rooms have a classic, elegant vibe with dark wood furniture and comfy beds. Couples or small families might do best booking a suite; otherwise, the cozier guest rooms can feel a little cramped. Amenities are your standard hotel fare—coffeemaker, hair dryer, cable television, and mini-refrigerator. Underground parking is also provided. Sadly, this hotel doesn't allow pets; with 27 rooms, it also fills up fast so call ahead to reserve a room.

The **Motel 6** (4835 Chiles Rd., 530/753-3777, www.motel6.com, $45–75) may not win style points, but it's a clean, convenient place to stay if you're visiting Davis. The rooms have simple furniture and basic amenities like wireless Internet and cable television; the hotel also has a coin-operated laundry and an outdoor pool. Don't expect the Ritz; this is definitely a budget option and also isn't really within walking distance of UC Davis.

Food

The delicious food at **Delta of Venus** (122 B St., 530/753-8639, www.deltaofvenus.org, 7:30 A.M.–10 P.M. Mon.–Wed., 7:30 A.M.–midnight Thurs.–Fri., 7:30 A.M.–6 P.M. Sat.–Sun., $4–11) is just part of this funky café's charm. Visiting feels like stopping by a colorful neighbor's house; artwork adorns the walls and students lounge on the tree-covered patio. With such a relaxed vibe, it's easy to spend a whole afternoon here sipping coffee or a beer, and many people do just that. You can grab meals here all day long; dinner is Caribbean fare and shouldn't be missed—try the tofu with ginger and citrus chili sauce or the coconut chicken with Jamaican curry. For breakfast, you can get omelettes and breakfast burritos; lunch is mostly salads and sandwiches like the vegetarian-friendly Blue Lagoon, served with blue cheese, tomatoes, and marinated artichoke hearts. The café often hosts live bands, and if you're in town, Delta of Venus is worth adding to any pub crawl.

With a name like **Burgers and Brew** (403 3rd St., 530/750-3600, http://burgers-brew.com, 11 A.M.–midnight Sun.–Wed., 11 A.M.–3 A.M. Thurs.–Sat., $8), you wouldn't expect many surprises. In fact, this is no ordinary brewpub: The burgers are made with all-natural meat and topped with plenty of mouthwatering fixings. Ever had a buffalo burger? You can here, although the Greek-styled lamb burger is just as good: Served with feta cheese, roasted garlic, olive oil, and a dash of yogurt sauce, you'd swear it came straight from Mt. Olympus. Wash it down with one of the roughly 20 craft beers on tap or select something from the long list of bottled brews; for dessert, spoil your taste buds with a slice of Nutella cheesecake. If you're bringing children, there's a kids menu, although it's pretty basic with burgers, hot dogs, and a grilled cheese sandwich.

There's more than just crepes at **Crepeville** (330 3rd St., 530/750-2400, www.crepeville. com, 7 A.M.–11 P.M. daily, $6–10, cash only). Run by the same folks who own Burgers and Brew, the restaurant also serves delightful omelettes, egg scrambles, and sandwiches. Still, you can't visit Crepeville without trying a homemade breakfast or dessert crepe; the Hawaiian is especially good if you're ordering breakfast, otherwise the banana chocolate crepe will have your eyes rolling in ecstasy. Grab a cold pint of freshly squeezed orange and carrot juice to go with your crepe or ask for a glass of local wine to truly enjoy a Crepeville meal.

Information and Services
The **Yolo County Visitors Bureau** (604 2nd St., 530/297-1900, www.yolocvb.net, 8:30 A.M.–4:30 P.M. Mon.–Fri.) provides information on the Davis, Woodland, and Winters area. Pop into the office while you're visiting or go to the website for a full list of events and attractions in Davis or if you need directions on navigating the array of local bike paths.

Grab a copy of the daily **Davis Enterprise** (www.davisenterprise.com) for a local perspective on the town; for a more collegiate take, UC Davis students publish *The California Aggie* (www.theaggie.org) four days a week. To stay updated on Davis nightlife, check out *The Davis Dirt* (www.davisdirt.blogspot.com), a local blog with its finger on the Davis arts and entertainment scene.

You can find plenty of ATMs and bank branches in Davis; the **Golden One Credit Union** (503 2nd St., www.golden1.com) is conveniently located near the Amtrak station and UC Davis. There's a **post office** (9:30 A.M.–4:30 P.M. Mon.–Fri., 9:30–11 A.M. Sat.) at 424 3rd Street.

If you need medical attention in Davis, the major hospital is **Sutter Davis Hospital** (2000 Sutter Place, 530/756-6440, www.sutterdavis. org). You can find a wide array of services at this hospital, including emergency and urgent care, pediatric care and a birthing center.

Getting There and Around
Davis lies directly on I-80, 14 miles west of Sacramento; the Richards Boulevard exit provides easy access downtown.

The closest airport is in Sacramento and the **Davis Airporter** (530/756-6715, www.davisairporter.com) provides door-to-door shuttle service.

The *Capitol Corridor* **Amtrak** line (840 2nd St., Davis, 530/758-4220 or 800/872-7245, www.amtrak.com) stops daily in downtown Davis. **Unitrans** (1 Shields Ave., Davis, 530/752-2877, http://unitrans.ucdavis.edu, $1) provides student-run public transit through Davis and the university campus.

Davis Pedicab (530/771-7405, 7 P.M.–3 A.M. Thurs.–Sat., 2–10 P.M. Sun.) is a fun and reliable human-powered option for getting around Davis. Hours change during warmer months, and service can also extend to Wednesdays; if you have a special request, usually Davis Pedicab can make arrangements ahead of time.

FOLSOM
Yes, that Folsom, as in the prison. Thanks to Johnny Cash and his 1955 song about this small city's infamous penitentiary, Folsom (pop. 72,000) will forever be stuck with that connection. If only the Man in Black had also written about Folsom's Gold Rush past or the old powerhouse—maybe the town would have an entirely different reputation. Folsom's namesake was a local ranch owner who successfully lobbied in the 1850s for a railroad to connect Sacramento with this small outpost on the American River. The same year Cash released his song, Folsom Dam created

a massive lake 4.8 miles long on the river. These days, Folsom has become a recreation hot spot for boaters and anglers. You can also find a bustling downtown area with bistros and cafés in the city's gnarly Gold Rush buildings.

Folsom Prison Museum

In 1955, Johnny Cash sang a country ballad about a lonesome desperado serving time in Folsom Prison after he had "shot a man in Reno, just to watch him die." Cash eventually played a famous concert here in the late 1960s after inmates wrote to him and requested a visit. By then, Folsom Prison, constructed in 1880, had earned quite a grisly reputation. From 1895 to 1937, 93 prisoners were executed by hanging inside these walls. Riots and violent escape attempts have occurred with startling frequency throughout the years. As one of California's first maximum security prisons, it was more like a medieval dungeon, even though it was the Golden State's first penitentiary with electricity. Inmates lived in stone cells behind boilerplate doors with small eye slots, and an imposing granite wall surrounded the place. Since then, Folsom Prison has expanded with an additional wing to house more prisoners, and the penitentiary remains in use today.

You can learn more about the long and bloody history of the penitentiary at the Folsom Prison Museum (300 Prison Rd., Represa, 916/985-2561, www.folsomprisonmuseum. org, 10 A.M.–4 P.M. daily, adults $2, children free). Really, it's not worth an extra drive from Sacramento unless you're already in Folsom for the day. The museum houses some artifacts from retired correctional officers, some photos, and plenty of gruesome stories about the place. They only take cash, no credit cards, for the entrance fee. Make sure to get a photo with the old granite guard towers in the background if you can.

Folsom Powerhouse State Historic Park

If you're in town, check out Folsom Powerhouse State Historic Park (9980 Greenback Ln., 916/988-0205, www.parks. ca.gov, noon–4 P.M. Wed.–Sun., free, parking $5). Built in 1895 and operated until 1952, this stately brick edifice supplied the first electricity to Sacramento along the country's longest transmission line. Water from the American River was fed to four hulking eight-foot-tall General Electric generators that pumped out hydroelectric power. Visitors can see those decommissioned generators, along with the canal system and forebays that brought water into the plant.

Folsom City Zoo Sanctuary

In 1963, a Folsom Park superintendent adopted an orphaned bear cub named Smokey from a UC Davis veterinarian. With that first animal the Folsom City Zoo Sanctuary (403 Stafford St., 916/351-3527, www.folsom.ca.us, 9 A.M.–3 P.M. Tues.–Sun. June 1–Aug. 31; 10 A.M.–4 P.M. Tues.–Sun. Sept. 1–May 31, adults $5–6, children $4–5) was born. The zoo only adopts critters that can't be returned to the wild. They may have been orphaned in the wild or rejected as pets. Here every creature in the sanctuary receives care and attention for the rest of its life, and they aren't forced to breed. Some of the animals here include bears, squirrels, tigers, cougars, bobcats, wolf hybrids, and monkeys.

Entertainment and Events

The **Three Stages** (10 College Pkwy., Folsom, 916/608-6888, www.threestages.net, $12–80) is a spanking new addition to the region's performing arts scene. It's worth taking the 25-minute drive from Sacramento to watch local community theater, concerts by pop performers like Kenny Loggins, and appearances by the Sacramento Philharmonic. Frankly, the performance quality is as good if not better than some stuff you'll see in Sacramento.

For a small bandbox more than 3,000 miles away from New York, **Sutter Street Theatre** (717 Sutter St., Folsom, 916/353-1001, www. sutterstreettheatre.com, adults $17–23, seniors $15–21, students $18, children $13–15) doesn't seem so far from Broadway. This is community theater at its finest and you can catch plays like *The Odd Couple, Our Town,* and *The Producers.* Located in downtown Folsom, this place is *tiny* and gets stuffy on hot summer evenings; they serve free glasses of wine but you're better off with something cold.

There's always something going on at **Powerhouse Pub** (614 Sutter St., 916/355-8586, www.powerhousepub.com, 3 P.M.–1 A.M. Mon.–Thurs., noon–1:30 A.M. Fri.–Sat., noon–midnight Sun.). It's not really a club, but not really a pub either. There's a narrow dance floor and a stage where local country, blues, and rock cover bands play on weekends. Powerhouse describes itself as a former "mama biker's bar," but the place has been renovated and now boasts a funky Wild-West-meets-Vegas theme. If there's a big game playing or you happen to arrive during Super Bowl week, they have 15 TVs and a big screen.

The Cellar Wine Bar (727 Sutter St., Folsom, 916/293-9332, http://thecellarwine-bar.com, 4–10 P.M. Tues.–Thurs., 4 P.M.–midnight Fri.–Sat., 2–8 P.M. Sun.,) pours flights of local wine inside this spiffed up rustic cubbyhole in downtown Folsom. Hungry wine drinkers can munch on finger food like cheese plates and chocolate truffles. Glasses of wine are $2 cheaper during their happy hour.

Sports and Recreation

Folsom Lake State Recreation Area (www. parks.ca.gov, summer 6 A.M.–9 P.M., certain areas 7 A.M.–8 P.M.; winter 7 A.M.–6 P.M., certain areas closed, $5–12) surrounds a 4.8-mile-long lake and becomes mobbed with locals on summer weekends. Freeways become thronged with boat trailers headed out to fish or water-ski on this beautiful stretch of water. It's an artificial lake, created in 1955 when local water authorities built a 340-foot-high dam across the American River. Bring a rod and troll for trout, catfish, perch, and two species of bass. If you're bringing a boat, you can launch from one of several spots; the closest put-ins near Folsom are **Folsom Lake Marina** (www.folsomlakemarina.com) at Brown's Ravine, and **Folsom Point** off East Natoma Street.

The lake also has awesome hiking and mountain biking trails. I recommend the **Old Salmon Falls Loop** (2.2 miles, easy), a nice trek from Salmon Falls Road through some oak woods down to the lake. For some fat tire fun, drive north on Salmon Falls until you cross a bridge over the American River; the trailhead for the **Darrington Salmon Falls Trail** (16–20 miles, moderate to technical) is on the left. From this dusty, often rocky single-track, you'll have spectacular views over the river.

Just below Folsom is **Lake Natoma** (Hazel Ave. and U.S. 50, 916/988-0205, www.recreation.gov, 6 A.M.–9 P.M. daily Apr. 1–Oct. 15; 7 A.M.–7 P.M. daily Oct. 16–Mar. 30), a short stretch of calm water between Folsom and Nimbus Dams. It's a great place for kayaking, sailing, and swimming. You can rent watercraft at the **Sacramento State Aquatic Center** (1901 Hazel Ave., 916/278-2842, www. sacstateaquaticcenter.com, kayaks $9, canoes $14, peddle boat $14, paddle boards $12).

Accommodations

Built in 1859, **Bradley House Bed and Breakfast** (606 Figueroa St., 916/355-1962, http://bradleyhousebandb.us, $90–120) offers some of the oldest lodgings in the Sacramento area. Inside this Victorian farmhouse are four country-style rooms with antique furniture, wrought-iron headboards, and quilted comforters. Out back you'll find a peaceful garden area

Tempe Public Library

(480)350-5500
tempepubliclibrary.org

Check out receipt

Date: 3/12/2022 2:35:28 PM

1. Moon handbooks.
   Sacramento &the gold
   country
   Barcode 32953011926641
   Due by 4/2/2022
   USD 0.00
   Item checkout ok. You just saved
   $17.00 by using your public library.
   You saved $2,340.56 this year!

Hours

Monday - Wednesday 9:00 AM - 8:00
PM

Thursday - Saturday 9:00 AM - 5:00
PM
Sunday - 12:00 PM - 5:00 PM

Thank you
For Visiting the
Tempe Public Library!

with comfortable benches and a white picket fence. There's a full breakfast served every morning, although downtown Folsom is only a block away if you're thinking about eating somewhere else.

For a more contemporary place to stay there's **Lake Natoma Inn** (702 Gold Lake Dr., Folsom, 916/351-1500, www.lakenatomainn.com, $120–300). True to its name, the inn overlooks Lake Natoma, and downtown Folsom is just a few blocks away. Amenities include pillow-top beds, coffee pot, ironing board, flat-screen TV, and a mini-fridge. Some rooms have a whirlpool tub next to queen- or king-size beds. If you need to cool off, there's a pool outside; fitness geeks can use the indoor sauna and the 24-hour fitness room.

For reliable and clean accommodations, try any of these hotels: **Hampton Inn and Suites** (155 Placerville Rd., Folsom, 916/235-7744, www.hamptoninn.com, $95–135), the **Hilton Garden Inn** (221 Iron Point Rd., Folsom, 916/353-1717, www.hiltongarden.com, $90–150), and **Larkspur Landing** (121 Iron Point Rd., 916/355-1616, www.larkspurhotels.com, $110–180). Each boasts streamlined corporate chain amenities within a short drive of downtown Folsom.

If you'd like to sleep by the calm waters of Folsom Lake, there are two campgrounds nearby. At **Beals Point Campground** (north of Folsom Dam, 9899 Folsom-Auburn Rd., Granite Bay, 916/988-0205 or 800/444-7275, www.reserveamerica.com, $28–48). The Jedediah Smith Bike Trail (32 miles, easy) starts here, and overnighters can reserve one of 57 spots near the water. Amenities include picnic tables, cooking grills, toilets, and showers. Across the lake, there's **Peninsula Campground** (end of Rattlesnake Bar Rd., 916/988-0205 or 800/444-7275, www.reserveamerica.com, $28–33) near Rattlesnake Bar. You'll find 100 campsites on this long land spit jutting out into the lake. Amenities

are limited; there are picnic tables, flush toilets, fire rings, and showers.

Food

For a cold pint of beer and a burger there's **Samuel Horne's Tavern** (719 Sutter St., Folsom, 916/293-8207, www.samuelhornestavern.com, 11:30 A.M.–9 P.M. Sun.–Wed., 11:30 A.M.–midnight Thurs.–Sat., $8). This friendly spot has an English pub vibe with dark leather booths and a rustic-looking wooden bar. They pour 16 brews on tap, and grub includes hot dogs, steak sandwiches, and burgers slathered in bourbon-espresso sauce.

Manderes (1004 E. Bidwell St., #600, Folsom, 916/986-9655, www.manderes.com, 11 A.M.–11 P.M. Mon.–Sat., noon–11 P.M. Sun., $15) does upscale American bar food like the Bulgogi Hoagie, a sandwich made with thin strips of steak marinated in Korean steak sauce. The menu also includes gorgonzola-stuffed ravioli, chicken Alfredo, and steak kabobs. An eye-popping wall of shiny taps pours 19 different craft brews; besides beer, there's a wine list full of international and West Coast vino.

For a classy steak dinner, **Sutter Street Steakhouse** (604 Sutter St., Folsom, 916/351-9100, www.sutterstreetsteakhouse.com, 4:30–9 P.M. Tues.–Thurs., 4:30–10 P.M. Fri.–Sat., 4:30–8:30 P.M. Sun., $20–40) grills hand-cut tenderloin and top sirloin with fancy sides like grilled prawns or Maine lobster tail. For my money, the desserts are reason enough to eat here—think banana cheesecake, white chocolate brownies, butterscotch pot de crème and seasonal gelato.

La Fiesta Taqueria (1008 E. Bidwell St., Folsom, 916/984-3030, www.lafiestataqueria.com, 8:30 A.M.–10 P.M. daily, $3–10) is the closest thing to a Tijuana taco stand that you'll find in Folsom. Order a burrito drenched in red sauce and cheese; wash it down with a tall cup of horchata.

Lake Forest Cafe (13409 Folsom Blvd., 916/985-6780, www.lakeforestcafe.com, 7 A.M.–1:45 P.M. Wed.–Sun., $7–15) serves up classic American breakfast food. They offer 40 different kinds of omelettes, scrambles, and specialties like latkes and matzo flatbread.

Information and Services

Folsom lies within the great urban sprawl of Sacramento and so has all the conveniences you'd expect from a modern suburb. There's seemingly a gas station or a bank on every corner, and plenty of shopping centers with big-name brands. To mail a letter, there's a **post office** at 1015 Riley Street (9 A.M.–5 P.M. Mon.–Fri., 10 A.M.–2 P.M. Sat.).

The local rag is the *Folsom Telegraph* (www.folsomtelegraph.com), which covers high school sports and city politics on a weekly basis. The *Sacramento Bee* is the most timely option for daily news, while the *Sacramento News and Review* posts music showtimes and reviews for hometown bands.

For emergency medical assistance, **Mercy Hospital of Folsom** (1650 Creekside Dr., 916/983-7400, www.mercyfolsom.org) has an emergency room that provides 24-hour treatment and minor urgent care facilities.

Getting There and Around

Folsom is located right off U.S. 50 about 25 minutes east from Sacramento and 25 minutes west of Placerville. Sometimes winter traffic can snarl the freeway when folks are heading back from the slopes, but usually you won't run into many problems out this way. Check weather, road condition, and traffic reports (www.caltrans.org) to make sure.

There's a good deal of public transportation in the region. You can take the **Sacramento Regional Transit** light-rail (916/321-2877, www.sacrt.com, $2.50) between Sacramento and downtown Folsom, a journey that takes 66 minutes. The **Folsom Stage Line** (916/355-8395, www.folsom.ca.us, $2.50) has bus routes that run through town.

The closest major airport is in Sacramento, about 34 miles to the west.

THE NORTHERN GOLD COUNTRY

The Northern Gold Country is a rugged triangle of mountain ridges, thickly forested valleys, and a spiderweb of emerald-green rivers bounded by I-80 in the northwest, Highway 49 from north to south, and U.S. 50 to the southeast. These major highways pass through the area's most popular destinations, and travelers have the luxury of choosing among several different routes to Grass Valley, Nevada City, Auburn, and Placerville, all of which lie on at least one of these thoroughfares.

While Gold Rush miners hit pay dirt throughout the Sierra Nevada foothills, the richest mines were up north in Grass Valley and Nevada City. These days, you can learn more about local history and see fascinating mining relics at the Empire Mine State Historic Park, one of the most extensive museums in the Gold Country. Still, there's more to Grass Valley and Nevada City than just gold mining. A walk through each town's historic quarter reveals cosmopolitan restaurants, quirky boutique stores, and one-of-a-kind art galleries.

Farther south in the postcard-worthy American River canyon, die-hard adrenaline junkies will flock to the Auburn State Recreation Area for bungee jumping, mountain biking, kayaking, dirt biking, and cliff diving; more laid-back adventures include hiking, horseback riding, and fishing. After a day

HIGHLIGHTS

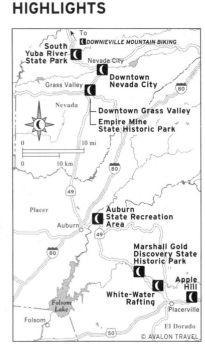

LOOK FOR ◖ TO FIND RECOMMENDED SIGHTS, ACTIVITIES, DINING, AND LODGING.

◖ **Downtown Nevada City:** Stroll past gas lamps, horse-drawn carriages, and 19th-century buildings in this romantic Victorian village (page 145).

◖ **South Yuba River State Park:** Come visit the longest covered single-span bridge in the world and take a wildflower hike through groves of oaks and ponderosa pines (page 152).

◖ **Downtown Grass Valley:** Travel back to the 1950s with a walk down historic Main Street in this Gold Rush town (page 161).

◖ **Empire Mine State Historic Park:** The best example of Gold Country mining is at this living history museum and park (page 162).

◖ **Downieville Mountain Biking:** Hold on to your handlebars while riding the rugged Downieville Downhill that drops roughly 17 miles from the snowcapped Sierra Buttes back into town (page 174).

◖ **Auburn State Recreation Area:** Copious activities await you in the American River canyon: mountain biking, swimming, dirt biking, hiking, and much more (page 187).

◖ **Apple Hill:** East of Sacramento lies this rural swath of heaven with dozens of orchards, vineyards, and pit stops for dining and relaxing (page 213).

◖ **Marshall Gold Discovery State Historic Park:** Stand in the exact spot where one man's find sparked arguably one of the greatest migrations in history (page 217).

◖ **White-Water Rafting:** The Gold Country has several mighty rivers with churning Class III-V rapids. Anyone from rookie rafters to experienced paddlers will find numerous rafting opportunities, especially on the American River near Coloma (page 218).

filled with outdoor fun, leave the canyon and drive into Auburn for some of the best fine dining in the region.

Finally, a trip to the Gold Country isn't complete without checking out Placerville. Known affectionately as "Hangtown" among locals for the town's wild past, Placerville has kept its edgy vibe while evolving into a hot spot for shopping and upscale eateries. Better yet, the town is just 10 minutes from the wineries and orchards of Apple Hill, a fun destination for all ages especially during fall, when farms offer hayrides, fresh pies, caramel apples, and craft fairs hosted by local artisans.

PLANNING YOUR TIME

Driving from town to town in the Northern Gold Country is fairly easy, but you should

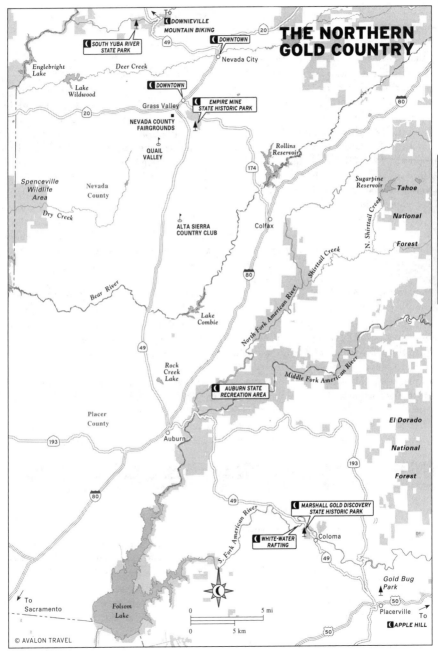

THE NORTHERN GOLD COUNTRY

To DOWNIEVILLE
MOUNTAIN BIKING

DOWNTOWN

SOUTH YUBA RIVER
STATE PARK

Englebright
Lake

Deer Creek

Nevada City

Lake
Wildwood

DOWNTOWN

EMPIRE MINE
STATE HISTORIC PARK

Grass Valley

NEVADA COUNTY
FAIRGROUNDS

QUAIL
VALLEY

Rollins
Reservoir

Sugarpine
Reservoir

Tahoe

Spenceville
Wildlife
Area

Nevada
County

National

Dry Creek

ALTA SIERRA
COUNTRY CLUB

Colfax

Forest

Shirttail Creek

N. Shirttail Creek

Bear River

Lake
Combie

North Fork American River

Middle Fork American River

Rock
Creek
Lake

AUBURN STATE
RECREATION AREA

Placer
County

El Dorado

National

Auburn

Forest

Folsom
Lake

S. Fork American River

MARSHALL GOLD DISCOVERY
STATE HISTORIC PARK

WHITE-WATER
RAFTING

Coloma

Gold Bug
Park

To
Sacramento

0   5 mi

0   5 km

Placerville

To

APPLE HILL

plan ahead before traveling. Many of the smaller towns and recreational adventures lay far off the beaten track, and what looks like a short distance on a map becomes far longer once you're navigating a car along winding, narrow roads. There's no way to see everything in one day. Instead, take time to savor each remote foothill town and historic attraction as you pass through beautiful country—skirting deep, blue-dark river canyons and rugged ponderosa forests where sunshine dapples the highway. With enough time, you'll find the Northern Gold Country becomes a magical and quite memorable place.

Most of the Northern Gold Country is fairly accessible from Sacramento. The twin hamlets of **Grass Valley** and **Nevada City** are an hour's drive up I-80 and Highway 49, while **Auburn** is only 40 minutes from the capital. To the east, **Placerville** is a 45-minute drive up U.S. 50 from Sacramento.

Any of these Gold Country towns makes an excellent base for exploring more remote destinations, whether for **white-water rafting** on the American River or visiting restored mining camps like **Marshall Gold Discovery State Historic Park.** Plan on spending at least one full day in each town, with extra time for **mountain biking** in Downieville, hiking and swimming in the **South Yuba River State Park,** rafting through the **Auburn State Recreation Area,** or wine-tasting at one of **Fair Play**'s family-owned wineries.

ORIENTATION

The Northern Gold Country stretches from Nevada City in the north to Auburn and Placerville farther south. The region lies northeast of Sacramento off I-80 and directly east on U.S. 50. Traveling northeast on I-80, the first major town you'll reach is **Auburn** in Placer County, about 33 miles north of Sacramento. Auburn is where Highway 49 splits the Northern Gold Country in two. Head north on Highway 49 to the towns of **Grass Valley** and **Nevada City,** or follow Highway 49 southeast to meet up with Placerville and U.S. 50. **Colfax** is farther along I-80, almost 20 miles north of Auburn.

Placerville is 45 miles east of Sacramento on U.S. 50 in El Dorado County. The small town of **Coloma** lies almost 10 miles north of Placerville along Highway 49, which continues north to Auburn for another 20 miles. The **Apple Hill** region runs parallel to U.S. 50 northeast of Placerville for about eight miles to the tiny burg of **Camino.** Farther south, take either Newton Road or Cedar Ravine Road from Placerville to reach **Fair Play,** about 18 miles south along narrow country lanes.

Nevada City

When people think of the Gold Country, most likely it's the dapper little town of Nevada City (pop. 3,000) that comes to mind. This well-preserved hamlet is packed with 19th-century Victorian townhomes and brick storefronts that haven't changed much since the town welcomed thousands of gold-hungry miners in the wild 1850s. Back then, Nevada City's founding fathers kept a lid on the unlawful behavior that plagued other gold camps and instead promoted a more cosmopolitan vibe. As a result, the town became a cultural bellwether for the region, building a theater where luminaries such as Mark Twain and Lola Montez performed and a stately hotel that is one of the West's oldest lodgings.

Today Nevada City still has a refined (if somewhat quirky) energy that defines its place in the Gold Country. It's the kind of town where honeymooners and Harley-Davidsons

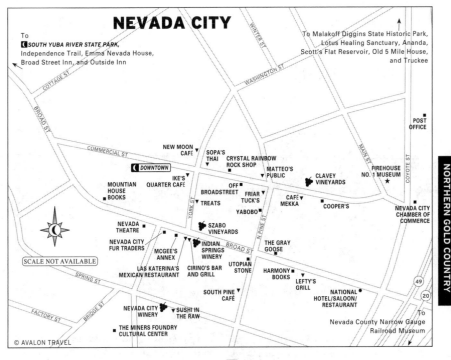

NEVADA CITY

To
⟨ *SOUTH YUBA RIVER STATE PARK,*
Independence Trail, Emma Nevada House,
Broad Street Inn, and Outside Inn

To Malakoff Diggins State Historic Park,
Lotus Healing Sanctuary, Ananda,
Scott's Flat Reservoir, Old 5 Mile House,
and Truckee

POST
OFFICE

NEW MOON
CAFÉ
SOPA'S
THAI
CRYSTAL RAINBOW
ROCK SHOP
MATTEO'S
PUBLIC
CLAVEY
VINEYARDS
FIREHOUSE
NO. 1 MUSEUM
★

⟨ *DOWNTOWN*
IKE'S
QUARTER CAFÉ
OFF
BROADSTREET
TREATS
FRIAR
TUCK'S
CAFÉ
MEKKA
COOPER'S
NEVADA CITY
CHAMBER OF
COMMERCE

MOUNTIAN
HOUSE
BOOKS
YABOBO

NEVADA
THEATRE
SZABO
VINEYARDS

NEVADA CITY
FUR TRADERS
MCGEE'S
ANNEX
INDIAN
SPRINGS
WINERY
THE GRAY
GOOSE

SCALE NOT AVAILABLE
LAS KATERINA'S
MEXICAN RESTAURANT
CIRINO'S BAR
AND GRILL
UTOPIAN
STONE
HARMONY
BOOKS
LEFTY'S
GRILL

SOUTH PINE
CAFÉ
NATIONAL
HOTEL/SALOON/
RESTAURANT

49

20

To
Nevada County Narrow Gauge
Railroad Museum

NEVADA CITY
WINERY
SUSHI IN
THE RAW

THE MINERS FOUNDRY
CULTURAL CENTER

© AVALON TRAVEL

easily mingle. It hosts annual Victorian Christmas street fairs and one of the West's premier races, the Nevada City Bicycle Classic. Hippies also seem to love Nevada City; if you're running low on rune stones and New Age remedies, chances are good that you'll find a shop selling both here. And of course, there's plenty of Gold Rush exploring to do at Malakoff Diggins State Historic Park and along the gin-clear Yuba River.

SIGHTS

Nevada City is a must-see on any traveler's list for its twinkling gaslights, old-fashioned carriage rides, and Victorian architecture that seem inspired by Dickens. The entire downtown area is a national historic landmark bustling with art galleries, boutique shops, world-class restaurants, and the occasional oddball character performing in the street.

⟨ Downtown

It's hard to imagine now, but downtown Nevada City (www.downtownnevadacity.com) started out as a meager encampment of pine shanties and mule trails in 1849. The Gold Rush gave the town a metallurgical shot in the arm as mine owners and local merchants built beautiful Victorian homes and elegant brick storefronts in the thriving commercial district. When gold mines finally went bust in the mid-20th century, the town's historic buildings were left alone while other Gold Country hamlets went on a concrete building spree. The result? Nevada City feels like a Dickensian blast from the past, and travelers to the Gold Country should make every effort to visit. Many of the Victorian townhomes have been converted into bookshops or vibrant bistros, while Broad and Commercial Streets—downtown's two main drags—are lined with cozy boutiques.

downtown Nevada City

© CHRISTOPHER ARNS

At night, old-fashioned gaslights flicker to life, lighting the way for a stroll to one of Nevada City's renowned restaurants—an experience best enjoyed during the holidays at the annual Victorian Christmas street fair.

For a walking tour, start at the bottom of Broad Street, near Highway 49, and stroll uphill while browsing shops and art galleries. At the top of the hill, head back down the other side of Broad Street or mosey down shadowy Commercial Street to find more cafés and a few more stores.

Nevada County Narrow Gauge Railroad Museum

Explore the long-lost history of the Gold Country's trains at the Nevada County Narrow Gauge Railroad Museum (5 Kidder Ct., 530/470-0902, www.ncngrrmuseum. org, 10 A.M.–4 P.M. Fri.–Tues. May 1–Oct. 31; 10 A.M.–4 P.M. Sat.–Sun. Nov. 1–Apr. 30, free). During the Gold Rush, local mines needed to

ship precious cargo east to connections with the transcontinental railroad. They had to build a special narrow gauge line that passed 22 miles through Grass Valley and Nevada City before ending in the important town of Colfax in Placer County. The narrow gauge railroad lasted 66 years, hauling more than $200 million in gold and shipping needed machinery and capital back to the mines. Most of the line's gleaming locomotives were stripped of parts long ago, but several narrow gauge cars remain at this ambitious little museum. Don't miss Locomotive 13, a fully operational steam engine completed by volunteers in 2009, and Engine 5, an 1875 Baldwin used by Hollywood in the first scene of *The Spoilers,* a 1942 John Wayne movie. Some exhibits might surprise visitors, such as the revelation that Nevada County had one of the country's first commercial airports, or that a streetcar line ran 4.8 miles from Grass Valley to Nevada City at the turn of the 20th century. There's always

Firehouse No. 1 Museum

display of Nisenan Indian artifacts, including baskets and photographs; the Nisenan populated Nevada County long before European settlers arrived, and their descendants still live there. Grass Valley was also home to a thriving Chinese community during the Gold Rush, and the museum has a large display of cooking utensils, clothing, and religious artifacts from the local Hou Wang and Kuan Yin temples.

WINERIES

Nevada County has a small but thriving wine scene that lives on friendly service and good, if not great, wines. Visiting tasting rooms in Nevada City isn't necessarily a must, but can be a worthwhile stop during a long afternoon.

Clavey Vineyards

Clavey Vineyards (232 Commercial St., 530/906-1394, www.claveywine.com, noon–6 P.M. Wed.–Thurs., noon–8 P.M. Fri., 11 A.M.–8 P.M. Sat., 11 A.M.–5 P.M. Sun., tasting $5) produces memorable reds from vineyards near the craggy Bear River. It's a family-owned wine company with ties to Nevada County. The wine is decent—and if you love syrah, you'll be in heaven at Clavey because they always seem to have at least several different peppery vintages on hand.

Indian Springs Winery

Founded in 1982, Indian Springs Winery (303 Broad St., 530/478-1068, www.indianspringswines.com, 11:30 A.M.–5 P.M. Sun.–Thurs., 11:30 A.M.–6 P.M. Fri.–Sat., tasting $5) is one of the oldest wineries in town, and the tasting room has a warm, friendly atmosphere. The wines are decent—blends are best, like the Hog Wild White and Hog Wild Red; an earlier vintage of the syrah port won gold at the 2005 *San Francisco Chronicle* Wine Competition.

Nevada City Winery

You've heard of garage bands, but what about

something fun happening at the museum, especially in the workshop where volunteers are usually restoring a rusted train car back to its former steam-powered glory. Call for information about tours and events; the gift shop is a fantastic place to pick up gifts for railheads.

Firehouse No. 1 Museum

Not one, not two, but seven terrible fires ravaged Nevada City during the Gold Rush. At Firehouse No. 1 Museum (215 Main St., 530/265-5468, www.nevadacountyhistory. org, 1–4 P.M. Wed.–Mon., May 1–Oct. 31, free), the town's combustible past is laid out in vivid exhibits. This beautiful museum (the building has a white Greek Revival–style facade) was Nevada City's first fire station and was home to Nevada Hose Company No. 1 for 80 years. Besides retelling the town's struggles with natural disasters, this wonderful building also displays several rooms of other historical tidbits from Nevada County. There's a sizable

© CHRISTOPHER ARNS

the Nevada City Winery's barn and tasting room

garage wine? Nevada City Winery (321 Spring St., 530/265-9463, www.ncwinery.com, noon–5 P.M. Sun.–Thurs., noon–6 P.M. Fri.–Sat., tasting $5) first started producing in 1980 and was actually founded in a Nevada City garage. The wine is good, but the photogenic tasting room, located in the former Miners Foundry Garage, is another great reason to stop by. Zinfandel is king here—the 2012 vintage won double gold at the California State Fair. Also try the Director's Reserve Syrah, a richly flavored varietal produced from a collection of different Nevada County vineyards.

Szabo Vineyards

Szabo Vineyards (316 Broad St., 530/265-8792, www.szabovineyards.com, noon–5 P.M. Thurs. and Sun., noon–7 P.M. Fri.–Sat., tasting $5) only produces wine from their own sustainably grown grapes. The family-owned outfit has 40 acres of vineyards planted between Grass Valley and Nevada City. The wines are

something special; the zinfandel is the specialty here, with balanced notes of black cherry and licorice.

ENTERTAINMENT AND EVENTS

The nightlife is certainly offbeat in Nevada City, where you can catch a Broadway-inspired play or grab pints of beer a few steps away at a local dive bar. My advice? Just go with it—the arts scene is rugged yet refined, run by friendly locals who put their heart into everything.

Nightlife

You can smell **Cooper's** (235 Commercial St., 530/265-0116, www.coopersnclive.com, noon–midnight Mon.–Wed., noon–2 A.M. Thurs.–Sat., noon–11 P.M. Sun.) from Commercial Street; the place reeks of old wood, beer, and fun. It's not really a biker bar, but don't be surprised if the sidewalk has a few Harleys parked on it. Cooper's is definitely a local's hangout

© CHRISTOPHER ARNS

The Nevada Theatre has staged performances since 1865.

and is slightly rough around the edges, but mostly in a friendly way. Live music usually happens on weekends and happy hour lasts all day on Sunday.

McGee's Annex (315 Broad St., 530/265-3205, www.mcgeesannex.com, 11 A.M.–2 A.M. daily) claims the largest big screen in town for sporting events, and I'm certainly not going to argue with them. McGee's is another scruffy joint with a local crowd, although tourists usually fill the place on weekends—maybe they're drawn by the DJ dance party on Friday and Saturday nights. If that sounds fun, there's a huge area for dancing (for a dive bar anyway), plus a big jukebox stuffed with good tunes and a pool table in the back for more laid-back evenings.

The town's original dive bar is the **National Hotel Saloon** (211 Broad St., 530/265-4551, http://thenationalhotel.com, 10 A.M.–midnight Mon.–Fri., 11 A.M.–midnight Sat.–Sun.). The hotel first opened more than 130 years ago, and

once you're inside, it doesn't feel like a day has gone by since. The old photos and historical knickknacks are nice touch, but the old weathered bar is the real star. Grabbing a cocktail here is fun while you wait to book a room upstairs, but if you're staying somewhere else, go wild.

The Arts

The Miners Foundry Cultural Center (325 Spring St., 530/265-5040, http://minersfoundry.org, $10–30) usually presents an eclectic mix of the performing arts and other cultural events. Depending on the time of year, you might find a traveling mime troupe or a black-and-white photography exhibit on the calendar. The setting is impressive; the stone building once housed the Nevada Iron and Brass Foundry and resembles a Viking mead hall.

The show has gone on for nearly 150 years at the **Nevada Theatre** (401 Broad

St., 530/265-6161, www.nevadatheatre.com, $8–25). This hulking stone building was originally constructed in 1865 and is one of California's oldest theaters; cultural glitterati from Mark Twain to Emma Nevada have trod the stage here. (It's sort of like grunge theater, but in a good way.) Shows include traditional drama and Broadway fare done with a twist; think edgy, modern interpretations of Shakespeare or rock musicals like *Next to Normal*. Since 1909, the Nevada Theatre has also been a full-fledged movie house, showing Oscar-winning indie flicks, short films, and documentaries. The interior is bare, almost spartan, like a typical New York playhouse, and it's actually kind of cool: the raw vibe gives performances even more intensity. During the summer, don't miss the **Nevada City Film Festival** (www.nevadacityfilmfestival.com, Aug.) for the latest flicks from cutting-edge directors such as Stacy Peralta, Kat Coiro, and Jonathan Demme, plus emerging filmmakers like Christina Choe and James Francis Khehtie.

Need something a bit lighter? The plays at **Off Broadstreet** (305 Commercial St., 530/265-8686, www.offbroadstreet.com, $23–25) are funny, irreverent, and usually a blast. Tucked down narrow Commercial Street, Off Broadstreet doesn't take itself seriously, but the productions are clever and are directed with a professional flair. Comedies or comedic musicals are presented in a "dessert theater" format; patrons can sip local wines while catching zany productions such as *Angry Housewives* and *The Great Northwest Mining and Doo Wop Co.* The mostly local actors give inspired performances, and theater fans with a sense of humor will enjoy this place.

Festivals and Events

The **Nevada City Bicycle Classic** (www.nevadacityclassic.com, mid-June) is the West's oldest and most prestigious road bike race. Top riders like Greg LeMond and Levi Leipheimer have won it, and the country's most competitive cyclists usually show up every year. The peloton starts at Pine and Broad Streets and loops dozens of times around a hair-raising 1.1-mile circuit through town. The setting is electric; spectators pack sidewalks along the course, cheering riders on as they careen down Broad Street at 50 mph. Just in case you feel like challenging the best, there are five different divisions, including one just for women; the road rash, on the other hand, is felt by everyone.

Every holiday season, Nevada City dresses up like Oliver Twist. The town's annual **Victorian Christmas** (530/265-2692, www.nevadacitychamber.com, Wed.–Thurs. Dec., free) is a top-hatted, frock-coated, roasted chestnut-eating kind of street fair. Nevada City already evokes a Dickensian vibe anyway, so this old-fashioned event—complete with costumed carolers, minstrels, and other street performers—is a fun throwback to days before TV and malls. Local vendors and artisans usually set up booths where fairgoers can browse handicrafts before taking a carriage ride around Nevada City. If you're lucky, there might be a light dusting of snow to complete the Christmas spirit.

SHOPPING

Nevada City is a great place for Christmas shopping because the downtown area is chock-full of tiny boutiques, bookstores, and quirky gift shops. **Broad Street** is the main drag, and most of Nevada City's homey little stores line the sloping sidewalk; **Commercial Street** also has a few shops. Parking can be a challenge, so be patient and check side streets like Coyote or North Pine for empty spots.

Books

Harmony Books (231 Broad St., 530/265-9564, 10 a.m.–6 p.m. Mon.–Sat., 11 a.m.–4 p.m. Sun.) is a bit of a

© CHRISTOPHER ARNS

A trip to the Crystal Rainbow Rock Shop is like finding a gnome's secret stash.

throwback—an indie bookstore stocked with volumes of new books that feels more like a private library. Head to the back if you're with kids and spend some time browsing with them in the children's literature section.

Mountain House Books (418 Broad St., 530/265-0241, http://mountainhousebooks. com, noon–5 P.M. Sat.–Sun.) is a dusty gold mine of used and rare tomes. Most of the books focus on California and the West, and quite a few of them are out of print. It's hard to discover priceless stores like this one, and serious bookworms will find it worthwhile to visit.

Gifts

With a great selection of imported drums and trinkets from West Africa, **Yabobo** (107 N. Pine St., 530/478-9114, 10:30 A.M.–6 P.M. Mon.–Sat., 11 A.M.–6 P.M. Sun.) is like going on safari. Besides drums, there's a ton of imported clothing from Asia and South America, Moroccan tea ware, and enough incense to fill

a Buddhist temple. The shop probably leans to the hippie side, but doesn't everyone need a little more Nag Champa in their life?

The tiny shack known as the **Crystal Rainbow Rock Shop** (310 Commercial St., 530/265-3784, noon–5 P.M. daily) feels like a gnome's secret hideaway. The Rock Shop has shelves of glittering crystals, fossils, and geodes for reasonable prices; a purchase here makes a fine gift. The shop has been tucked down Commercial Street for almost 30 years and sometimes closes inexplicably, but finding it open is a treat.

Need something irreverent for a boss or brother-in-law? Chances are, **The Gray Goose** (230 Broad St., 530/265-5909, www.graygoose.com, 10 A.M.–5:30 P.M. Mon.–Sat., 11 A.M.–4 P.M. Sun.) has inappropriate gifts for any occasion, like "The Cannabis Cookbook" or "Penis Pokey" board book. This eclectic and funny store has gads of other interesting items—spooky Day of the Dead decorations, goofy greeting cards, and a display case filled with bohemian-style jewelry.

If you've always dreamed of surrounding yourself in leather and fur, **Nevada City Fur Traders** (319 Broad St., 530/265-8000, www. furtraders.com, daily 10 A.M.–6 P.M.) will satisfy that craving. From the fringed to the furry, Fur Traders probably has something to catch your eye. Since one store obviously wasn't enough, there are actually three Fur Traders on Broad Street within a block of each other and each store has slightly different merchandise if you're on a mission for something specific. Want something unique? For about $1,000, you can order a mounted buffalo head.

Jewelry

At **Utopian Stone** (301 Broad St., 530/265-6209, www.utopianstone.com, daily 10 A.M.–5:30 P.M.) the jewelers divide their work into two categories: one of a kind and everything else. Five master goldsmiths produce some of the most luminous fine jewelry you'll ever see—and if you don't see it, they'll commission anything by request. Some of their gold comes from nuggets found in the nearby Yuba River and quartz from Nevada County mines. Besides the gold work, Utopian Stone's superb gemstone carvings are also quite unique.

SPORTS AND RECREATION

Nevada City was named one of *Outside Magazine*'s Best River Towns of 2012. Adrenaline junkies can thrive on 120 miles of single-track in nearby Tahoe National Forest or plunge into the Yuba's churning whitewater rapids and countless swimming holes.

Malakoff Diggins State Historic Park

Take a hike through the eerie but colorful canyon at Malakoff Diggins State Historic Park (Tyler Foote Rd., 26 miles north of Nevada City, 530/265-2740, www.parks.ca.gov,

sunrise–sunset, day-use $8 per vehicle), once the site of California's largest hydraulic mine. During the Gold Rush, miners blasted the hillsides with water to find gold buried deep in the ground, leaving behind strange land formations streaked with red and orange mineral deposits. There is an on-site museum (10 A.M.–4 P.M. Fri.–Sun.), and park tours are available (1:30 P.M. Fri.–Sun.).

The best way to see the park is by taking the **Diggins Loop Trail** (three miles round-trip), which is also the easiest route if you have kids. Hydraulic mining stripped away immense quantities of topsoil during the mid to late 19th century, and completely changed the landscape while creating a deep basin where pools of standing water gleam a weird green color. The trail descends into that basin and traverses past a pond and an old drainage tunnel which hikers can check out.

The park also includes the ghost town of **North Bloomfield,** which has several historic structures including a one-room schoolhouse, an old cemetery, St. Columncille's Church, and a small museum.

Malakoff Diggins is about 26 miles north of Nevada City, but it can take almost an hour to drive here. To reach the park from Nevada City, take Highway 49 north for 11 miles toward the small town of Downieville. Turn right onto Tyler-Foote Road and follow the road into the park.

◖ South Yuba River State Park

Looking to cool off after traipsing through the foothills? Head to the South Yuba River State Park (17660 Pleasant Valley Rd., Penn Valley, 530/432-2546, www.southyubariverstatepark.org, sunrise–sunset, free). This 20-mile stretch of the Yuba River winds all the way from Malakoff Diggins State Historic Park to the picturesque covered bridge at Bridgeport—the longest of its kind in the world. There are plenty of Gold Rush ruins

GHOST TOWNS OF THE FOOTHILLS

While some Gold Rush towns were well-populated, with dozens of saloons, hotels, and even opera houses, too often these small foothill burgs faded away as swiftly as they formed. The following abandoned "ghost towns" form a trail back to California's wildest days and while many are overgrown, a few offer a vivid glimpse into the booming days of 1849.

- **North Bloomfield** had humble beginnings. But in 1853, everything changed when a prospector blasted water at local hillsides to loosen gold ore from the dirt and hydraulic mining was born. A federal judge banned hydraulic mining in 1884 and just like that, North Bloomfield went bust. Today, it's part of the Malakoff Diggins State Park. Some of the original buildings include St. Columncille's Catholic Church and the North Bloomfield School, which has an old cemetery in back. North Bloomfield is 15 miles northeast of North San Juan. Take Highway 49 to Oak Tree Road and turn left on Tyler Foote Road. After six miles (and passing through North Columbia, another ghost town), turn right onto Cruzon Grade and continue when it turns into Backbone Road. Turn right after 5.7 miles onto Derbec Road and drive 0.7 mile. Turn right again onto North Bloomfield Road; the town is 1.3 miles ahead.

- Between Cool and Coloma, keep your eyes peeled for a crumbling brick manor with boarded windows just off Highway 49. That's the **Bayley House,** a former hotel that opened in 1861. More than 300,000 bricks were made on-site, lumber was milled from the surrounding countryside, and additional features were imported from England. Owner A. J. Bayley thought the First Transcontinental Railroad would

pass by here, but the Big Four decided to lay tracks farther north, so the hotel never got off the ground.

- About 30 miles east of Auburn is **Georgetown** (pop. 2,300), a little burg high in the upper foothills. Georgetown was known as "Growlersburg" during the 1850s when the town housed about 3,000 people. The main attraction here is the Pioneer Cemetery, off Highway 193. Also check out the hulking 1859 I.O.O.F. Hall, 1852 Wells Fargo Building, and the grizzled **Georgetown Hotel and Bar** (6260 Wentworth Springs Rd., 530/333-2848, 11 A.M.-10 P.M. daily), a former brothel built in 1849. From Auburn, take Highway 49 to Cool and turn east on Highway 193 for 12 miles to reach Georgetown.

- Back in the day, you wouldn't mess with folks from Moke Hill, now **Mokelumne Hill** (pop. 650). After Jackson became the Calaveras County seat in 1866, they formed a lynch mob and tried to capture the judge who made the decision. Moke Hill peaked at 15,000 residents in the 1850s, when gold claims were restricted to 16 square feet because so many people were striking it rich. Crime was rampant, murders happened weekly, and the famous bandit Joaquin Murrieta stopped by occasionally to gamble in the bawdy saloons. Gold claims eventually petered out, and people left. Today, Mokelumne Hill is a cluster of brick buildings with rusted steel shutters, the 1854 I.O.O.F. Hall (reportedly California's first three-story building), and the Pioneer Jewish Cemetery where gravestones are carved in Hebrew. Mokelumne Hill is located on Highway 49 between Jackson and Angels Camp.

on the river, including an old mining camp and several sections of the **Virginia Turnpike,** a 14-mile-long toll road. Take a short nature walk through oak woodlands and wildflowers like California poppies and purple lupine; during spring, the visitor center (Thurs.–Sun. 11 A.M.–3 P.M.) offers guided wildflower walks

on weekends. If you come on the last Sunday in April and October, the park offers wagon rides and exhibits on pioneer life and the native Maidu people that lived in the canyon before gold was discovered. In summer, you can find a small gravel beach and jumping rocks for more adventurous visitors just a short hike east of the covered bridge. Parking (10 A.M.– sunset daily, $5) is permitted in the fenced lot; street parking on Pleasant Valley Road is not allowed.

One of the most beautiful walks in the South Yuba River State Park is the **Independence Trail** (Hwy. 49, 5.5 miles north of Nevada City, 10 miles round-trip, easy), which was used as an old mining flume during the Gold Rush and has been converted into a flat stroll along the river canyon. The best time to visit is during spring when black oaks cover the path in a lime-green canopy and wildflowers are in bloom. It's also the best time to spot California newts crawling on their orange bellies through puddles beside the trail. The trail is actually two separate hikes that both start from Highway 49; each one is roughly five miles round-trip. The eastern section ends near a bucolic picnic area with a creek and plenty of shade. To reach the trailhead, take Highway 49 north 5.5 miles from Nevada City. Parking is in turnouts along the highway, so keep an eye on traffic.

Boating and Fishing

Scotts Flat Reservoir (23333 Scotts Flat Rd., 530/265-5302, www.scottsflatlake.net, day-use $4–6.50, boat launch $9.25–13, boat rentals $12–125) is a mountain lake with fresh piney air and sparkling water. It's truly a beautiful setting at an elevation of 3,000 feet with bright blue skies and woods that come right down to the shore. Nine species of game fish swim in the reservoir's depths, including rainbow and brown trout, three species of bass, catfish, and kokanee salmon. Scotts Flat has seven miles of shoreline, so it's large enough for waterskiing and wakeboarding, with enough space left over for kayakers to serenely paddle along the shore. Like all reservoirs, the water line can fall drastically in dry years, exposing sandbars and rocks, so exercise caution while boating in late summer.

Mountain Biking

At nearly 3,000 feet and laced by jagged ridgelines, Nevada City is fat tire heaven for mountain bikers. There are at least a dozen known trails within a few miles of town. Most of the rides follow moderate to easy single track, potholed logging roads, and old irrigation ditches. In other words, clip those toes in and hold on. **The Tour of Nevada City Bicycle Shop** website (www.tourofnevadacity.com) has a listing of local rides. One of the best is the **Upper Pioneer Trail** (10 miles, moderate) which starts at the White Cloud Campground on Highway 20 about 11 miles east of Nevada City. For an easier ride that beginners will enjoy, hit the **Champion Mine Road Trail** (10 miles, easy) off Old Downieville Highway southeast of town.

Selling two-wheeled fun since 1969, **Tour of Nevada City Bicycle Shop** (457 Sacramento St., 530/265-2187, www.tourofnevadacity.com, 10 A.M.–6 P.M. Mon.–Fri., 10 A.M.–4 P.M. Sat., 11 A.M.–4 P.M. Sun.) is the best place around for service, rentals, and new bikes. Loaner Trek mountain bikes are $45, and car racks are only $10.

Spas

Lotus Healing Sanctuary (20191 New Rome Rd., 530/265-8811, www.lotushealingsanctuary.com, by appointment) is a short jaunt out of town. This relaxing getaway in the woods specializes in drool-inducing ayurvedic massages that combine a delightful mix of organic herbs, flowers, oils, steam, and touch. Yoga classes and therapy sessions are also available.

Massage and Company (202 Providence Mine Rd., Ste. 103, 530/470-0202, www.massageandco.com, by appointment) offers more traditional massage treatments that include deep tissue, Swedish, hot stone, and aromatherapy. They also offer clay wraps and body polish sessions.

Ananda (14618 Tyler Foote Rd., 530/478-7560, www.ananda.org, call for schedule) isn't for everyone, but hard-core yoginis should look into this peaceful retreat in the woods. Ananda is the real deal—a meditation and yoga village where some people stay for years. Obviously that's not an option for travelers passing through town, but the village's Expanding Light Retreat has classes and workshops that last only a few days. There's also a weekend course for yoga newcomers.

ACCOMMODATIONS
Under $100
Located just a short stroll from downtown Nevada City, the **Outside Inn** (575 E. Broad

SWIMMING HOLES

Nothing beats a dip in cool waters during a summer heat wave. Luckily, the Northern Gold Country's abundant rivers and rushing creeks provide plenty of excellent swimming holes for summer fun.

BRIDGEPORT
Located in the **South Yuba River State Park** west of Nevada City, this swimming hole is just a short hike from the longest single-span covered bridge in the world. Bring cash to pay the iron ranger for parking; street parking isn't allowed. Hike east from the parking lot for about 200 yards and ford the river to the gravelly beach. The swimming hole has a gentle current, crystal-clear water, and a few jumping rocks—but be careful!

MOUNTAIN DOG
This scenic 20-foot waterfall on the **South Fork of the Yuba River** is a beautiful spot deep in a heavily wooded canyon, bracketed by a few rushing rapids and mossy boulders. From Nevada City, head north toward Edwards Crossing, where you'll park, and hike one mile downstream to Spring Creek to reach the falls. Just a heads-up: The swimming hole has a reputation for being clothing-optional, so think twice about coming here if you're squeamish about that kind of thing.

CLARK'S HOLE
You'll find this spot beneath the towering Foresthill Bridge in the **Auburn State Recreation Area.** From Auburn, take Highway 49 into the American River canyon but continue straight instead of turning right for Coloma and Placerville. Park along the road and hike up the North Fork for about 0.3 mile to this large swimming hole. There's a narrow strip of sandy beach and a few jumping rocks, but the awesome view of the 730-foot-high bridge makes this spot the most picture-worthy of them all.

HAPPY VALLEY
This family-friendly pool along the **Cosumnes River** is a beautiful spot to swing on ropes and relax in the frothy bubbles created by a small waterfall. From Placerville, take Pleasant Valley Road south and turn right on Mt. Aukum Road. Head south for two miles and turn left on Happy Valley Cutoff Road. Park anywhere before the second bridge; there are several swimming holes along the river just below the road and less than 0.5 mile away. Most of the property here is privately owned, so please stay on clearly marked trails and respect the neighbors.

UNIVERSITY FALLS
An urban legend for years, a number of people have finally been able to verify that, yes, this place does exist. University Falls is a series of thrilling natural rock waterslides that cascade into pristine emerald pools on **Pilot Creek;** the waterslides are 40-80 feet wide and about 12-15 feet deep. Make sure to be careful on the rocks, and whatever you do don't take the fourth slide—it's extremely dangerous and has caused serious injury to several people. From Auburn or Placerville, follow Highway 193 for 30 miles northeast to the semi-ghost town of Georgetown. Continue northeast for 12 miles on Wentworth Springs Road to the tiny hamlet of Quintette. Park on the left side of the road near a large yellow gate; if you pass the Blodgett Forest Research Station you've gone too far. From here, it's a 90-minute hike to the falls, but it's worth it. The falls are on private property, so please pick up your trash or any debris and leave the glass bottles at home.

St., 530/265-2233, www.outsideinn.com, $80–200) is a family-owned throwback to the days when road trips felt more like pleasure cruises. Converted from a 1930s motor court motel, each room has a different outdoors theme, including the Single Track Room and the romantic Creekside Hideaway cabin—officially Nevada City's smallest house. A natural creek gently runs through the laid-back patio area, which includes a pool and brick fire pit. If that still doesn't sound relaxing, kick back in one of the hammocks outside your room. You can even bring your dog because the Outside is pet-friendly. For kids, ask about the quirky scavenger hunt for lawn trolls hiding in the neatly tended hotel grounds.

The oldest continuously operating hotel west of the Rockies is the **National Hotel** (211 Broad St., 530/265-4551, http://thenationalhotel.com, $75–150). More than 130 years of guests have passed through the hallways here. Some say they never left; at least one TV show has documented ghostly activity at the National, and visitors report seeing the specter of a little girl in the hallways. Ghosts aside, the hotel feels more like a museum with display cases of sepia-toned photographs and 19th-century artifacts. Truth be told, the National hasn't aged well; it gets rowdy at night from all the saloon noise, and the musty-smelling rooms are badly in need a makeover.

$100-150

The **◖ Broad Street Inn** (517 W. Broad St., 530/265-2239, http://broadstreetinn.com, $110–120) isn't a bed-and-breakfast because it doesn't serve meals, but the vibe is similar to a cozy cottage. The Victorian-style building dates back to 1870, but the six rooms have been spruced up with warm earthy colors and plush modern linens on the queen-size beds. The word here is quaint; you won't find many

Find peace within at the Broad Street Inn.

electronic amenities (other than a TV) cluttering the rooms, although there's coffee, a microwave, and a fridge in the inn's common room if needed. Step out back onto the garden patio for a little relaxation time in the sun, or bundle up next to the fire pit during cooler months. Don't worry about the bathrooms; even though the building is old, the Broad Street Inn has private commodes and tub showers.

$150-200

If you can, stay at the ❰ **Emma Nevada House** (528 E. Broad St., 530/265-4415, www.emmanevadahouse.com, $170–250). This romantic 19th-century Victorian-style home has been beautifully restored into a luxurious inn that's just steps from downtown Nevada City. The six guest rooms effortlessly combine comfort with antique sensibilities; amenities include queen-size beds lavished with plush linens, claw-foot tubs, and polished antique furnishings. In the morning, step onto the sundeck for a gourmet breakfast of French toast, fresh fruit, or cheese soufflé. The inn is conveniently located a block away from Nevada City's shops and restaurants.

Just minutes away from downtown Nevada City, the **Red Castle Inn** (109 Prospect St., 530/265-5135, www.redcastleinn.com, $155–210) is like stepping into a Gilded Age time capsule. The restored 1860 Gothic Revival building is surrounded by a fragrant grove of cedar trees and beautiful terraced garden. Inside, five comfy and air-conditioned rooms offer amenities such as canopied featherbeds, clawfoot tubs, 19th-century antique furniture, and arched windows with a view of downtown Nevada City. Breakfast is a treat—six courses of gourmet fare, from mushroom crepes to ham-and-cheese blintzes to gingerbread muffins. Tea is served daily underneath a shimmering crystal chandelier in the decadent Victorian parlor. On the downside, pets are not allowed and there's no elevator to reach the third floor; be ready to lug your bags up the stairs. A stay of least two nights is required, but sometimes they'll squeeze in visitors if there's a last-minute cancellation.

One of the friendliest places to stay is at ❰ **Deer Creek Inn** (116 Nevada St., 530/264-7038, www.deercreekinn.net, $160–200), where your hosts bubble over with knowledge and friendly tips about the town. The restored Queen Anne Victorian was constructed in 1860 and is just a short walk from downtown Nevada City. Five elegant rooms are decked out with modern amenities—flat-screen TVs, dual showerheads in the bath, ceiling fans, air conditioning, free Wi-Fi—while still retaining a tasteful charm. Breakfast is a four-course affair with dishes such as eggs Florentine, chicken pecan quiche, and Italian omelettes and a complimentary wine service is served every day. The inn gets its name from the gently rushing creek out back, which flows beneath a towering forest of 150-year-old maples, dogwoods, and cedars, along with one of Nevada County's tallest cherry trees. It's a fantastic place to grab a book and relax by the peaceful rose garden and immaculate lawn. Two-night stays are required; rates are often lower in winter.

Camping

Scotts Flat Reservoir (23333 Scotts Flat Rd., 530/265-5302, www.scottsflatlake.net, $19–35) has fresh air and brilliant views of the lake. The 171 campsites have fire pits and picnic tables, plus access to shower facilities ($0.25 for three minutes) and decent bathrooms. But the greatest thing about Scotts Flat is the water, and all the campsites are close to the shore. Bears have been spotted here; the campsites don't have bear-proof lockers, so avoid stashing food in tents and keep everything (even toothpaste) in the car and out of sight.

FOOD
American

The name might not give it away, but **Lefty's**

Grill (221 Broad St., 530/265-5838, www. leftysgrill.com, 11:30 A.M.–9 P.M. daily, $15), has some of the best upscale bar food you'll ever sink your teeth into. The restaurant's handsome brick building is a historic landmark and was a former bank during the Gold Rush. Inside, cheerful lighting and spotless white tablecloths give a hip urban feel, and the food definitely measures up. Start with a side of sweet-potato fries slathered in apricot-chipotle sauce, but leave room for the Napa pizza—named Best in the West at the 2009 International Pizza Expo. Children are welcome, and the restaurant has an extensive kids menu.

Friar Tuck's (111 N. Pine St., 530/265-9093, http://friartucks.com, 5–9 P.M. daily, $13–42) has literally been through fire; local diners wrung their hands when this beloved establishment burned down in 2002. Luckily, Friar Tuck's was rebuilt to its former glory. Diners will pick up a mom-and-pop vibe in the Sherwood Forest–like dining room, artistically decorated with a real tree and a trellis reaching up to the ceiling. The menu is a meat lover's dream, bristling with steak, prime rib, lamb, and fish; the salmon roasted on Oregon cedar is highly recommended. After dinner, wander over to the massive mahogany bar and order a glass of Nevada County zinfandel or syrah.

National Hotel Restaurant (211 Broad St., 530/265-4551, http://thenationalhotel. com, 8 A.M.–2 P.M. and 5:30–9:30 P.M. Mon.–Fri., 7 A.M.–3 P.M. and 5:30–9:30 P.M. Sat., 10 A.M.–3 P.M. and 5:30–9:30 P.M. Sun., $13–25) serves traditional American cuisine that leans heavily toward surf and turf. Meals include lobster tail, buffalo short ribs, steaks, and chicken. If you're staying at the hotel and find yourself taken with the ancient building's ambience, it's worthwhile to try for dinner.

A gnarly-looking mountain lodge off Highway 20, **Old 5 Mile House** (18851 Hwy. 20, 530/265-5155, www.theold5milehouse. com, 11 A.M.–9 P.M. Tues.–Sun., brunch Sat.–Sun., $11–24) has been around since 1890. Once a stagecoach stop and inn, the place now serves basic American cuisine like pizza and pasta, plus random other dishes that might seem out of place; each month features a different theme such as Spanish or Middle Eastern. This is a great place for a quick bite or a drink if you can grab a chair on the patio, although Nevada City's restaurants should be given higher priority.

Asian

The last thing you might expect in Nevada City is high-quality sushi. But **Sushi in the Raw** (315 Spring St., 530/478-9503, 5:30–9 P.M. Tues.–Sat., $6–15) is *that* good. Before opening his own restaurant in 2002, owner Ru Suzuki already had a dedicated following in the Gold Country as one of the region's premier sushi chefs. He's topped himself with this cozy, authentic location where the fish competes with anything you'd find in a larger city. Start with the scallop shooters and then order Ru's white-truffle sashimi; your taste buds will swear they're in Tokyo. Call several days ahead for a reservation; the restaurant is small and very popular with locals. The restaurant opens at 5 P.M. in winter.

Bakeries and Cafés

Café Mekka (237 Commercial St., 530/478-1517, 7 A.M.–10 P.M. Mon.–Fri., 8 A.M.–midnight Sat.–Sun., $5) is more than a coffee shop—it's an eye-opening coffee experience for people tired of corporate espresso joints. Inside this funky café are black wooden moveable walls and overstuffed furniture—it's more like a theater production than a café. Mekka usually attracts a scruffy street performer or two, but don't be intimidated by any vagabonds lounging on the sidewalk. The espresso drinks are perfect, and the chalkboard menu reads like a Salvador Dalí exhibit; typical concoctions include the Café Borgia (double mocha steamed

NORTHERN GOLD COUNTRY

Matteo's Public

with orange peel) and the Fairy Tea (steamed rice milk with white chocolate and cinnamon). Some pastries are made locally by famed truffle wizard Willem Degroot; they are, simply put, amazing.

South Pine Café (110 S. Pine St., 530/265-0260, http://southpinecafe.com, 8 A.M.–3 P.M. daily, $8–12) is a homey little breakfast spot serving healthy food made with local produce. The slightly exotic fare features dishes with a Southwestern theme (the corn cakes come highly recommended), while others are more international. The South Pine also boasts a fantastic lunch menu with the same international theme.

Californian

Ike's Quarter Café (402 Commercial St., 530/265-6138, www.ikesquartercafe.com, 8 A.M.–3 P.M. Thurs.–Mon., 3–8 P.M. Fri.–Sat., $10–23) serves Cajun-Californian cuisine in a cheerful setting. Ike's has filled its menu with

dishes like the veggie BBQ bacon burger and the tofu melt. I recommend the breakfast, especially the spicy Hang Town Fry frittata (okra, crawfish, andouille sausage with peppers, and caramelized onions). The food is tasty, but expect to pay tourist prices.

At first, **Matteo's Public** (300 Commercial St., 530/265-0782, http://matteospublic.com, 11:30 A.M.–9:30 P.M. Tues.–Thurs. and Sun., 11:30 A.M.–11 P.M. Fri.–Sat., $10–31) sounds pretty granola. Waste is composted, the staff uses chemical-free cleaning supplies, and almost everything on the menu comes from local farms and vendors; most of the food is organic. However, the Public feels more like an old brick saloon than a tofu co-op. Tall, old-fashioned windows give diners a view of downtown Nevada City and worn plank floors creak as new guests trickle in. The food is mostly burgers and sandwiches, typical pub fare but fancy; try the Kobe beef sliders or the pulled-pork sandwich. The only quibble is with the prices, which are definitely skewed to the tourist crowd.

Dessert

If you notice someone clutching an ice cream cone on Nevada City's sidewalk, most likely they've just come from ◖ **Treats** (110 York St., 530/913-5819, http://treatsnevadacity.com, noon–9 P.M. Sun.–Thurs., 11 A.M.–10 P.M. Fri.–Sat. in summer; noon–5 P.M. Sun.–Thurs., noon–8 P.M. Fri.–Sat. in winter, $2–6). This isn't just any ice cream. Treats makes several ice cream flavors in-store from local, organic ingredients, whipping up unbelievably creative delights such as Earl Grey, Chai, and Mint Chip; the last flavor contains real peppermint leaves. Other goodies include freshly baked cookies, smoothies, cupcakes, and ice cream sundaes. For those with special dietary needs, the shop also serves vegan, gluten-free, and sugar-free sweets.

Fine Dining

New Moon Café (203 York St., 530/265-6399, www.thenewmooncafe.com, 11:30 A.M.–2 P.M. and 5–8:30 P.M. Tues.–Fri., 5–8:30 P.M. Sat.–Sun., $21–30) has been whipping up culinary magic in Nevada City for more than a decade with a menu that rivals established eateries in foodie capitals like San Francisco or Seattle. Entrées range from raspberry duck to chorizo prawns. Much of the food is organic and comes from local farmers when available. Although New Moon is one of the more exclusive restaurants in town (reservations are a must), word on the street says this place isn't what it used to be.

Italian

The Italian food at **Cirino's Bar and Grill** (309 Broad St., 530/265-2246, www.cirinosbarandgrill.com, 5–9 P.M. Sun.–Thurs., 11:30 A.M.–4:30 P.M. and 5–10 P.M. Fri.–Sat., $20) is hearty and very traditional. The cuisine is heavily

Northern Italian with dishes like linguine, risotto, and spaghetti; they also have pizza nights (5–9 P.M. Wed. and Sun.). However, the interior feels more like an old-school bar or surf and turf place. Cirino's has been around since the 1980s, so it's a local's favorite and the service is pretty attentive.

Mexican

Las Katerinas Mexican Restaurant (311 Broad St., 530/478-0275, 11 A.M.–8:30 P.M. Wed.–Sun., $10–15) dishes up traditional Mexican fare, something that's certainly unique in this former Gold Rush town. It's nothing fancy, but the spicy burritos are pretty good and the service is usually fast and friendly.

Thai

Eating at **Sopa's Thai** (312-316 Commercial St., 530/470-0101, www.sopathai.net, 11 A.M.–3 P.M. and 5–9:30 P.M. Mon.–Fri., noon–9:30 P.M. Sat.–Sun., $10–15) is the closest thing you'll find to dining in Bangkok. Sopa's serves mouthwatering curries, pad Thai, and salads with the restaurant's popular peanut dressing. Owner Sopa Savedra imported most of the furniture and decorations from her native Thailand, including the triangle pillows that separate diners from each other. On a summer night, sit outdoors in the balmy Asian garden patio.

Vegetarian

For a healthy change of pace, **Fudenjüce** (815 Zion St., 530/265-5282, www.fudenjuce.com, 8 A.M.–7 P.M. Mon.–Fri, 10 A.M.–7 P.M. Sat., $5–8) has an all-veggie menu and long list of fresh fruit juices. It's a typical Nevada City joint, serving alternative food in a breezy, bohemian atmosphere. For dinner or lunch, try either the rice bowls or a wrap. Fudenjüce is all-natural and free of chemicals; the kitchen doesn't even have a microwave. They also make great smoothies.

INFORMATION AND SERVICES

The **Nevada City Chamber of Commerce** (132 Main St., 530/265-2692, www.nevadacitychamber.com, 9 A.M.–5 P.M. Mon.–Fri., 11 A.M.–4 P.M. Sat., 11 A.M.–3 P.M. Sun.) has gads of information about local recreation and cultural happenings, including maps of the area and tips for self-guided walking tours.

GETTING THERE AND AROUND

Nevada City sits on fragrant pine-covered hillsides about 61 miles northwest of Sacramento and 28 miles west of Auburn. From Sacramento travel east on I-80 and at Auburn head north on Highway 49. For a more scenic ride, head east all the way to the small Gold Rush town of Colfax on I-80 and go west on Highway 174.

Grass Valley

According to local legend, Grass Valley (pop. 12,400) has a long-standing rivalry with nearby Nevada City. During the Gold Rush, most prospectors made their home in Grass Valley while the upper class—consisting of mine owners, merchants, and professionals—took up residence in the blue-blooded Victorian neighborhoods of Nevada City. Perhaps because of its scruffy background, Grass Valley has always remained in the shadow of its more well-to-do neighbor. But bypassing this town would be a mistake. Grass Valley has grown up, and travelers will find a thriving arts scene, antique shops stuffed with Americana, and wonderful used bookstores situated among these picturesque streets.

Grass Valley is arguably the best place in the foothills to explore Gold Rush mining history. Hardrock shafts deep below the town pumped out more gold than anywhere else in California. At nearby Empire Mine, now a historic state park, more than 5.6 million ounces of gold were extracted from nearly 370 miles of mine shafts and tunnels. At local museums, visitors can check out exhibits of gigantic steam-powered mining equipment that serviced the region's industrial golden age. Culinary tourists can try pasties, the local delicacy brought by 19th-century Cornish miners who immigrated to work the goldfields. But there's more to Grass Valley than the many industrial and cultural artifacts left behind by prospectors. Recreation has become the new gold for mountain bike enthusiasts, hikers, and boaters who flock to Grass Valley's nearby reservoirs and trails.

SIGHTS
◖ Downtown

If Nevada City is a throwback to the late 19th century, then visiting Grass Valley's old movie house, friendly diners, and used bookshops is like taking a walk through vintage 1950s Americana. The city's downtown (www.historicgrassvalley.com) is just as fascinating as its northern neighbor. While Grass Valley's past is laced with industrial influences from the nearby gold mines, today visitors will find a charming, laid-back foothill burg dotted with luxurious Victorian-style inns. The growing Nevada County wine scene has its roots in downtown Grass Valley, where local wineries have begun opening tasting rooms to showcase varietals that are slowly earning more fans across California. Most of the action in downtown Grass Valley is on Mill Street, where eateries and shops are situated; to see the most of town, start by walking up West Main Street and turn left on Mill. There's a brilliant self-guided walking tour online (www.nevadacountygold.com) that hits most of the town's main landmarks.

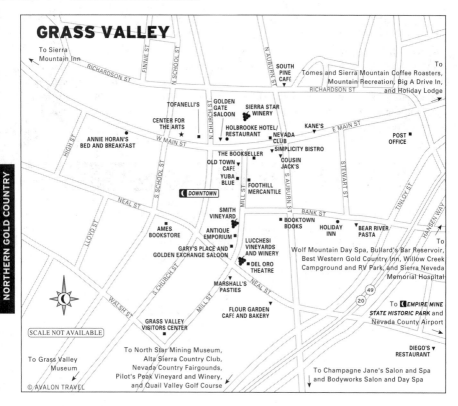

GRASS VALLEY

To Sierra Mountain Inn

RICHARDSON ST

FINNIE ST

N SCHOOL ST

N CHURCH ST

N AUBURN ST

SOUTH PINE CAFE

To Tomes and Sierra Mountain Coffee Roasters, Mountain Recreation, Big A Drive In, and Holiday Lodge

RICHARDSON ST

TOFANELLI'S

GOLDEN GATE SALOON

SIERRA STAR WINERY

CENTER FOR THE ARTS

ANNIE HORAN'S BED AND BREAKFAST

W. MAIN ST

HOLBROOKE HOTEL/ RESTAURANT

NEVADA CLUB

KANE'S

E MAIN ST

POST OFFICE

HIGH ST

THE BOOKSELLER

OLD TOWN CAFÉ

SIMPLICITY BISTRO

COUSIN JACK'S

YUBA BLUE

FOOTHILL MERCANTILE

S AUBURN ST

STEWART ST

TINLOY ST

DOWNTOWN

S SCHOOL ST

NEAL ST

SMITH VINEYARD

BANK ST

BOOKTOWN BOOKS

HOLIDAY INN

BEAR RIVER PASTA

HANSEN WAY

LLOYD ST

AMES BOOKSTORE

ANTIQUE EMPORIUM

LUCCHESI VINEYARDS AND WINERY

GARY'S PLACE AND GOLDEN EXCHANGE SALOON

Wolf Mountain Day Spa, Bullard's Bar Reservoir, Best Western Gold Country Inn, Willow Creek Campground and RV Park, and Sierra Nevada Memorial Hospital

To

DEL ORO THEATRE

S CHURCH ST

MILL ST

MARSHALL'S PASTIES

NEAL ST

49

20

To **EMPIRE MINE STATE HISTORIC PARK** and Nevada County Airport

FLOUR GARDEN CAFÉ AND BAKERY

WALSH ST

GRASS VALLEY VISITORS CENTER

SCALE NOT AVAILABLE

DIEGO'S RESTAURANT

To Grass Valley Museum

To North Star Mining Museum, Alta Sierra Country Club, Nevada Country Fairgrounds, Pilot's Peak Vineyard and Winery, and Quail Valley Golf Course

To Champagne Jane's Salon and Spa and Bodyworks Salon and Day Spa

© AVALON TRAVEL

◖ Empire Mine State Historic Park

Gold Country takes on new meaning at Empire Mine State Historic Park (10791 E. Empire St., 530/273-8522, www.empiremine.org, 10 A.M.–5 P.M. daily, adults $7, children $3, tours included), the richest gold mine in the foothills. During a span of 100 years, the operation yielded 5.6 million ounces of gold—around $400 million, not a bad profit considering the mining rights were originally sold for a measly $350 in 1851. As small-time gold panning slowly gave way to industrial mining, the area around Grass Valley experienced a technological revolution: In order to bore into the tough granite bedrock, mine operators blasted deep into the mountain to reach sheets of gold-bearing quartz. Extracting the gold was a never-ending process; sky-high stamp mills pounded thousands of pounds of ore 24 hours a day and seven days a week, creating an ear-splitting racket heard by folks nearly three miles away. Today these awesome machines sit quietly in a huge plaza by the park's main entrance, and visitors can stroll past a majestic Pelton wheel, ore carts that ferried miners deep underground, sepia-colored engines called steam donkeys, and a two-story rusting head frame that hoisted equipment out of the mine. You'd never know it, but the ground beneath the park is riddled with 367 miles of flooded mine shafts and tunnels; for now, visitors can only peek at the closed mineshaft or check out a perfect scale model of every

© CHRISTOPHER ARNS

mining machinery in the main yard at Empire Mine State Historic Park

underground cavern below the compound. In 2013, park rangers plan to begin underground tours through Empire Mine's hidden depths.

The mining artifacts are definitely spectacular, but don't miss the estate grounds—a walk through the Gatsby-like estate is a must. This is where the mine owner and superintendent lived, among lush grassy lawns sprawling under a canopy of Italian cypress, hawthorne, southern magnolias, and birch trees. The highlight is the Bourn Cottage, a 19th-century stone manor perched on an immaculately tended hillside overlooking the mine. Thirteen acres of gardens explode with color during summertime as 950 roses bloom, hedged by English holly and lovingly preserved stone walls. Make sure to join the free tours offered by park docents; larger groups might want to call ahead for reservations.

North Star Mining Museum

Much smaller and more intimate than Empire Mine, the North Star Mining Museum (10933 Allison Ranch Rd., 530/273-4255, www. nevadacountyhistory.org, 10 A.M.–4 P.M. Tues.–Sun. May 1–Oct. 31, free but donations encouraged) is a low-key alternative. History fans will love this fascinating tribute to the industrial machinery that once powered the North Star Mine in Grass Valley, one of California's most successful mines during the Gold Rush. In those days, miners used some of the most advanced technology of the era to construct sprawling hydraulic operations or burrow deep into the hillsides to find the quartz deposits there. Imagine gigantic water cannons blasting canyon walls with thousands of gallons per minute and you'll get the idea. The museum has plenty of mining relics from those operations—like the largest Pelton wheel in the world, a crude form of hydraulic power that once helped power the North Star. The museum even has a working stamp mill, a towering machine once used to crush hundreds of

© CHRISTOPHER ARNS

North Star Mining Museum

tons of gold ore per day with an awe-inspiring engine of gears and pistons.

The museum is closed in winter (Nov. 1– Apr. 30), so plan your visit accordingly. Some of the machines are outside, so you can still walk around the grounds and have a look if the museum isn't open. It's an easy walk on dirt and gravel paths, but part of the museum is on a slope; families with strollers or individuals with walking difficulties might have trouble. If you have kids, ask the helpful park guides to demonstrate how some of the machinery works. There's also a shady picnic area next to a rushing creek, so pack a lunch and enjoy the leafy setting next to the museum.

Grass Valley Museum
Check out an undiscovered gem at the Grass Valley Museum (410 S. Church St., 530/272-4725, www.saintjosephsculturalcenter.org, 12:30–3:30 P.M. Wed.–Sat. Apr. 15–Dec. 15, by appointment, free), a cluttered time capsule

of Victorian-era artifacts from Grass Valley's yesteryears. Savvy travelers can spend hours exploring six rooms packed with furniture exhibits, clothing, knickknacks, and art. This slightly unorganized abode is packed with souvenirs and mementos spanning nearly a century; you can even gaze at a bathtub owned by famed vaudeville performer Lola Montez. Highlights include a lace-making exhibit and a hall of vintage photographs. Call ahead for tour information.

WINERIES
Nevada County's wine industry is surprisingly competitive. While the region's wineries are still a step behind Amador and El Dorado County varietals, they are certainly improving every year; some labels have even started earning gold and double gold medals at California wine competitions. There are several wineries with tasting rooms in downtown Grass Valley, along with a few more just outside of town.

Lucchesi Vineyards and Winery

Fans of white wine will enjoy Lucchesi Vineyards and Winery (167 Mill St., Grass Valley, 530/274-2164, www.lucchesivineyards.com, 11 A.M.–6 P.M. daily, tasting $5). Most other Nevada County wineries focus on reds but Lucchesi produces pinot grigio, two different chardonnays and a sauvignon blanc. Out of all the wines here, the best may be the award-winning port, which has won silver at the San Francisco Chronicle Wine Competition.

Pilot's Peak Vineyard and Winery

It's not in town, but Pilot's Peak Vineyard and Winery (12888 Spenceville Rd., Penn Valley, 530/432-3321, www.pilotpeak.com, noon–5 P.M. Sat.–Sun., free) is worth the drive. The winemakers have developed sophisticated, balanced reds that combine nicely in the winery's Paramour blend, a mix of Pilot Peak grenache, syrah, mourvèdre, and petite syrah. The winery also has live music on weekends.

Sierra Star Winery

Sierra Star Winery (124 W. Main St., 530/477-8282, www.sierrastarrwine.com, noon–5 P.M. daily, tasting $5) opened the first tasting room in downtown Grass Valley. For those a little sick of zinfandel and syrah, this winery has a very diverse roster that includes sparkling peach wine, almond champagne, and port. The Jack's Blend (mostly a mix of reds but with a splash of viognier) also stands out. The tasting room's dark wood bar and rough brick walls make a beautiful setting.

Smith Vineyard

Smith Vineyard (142 Mill St., 530/273-7032, http://smithvineyard.com, noon–6 P.M. Wed.–Fri., noon–7 P.M. Sat., 1–5 P.M. Sun., noon–6 P.M. Mon., tasting fee $5) is a family-owned winery with very friendly staff. The wine from this vineyard is pretty standard

for the area; chardonnay, syrah, and cabernet sauvignon fill out the list. Do try the Three Brothers vintage, which is a balanced blend of merlot, primitivo, and cabernet.

ENTERTAINMENT AND EVENTS

For a small foothill town, you might expect Grass Valley to be a little, well, dead. Not so; it's really a happening place that attracts well-known performers and top-notch events. But those scruffy mining roots are never far away, and Grass Valley nightlife usually revolves around a handful of busy dive bars or flicks at the Del Oro Theatre.

Nightlife

Not even Prohibition could stop the **Golden Gate Saloon** (212 W. Main St., 530/273-1353, http://holbrookehotel.com/saloon, 11 A.M.–2 A.M. daily), the oldest saloon west of the Mississippi still in operation. It's located in the Holbrooke Hotel and first opened in 1852. And what a gem; part of the majestic wooden bar was imported from Italy and bears Neoclassical onyx pillars and stained glass. Most likely, this is where onetime guests Mark Twain and Bret Harte had cocktails during their stay. Stop by Thursday through Saturday for live music.

The **Nevada Club** (108 W. Main St., 530/274-0947, 9 A.M.–2 A.M. daily) may not be for everybody. Women's delicates hang from a moose head mounted over the bar, and the crowd is a little rough around the edges. If you go, Nevada Club has a daily happy hour and two pool tables.

Gary's Place and Golden Exchange Saloon (158 Mill St., 530/272-5509, 7 A.M.–2 A.M. daily) is a little more upscale, but it's still a scruffy dive at heart. There's a pool table in back and a jukebox with copious amounts of classic rock and country.

The Arts

Famous performers are common at **Center for the Arts** (314 W. Main St., 530/274-8384, www.thecenterforthearts.org, $12–58). Shows include a wide range of events, from Willie Nelson concerts to book readings with writer David Sedaris; acts can include comedy troupes like Second City or interpretive dance companies. Many of these shows sell out far in advance because they attract crowds from Sacramento and even the Bay Area; check the website before visiting.

Cinema

The **Del Oro Theatre** (165 Mill St., 530/272-1646, www.sierracinemas.com, $7–9) screened its first film in 1942, and the stately movie house still looks great. From the outside, Del Oro splits the Grass Valley skyline with a needlelike spire that's just as eye-catching at night when the old-fashioned marquee gleams neon. Inside, art deco murals painted in muted earth tones cover the walls and ceiling; it feels like Gary Cooper or Rita Hayworth might stroll in. There are usually three new flicks showing at the Del Oro.

Festivals and Events

Locals are extremely proud of **Cornish Christmas** (www.grassvalleychamber.com, Fri. late Nov.–late Dec., free), a holiday street fair that's very similar to Victorian Christmas in Nevada City. One big difference is the name, which honors the 19th-century Cornish miners who immigrated to Grass Valley during the Gold Rush. Mill Street shuts down for the Cornish Carolers (descendants of the town's original miners) and the Tommyknocker Cloggers, who bang out a deafening rhythm with their wooden shoes. Many of the shops and wine bars stay open for the event, which starts Friday evening after Thanksgiving and continues weekly until just before Christmas. Nibble on roasted chestnuts and peek inside

booths where local artisans sell wooden and ceramic handicrafts, art, and handmade jewelry. For kids, there are pony races, go-kart races, and a bouncy house.

Every small town seems to have a local fair, but the **Nevada County Fair** (11228 McCourtney Rd., 530/273-6217, www.nevadacountyfair.com, early Aug., adults $9, children $6) stands out for folksy atmosphere. For one week every August, this rustic and charming little fair takes place under a shady canopy of towering evergreens high in the foothills. There's the usual assortment of carnival games for kids, plus crafts, musical acts, art exhibitions, a rodeo, and appearances by the Budweiser draft horses. Stop by the food court and visit the booth run by the local Job's Daughters chapter to grab a homemade corn dog. Don't miss the livestock exhibits from Nevada County farms and local high school FFA clubs, many of whom earn top prizes at the California State Fair. While the fair is a great place for families and kids, pets are not allowed. If you visit in the evening, make sure to pack a light jacket—the foothills can be slightly chilly, even in August. Children under age five are free; on Thursday during the fair, all children under 13 years old are free.

SHOPPING

Grass Valley is the capital of the Gold Country's indie bookstores, but you can also spend a long afternoon hunting for antiques and gifts at many of the family-owned shops along Main and Mill Streets. Parking is tough by mid-afternoon; try side streets if needed, as the town is short on public lots.

Antiques

Antique Emporium (150 Mill St., 530/272-7302, 10 A.M.–5 P.M. daily) is like a big barn cluttered with heirlooms and long-lost trinkets. Everything antiques hunters would want is

© CHRISTOPHER ARNS

Booktown Books

here—from fine glassware and china to bulky wood armoires packed with old watches, lamps, and silverware. Best of all, the prices are extremely reasonable, especially compared to other shops across the Gold Country.

Books

The grizzled war hero among Grass Valley's bookshops is **Ames Bookstore** (309 Neal St., 530/273-9261, 10 A.M.–6 P.M. Tues.–Sat.). This one-story building doesn't look like much from the outside, but inside it's packed with books. Songbirds chirp from their cages as you browse endless tunnels and rooms of bookshelves, filled with every genre imaginable.

Booktown Books (107 Bank St., 530/272-4655, 10 A.M.–6 P.M. Mon.–Sat., 11 A.M.–5 P.M. Sun.) is truly the mother lode for rare and used tomes. More co-op than store, 12 independent booksellers share the same open space. Every genre is represented—from science fiction to romance to comic book art. Pressed for time?

Grab a store directory at the front counter to find each bookseller (nothing separates them and the different sections blend together).

The Bookseller (107 Mill St., 530/272-2131, www.thebookseller.biz, 10 A.M.–7 P.M. Mon.–Fri., 10 A.M.–5:30 P.M. Sat., 11 A.M.–4 P.M. Sun.) is another longtime Grass Valley bookshop selling new books, including a well-stocked section of children's titles. Ask to see their selection of autographed volumes that includes bestsellers and works by newly published authors.

Tomes and Sierra Mountain Coffee Roasters (671 Maltman Dr., #3, 530/273-4002, www.tomesgv.com, 7 A.M.–5 P.M. Mon.–Fri., 8 A.M.–5 P.M. Sat., 9 A.M.–4 P.M. Sun.) is a double threat: a used bookstore hidden inside a coffee shop. Budding philosophers will dig the outsize section on religion and philosophy. The store also specializes in literature, art, history, and politics, along with a decent offering of kids' books.

Gifts

For a unique gift for any occasion, stop by **Yuba Blue** (116 Mill St., 530/273-9620, www.yubablueonline.com, 10 A.M.–6 P.M. daily). Part boutique and part knickknack novelty, the store has everything from exquisite jewelry and clothing to housewares and decorations. If you can't find something, ask the friendly staff for help. Some of the items do seem a little random—like the stack of gourmet jellies next to the gag books section—but that's part of the fun.

Foothill Mercantile (121 Mill St., 530/273-8304, www.foothillmercantile.com, 9:30 A.M.–6 P.M. Mon.–Fri., 9:30 A.M.–5 P.M. Sat., 11 A.M.–4 P.M. Sun) is a throwback to general stores that sold candy, toys, and other dry goods. Kids will love the second floor, which is entirely devoted to Thomas the Tank Engine, Breyer plastic horses, science kits, and other toys. Downstairs, you'll find a varied selection of gifts, including a whole wall devoted to kitschy Department 56 decorations. You can also find a decent assortment of greeting cards.

Outdoor Equipment

Grass Valley's best outdoor shop is **Mountain Recreation** (491 E. Main St., 530/477-8006, www.mtnrec.com, 10 A.M.–6 P.M. Mon.–Sat., 10 A.M.–5 P.M. Sun.). You can rent snowboards and skis ($30) during the winter season; snowshoes and cross-country skis (both $15) are also available. This shop carries a decent selection of footwear, camping gear, and apparel. The selection is smaller than what REI might have, but it's just right for a small town like Grass Valley. If you call ahead during summer, sometimes the shop will allow wakeboarders to demo new equipment.

SPORTS AND RECREATION
Empire Mine State Historic Park

More gold was found at Empire Mine State Historic Park (10791 E. Empire St.,

530/273-8522, www.empiremine.org, sunrise–sunset daily) than at any other mining operation. Once you've explored Empire Mine's stately mansion and fascinating Gold Rush artifacts, go for a hike on the park's 14 miles of trails crisscrossing 845 acres of shady black oaks, manzanita bushes, and towering ponderosas. The well-maintained trails are open year-round; dogs are welcome on a leash. You can also go mountain biking on some designated trails and horseback riding is also allowed. A good hiking trail that meanders over a sizable chunk of the park is the **Hardrock Trail** (three miles, moderate), which follows an abandoned rail line once connected to the mines. It's a stunning trail in fall when the black oaks become a kaleidoscope of orange and yellow, and it passes a virtual graveyard of rusting 19th-century mining equipment and old foundations. For mountain biking, try the **Union Hill Trail** (four miles, moderate); it's mostly a network of fire roads that's perfect for beginning to intermediate cyclists.

Boating

Bullard's Bar Reservoir (12571 Marysville Rd., Dobbins, 877/692-3201, http://bullardsbar.com, free) is an artificial lake in western Nevada County that draws boaters from all over California. The surrounding foothills are part of the Tahoe National Forest, and the setting—forested ridgelines that grow darkly blue at night, pine-scented air, and dazzling water—is simply brilliant. The reservoir has been ranked as one of the best recreation lakes in the country; there's bass and kokanee salmon fishing, mountain biking, and waterskiing.

Houseboating is big at Bullard's Bar, and visitors can rent from the marina ($500–4,000, three-day minimum). The marina also rents ski boats ($290–375 per half-day, $400–525 full day) or smaller watercraft like Jet Skis and small Speedsters boats ($280–290 per half-day, $350–400 full day). Look into staying overnight at one of the five campgrounds ($22 individual sites, $44–180 group camping, $7.50 fee phone reservations) spread out around the reservoir and often situated right next to the water.

Golf

Swing the sticks at **Alta Sierra Country Club** (11897 Tammy Way, Alta Sierra, 530/273-2868, www.altasierracc.com, open to public after noon, $40–50), the premier course in western Nevada County. This semipublic course opens to nonmembers by early afternoon, which is perfect for golfing in summer when the sunlight lasts into the late evening. The par-72 championship-style course is a challenging loop through black oak and pines; because Alta Sierra is at 2,000 feet, the tee boxes are often high above the greens and can play tricks on a golfer's sense of distance. Keep an eye out for Canada geese, blue herons, and other wildlife on the immaculate fairways, as the country club is one of 31 courses in California to be named a Certified Audubon Cooperative Sanctuary. Book tee times in advance in warmer months when the course is busy.

Weekend warriors can play a quick round at **Quail Valley Golf Course** (12594 Auburn Rd., 530/274-1340, $10). Expect a typical nine-hole executive layout with a few bunkers and water hazards. The green on the final hole is hidden behind a barn, so golfers are faced with a tricky blind lie. Overall, it's a great course for casual golfers who care more about fun than burnishing that handicap.

Spas

If you're pining for a mani-pedi in the Northern Gold Country, **Champagne Jane's Salon and Spa** (477 S. Auburn St., 530/273-0477, http://champagnejanesalonspa.com, 9 A.M.–7 P.M. Mon.–Sat.) is the place to go. They also do hair and nails, along with a full range of traditional salon services like waxing, eyebrow tinting, and airbrush tanning.

Bodyworks Salon and Day Spa (267 S. Auburn St., 530/273-2099, www.salonbodyworks.com, 9 A.M.–1:30 P.M. Mon., 9 A.M.–5 P.M. Tues.–Sat.) provides the full works, including hair and nail care, plus skin treatments. They also have several different massages including a relaxing scalp, feet, and hands treatment.

Wolf Mountain Day Spa (110 E. Main St., 530/477-2340, www.wolfmountaindayspa.com, 11 A.M.–4 P.M. Mon., 10 A.M.–6 P.M. Tues.–Fri., 9 A.M.–5 P.M. Sat., noon–5 P.M. Sun.) has holistic treatments, including Reiki wraps and infrared sauna sessions. Other services are more traditional—manicures, pedicures, haircuts, and massages. Wolf Mountain offers facials and massages just for guys.

ACCOMMODATIONS
Under $100

Annie Horan's Bed and Breakfast (415 W. Main St., 530/272-1516, www.anniehoran.com, $85–120) is among the most delightful places to stay in the Gold Country. From the moment you step through Annie Horan's iron gate into the rose garden, it's obvious this place is special. Four rooms are exquisitely decorated with antique bed frames, linens in warm earth tones, bay windows, and a claw-foot tub. All rooms have free wireless Internet and air-conditioning to keep guests cool during the summer. The gourmet breakfast is incredible; in the morning, homemade cinnamon rolls, delicious scrambled eggs, pastries, veggie frittatas, and freshly squeezed juice await. Unfortunately, pets are not permitted.

For simple yet comfortable rooms, check out the **Sierra Mountain Inn** (816 W. Main St., 530/273-8133, www.sierramountaininn.com, $80–180). Just minutes from downtown Grass Valley, these charming motel-style accommodations offer a romantic and relaxing option to get away from it all. Rooms combine rustic decor with luxurious touches like marble baths and vaulted ceilings for a quirky farmhouse vibe. Most rooms offer kitchenettes with a mini-fridge, sink, and microwave. If you plan to stay only one night, call and reserve over the phone instead of online—the inn usually requires a two-night minimum stay. Note that if you bring a dog, it's at least an extra $25 depending on the room.

Best Western Gold Country Inn (972 Sutton Way, 866/839-6035, www.bwgrassvalley.com, $85–140) has clean, hassle-free lodgings within a short drive of downtown Grass Valley. Standard amenities include a hair dryer, fridge, coffeemaker, and microwave. Grass Valley gets hot during summertime, and luckily the Best Western has an outdoor pool where you can cool off; there's also a spa. Make sure to ask for a nonsmoking room, as the hotel does offer both smoking and smoke-free lodgings.

Holiday Lodge (1221 E. Main St., 530/273-4406, www.holidaylodge.biz, $60–120) is a simple, clean place offering budget accommodations near downtown Grass Valley. The 13 rooms each have a different, quirky theme; the decor is corporate motor coach meets rustic country inn. Some rooms might resemble a college dorm (like the NASCAR room), while others (the Miner's Cabin room) are adorned with old photographs, antique curios on the walls, and quilted bedspreads. The owners take magnificent care of the Holiday, and despite the somewhat offbeat decor, this hotel is perfectly suited for either a family or couple.

$100-150

Presidents and Gold Rush celebrities alike have stayed at the **Holbrooke Hotel** (212 W. Main St., 530/273-1353, www.holbrooke.com, $119–249) in downtown Grass Valley. One of the oldest hotels in California, the Holbrooke has

© CHRISTOPHER ARNS

The Holbrooke Hotel in downtown Grass Valley has hosted several U.S. presidents.

been delightfully restored to its former grandeur without losing any character. First built in 1862, the hotel has hosted famous 19th-century figures such as U.S. presidents Ulysses S. Grant and Grover Cleveland, writers Mark Twain and Bret Harte, prizefighter James "Gentleman Jim" Corbett, and entertainers Lotta Crabtree and Lola Montez. Expect updated amenities in all 28 rooms, which are fully stocked with modern conveniences like cable TV, free wireless Internet, a coffeemaker, and a hair dryer. Each room has a private bath—something you can't take for granted in older Gold Rush–era buildings. The Holbrooke's Victorian-era decor is what stands out; some rooms have balconies or fireplaces, and most have antique claw-foot tubs. The hotel has central heating and air, although the climate is controlled by the staff and not in each room. Pets are allowed, but the hotel does charge $50 for furry friends.

The **Holiday Inn** (121 Bank St., 530/477-1700, www.hiexpress.com, $140–470) is the most modern place to stay in town. It's also extremely convenient because it's located in downtown Grass Valley. Expect to find modern amenities in the rooms (microwave, minifridge, coffeemaker) and in the lobby (fitness center, business services such as a printer, available PC, and UPS shipping); every room also has free wireless Internet. In the morning, there's a complimentary breakfast buffet with simple fare like scrambled eggs and hash browns; the hotel also offers a free cocktail hour with beer and wine in the afternoon.

Camping

Headed to Bullard's Bar? Check out **Willow Creek Campground and RV Park** (17548 Hwy. 49, 530/288-0646, http://willowcreek-campground.net, $25–125). In addition to five campgrounds, Willow Creek has 13 tent sites, 6 cabins, and roughly 20 RV spots. The location is beautiful, and there's a small creek not far from the campground. Expect a comfortable

stay with showers, laundry, clubhouse, and wireless Internet. Pets are welcome with a $25 refundable deposit and a daily fee.

FOOD
American

Simplicity Bistro (111 W. Main St., 530/205-9365, www.simplicitybistro.net, 11 A.M.–3:30 P.M. and 5–9 P.M. Tues.–Sat., $10–21) is known for hearty comfort food. Dishes include basic American cuisine that leans toward the healthy side such as chicken potpie, naturally raised steak, and vegetable lasagna.

Right in the heart of downtown Grass Valley, **Old Town Café** (110 Mill St., 530/273-4303, 7 A.M.–3 P.M. Mon.–Sat., 7:30 A.M.–2:30 P.M. Sun., $8) is an authentic diner with homespun service. There's been a restaurant at this site since the 1920s, and there's no better place to experience Grass Valley's Norman Rockwell vibe. The café serves breakfast and lunch, along with soda fountain treats like root-beer floats. Most folks go for the pancakes, which are bigger than hubcaps. If you can, grab a stool at the counter for a true diner experience.

Drive-ins aren't dead, at least not in Grass Valley. The **Big A Drive In** (810 E. Main St., 530/273-3243, 8 A.M.–9 P.M. daily, $5–9) is the kind of place where poodle skirts and Elvis would fit right in. A menu filled with classic 1950s-style fast food features cheeseburgers, Philly cheesesteaks, corn dogs, and BLT sandwiches. Probably not something your personal trainer would recommend, but neither are the desserts—sundaes, milk shakes, and banana splits.

Bakery and Café

A local favorite and one of the best coffee shops in town is ◖ **Flour Garden Café and Bakery** (999 Sutton Way, 530/272-2043, www.fourgarden.com, 5 A.M.–7 P.M. Mon.–Sat., 6 A.M.–6 P.M. Sun.). Pastries are baked fresh onsite daily, including scones, croissants, cakes, and pies. Some people forget that Flour Garden serves lunch, but the sandwiches and soups are among the best in town. The coffee is organic and certified free trade. Also check out the location in downtown Grass Valley (109 Neal St.) and the Auburn store (340C Elm Ave.).

Californian

A place that combines hip decor with genuinely healthy food is **South Pine Café** (102 N. Richardson St., 530/274-0261, http://southpine-cafe.com, 8 A.M.–3 P.M. daily, $8–12). The menu combines Southwestern, Asian, and Caribbean influences for breakfast and lunch. A typical entrée might be the Smoldering Pine Burger, topped with bacon, chipotles, grilled onions, mushrooms, Swiss cheese, and chipotle mayonnaise. Locals rave about the potato pancakes topped with pesto for breakfast, but the spicy Mexican chicken scramble is also pretty good.

Chilean

The relaxed vibe at **Diego's Restaurant** (217 Colfax Ave., 530/477-1460, 11 A.M.–9 P.M. daily, $14) will make you feel right at home. This eatery leans heavily to the local crowd, and with an eclectic, funky interior, it's a nice break from touristy joints. The cuisine is Chilean with a Californian flair—which might seem random for a small foothill town, but shouldn't be missed. Try the *panqueque especial,* a tasty mishmash of pineapple, chorizo, cheese sauce, and rice, rolled in a crepe and slathered with tomatillo sauce. The menu has a few vegetarian options beside salads, like the stuffed portobello with tofu and quinoa, but most entrées are meat-heavy.

Cornish

Any trip to Grass Valley would be incomplete without visiting ◖ **Cousin Jack's** (100 S. Auburn St., 530/272-9230, www.historichwy49.com, takeaway 10:30 A.M.–6 P.M. Mon.–Sat., 11 A.M.–5 P.M. Sun., sit-down

11 A.M.–5 P.M. Mon.–Sat., 11 A.M.–4:15 P.M. Sun., $6). Opened in 1989, this adorable café serves up delicious pasties, hearty meat pies filled with piping-hot ingredients. Try the turkey pasty or look for unusual specials; if the café is serving Greek pasties, they're amazingly good. Cousin Jack's is also a savory way to experience Grass Valley history—the pasty was introduced by Cornish mine workers who immigrated to the area during the Gold Rush. You can also order traditional British fare like fish-and-chips and English tea. If you're in a hurry, call ahead and arrange takeaway.

Grass Valley's mouthwatering Cornish roots can also be tasted at **Marshall's Pasties** (203 Mill St., 530/272-2844, 9:30 A.M.–6 P.M. Mon.–Fri., 10 A.M.–6 P.M. Sat., $5). Pasties were first introduced by 19th-century miners from Cornwall who immigrated to Nevada County. On the job, they filled their bellies with these meaty treats and passed down the recipe through the generations. Among the most popular pasties at Marshall's are the ham and cheese and the apple dessert pasty, which is kind of like a strudel. The shop is a tiny hole in the wall so ordering to go is recommended.

Deli

Bear River Pasta (109 Bank St., 530/274-1760, www.bearriverpasta.com, 10 A.M.–9 P.M. Mon.–Sat., 11 A.M.–6 P.M. Sun., $6–13) is Grass Valley's best imitation of a Mediterranean deli. The pastas and sauces are homemade by the friendly staff at this family-owned joint, which has a unique format: Choose your food in the display case and then heat it in a microwave. Somehow it works, and this little café has become a favorite among locals.

Fine Dining

Most diners looking for upscale meals with a side of history go to **The Holbrooke** (212 W. Main St., 530/273-1353, www.holbrooke.com, 11 A.M.–9 P.M. Sun.–Thurs., 11 A.M.–midnight

Fri.–Sat., $15–32). It's located in the ancient Gold Rush hotel of the same name. It's also one of the most convenient places to grab a meal in downtown Grass Valley. Entrées tend toward typical American surf and turf with steaks, roasted chicken, scampi, pasta, and burgers. Try to grab a window table for a view of Main Street.

Italian

Kane's (120 E. Main St., 530/273-8111, www. kanesrestaurant.net, 11 A.M.–9 P.M. Mon.–Thurs., 11 A.M.–9:30 P.M. Fri.–Sun., $8–35) is an old-school joint with some culinary blue blood running through its veins. John Kane is the head chef who learned his trade at the famed University Club of San Francisco. The food is upscale Italian, although there are also traces of Asian influences and California fusion. Call it Italasian if you will, but don't call it cheap; eating here is pricey.

Call **Tofanelli's** (302 W. Main St., 530/272-1468, www.tofanellis.com, 8 A.M.–9 P.M. Sun.–Thurs., 8 A.M.–10 P.M. Fri.–Sat., $10–26) an Italian-inspired restaurant because it refuses to be pigeonholed. They serve lamb shanks, different cuts of beef, seared ahi, meatloaf, and yes, lots of pasta dishes. The claim to fame here is the omelette menu, which features 101 different variations of the eggy dish. Folks like to sit on the patio here where it's a little quieter during busy hours.

INFORMATION AND SERVICES

For maps and a visitor's info packet, stop by the **Grass Valley Visitors Center** (248 Mill St., 530/273-4667, www.grassvalleychamber. com, 9 A.M.–5 P.M. Mon.–Fri.) in the historic Lola Montez House.

For a local take on Grass Valley, read *The Union* (www.theunion.com), the Nevada County daily, or check **Nevada County Gold** (www.ncgold.com) online.

There is a **post office** (8:30 A.M.–5 P.M. Mon.–Fri.) at 185 East Main Street.

The major hospital with an emergency room is **Sierra Nevada Memorial Hospital** (155 Glasson Way, Grass Valley, 530/274-6000, www.snmh.org).

GETTING THERE AND AROUND

Grass Valley lies in a woodsy basin 24 miles north of Auburn and 57 miles northeast of Sacramento. To reach the area by car, take I-80 east to Auburn and follow Highway 49 northwest (it is also called Golden Chain Highway). Grass Valley appears in less than 25 miles, and Nevada City lies four miles farther north. Note that weekend traffic on I-80 between San Francisco and Tahoe can be quite congested and the area can receive heavy snowfall in winter. Check weather, road condition, and traffic reports (www.dot.ca.gov) before heading out.

The local airport is **Nevada County Airport** (13083 John Bauer Ave., Grass Valley, 530/273-3347, www.nevadacountyairport.com). Car rentals are available through **Hertz** (530/272-7730, www.hertz.com) and **Enterprise** (530/274-7400, www.enterprise.com).

The **Gold Country Stage** (http://new.myne-vadacounty.com/transit, adults $1.50, children under 6 free, day pass $4.50) runs buses and minibuses through Nevada City, Grass Valley, down south to Auburn, and up to points north of the Gold Country.

DOWNIEVILLE

One of the West's most fabled destinations for mountain biking and outdoor recreation almost became the capital of California. Back in 1853, several cities were considered for the new state's government seat, and Downieville, an up-and-coming town with 5,000 people, 15 hotels, 6 saloons, and seemingly loads of gold, received just 10 fewer votes than Sacramento. It's actually kind of mind-boggling. Downieville (pop. 282) is about 45 minutes north of Nevada City at the bottom of a steep canyon; picturing this rustic little hamlet as California's capital city just doesn't fit. Instead, imagine spending a weekend exploring miles of the purest single track you'll ever find, just a stone's throw from active mining claims on the North Fork of the Yuba River. Rafting is also popular on the North Fork in both late spring and early summer. An evening spent here, listening to the Yuba and Downie Rivers rush through town and watching stars wink into the clearest cobalt sky, is tough to beat. Downieville is technically in Sierra County and certainly seems miles away from civilization, but it makes an easy day trip from Nevada City and Grass Valley.

Downieville Museum

Nothing is very large in Downieville and neither is the Downieville Museum (330 Main St., 530/289-3423, 11 A.M.–4 P.M. daily, Memorial Day–Labor Day, free), but it gives a comprehensive look at the town's important place in the region's mining history. The museum was originally a store built by Chinese immigrants in 1852. Exhibits include a scaled replica of Downieville from 1900, snowshoes for horses, a collection of pioneer portraits, and photos showing old Downieville during the boom years. Time passes a little differently in this small burg, so call ahead to make sure the museum is open.

Entertainment and Events

There's not a whole lot to do in Downieville. The nightlife revolves around a saloon and a few restaurants. But in summer, everything stops for the **Downieville Classic** (http://downievilleclassic.com, summer), a renowned festival and mountain bike race that draws some of the world's most accomplished riders to this Gold Country village for six days. There's a bike expo and street fair in Downieville's old streets, live music at night, a log pulling competition, and different stunts involving ramps, a bike, and the Yuba River. But the most fun comes from volunteering as a race marshal or a shuttle driver; volunteers get free food, free camping, and a T-shirt, plus the unbeatable camaraderie that comes from patrolling near anarchy for half a week. That said, the real action is the racing; nine classes of riders, both men and women, slash their way down brutal single track in pursuit of the All-Mountain Championship, a two-stage rally combining the Downieville Downhill trail and a cross-country challenge.

St. Charles Place (203 Main St., 530/289-3237, www.stcharlesplace.com, 11 A.M.–2 A.M. daily) has a checkered past. Situated in the old Craycroft building, the location was a courthouse and jail during the Gold Rush and Downieville's first district attorney was shot outside the building by a 19th-century lynch mob. That kind of history hangs heavily in the air once you're inside the St. Charles. The saloon looks much the same as it did 150 years ago: worn plank floors, a glass mountain of liquor bottles on the back bar, a pool table, and mounted hunting trophies on the wall. It has the town's only full bar and really the only regular entertainment, holding weekly poker and pool tournaments.

Sports and Recreation
◖ MOUNTAIN BIKING

Summer weekends are busy in Downieville, and that's because fat tire fanatics flock to the miles of plunging single track that loop through these hills. Some claim that Downieville is second only to Utah's Moab Desert as a hot spot for mountain biking. The scenery, the elevation drops, and the granite-filled gullies definitely combine for one heck of an adrenaline rush. What makes Downieville so special—other than technical trails that cling to rocky cliffs above the river—is the infrastructure developed by locals that includes a shuttle system and a spaghetti bowl of ever-expanding routes. Trails are maintained but hard; riders often gear up like medieval knights with motorbike helmets, elbow guards, and shin protectors. The most famous trail is the **Downieville Downhill** (14–17 miles, moderate to challenging), which begins within sight of the snowcapped Sierra Buttes and eventually drops almost 5,000 feet before ending back in town. Frankly, this might be the most underrated outdoor experience in Northern Gold Country. Locals have added new trails in the past several years, including the spanking new **North Yuba River Trail** (15 miles one way, moderate to challenging), which eventually will stretch all the way to Bullard's Bar Reservoir.

Mountain bikers will need a shuttle to access the Downieville Downhill trail that begins near the Sierra Buttes. Outfitters strap bikes to vans and ferry riders almost every hour on summer weekends, less frequently during the week. The service shuts down after October when the weather starts getting too cold and reopens around Memorial Day. Both **Yuba Expeditions** (208 Main St., 530/289-3010, www.yubaexpeditions.com, 8 A.M.–5 P.M., daily Memorial Day–Labor Day; Mon.–Thurs. spring and fall, closed in winter) and **Downieville Outfitters** (114 Main St., 530/289-0155, www.downievilleoutfitters. com, 9 A.M.–5 P.M. Mon.–Thurs., 8 A.M.–6 P.M. Fri.–Sun. May 15–Oct. 31) run shuttles for $20 to the trailhead, a trip that takes about 25 minutes. Both outfitters offer bike tune-ups and service; Downieville Outfitters also rents Specialized bikes for $60 per day.

RAFTING

The North Fork of the Yuba River is one of the most challenging runs in the Northern Gold Country. It's not for the weak-kneed, that's for sure. Rapids on this stretch of the Yuba are Class III–V and shouldn't be attempted without prior rafting experience. Guided trips only run between April and June when the water is cold and unforgiving. Locals like to joke about updating your will before heading onto the river; at least, I think they're joking.

Tributary Whitewater Tours (800/672-3846, www.whitewatertours.com, Apr.–July, full day $128–158, two days $275–304, three days $388–418) has been guiding rafting trips into local white water since 1978. Rafters with Class V experience can sign up for the **Wild Plum Run** (Class V+, eight miles) through Ladies Canyon, a death-defying stretch of river and the toughest run on the North Yuba. Tributary offers five thrilling options for attacking Downieville's white water.

Whitewater Voyages (800/400-7238, www. whitewatervoyages.com, May–July, full day $160–170 adults, $145–154 youth, $128–136 groups) has two different rafting trips down the North Fork of the Yuba, including a plunge through Big Dummy rapids. Only strong swimmers and experienced rafters are allowed on these trips.

Accommodations

Riverside Inn (206 Commercial St., 888/883-5100, www.downieville.us, $90–180) is a homey lodge with a long veranda overlooking the river. Eleven rooms are outfitted with modern amenities; some features include cable TV, a fireplace, microwave, fridge, and futon. Pets are allowed if you pay a $10 fee. In the morning, wake up to a continental breakfast before heading off for some mountain biking or fishing.

Riding mountains all day can be tiring, but your aching legs won't walk far to **Carriage House Inn** (110 Commercial St., 530/289-3573, www.downievillecarriagehouse.com, $90–175). The country-style lodgings include eight rooms with quilts, wrought-iron bed frames, and ceiling fans. Wood-paneled walls make the place feel rustic, but each room has modern stuff like a microwave, fridge, and TV.

Make sure to ask for a private bath; otherwise you'll be hiking down the hallway to shower.

Staying at the **Downieville River Inn and Resort** (121 River St., 530/289-3308, www.downievilleriverinn.com, $90–225) resembles a summer camp for adults. Dive in the resort's swimming pool, get sweaty in the sauna, and grill some grub at the picnic area. Suites have fully equipped kitchens and private decks; smaller rooms have standard amenities like a microwave and fridge. It's comfortable if a little outdated, unless brown shag carpeting is coming back soon; just pretend you're at Grandma's house.

During the earliest days of the Gold Rush, prospectors built pinewood shanties near their claims on the river. **The Lure Resort** (100 Lure Bridge Ln., 530/289-3465, www.lureresort.com, $165–260) is an updated throwback to those good ol' days. Nine log cabins are strung out along 14 acres of prime North Yuba riverfront. Some cabins have a microwave, toaster, and coffeemaker, but others are more spartan. Bring a fishing rod and cast a line in the water, which rushes by within sight of the cabins. Pets are welcome.

Die-hard mountain bikers will love the **Downieville Loft** (208 Main St., 510/501-2516, http://downievilleloft.com, $185–325). It's right above Yuba Expeditions, so it's easy to roll out of bed and jump on the shuttle. And it gets better: rafting trips also put in the North Yuba behind the loft and there's a swimming hole nearby. This isn't a bed-and-breakfast or an inn; it's a modified guesthouse that can accommodate up to eight people. But the location is unbeatable and the amenities are also pretty sweet; three queen beds, a fully stocked kitchen, artisan furnishings made from recycled wood, two fireplaces, and a giant basement with a Ping-Pong table and dartboard, plus storage for bikes or rafts. Finally, the downstairs is called the "Yuba Lounge," a meeting place for bikers to converge after riding the trails; there's a big-screen TV with a library of 200 DVDs, pool table, foosball, and inner tubes for the river.

Let's be honest—Downieville is deep in the mountains and far from civilization. The cottages at **Sierra Shangri-La** (12 Jim Crow Canyon Creek Rd., 530/289-3455, www.sierrashangrila.com, $115–260) make guests feel more at home. This place feels just like a fly-fishing or hunting lodge. Ten homespun cottages have newly buffed wooden floors and walls, woodstoves or stone fireplaces, and a view of the river. Kitchens are fully stocked with modern appliances along with a coffeemaker, and there's a barbecue on each cottage deck. There is a two-night minimum stay on weekends, and no pets are allowed.

Sierra Streamside Cabins (21792 Hwy. 49, 530/289-3379, www.sierrastreamsidecabins.com, $110–300) are right on the gin-clear North Yuba. The five cabins are within walking distance (over a cable suspension bridge) of RV spaces and a duplex for larger parties.

Hard-core campers will enjoy roughing it at **Union Flat Campground** (five miles northeast of Downieville on Highway 49, 530/862-1368, www.recreation.gov, end of Apr.–end of Oct., $21) in the Tahoe National Forest, where 11 rustic sites open up to pristine views of the river canyon and a woodsy canopy of maple, oak, pine, and cedar trees. This place isn't for city dwellers with shower anxiety; there are vault toilets, picnic tables, water, and fire pits, and that's it. Bring inner tubes or kayaks to enjoy the river, which is right next to the campground. Make sure to watch for bears and keep food in approved containers.

Ramshorn Campground (five miles southwest of Downieville on Highway 49, 530/862-1368, www.recreation.gov, end of Apr.–end of Oct., $21) is another camping spot that's deep in the Tahoe National Forest with few modern amenities. It's definitely deep; staying at these bare-bones campsites gets visitors closer to nature. No showers, just vault toilets and drinking water are provided. Don't focus on the minimal conveniences; instead, enjoy picking blackberries underneath soaring fir and cedar trees, or swimming in the nearby river. Take a hike on the Halls Ranch Trail (5.8 miles, easy/moderate), part of a spider's web of walking tracks close to the campground. Again, watch for bears and secure anything that smells like food.

Food

Yes, they have Mexican food way out in the sticks. **La Cocina De Oro** (322 Main St., 530/289-3584, 11 A.M.–8:30 P.M. Thurs.–Sat., 11 A.M.–5 P.M. Sun., $5–13) serves genuine food from south of the border, like tacos, burritos, and tostadas. The restaurant doesn't have a liquor license for margaritas, which is too bad, but they do have a pretty chill patio in the back that overlooks the river.

You'll get a friendly Downieville welcome at **Two Rivers Café** (116 Main St., 530/289-3540, 11:30 A.M.–8 P.M. Wed.–Mon., 11:30 A.M.–3 P.M. Tues., $9–20). Eating here is like having a summer cookout. You can chow down on burgers, sandwiches, and pizzas. On weekends, there's a kick-ass breakfast buffet that's popular; make sure to try the tasty eggs Benedict.

Expect good, hearty food at **The Grubstake Saloon** (315 Main St., 530/289-0289, 4–9 P.M. Mon.–Tues. and Thurs.–Fri., 11 A.M.–3 P.M. and 4–9 P.M. Sat.–Sun., $7–32). Like a chuck wagon with four walls, this restaurant exudes a pioneer spirit; maybe it's the sepia-toned photos depicting old Downieville. Maybe it's the mounted deer above your table; whatever it is, the Grubstake is one of a kind. Meals are made from scratch and mostly with local, all-natural ingredients. The food is typical American barbecue fare: burgers, sandwiches, pasta, and steak. If you're really adventurous, try the liver and onions; I think it's the best thing on the menu.

Coyoteville Cafe (15921 Hwy. 49,

530/289-1820, 7 A.M.–1 P.M. daily, $10–15) dishes up sizzling breakfast plates year-round. It's a great place for a beer on a hot day or after a long bike ride; in the morning, the flapjacks come highly recommended.

Information and Services

Downieville is considered "the sticks" for people in Sacramento because the town lacks basic modern stores and amenities like banks or supermarkets. Visitors should stock up on groceries in Nevada City or Grass Valley before trekking out here. You can find gas pumps at **Unocal 76** (114 Main St., 530/289-3431), and there's also a **post office** (301 Main St., 8 A.M.–4 P.M. Mon.–Fri.).

The Mountain Messenger is one of California's oldest weekly newspapers. It's so old apparently it doesn't have a website, but it does print every Thursday.

There's no visitors bureau in Downieville but the **Sierra County Chamber of Commerce** (http://sierracountychamber.com) has a fairly informative website with long list of recreation tips.

Getting There and Around

Downieville is about an hour northeast of Nevada City. To get there, take Highway 49 to where it splits with Highway 20. Turn west on Highway 49 and keep going until Downieville appears through the trees.

Visitors will need a car to get here. There's no public transportation from Nevada City, although you could rent a car in Grass Valley to drive here. During the winter, Downieville does receive about 40 inches of snow per year so prepare for colder weather and bring chains during winter storms. Check Caltrans (www.dot.ca.gov) for updated traffic info.

WASHINGTON

The hard-boiled little village of Washington (pop. 185) is remote, rustic, and seems stuck in some kind of time warp. In other words, it's a blast. Crouched in a thickly forested river canyon, it's a great place to escape big-city life and modern hassles. Two campsites are situated nearby, and anglers can cast their lines in the Yuba River's shallow riffles. Hiking is also becoming more popular; there's a long hike that winds along the bracingly cool waters of the Yuba's South Fork, all the way back to Nevada City. The Gold Rush doesn't seem so distant in Washington, and on lazy summer afternoons, time seems to slow down to a crawl.

Accommodations

Don't expect a wide variety of lodgings in Washington's tiny business district. Folks come here for camping or the old-timey Washington Hotel, not for luxurious bed-and-breakfasts.

Everything in town revolves around the ancient **Washington Hotel** (15432 Washington Rd., 530/265-4364, www.washingtonhotel. net, $65–180). A Dutch immigrant built the place in the late 1850s when Washington's vibrant mining industry was serviced by several stagecoach lines. It's been rebuilt twice, both times after fires roared through the building in the late 19th century. The current structure dates back to 1896. The hotel's 15 rooms are small and simple; most have wrought-iron or wooden headboards squeezed between a dresser and narrow walls, and all but two rooms have shared baths. After leaving your room, hop down the steps out back to the Yuba River which runs behind the hotel.

River Rest Resort (152 Washington Rd., 530/265-4306, www.riverrestresort.com, $30–45) has camping right on the South Yuba's banks. This place has everything; horseshoe pits, tether ball for kids, a dance pad, showers, picnic tables, and barbecue grills. Call ahead; the campground has 107 tent sites but gets popular during the summer.

White Cloud Campground (11 miles east of Nevada City and 8 miles south of Washington off Highway 20, 530/478-0248, www.recreation.gov, May–Sept., $21) is a pretty destination between Washington and Nevada City in the Tahoe National Forest. The 46 sites are raked spotlessly clean; no modern amenities, just vault toilets, water, and picnic tables. The trailhead for the **Pioneer Trail** (10 miles, moderate) begins from the campground's parking lot. From here, it's easy to explore Nevada City, Malakoff Diggins, Scotts Flat Reservoir, or Washington.

Food

Looking for grub in Washington? About the only place to eat is the café at the **Washington Hotel** (15432 Washington Rd., 530/265-1990, www.washingtonhotel.net, 8:30 A.M.–9 P.M. Thurs.–Mon., $10–25; saloon 11 A.M.–10 P.M. Sun.–Thurs., 11 A.M.–2 A.M. Fri.–Sat.). Inside, the walls (and white paneled ceiling) are covered in logging and mining tools. The food is decent, mostly grill food like burgers and steaks, and you can get a meal any time of day.

Information and Services

Washington is another burg that's escaped the clutches of modern civilization. Forget about grocery stores, banks, or gas stations; make sure to stock up on everything before heading out here. Visitors who need to mail a letter will find a **post office** at 15274 Washington Road (8 A.M.–4 P.M. Mon.–Fri. and 11:30 A.M.–1:30 P.M. Sat.).

Getting There and Around

The turnoff for Washington is roughly 13 miles northeast of Nevada City on Highway 20. At Washington Road, turn north and drive 5.6 miles to reach the town. Public transportation doesn't travel here, so visitors will need a car. During the winter, check with Caltrans (www.dot.ca.gov) to see if the road is open or if drivers need chains for their vehicles.

Auburn

Visitors won't find a better place in the Gold Country for going really fast down steep hills. Placer County's topography drastically changes between Roseville, which is located at 164 feet elevation in the Sacramento Valley, to the summit of Mt. Baldy at 9,000 feet overlooking Lake Tahoe. There's so much to see and do here, from mountain biking, hiking, and swimming to rafting and horseback riding. Outdoor enthusiasts often talk about Placer County like wine lovers extol the virtues of their favorite vintage. One thing is definitely for sure: With such a smattering of activities, visitors won't get bored here.

SIGHTS
Old Town

There are traces of Tinseltown in Old Town Auburn, where visitors might recognize scenery from the 1996 film *Phenomenon*. The town goes back even further to the early days of the Gold Rush when the precious metal was discovered in a nearby ravine. In Auburn, you'll also find the usual mix of dive bars, quirky cafés, and scattered antiques shops common to most Gold Country villages; the close proximity to busy I-80 takes away some ambience unless you're a big fan of freeway noise. Foodies, on the other hand, will love the fine dining in Old Town, which ranks among the best in the Northern Gold Country. History-wise, there are two obvious attractions in Old Town: The state's oldest continuously operating **post office** is a must-see, and the town's first firehouse, complete with Model A fire truck, is also fun to check out.

Downtown

Yes, Downtown is different than Old Town; the dueling town centers are actually about a half-mile away from each other. Where Old Town feels provincial and ancient with 150-year-old brick buildings, Downtown has a *Happy Days* vibe with barber shops, a vintage soda fountain, and weekly **Cruise Nites,** when locals show off their hot rods and restored classic cars every Thursday during the summer. If you only had time for one part of Auburn, I'd recommend Old Town for the history, but Downtown has several worthy boutiques and galleries if you can swing an extra hour or two.

Bernhard Museum

It's easy to miss the Bernhard Museum (291 Auburn-Folsom Rd., 530/889-6500, www. placer.ca.gov, 11 A.M.–4 P.M. Tues.–Sun., free). The complex sits on a busy highway between a baseball field and the Gold Country Fairgrounds. That's too bad; home to one of Placer County's oldest buildings, this former guesthouse and traveler's inn has been renovated extensively over the past decade and now sparkles with Gold Country charm. There are several fun facts to learn about this museum, including its historic place in local viticulture; one of the first owners started a winery here in 1874, and visitors can check out old winemaking artifacts inside an ancient stone processing plant. Inside the museum's gleaming white Victorian house, rooms have been lovingly restored to resemble a 19th-century family home, complete with handmade linens and furniture. During the school year, prepare for an invasion of elementary students dressed like tiny pioneers; the museum is part of Placer County's Living History program that hosts field trips from local elementary schools.

Placer County Museum

Located on the first floor of the historic Placer County courthouse, the Placer County

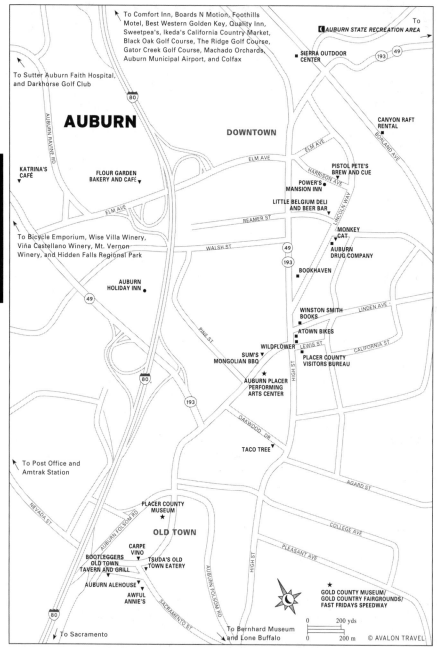

To Comfort Inn, Boards N Motion, Foothills Motel, Best Western Golden Key, Quality Inn, Sweetpea's, Ikeda's California Country Market, Black Oak Golf Course, The Ridge Golf Course, Gator Creek Golf Course, Machado Orchards, Auburn Municipal Airport, and Colfax

To AUBURN STATE RECREATION AREA

To Sutter Auburn Faith Hospital, and Darkhorse Golf Club

SIERRA OUTDOOR CENTER

193 49

80

AUBURN

DOWNTOWN

CANYON RAFT RENTAL

KATRINA'S CAFÉ

FLOUR GARDEN BAKERY AND CAFÉ

ELM AVE

ELM AVE

BORLAND AVE

PISTOL PETE'S BREW AND CUE

HARRISON AVE

POWER'S MANSION INN

LITTLE BELGIUM DELI AND BEER BAR

ELM AVE

REAMER ST

To Bicycle Emporium, Wise Villa Winery, Viña Castellano Winery, Mt. Vernon Winery, and Hidden Falls Regional Park

WALSH ST

LINCOLN WAY

MONKEY CAT

AUBURN DRUG COMPANY

49
193

BOOKHAVEN

AUBURN HOLIDAY INN

49

WINSTON SMITH BOOKS

LINDEN AVE

PINE ST

ATOWN BIKES

LEWIS ST

CALIFORNIA ST

WILDFLOWER

80

SUM'S MONGOLIAN BBQ

HIGH ST

PLACER COUNTY VISITORS BUREAU

193

AUBURN PLACER PERFORMING ARTS CENTER

OAKWOOD DR

TACO TREE

To Post Office and Amtrak Station

AGARD ST

NEVADA ST

PLACER COUNTY MUSEUM

COLLEGE AVE

AUBURN FOLSOM RD

OLD TOWN

PLEASANT AVE

CARPE VINO

BOOTLEGGERS OLD TOWN TAVERN AND GRILL

TSUDA'S OLD TOWN EATERY

AUBURN FOLSOM RD

HIGH ST

AUBURN ALEHOUSE

AWFUL ANNIE'S

GOLD COUNTRY MUSEUM/ GOLD COUNTRY FAIRGROUNDS/ FAST FRIDAYS SPEEDWAY

80

SACRAMENTO ST

To Sacramento

To Bernhard Museum and Lone Buffalo

0   200 yds

0   200 m   © AVALON TRAVEL

Old Town Auburn

Museum (101 Maple St., 530/889-6500, www.placer.ca.gov, 10 A.M.–4 P.M. daily, free) offers a glimpse into the town's rustic past. While small, the museum is a worthwhile stop before heading higher into the Gold Country to visit other historical sites. The exhibits span different themes and time periods in Placer County history, like the women's jail, the re-created sheriff's office, and the stagecoach that ran from Auburn up into the mountains. There's also a video on the history of I-80, the transcontinental highway running through Auburn, plus different art pieces depicting the native Maidu and Miwok tribes that lived in the Auburn area for thousands of years before pioneers arrived. Outside the museum, views from the courthouse are picture-worthy, and it's just a short walk to restaurants and bars in Auburn's Old Town. The museum is closed on holidays so call ahead to make sure it's open.

Gold Country Museum

Rich in Gold Rush history, Auburn was one of California's first mining settlements built after the precious metal was discovered in 1848. Learn more about that history at the Gold Country Museum (1273 High St., 530/889-6500, www.placer.ca.gov, 11 A.M.–4 P.M. Tues.–Sun., free). Many of the standard Gold Country exhibits are on display, including a reconstructed mine, a stamp mill, and a mining camp saloon. Kids can pan for gold in the museum's indoor stream, although it costs $3. You might be underwhelmed by the displays here after visiting some of the region's larger historic sites, but the docents are knowledgeable and attentive to anyone excited to learn about Auburn's place in Gold Rush lore. Note that finding the museum can be challenging; it's tucked near the back of the Gold Country Fairgrounds in a one-story building. You should also call ahead if it's a holiday to see if the museum is open.

AMAZON WARRIORS OF AUBURN

© CHRISTOPHER ARNS

Get ready for possibly the most inexplicable sight in the Northern Gold Country: giant statues of Amazon warriors. Located in Auburn, these statues are at least two- or three-stories tall and loom over Auburn Ravine Road between I-80 and Highway 49.

A local dentist and bohemian sculptor named Kenneth Fox placed them outside his office in the late 1960s, along with two smaller statues of Prometheus and a nude woman in prayer (supposedly modeled after one of his employees). But the Amazons always get the most attention. One is shown brandishing a spear at some imaginary foe, while the other scowls and aims her bow and arrow.

Half nude and wearing only flimsy loincloths, these behemoths forced the town prudes to reroute school buses for years while locals wailed and gnashed their teeth over the "obscene" sculptures. "Make them wear some clothes!" they implored, but Fox refused and eventually locals got used to them. They still stand there today and probably will for decades as Fox had them commissioned in concrete.

WINERIES

I know, I know—you're probably tired of hearing about the next Napa Valley hidden somewhere in the Gold Country. Don't worry; Auburn's wineries aren't in the same class. That's actually a very good thing; it keeps away the wine snobs and encourages travelers to bond with winemakers who staff their own tasting rooms. On the **Placer County Wine Trail** (www.placerwine.com) and nestled among shady oak woodlands, you'll find small, family-owned wineries that feel more like boutiques than grandiose estates. And the wine? Well, it's actually quite good. Pack a picnic and plan on spending an easygoing afternoon in Auburn's endearing little wine country.

Lone Buffalo

You've probably heard of wine bars—but how about a "sensory" bar? Before sampling the reds and whites at Lone Buffalo Vineyards (7505 Wise Rd., 530/663-4486, www.lonebuffalovineyards.com, noon–5 P.M. Fri.–Sun., tasting free), tasters can first sniff a row of glasses, each containing an object with distinct aromas found in wine. That means you could be sniffing a glass with a cigar butt or an herb; that might sound weird, but it actually helps you develop a keener palate for wine-tasting. Once you're finished with the sensory bar, try Lone Buffalo's estate-grown reds, including the fruit-forward zinfandel and the rustic petite syrah.

© CHRISTOPHER ARNS

The Placer County Museum is located on the first floor of the Placer County courthouse.

Mt. Vernon Winery

If you really, absolutely, must have a typical big-estate experience in Placer County, Mt. Vernon Winery (10850 Mt. Vernon Rd., 530/823-1111, http://mtvernonwinery.com, 11 A.M.–5 P.M. Thurs.–Sun., tasting $6) is the closest thing you'll find. It's the largest (and usually most crowded on weekends) winery near Auburn, but it's also homegrown; winemaker Ryan Taylor went to a local high school before helping his parents start Mt. Vernon. The best wines here are bold reds like the full-bodied zinfandel and cabernet sauvignon, although the winery has also started producing a viognier-roussanne blend that's starting to earn some buzz.

Viña Castellano Winery

Some of the Gold Country's best Spanish-style wines are produced at Viña Castellano Vineyard and Winery (4590 Bell Rd., 530/889-2855, http://vinacastellano.ewinerysolutions.

com, noon–5 P.M. Thurs.–Sun., tasting $3). I recommend heading straight for the spicy but smooth tempranillo, easily the flagship wine here (and a gold medal winner); the subtle but savory mourvèdre is also a treat and makes a mouthwatering pairing with steak. Make sure to call ahead for the tapas, although you can always bring a picnic, grab a bottle, and spread out by the tranquil pond behind the winery.

Wise Villa Winery

Wise Villa Winery (4100 Wise Rd., Lincoln, 530/543-0323, www.wisevillawinery.com, 11 A.M.–5 P.M. Thurs.–Sun., tasting $5) is one estate in Placer County that oozes Napa Valley chic. From the sprawling Mediterranean-style villa that overlooks the Sacramento Valley to the gourmet finger food served in the tasting room, there's definitely an upscale, we're-trying-to-be-the-best vibe here. But you won't get that attitude from the friendly staff. The wine itself lives up to all the hype; award-winning reds like the cabernet sauvignon (notes include vanilla, mulberry, spice, and tea) are among the best in the Sierra Nevada Foothill appellation. If you love dessert wines, make sure to try the sultry Eclipse port, which has delicious hints of blackberries, chocolate, and cola.

ENTERTAINMENT AND EVENTS

Nightlife in Auburn is still rough around the edges; the dives have plenty of attitude, while the cocktail lounges are full of old codgers who like to talk trash. If you like chatty bartenders, this probably isn't your scene. On the other hand, if you're looking for a game of pool, darts, or shuffleboard, Auburn's bars will keep you entertained all evening long. But if the bar scene isn't your thing, there's usually a family-themed event happening at the Gold Country Fairgrounds (www.goldcountryfair.com).

Nightlife

The best place in Auburn for live music is **Pistol Pete's Brew and Cue** (140 Harrison Ave., 530/885-5093, 11 A.M.–2 P.M. daily), where you can catch blues acts and cover bands playing mostly old-school classic rock. Pete's is a sizable joint with five pool tables and an outdoor patio, so it's a great place to take groups. Make sure to come thirsty for the 24 beers on tap, which include several Placer County brews.

Club Car (836 Lincoln Way, 530/887-9732, www.clubcarauburn.com, 11 A.M.–midnight Sun.–Tues., 11 A.M.–1 A.M. Wed.–Thurs., 11 A.M.–2 A.M. Fri.–Sat.) also offers live tunes, although the talent is hit-and-miss. I think they'll let anybody on the tiny stage here, meaning there's an entirely different level of entertainment available if you have an open mind. Honestly, the food is the best thing about Club Car, and I recommend the burgers, which are actually pretty darn good: juicy and served with mouthwatering fixings.

A great place to watch a game is the **Auburn Alehouse** (289 Washington St., 530/885-2537, http://auburnalehouse.com, 11 A.M.–10 P.M. Mon.–Tues., 11 A.M.–11 P.M. Wed.–Thurs., 11 A.M.–midnight Fri., 9 A.M.–midnight Sat., 9 A.M.–10 P.M. Sun.). They have racks of big-screen TVs and pitchers of Alehouse microbrew. During the summer, blues and rock bands often play outside on the patio overlooking Old Town.

Who doesn't love a little mud in their beer? At **Fast Fridays Speedway** (1273 High St., 530/878-7223, www.fastfridays.com, 8 P.M. Fri. May–Oct., adults $12, children and seniors $10), nothing says TGIF like the sound of 500cc motorcycle engines tearing around a dirt racetrack on a summer's eve. This is definitely the loudest, dirtiest spectator sport in the Gold Country—and possibly the most fun you can have on Friday nights in Auburn. During the race, riders can reach speeds of up to 70 mph using dirt bikes tricked out with just one gear and no brakes; the result often leads to spectacular wipeouts on the treacherous dirt speedway. If you feel like staying clean and avoiding the riders' dust, just don't sit by the track; you'll be fine higher up in the grandstand seats.

The Arts

Brilliantly restored, the **Auburn Placer Performing Arts Center** (985 Lincoln Way, 530/885-0156, www.livefromauburn.com, tickets $5–25) brings a dash of Hollywood glamour to the foothills. The center offers concerts, community theater productions, and you can watch classic flicks like *Dirty Harry* or catch more recent films like the *Shawshank Redemption*. Located in the historic State Theatre, the building first opened in 1930 and the renovated marquee conjures up memories of glitzy movie premieres from a bygone era. On stage, the center hosts a bevy of musical and dramatic events, from country music crooners

© CHRISTOPHER ARNS

The Auburn Placer Performing Arts Center is located in the historic State Theatre.

to Shakespeare. Have kids with you? There are even family-friendly improv performances that will keep you cracking up all evening. The performance hall currently has 130 seats, so order tickets online if you're worried about missing a show.

Festivals and Events

Every September, Auburn puts on a show during the **Gold Country Fair** (1273 High St., 530/823-4533, www.goldcountryfair. com, first week of Sept., adults and youth $10, seniors $8, children free). Just like any small-town carnival, you'll find all the usual midway games, with stomach-churning rides like the Gravitron and the Zipper. But I always head straight for the local exhibits to see who won blue ribbons among the craft and baking entries in Placer Hall. Auburn's agricultural roots are also on full display during the fair, as local FFA chapters and 4-H clubs show off their horses, heifers, and prize hogs

in the Junior Livestock Auction. Usually the fair books plenty of local musical talent; expect entertainment from the likes of Beatles tribute bands, bluegrass groups, country acts, and seemingly endless classic rock cover bands. If you're around on the fair's last day, the event ends with a bang with the annual demolition derby; it's an open competition, so feel free to enter if there's an old clunker rusting in your driveway at home.

Think you can jog 100 miles? How about on horseback? Billing itself as the "Endurance Capital of the World," Auburn hosts two prestigious and grueling races each year. Every June, at the ultramarathon known as the **Western States Endurance Run** (http://ws100.com, last full weekend in June), participants slog a full century from Lake Tahoe to Auburn's Placer High School while braving ice-cold rivers, fierce mountain lions, and 40,000 feet in elevation changes—all in one day. Just reading about the grueling event could make a person tired. If you're into running really, really far distances, the event—also known as the Western States 100—is one of the most famous races in the world. Hard-core athletes can finish the course in 16 or 17 hours; most entrants shoot for a goal of 24. The Western States isn't even the oldest endurance competition in Auburn; that title belongs to the **Tevis Cup** (www.teviscup.org, midsummer), a legendary equestrian trail ride through the Sierra Nevada. The trail follows much the same route as the Western States ultramarathon, meaning participants pass through treacherous wilderness and terrain. Riders earn a coveted silver belt buckle if they finish the grueling course within 24 hours. The race usually takes place in late July or early August, starting near Truckee and finishing at the Gold Country Fairgrounds in Auburn. If it sounds easy because the horse does all the work, imagine being saddle-bound for a full day; yeah, this race is legit.

SHOPPING

Most seasoned travelers would say Auburn's shopping districts lack the charm of fellow Gold Rush cities like Grass Valley and Nevada City, and they're probably right—but that doesn't mean you should avoid stopping here. The shopping scene in Auburn is split between Downtown and Old Town, and both locations are bristling with boutique gift shops, art galleries, and merchants selling wares from local artisans. If you're headed into the foothills' rugged outdoors for some hiking or mountain biking, skip the historic town center; most of the gear suppliers are spread throughout "greater" Auburn on Highway 49 or I-80.

You'll expect the Fonz to show up at the **Auburn Drug Company** (815 Lincoln Way, 530/885-6524, 9 A.M.–6 P.M. Mon.–Fri., 9 A.M.–5 P.M. Sat.), a charming soda fountain, gift shop, and working pharmacy that's been around since 1896. The first thing that

Kids have been enjoying ice cream at the Auburn Drug Company since 1896.

hits you is the smell—the aroma of creamy ice cream and buttery popcorn waiting to be eaten. Having treats here is a trip down nostalgia lane; grab one of the worn wooden stools and order an old-fashioned Irish soda or a chocolate sundae at the vintage marble bar. In case you're shopping for gifts, the store has lately branched into selling upscale mementos like kitchen knickknacks, candles, handbags, and beautiful throw blankets hanging from the walls.

If you're in a pinch and need a last-minute baby shower gift or wedding present, **Wildflower** (809 Lincoln Way, 530/823-8220, 10 A.M.–6 P.M. Mon.–Fri., 10 A.M.–5 P.M. Sat., noon–4 P.M. Sun.) is procrastinator's dream. This place is stocked with tasteful, upscale items like artisan stationery, jewelry, candles, and body care products produced by vendors based in the United States.

If you need a used book for your travels, aim the car for **Winston Smith Books** (933 Lincoln Way, 530/823-5940, www.winstonsmithbooks. com, 10 A.M.–5 P.M. Mon.–Sat., noon–5 P.M. Sun.). This independent bookstore with a light, airy layout has plenty of tall stacks jam-packed with pulp paperbacks, romance novels, literary classics, and rare tomes for collectors. There's more than 3,000 square feet of well-organized space, making this shop a fun and leisurely spot for some quiet browsing. Winston Smith will even take trades and buy those dusty volumes you've been storing at home.

On the other hand, if you're looking for the latest bestseller, head to **Bookhaven** (884 Lincoln Way, 530/888-0229, 10 A.M.–5 P.M. Mon.–Sat.). More like a cozy nook than a bookstore, you can certainly waste a lazy afternoon scanning the hundreds of titles. Make sure to check out the clearance boxes near the front door; there's usually a fair assortment of used paperbacks and dime-store thrillers on sale for just a few bucks.

Instead of wasting hours in line to rent gear on the slopes, pick up your snowboard rentals at **Boards N Motion** (13417 Lincoln Way, 530/888-7873, www.boardsnmotion.com, 10 A.M.–7 P.M. Mon.–Sat., 11 A.M.–6 P.M. Sun.). Board rentals are about $10 cheaper than equipment you could find on the mountain, and the Auburn shop takes better care of their stuff. Think you're a top-notch boarder? The shop will let you demo new boards by top brands like Burton, Forum, and K2; with a credit card deposit, you can try them out for a day. Besides snowboards, this place also stocks a kick-ass supply of wakeboards. If you're just looking for new swag, like shirts, hoodies, caps, or a new parka, Boards is the go-to place in the foothills.

SPORTS AND RECREATION
◖ Auburn State Recreation Area

Tucked inside the stunning American River canyon, the Auburn State Recreation Area (www.parks.ca.gov, day-use 7 A.M.–sunset) should be a priority for outdoorsy types. More than 100 miles of trails wind through leafy oak woodlands, California poppies in springtime, and past seasonal waterfalls like Codfish Falls for use by hikers, joggers, mountain bikers, dirt-bikers, and horseback riders. Start at the confluence of the river's North and Middle Forks where it's easier to park and also where most of the trails begin. This area is also arguably one of the best places for water sports in the area; rafting, kayaking, and boating are all available along various stretches of the river. In summer, pack a swimsuit and enjoy the cooling waters of the river confluence, which has plenty of swimming holes and jumping rocks. Keep your eyes peeled for wildlife; white-tailed deer, bald eagles, river otters, black bears, and even the occasional mountain lion roam the park.

History buffs will also enjoy discovering Gold Rush history here, like the ancient railroad bridge spanning the lower Middle Fork. Farther upriver at **Upper Lake Clementine** (Apr. 15–Oct. 15), look for a jagged rock

© CHRISTOPHER ARNS

The American River flows through the Auburn State Recreation Area.

formation named Robbers Roost—local outlaws once used it for a hideout. The lake widens farther south to allow motorboats and small fishing craft to troll the water. If you're on a mountain bike, the **Lower Clementine Trail** (10.5 miles, moderate) is an exhilarating way to check out the canyon's scenery. Part of the trail plunges down an old stagecoach road, providing unrivaled views of the canyon.

Clark's Hole Trail (0.2 mile one-way, easy) is a short walk from the confluence of the North and Middle Forks of the American River to a small beach that Auburn city officials once ran as a municipal swimming pool with lifeguards and snack bars. Those things are long gone, but the warm water, tall jumping rocks, and narrow slip of sandy beach make this place a fun spot.

One word of caution: while most of the activities in the park are family-friendly, beaches south of the Highway 49 bridge—about 0.5-mile downstream from the river

confluence—are unofficially clothing optional. Parking is limited and costs $10 for day use, so arrive early in the summer to find a good spot close to the confluence. Hours within the park are slightly different for off-road vehicles and boating access so check the park's website for current use schedules.

Hidden Falls Regional Park

Hidden Falls Regional Park (7587 Mears Place, 530/889-6808, www.placer.ca.gov, open one half-hour before sunset to one half-hour after sunset, daily) is an undiscovered gem, even for locals; the parking lot is usually quite empty, probably because this rugged 1,200-acre preserve is in the middle of nowhere. That said, it's an easy drive from the center of Auburn to reach the park. There are seven miles of easy to moderate trails that meander through blue oak woodlands to the bottom of a deep creek canyon. Stop for a while to pick blackberries or keep an eye out for red-shouldered hawks that

THE ENDURANCE CAPITAL OF THE WORLD

Imagine a town that prides itself on making people suffer. What an awful place—but not for ultramarathon runners and trail riders! For these athletes, Auburn is the Louvre, the Eiffel Tower, and Mount Everest all rolled into one.

Auburn likes to call itself the Endurance Capital of the World, and it's not hard to see why. The **Auburn State Recreation Area** (www.parks.ca.gov) boasts 100 miles of trails for mountain biking, running, and horseback riding through the rugged American River canyon, including parts of the venerable **Western States Trail** to Lake Tahoe.

Every year, the town hosts two famous 100-mile endurance races—one on horseback, the other on foot. Both competitions have been torturing contestants for more than 30 years. The quickest finishers in the **Western States 100** (http://ws100.com) take about 15-20 *hours* to run a "century," as the races call it.

Using a horse instead might not sound so bad, unless you've ever tried riding Western style for a few miles—then suddenly it's no joke. Now try sliding down scree-filled cliffs, fording ice-cold white water, and outrunning pissed off mountain lions through 100 miles of remote Sierra Nevada backcountry. Racers might do all three in the **Tevis Cup** (www.teviscup.org), in which participants ride trail horses from Lake Tahoe to Auburn. The Cup actually helped inspire the ultramarathon. In 1974, a local chiropractor named Gordon Ainsleigh ditched his horse when it pulled up lame in the Cup and decided to finish the course on foot. He came in at just under 24 hours, and a new race was born.

Since Tevis Cup's first race in 1955, grueling races have cropped up to burnish Auburn's endurance brand. The **Auburn Century** (www.wildestride.com) is a road bike competition, which is actually four different races roughly 100 miles and longer through Placer County's steep canyons. The **Auburn Triathlon** (www.auburntriathlon.com) challenges participants to complete a 1.2-mile swim, 56-mile bike ride, and a half marathon. Mountain bikers can also punish themselves with the muddy **Cool Mountain Bike Race** (www.auburnbikeworks.com). Auburn's other endurance races include the **American River Classic** (www.americanriverclassic.com), **American River 50-Mile Run** (www.ar50mile.com), and the **Way Too Cool 50K Run** (www.wtc50k.com).

soar overhead. Once you reach the 30-foot falls, rest on the large wooden overlook clinging to the cliff side and watch the water plunge down a series of small drops into a glistening emerald pool. Just below the falls, there's a fork in the creek with decent-size swimming holes; if you walk farther upstream on Coon Creek, there are several places to fish. Don't want to walk? Many of the trails are open to horseback riders or cyclists; hikers just need to yield the trail if they happen upon equestrians in the park.

To reach the park, take Grass Valley Highway to Atwood Road and head west for 1.7 miles. Atwood Road becomes Mt. Vernon Road; continue going straight on Mt. Vernon for another 2.7 miles and turn right on Mears Road. Stay on Mears for one half of a mile and take the first right; the turnoff for the park is another 1,000 feet down the road.

Biking

Cycling fanatics will love the **Auburn Century** (early June, www.wildestride.com, $40–95), a one-day cycling event that cruises through many of the region's historic mining towns. It's no easy pedal; riders choose one of four grueling courses, the shortest of which is 40 miles and climbs 3,000 feet. There are no bike lanes, and you'll ride all day on hair-raising backcountry roads, so it's best to have some cycling experience before trying the Century. Still, it's a chance to bike through picturesque scenery and historic Gold Rush cities, including ghost towns like Gold Run and Iowa Hill.

Hidden Falls Regional Park, near Auburn

Participants get a souvenir cycling jersey and bragging rights for braving one of the toughest bike rides in the West.

Forgot your mountain bike at home? Relax—you can still hit Auburn's famed single track with a fat tire rental from one of the local bike shops. **Bicycle Emporium** (483 Grass Valley Hwy., 530/823-2900, www.bicycleemporium.com, 10 A.M.–6 P.M. Mon.–Fri., 9 A.M.–5 P.M. Sat., 11 A.M.–4 P.M. Sun.) will rent Trek bikes for the heart-stopping plunge into the American River canyon. A day's rental costs $45. Think you'd rather just buy? The shop specializes in higher-end mountain bikes like Santa Cruz and Intense, but they also offer reasonably priced Treks for under $500. If you're starting from downtown Auburn, pick up a rental from **Atown Bikes** (943 Lincoln Way, 530/820-3375, http://atownbikes.net, 10 A.M.–6 P.M. Tues.–Fri., 9 A.M.–5 P.M. Sat.). Duke, the shop's friendly owner, loans out high-end GT mountain bikes for $8 per hour

and $40 per day. And I think this is pretty cool: Sometimes Atown stocks a decent selection of used bikes for sale in case you're looking for a fresh set of wheels.

Hiking

The **Olmstead Loop and Pointed Rocks Trail** (9.8 miles one-way, moderate/strenuous) climbs through oak woodlands and grassy meadows on its way to the little town of Cool. The views take in most of the American River canyon and Auburn State Recreation Area. Along the way, you'll pass the picturesque old Mountain Quarries Railroad bridge (most locals call it No Hands Bridge); make sure to bring a camera. The Pointed Rocks Trail charges straight up a very steep hillside from the confluence to reach the canyon's topside and the Olmstead Loop before meandering through bluffs and rolling grassland. In spring, this entire area glows bright green with new grass and wildflowers pop up between March and June. You can find the trailhead 1.75 miles south of the Auburn State Recreation Area headquarters.

The **Quarry Road Trail** (5.6 miles one-way, easy/moderate) is like a Swiss Army knife of outdoor fun. You can hike, swim, fish, bike, and ride horses on this easily accessible trail. The trail follows a 19th-century mining flume and railroad line along the Middle Fork of the American River. The first two miles run along a flat road just above the water through oaks and ghost pines. Keep an eye out for river otters as you hike down the trail, which eventually starts climbing higher. If you're okay with adding an additional 2.5-mile detour, take the PG&E Road Trail up to an old rock quarry overlooking the canyon. The view up there is hard to match. Back on the trail, you'll trek along parts of the Western States Trail, first blazed by Paiute and Washoe Indians between Utah and Sacramento long before European pioneers arrived. Keep an eye out for Murderer's Bar rapids at the two-mile mark, which is named for a battle between prospectors and local Native Americans. You can find the trail two miles south of the Auburn State Recreation Area headquarters on Highway 49.

Golf

These links are the real deal: Designed by famed course architect Robert Trent Jones Jr., **The Ridge Golf Club** (2020 Golf Course Rd., 530/888-7888, www.ridgegc.com, $25–60) is one of the Northern Gold Country's most challenging and prestigious layouts. A round at the Ridge is certainly a scenic experience, with blue oak woodlands, reclaimed wetlands filled with blue herons and red-winged blackbirds, and rocky creeks where duffers could spend hours searching for lost Titleists. The golf's not so bad, either; the course is a dicey ramble down narrow fairways with hairpin doglegs and unforgiving boundaries. For that reason, golfing newcomers might find this course frustrating instead of exhilarating. Better to avoid the pricey greens fees and try a local executive nine-hole course instead. One tip: if you don't mind the late afternoon sun, the Ridge has discounted greens fees for golfers teeing off after 3 P.M.

Emerging from the blue oaks and hilly grasslands like a green mirage, **Darkhorse Golf Club** (24150 Darkhorse Dr., 530/269-7900, www.darkhorsegolf.com, $35–69) is quite frankly a beautiful place for golf. This par-72 championship course has challenging, narrow fairways peppered with bunkers on nearly every hole. It's not a true links course, but it bears similar features. The landscape's natural contours have been left unchanged, allowing wetlands and marshes to crisscross fairways, while the greens have been placed into gullies and small valleys. Not bad for a former cattle ranch. Golfers familiar with the area will agree that Dark Horse is among the best in the Northern Gold Country, but the course is still an undiscovered gem.

Duffers and pros alike will enjoy the well-manicured fairways at **Black Oak Golf Course** (2455 Black Oak Rd., 530/878-1900, www.golfblackoak.com, $12–15) a tidy nine-hole layout that plays more like the front nine of an expensive country club. The greens fees are cheap, but this isn't your average muni course. At this place, the groundskeepers do an excellent job—Black Oak's grass stays a glowing green, even during hot Gold Country summers. In other words, you'll rarely see large patches of brown tundra often found at other low-budget executive courses. This is a perfect place for beginning to intermediate golfers who want something challenging, but the course also has plenty of bunkers, water hazards, and elevation changes to give scratch players a run for their money.

Gator Creek Golf Course (14520 Musso Rd., 530/878-1110, $10) is a nine-hole course with wide fairways, few bunkers, and two or three strategically placed water hazards. Greens fees are cheap, and it's easy to knock out a round in about an hour if you don't dally. The course can get soggy in the morning, but by late afternoon it plays much better. Ambience isn't the greatest because I-80 runs right by Gator Creek; do try to resist the temptation to hit drives into the freeway.

White-Water Rafting

From Auburn, it's a 15–20 minute drive to either the Middle Fork or the North Fork of the mighty American River; the South Fork is about 30 minutes away. Most guided trips in the area are run by companies based near Placerville or in Calaveras County, and they will usually ask you to meet them just east of Auburn for river excursions. If guided tours aren't your thing, it's possible to rent rafts and kayaks from outfitters in Auburn sans guides, although it's best to steer clear of more dangerous Class IV–V rapids (especially on the North Fork) if that's your plan. The season usually runs from April to October, and outfitters will have advice on the best spots to put your raft onto the river.

If you'd rather hit the rapids without a guide, **Canyon Raft Rental** (133 Borland Ave., 530/823-0931, www.canyonraftrentals.com, rafts $42–250, kayaks $35–70) offers inflatable kayak and raft rentals. It's certainly much cheaper to go guide-less, but this option is best for rafters with some experience. Canyon Raft has a shuttle service providing transport to the Middle Fork and back to Auburn, but make sure to reserve it beforehand; occasionally, you can arrange shuttle pickup on the North Fork upon request. If you're not using the shuttle, it's easy to pack a raft into your trunk and inflate it at the river; air pumps are included with all rentals.

You can also rent equipment from **Sierra Outdoor Center** (440 Lincoln Way, 530/885-1844, www.sierraoutdoorcenter.com, rafts $80–235, kayaks $19–69). Rentals include paddles, helmets, air pump, and life jackets. If you're not sure where to ride the river, just ask the friendly staff; everyone in the shop has paddling experience. Just in case you need extra instruction before heading out on the water, Sierra Outdoor Center also offers lessons in basic kayaking and rafting.

ACCOMMODATIONS
Under $100

The **Best Western Golden Key** (13450 Lincoln Way, 530/885-8611, www.bestwesterngolden-key.com, $65–115) has tidy and comfortable accommodations. Nothing fancy here, but the location is perfect for exploring Auburn and nearby Gold Country attractions. There's a hot tub and a heated outdoor pool that's enclosed during chilly foothill winters. Free wireless Internet and a hearty continental breakfast are also perks. The hotel is also pet-friendly, but there's an additional $15 charge per night.

The **Quality Inn** (13490 Lincoln Way,

Sierra Outdoor Center rents kayaks and rafts.

530/885-7025, www.qualityinn.com, $60–95) is a clean, no-hassle kind of place that's perfect if you're just passing through town for a night. Nothing fancy here, but each room has a fridge, microwave, and coffeemaker—everything you'd expect of a roadside motel. In the morning, there's free breakfast and complimentary newspapers waiting in the lobby. If you need to escape the hot Gold Country sun or relax after a long day on Auburn's rugged trails, you can slip into the outdoor (but heated) swimming pool. Only certain rooms have access to wireless Internet, so ask the front desk if that's something you need.

The **Foothills Motel** (13431 Bowman Rd., 530/885-8444, www.foothillsmotel.ws, $55–78) is perfect for guests seeking a nostalgic stay at an old motor court dive. From the neon sign by the freeway to the low-slung '60s-style buildings, you can be sure that ex–Rat Pack groupies will feel right at home. Let's be honest: this isn't the ritziest place in town, but it's probably the best bargain. The rooms are spare but tidy, with modern amenities such as microwaves, refrigerators, and ironing boards; if you splurge, apparently hair dryers are available in "deluxe" rooms! Make sure your room has wireless Internet by asking at the front desk.

The **Comfort Inn** (1875 Auburn Ravine Rd., 530/885-1800, www.comfortinn.com, $80–130) is a decent place to hang your hat. Inside, you'll find clean rooms with few frills and basic amenities like microwaves, refrigerators, and wireless Internet in every room. It's also close to several restaurants and just a short drive from I-80. Perhaps the best thing about the Comfort is the piping-hot free breakfast, which includes eggs and waffles; perfect for loading up on carbs before white-water rafting or mountain biking at the nearby American River.

$100-250

The slightly more upscale **Auburn Holiday Inn** (120 Grass Valley Hwy., 530/887-8787, www.

auburnhi.com, $100–165) has an outdoor pool and large, well-equipped rooms with flat-screen televisions and king-size beds. Inside, the hotel is comfortable without being lavish, and it's the closest thing to luxury accommodations that you'll find in Auburn. The location is convenient—less than a mile from Auburn's historic town center—and you'll get a decent view of the town's historic courthouse from the hotel parking lot. If you're visiting on the Fourth of July, it's actually a great place to watch the fireworks display taking place at the nearby Gold Country Fairgrounds. Amenities include free wireless Internet, on-site laundry pickup, room service, and a fitness center. Pets are welcome with a onetime $20 surcharge.

Built in 1884, the **Power's Mansion Inn** (195 Harrison Ave., 530/885-1166, www.powersmansioninn.com, $200–250) is Auburn's only bed-and-breakfast. From the outside, this place is fantastic: With an eye-catching pink Victorian facade and beautifully manicured landscaping, the mansion measures up to any other Gold Rush–era inn. The ornate common areas—spruced up with period furniture, plush Persian rugs, and beautiful dark wood accents—feel like a Gilded Age parlor. Unfortunately, the same can't be said about the rooms, which are small, somewhat dingy, and haven't caught up to the exquisite renovation completed on the mansion's exterior. If you decide to stay here, make sure to sign up for the afternoon tea, which includes homemade quiche, sandwiches, and desserts like lemon bars and carrot cake.

FOOD
American
Katrina's Cafe (456 Grass Valley Hwy., 530/888-1166, 7 A.M.–2:30 P.M. Wed.–Sat., 7 A.M.–2 P.M. Sun., $5–12) serves arguably the most delicious home-cooked breakfast in the Gold Country. Famous for their awesome pancakes and mouthwatering eggs Benedict, this

place is legendary in Auburn for whipping up mouthwatering, belt-busting meals. I have no idea how they fit everyone into this tiny country shack on the side of Highway 49, but get there early to find a seat—it's that good. Even though this place is packed on weekends, the friendly staff always keeps their cool, even as they welcome large families. If you're a fan of oatmeal pancakes, I recommend asking for a secret item that's not on the menu; a delicious order of orange-oat flapjacks. One word of advice: bring plenty of cash because Katrina's doesn't take credit cards. If you're not a breakfast person, lunch is also served here.

The hearty breakfasts at **C** **Sweetpea's** (13498 Luther Rd., 5330/823-1818, 6 A.M.–3 P.M. daily, $10) will keep you full all day long. This place is famous for its six-egg omelettes, stuffed with several varieties of meat, roasted veggies, and melted cheese. The food is tasty, down-home country cooking—something you'd expect to gobble up on a cattle ranch. There can be quite a wait on weekend mornings, so I recommend showing up fairly early to grab a table, especially if you're bringing a larger party. Sweetpea's also serves lunch if you miss breakfast.

For standard surf and turf, the **Monkey Cat** (805 Lincoln Way, 530/888-8492, www.monkeycat.com, 11 A.M.–2 P.M. and 5 P.M.–close Mon.–Fri., 5 P.M.–close Sat.–Sun., $9–29) will satisfy your hunger. There's nothing especially original about the menu here, just your traditional American dishes like grilled salmon and pork tenderloin. The atmosphere is great; with vintage light fixtures and dark wood booths, Monkey Cat almost feels like an upscale restaurant in the tropics. Call ahead for a reservation on the weekend.

Some of the best burgers in town are served at the **Club Car** (836 Lincoln Way, 530/887-9732, www.clubcarauburn.com, 11 A.M.–10 P.M. Sun.–Thurs., 11 A.M.–midnight Fri.–Sat., $7–24). The place is first and foremost a dive bar,

but the restaurant area is actually fairly upscale with candlelight and white tablecloth settings. Kind of quirky, but somehow it works. Local favorites are the bison burger (lathered in barbecue sauce and fried onions) and the bistro burger, a heart-stopping mess of roasted garlic mayo and brie.

If you follow the tourist crowd, you're bound to end up at **Awful Annie's** (160 Sacramento St., 530/888-9857, www.awfulannies.com, 8 A.M.–3 P.M. daily, $10). Most trips to Old Town usually end with breakfast or lunch at this cheeky little eatery, which serves meaty sandwiches for lunch and plate-busting omelettes at breakfast. Truth be told, there are better breakfast joints in Auburn, but Awful Annie's has earned quite a following with Gold Country travelers. Mostly because the restaurant is so close to I-80, it's always busy, so try to get there early or between peak times.

Asian

Who would expect to find overflowing bowls of Mongolian noodles deep in the Gold Country? **C** **Sum's Mongolian BBQ** (958 Lincoln Way, Ste. A, 530/889-8948, 11 A.M.–2:30 P.M. and 5–8:45 P.M. Mon.–Thurs., 11 A.M.–2:30 P.M. and 5–9:15 P.M. Fri., 4–9:15 P.M. Sat., $6.75–9.50) will make sure you don't leave feeling hungry. This quirky Auburn eatery serves kick-ass barbecue from a huge steaming griddle facing the front window. There's rarely a long wait because the food is served buffet style; you grab a bowl, help yourself to noodles, meat, and vegetables, and then lather your creation with sauces. Dinner is all-you-can-eat, although even the hungriest barbecue fan would have trouble making a second round here. Afterwards, treat yourself to a tasty (if slightly random) helping of vanilla soft-serve ice cream.

Bakeries and Cafés

Skip the corporate coffee joints and head to **Flour Garden Bakery and Cafe** (340C Elm

Ave., 530/888-1012, www.flourgarden.com, 5 A.M.–7 P.M. Mon.–Sat., 6 A.M.–6 P.M. Sun., $2–10). I'll admit, it's not the hippest joint and cup sizes are simply known as small, medium, and large, but the pastries are damn good. The owners are recovering hippies, and it shows. Breads, pies, scones, and bagels are made from scratch every day with local organic wheat and produce. And the coffee is legit; 100 percent organic and free trade grown. Lunch food includes enchiladas, lasagna, quiches, salads, and sandwiches.

For upscale bistro food and a decent cup of joe, try **Tsuda's Old Town Eatery** (103 Sacramento St., 530/823-2233, www.tsudas. com, 8 A.M.–5 P.M. daily, $10). It's named for an old Japanese grocery store that operated on this site from 1918 to 2006. The Eatery serves Temple coffee, roasted in downtown Sacramento, and gourmet-style sandwiches with names like the Pear Affair and Veggie Wedgie.

Brewpubs

Consider yourself a hophead? If so, serious beer drinkers should check out the vast selection of craft brews at **Little Belgium Deli and Beer Bar** (780 Lincoln Way, 530/820-3056, 10 A.M.–10 P.M. Mon.–Wed., 10 A.M.–midnight Thurs.–Fri., 11 A.M.–midnight Sat., 11 A.M.–10 P.M. Sun., $8). This old-school deli serves 14 beers on tap and 40 bottled varieties with old-world names like Strubbe Flemish Red Ale Grand Cru and Lindeman's Framboise Raspberry Lambic. There's more than just beer—the sandwiches taste just like those that Mom makes. Make sure to try the Gobbler (turkey, cranberry sauce, jalapeños, and cream cheese) or the spicy Tuna Wasabi. One of the coolest things about this place: it's a chemical-free zone, meaning the restaurant uses all-natural food (no nitrates, MSG, or growth hormones in the sandwich meats) and organic cleaning supplies.

Love microbrews? The **Auburn Alehouse** (289 Washington St., 530/885-2537, http:// auburnalehouse.com, 11 A.M.–9 P.M. Mon.– Tues., 11 A.M.–10 P.M. Wed.–Thurs., 11 A.M.– 11 P.M. Fri., 9 A.M.–11 P.M. Sat., 9 A.M.–9 P.M. Sun., $9–20) won't let you down. Every pint is brewed in the gleaming silver tanks at the back of this bustling sports bar. For starters, try the beer sampler—for less than $10, you can sample every beer on tap. The cuisine is typical bar food, with burgers, sandwiches, and sides like sweet potato fries. During the summer, you can also catch live blues bands playing on the back patio. The Alehouse, bless their heart, serves food (and beer!) all day long on weekends.

Californian

Located in Old Town Auburn and inside a former Gold Rush saloon, **⚫ Carpe Vino** (1568 Lincoln Way, 530/823-0320, www.carpevino-auburn.com, 5–10 P.M. Wed.–Sat., $10–29) feels like a place John Wayne might have enjoyed had the Duke been a wine drinker. The building dates back to 1855 and the current owner took pains to restore the rustic vaulted ceiling and aged brick walls, giving Carpe Vino a polished Old West vibe. For the menu, Carpe Vino prepares sustainably grown ingredients from local farms and vendors; you'll find the red-wine braised beef, the Muscovy duck breast, and the roasted Angus strip loin are all standout dishes. If the restaurant is full, pull up a chair at the gleaming mahogany wine bar—it's a replica of the original from the old saloon. Carpe Vino also opens at noon from Tuesday to Saturday for wine-tasting only.

For delicious fast food with an Asian twist, head to **Ikeda's California Country Market** (13500 Lincoln Way, 530/885-4243, www. ikedas.com, 11 A.M.–7 P.M. Mon.–Thurs., 10 A.M.–8 P.M. Fri.–Sun., $8–10). This roadside burger joint and fruit stand has become a de facto rest stop for travelers headed to Lake Tahoe. The food is a culinary mash-up

Carpe Vino serves wine and fine cuisine in an Old West saloon.

between traditional diner fare and Japanese cuisine; menu options include everything from teriyaki chicken bowls to teriyaki bacon burgers. If teriyaki isn't your thing, ask for the pot-pie—an Ikeda's specialty, made fresh in Ikeda's on-site bakery. The turkey burger—showered with a tasty mix of secret spices—is also delicious. Finish off your meal with a slice of fresh fruit pie from the bakery, made with fruit from the Ikeda's family orchards. You should know that lunch and dinner hours can bring quite a crowd, so expect a short wait for your food.

Fine Dining

The grand old dame of Auburn's fine dining establishments is **Bootleggers Old Town Tavern and Grill** (210 Washington St., 530/889-2229, http://bootleggersauburn.com, 11 A.M.–9 P.M. Tues.–Thurs., 11 A.M.–10 P.M. Fri.–Sat., 4–9 P.M. Sun., $15–30). A local favorite, Bootleggers feels clubby and exclusive like an old country club, with varnished dark

wood trim, rough brick walls adorned with mounted deer heads, and a roaring fireplace; in my humble opinion, I'd say this place has some of the best dining ambience in town. On warm summer nights, ask for a seat outside on the patio and watch dusk fall on Old Town. Foodies with a keen palate may find the menu rather generic, but you can't go wrong with old standbys like the fried chicken or the Korean-style skirt steak. Make sure to call ahead for a reservation.

Mexican

Could it be that Auburn's best restaurant is actually a fast-food joint? For folks that know, **Taco Tree** (180 Oakwood Dr., 530/823-0969, 7 A.M.–11 P.M. daily, $1–5) is a serious contender for best bites in town. What makes this place so noteworthy? Well, it's everything you wouldn't expect from a large corporate chain; tacos made from fresh shells that don't taste like cardboard, savory burritos made with oh-so-soft tortillas and fresh veggies. According to locals, they'll drive miles out of their way just to eat at Taco Tree because it really is that damn good.

Orchards and Produce

You haven't lived without trying a homemade pie from **Machado Orchards** (100 Apple Ln., 530/823-1393, 8 A.M.–7 P.M. daily May–Dec., pies $15). This family-owned farm has been selling fresh produce and baked goodies in Auburn for several generations, and it's actually a local secret; there's rarely a crowd at their small grocery store even during harvest time, when the family cranks out the most delicious apple cider you'll ever drink. During the summer, Machado's is like an indoor fruit stand selling juicy white corn, peaches, melons, and fresh vegetables; most of the produce is also offered in dried snack packs, which make perfect treats for the road. But everything comes back

to the pies—oozing with fresh fruit from the Machado's family trees and baked with a light, flaky crust dusted with a touch of sugar. If you like fruit pies, I'd go with either the cherry or the peach; if you swing by during the holidays, the pumpkin and apple are second to none. Look for the small white blimp soaring above the orchards—it means Machado's is open.

INFORMATION AND SERVICES

Auburn has all the amenities of a small city, complete with gas stations near the highways, ATMs, big-box stores, and a **post office** (371 Nevada St., 9 A.M.–5:30 P.M. Mon.–Fri., 10 A.M.–3 P.M. Sat.). For travel tips and more good info about the town, there's the **Placer County Visitors Bureau** (1103 High St., 530/887-2111, www.visitplacer.com, 9:30 A.M.–4:30 P.M. Mon.–Sat., 11 A.M.–4:30 P.M. Sun.).

Auburn's daily newspaper is the *Auburn*

NORTHERN GOLD COUNTRY

© CHRISTOPHER ARNS

Machado Orchards sells pies and fresh produce from their ranch in Auburn.

Journal (http://auburnjournal.com), which covers foothill and Placer County government news. *Sierra Heritage* (http://sierraheritage.com), a travel magazine dedicated to the Sierra Nevada and the Foothill region, sometimes profiles Auburn and surrounding areas. A great website for local tourist information is the **Placer County Visitors Bureau** (www.visitplacer.com).

For medical assistance, **Sutter Auburn Faith Hospital** (11815 Education St., Auburn, 530/888-4500, www.sutterauburnfaith.org) offers an emergency room and a full range of hospital services.

GETTING THERE AND AROUND

Auburn is located directly off I-80 and provides access to both Highway 49 north and south. As such, it experiences heavy weekend traffic as well as snow in winter. Check weather, road condition, and traffic reports (www.caltrans.org) if you're unsure about making a trip.

The closest major airport is in Sacramento, 30 miles south. There is an **Amtrak** station (277 Nevada St.) serviced by the *Capitol Corridor* route, but there are no ticket services at the platform. The local airport is **Auburn Municipal Airport** (13626 New Airport Rd., 530/386-4211). Car rentals are available through **Enterprise** (530/823-5500, www.enterprise.com).

The **Gold Country Stage** (http://new.mynevadacounty.com/transit, adults $1, children under 6 free, day pass $4.50) runs buses and minibuses through Nevada City, Grass Valley, down south to Auburn, and up to points north of the Gold Country. You can also take **Placer County Transit** (530/885-2877, www.placer.ca.gov, $1.25) buses farther northeast up I-80, stopping at destinations like Weimar, Colfax, Gold Run, and Alta.

For bus rides around town, **Auburn Transit** (530/906-3700, www.auburn.ca.gov, $1) has daily service throughout Auburn and in some surrounding areas.

COLFAX

The arc of this little town's history can be followed along two steel rails. Colfax (pop. 2,000) was an important stop on the First Transcontinental Railroad; the Central Pacific and the Nevada County Narrow Gauge Railroad converged here, pumping gold back into the country's heartland in exchange for mining equipment and capital. People always seem to be coming and going through Colfax. The Gold Country's first stagecoach robbery happened here in 1852 when outlaws held up the Nevada City line for $7,000. As railroads gave way to the automobile in the 1920s, engineers built U.S. 40—one of the country's first cross-country highways—through town. So many roads and railroads make Colfax a great place for a pit stop, but you can find reasons to stick around. Colfax sits high above the American River canyon, offering quick access to rafting trips on the turbulent North Fork. Hiking trails are abundant in the thick ponderosa forests outside of town, including a couple with postcard-worthy waterfalls. And Rollins Lake, just five minutes north of Colfax, has some of the best boating and camping spots in Placer County.

Sports and Recreation
BOATING
Rollins Lake (five miles north of Colfax off Highway 174, day use $6.50) has 26 miles of pristine shoreline, perfect for waterskiing, tubing, or just swimming. The water stays an average temperature of 72 degrees, although the best time to visit is between May and October. Because Rollins is an artificial dam in the Bear River canyon, the lake twists around like a two-headed dragon; folds in the canyon have made small coves that are often deserted, letting boaters explore quiet groves of ponderosa

downtown Colfax

and black oaks. That also makes for some awesome fishing holes, and Rollins is a renowned trout, catfish, and bass fishery. To be honest, this lake gets packed during the summer, sometimes uncomfortably so. Try going earlier or later in the season to avoid unruly boaters who clog the water.

HIKING

Colfax is located high above the beautiful American River canyon at the far northern edge of the Auburn State Recreation Area. Take a camera because the views take in miles of jagged, bluish-colored ridgelines, blanketed in untouched ponderosa and oak forests, stretching all the way to Lake Tahoe. In other words, it's pretty damn spectacular. A hike through this scenery is worth a day trip from Auburn or Grass Valley; if you are staying in Colfax, it's almost mandatory to explore the steep river gorge for at least half a day.

Depending on your ambition to really get out there, the **Indian Creek Falls Trail** (2.8 miles round-trip, moderate) tracks out to a 30-foot cascade near the North Fork. It's not a long hike, but it takes some nifty driving on pot-holed and narrow Yankee Jim's Road (which is often impassable during the wet season), eventually crossing a one-lane suspension bridge that looks downright ancient. As an alternative, the **Indian Creek Trail** (2 miles one-way, easy/moderate) starts on the east side of the North Fork near Shirttail Creek; there's parking near the bridge.

Another fantastic hike is **Codfish Creek Falls Trail** (3.4 miles round-trip, moderate), about six miles south of the little community of Weimar with a 40-foot waterfall. Again, this road is treacherous when it rains so drive a high-clearance vehicle in spring or winter; it's just too bad because the waterfall is best when it rains! For a hike with much easier access, check out the **Stevens Trail** (N. Canyon Way, 6.4 miles round-trip, easy but strenuous), an old cable car route that switchbacks all the way to the North Fork. Expect to see the remnants of 19th-century mining activity littered along the trail, including an old suspension bridge and a stretch of the original Transcontinental Railroad. Along the Stevens Trail, keep an eye open for sweeping views up and down the North Fork; several miles downstream is the Iowa Hill suspension bridge.

WHITE-WATER RAFTING

Colfax is a short shuttle ride to the North Fork of the American River. This white water is gnarly, and the scenery (2,000-foot granite cliffs and sheer canyon walls) often leaves visitors speechless. Class IV and V rapids are typical in this stretch of canyon, meaning it's reserved for rafters with experience. Tumbling, stomach-churning rapids like Chamberlain Falls, Nutcracker, and Dominator can be widow makers for newbies. Book your trips between April and June when the white water is at its peak. A quintessential North Fork rafting trip is usually nine miles long and includes a lunch about four miles into the journey.

Tributary Whitewater Tours (800/672-3846, www.whitewatertours.com, Apr.–June, half day $100–120, full day $120–140, two days $270–300) has been guiding trips in the Northern Gold Country for more than 30 years. They cover miles of the North Fork canyon and offer several trips, including a half-day float on Class II rapids for beginners. In fact, most of their trips are a good balance between tougher Class IV drops and calmer Class II–III white water.

The folks at **All-Outdoors Whitewater Rafting** (925/932-8993, www.aorafting.com, full day $154–179) are also experienced; the company has been around for 50 years. They have only one North Fork trip so options aren't great for beginners, but white-water studs will love it.

Whitewater Connection (530/622-6446, www.whitewaterconnection.com, Apr.–May, $140–170) is another outfit that runs the North Fork. The route is similar to what other companies offer, dropping through frothy rapids with diabolical names like Devil's Staircase.

Whitewater Excitement (800/750-2386, www.whitewaterexcitement.com, Apr.–June, half day $110–130, full day $140–200, two days $270–320) offers a slate of adrenaline-charged North Fork rafting. They cater to full-blown (aka insane) rafters who enjoy not one but two runs down the same narrow canyon in one day. Screaming like a banshee is encouraged.

Accommodations

Most people pass through Colfax on the way to campsites or somewhere else in the Gold Country. For that reason, there are just a couple of options for non-camping lodgings. In the spirit of Colfax's place in transportation history, **Colfax Motor Lodge** (550 S. Auburn St., 530/346-8382, www.colfaxmotorlodge.com, $55–118) harks back to vintage motor court motels. The format is typical 1950s style with a freshly paved parking lot surrounded by smart one-story buildings. Once inside, the 18 rooms have been spruced up with modern electronics and amenities, so expect a fridge, cable TV, coffeemakers, and air-conditioning. No frills here, just a tidy place that's close to the road.

If you plan to kick back in Colfax for a few days, the laid-back **Sierra Sun Cloud Inn** (685 Coyote Hill Rd., 530/637-1083, www.sierrasuncloudinn.com, $125–180) is a full-fledged bed-and-breakfast. These large farmhouse-style accommodations are located on 18 acres of prime forestland; views include Sacramento's lights in the evening and distant mountain ranges during the day. Walking around the property, blanketed with wildflowers and rolling hills, feels like strolling through a park. The interior has four rooms with simple yet elegant bedding, antique wood furniture, and more spectacular views. There's also a game room with a pool table and potbellied woodstove. In the morning, breakfast is waiting for you and consists of gourmet crepes, frittatas, and fresh fruit. Note that smoking isn't allowed anywhere at the inn.

Orchard Springs Campground (19085 Larsen Rd., Chicago Park, 530/346-2212, www.osresort.net, $30–60), on Rollins Lake, has 91 campsites with access to a full range of convenient features such as showers, flush toilets, and RV hookups. It's also open all year long. Fishing licenses and firewood are available from the clubhouse, and all kinds of watercraft can put in from the dock, including boats, Jet Skis, and Waverunners. The campground is extremely easy to reach because it's less than five miles away from Colfax and I-80.

There's way too much fun stuff to do at **Peninsula Campground** (21597 You Bet Rd., Grass Valley, 530/477-9413, www.penresort. com, $33–175). Located on 300 acres near the northern end of Rollins Lake, the campground has horseshoe pits, volleyball courts, and paddleboat rentals ($10–12 per hour). Going fishing but didn't bring a boat? You can rent 14-foot fishing vessels to troll for trout, bass, and catfish. Note that Peninsula's camping season is from April through mid-September; pets are welcome on a leash.

Long Ravine Resort (26909 Rollins Lake Rd., 530/346-6166, www.longravineresorts. com, $30–100) is a tidy campground on Rollins Lake that's seemingly designed with families in mind. There's a swim platform and a marina with a fair number of boat slips; RV hookups are available, along with hot showers and flush toilets. The resort is somewhat removed from the raucous party scene that sometimes erupts on the northern side of the lake, and for that

reason, parents with smaller kids would probably prefer Long Ravine.

Greenhorn Campground (15000 Greenhorn Access Rd., 530/272-6100) has 40 sites on the lake, including spots for RVs ($35) and tents ($20). Greenhorn is known for being a little louder; sometimes there are bands with folks having a beer or two. This campground might not be great for families; on the other hand, it's perfect for a bachelor's weekend.

Food

Colfax's restaurant scene is slowing evolving from its fast-food roots. Most joints aren't polished eateries, but rather country-style diners or sports bars.

Tuck into some piping hot pie and a cup of joe at **Café Luna** (5 W. Depot St., 530/346-8833, 7 A.M.–3 P.M. Mon.–Fri., 8 A.M.–2 P.M. Sat.–Sun., $5). They open at the crack of dawn, which is nice for roadies leaving town early. Friendly atmosphere, a good mix of locals and tourists, and home-style pastries make Luna a fun place.

Blue Coyote Taqueria (212 Canyon Way, 530/366-5537, 10 A.M.–9 P.M. daily, $4–8) serves straight-forward Mexican food, the kind you'd expect from a San Diego taco stand— quesadillas, burritos, and damn tasty fish tacos. The food is cheap but good, and you can eat it on the back porch.

The oldest diner in town is **Colfax Max Restaurant** (555 S. Auburn St., Ste. E, 530/346-7404, http://colfaxmax.com, 11 A.M.–8 P.M. Sun.–Thurs., 11 A.M.–9 P.M. Fri.–Sat., $10). Folks like to order juicy burgers like the Biker, a full pound of Angus beef slathered in cheese, bacon, and steak sauce; or the Safari burgers, your choice of kangaroo, bison, elk, alligator, or Kobe beef. Since you've already crossed the Rubicon for your weekly junk food allowance, gulp down a 16- or 24-ounce milk shake (25 flavors include peppermint, eggnog, banana, and pineapple) for dessert.

Don't worry, you won't need Patrick Swayze for backup at **TJ's Roadhouse** (520 S. Auburn St., 530/346-1040, http://tjscolfax. com, 6:30 A.M.–8 P.M. Tues.–Thurs. and Sun., 6:30 A.M.–9 P.M. Fri.–Sat., 6:30 A.M.–2 P.M. Mon., $10–15). Hollywood's version of a "roadhouse" is a far cry from this homey shack on the side of I-80. Instead, expect generous helpings of burgers, like the Blue Cheese Bacon patty, steaks, soups and sandwiches, and hearty three-egg breakfast omelettes.

Situated in a rustic brick building in downtown Colfax, **Dottie's Restaurant** (38 N. Main St., 530/346-2828, 10 A.M.–9 P.M. Tues.–Thurs., 10 A.M.–10 P.M. Fri.–Sat., 10 A.M.–3 P.M. Sun., $10–22) is a friendly Italian restaurant, but the menu strays quite a bit. They serve button-busting portions of Caribbean-inspired food, burgers, and seafood. Yes, there's also pasta and it's not bad; service can lag a little bit even when it's slow.

The most upscale place in town is **Basement on Main Street** (46 N. Main St., 530/346-9550, http://basementwines.com, 11 A.M.–9 P.M. Mon.–Thurs., 11 A.M.–10 P.M. Fri.–Sat., 11 A.M.–8 P.M. Sun., $10–20). It's not a wine bar; more of a bistro serving pizzas along with California vino. Hipsters and homemakers would feel comfortable in this spacious, contemporary space; not too sleek but still modern, with wood floors and tables framed by brightly toned walls.

Information and Services

Colfax is smaller than Grass Valley or Auburn but does offer many of the same services. Visitors will find a grocery store, gas stations, and a few banks with ATM machines.

The **Colfax Area Chamber of Commerce** (99 Railroad St., 530/346-8888, www.colfaxarea. com, 10 A.M.–3 P.M. daily) can provide tourism info including tips on lodgings, recreation, and upcoming events. The **post office** can be found at 40 W. Church Street (9 A.M.–11:30 A.M. and 12:30–5 P.M. Mon.–Fri.). For quick cash, **Bank of America** (33 Depot St.) has an ATM and it's open 24 hours. There are several convenient gas stations just off the freeway in Colfax, including **Valero** (300 S. Canyon Way, 530/346-6661).

The local newspaper for sports, politics, and breaking news is the **Colfax Record** (http:// colfaxrecord.com), which is published weekly every Thursday. Most locals also subscribe to either the **Auburn Journal** or the **Union** to beef up their daily news intake.

Getting There and Around

Colfax is one of the Gold Country's most accessible towns. By car it's only 20 minutes northeast of Auburn off I-80. Highway 174 links Colfax with Grass Valley, which is a 25-minute drive to the northwest.

Amtrak's (www.amtrak.com) *California Zephyr* and *Capitol Corridor* trains provide service between Colfax and the Sacramento Valley twice a day. The station is located at 99 Railroad Street; there's no shelter, just a platform.

For coach service to and from Colfax, both Amtrak and **Greyhound** (www.greyhound. com) provide bus service several times daily. Check the websites for updated timetables and routes.

Placer County Transit (530/885-2877, www.placer.ca.gov, $1.25) runs two daily buses between Auburn and the Colfax Amtrak station between Monday and Friday.

Placerville

One of the most notorious towns in the foothills has a macabre past. Placerville (pop. 10,300) was first called Old Dry Diggins when it was founded in 1848, but quickly earned a reputation as "Hangtown." Why the grisly name? In 1849, a street jury (some would say a lynch mob) strung up three accused murderers from a giant white oak tree in the middle of town. Other hangings soon followed, adding to Hangtown's reputation for frontier justice. Scandalized citizens eventually changed the name and chopped down the tree, but nobody ever forget Placerville's lawless roots. And the infamous tree stump still lies underneath a building on Main Street.

These days Placerville has been spruced up for tourists. The El Dorado wine country has become big business for local shopkeepers and tasting rooms. In late summer and fall, Placerville hosts caravans of tourists headed to Apple Hill, a community of apple farmers who offer hayrides, pies, and harvest fun every year. Luckily, despite the town's popularity, Placerville's downtown—a collection of rugged stone and brick buildings—hasn't changed much since the Gold Rush, and visitors will love how authentically Western this place feels.

SIGHTS
Old Hangtown's Gold Bug Park

Just a mile north of downtown Placerville is Old Hangtown's Gold Bug Park (Bedford Ave., Placerville, 530/642-5207, www.goldbugpark.org, 10 A.M.–4 P.M. daily Apr.–Oct., adults $5, youth $3, children $2, audio tour $5), an old hard rock mine turned into a wonderful park and historical exhibit. During the Gold Rush, lucky prospectors would uncover a few nuggets while panning local rivers. Hard rock miners, on the other hand, burrowed thousands of feet into hillsides while hoping

to find a million-dollar quartz vein. No one knows how much wealth came from Gold Bug Mine, but prospectors surely found the mother lode; miners worked the claim from 1888 until World War II. Gold Bug is actually owned by Placerville—oddly enough, the only city in California to own a gold mine. The place feels a bit like a theme park. Visitors don helmets and head lamps before striding down wooden planks into the 352-foot horizontal shaft. A self-guided audio tour is available, but docents will also lead guided tours and offer bits of trivia about the mine. Make sure to visit the **Hendy Stamp Mill,** a giant iron dynamo that once crushed copious loads of quartz ore; a working model shows visitors how the process worked. Behind the stamp mill is a spanking new **blacksmith's shop** (10 A.M.–4 P.M. Wed.–Thurs.) with real smiths working the anvil. For visitors who book a guided tour, the **Priest Mine** is the real deal; a hand-dug wormhole that still bears pick marks from the prospectors who built it in the early 1850s.

Back above ground in the bright foothill sunlight, Gold Bug can make your Gold Rush fantasy come true. Grab a gold pan ($2) and "prospect" for amethysts, pyrite, and flecks of gold at a wooden trough. Explore the mine's past at **Hattie's Museum** and learn how miners and engineers tamed the local geology with 19th-century equipment. Afterward, lace up your hiking shoes and take a two-mile trek along the park's trails. During April and May, expect to see an explosion of California poppies, purple lupine, and wild iris; stay on the trail to avoid poison oak and rattlesnakes.

ENTERTAINMENT AND EVENTS

You'd expect roughneck dives in a place once known as Hangtown, and that's just what you

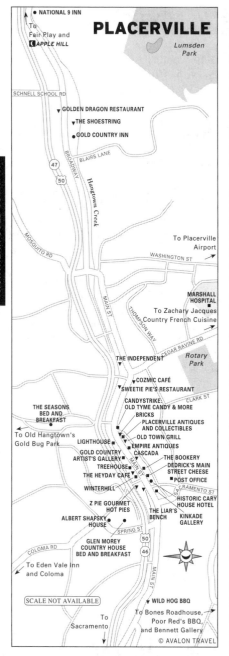

get. Placerville's downtown scene has two faces; one for the wine-tasting, foodie crowd and the other for leather-bound Harley riders. It's okay if you get confused because people here are mellow; don't expect parking lot showdowns with the Hells Angels.

Nightlife

Serving craft beer with a smile, **Brick Oven Pub** (2875 Ray Lawyer Dr., www.brickovenpub.com, 11 A.M.–9:30 P.M. Mon.–Thurs., 11 A.M.–10:30 P.M. Fri., 11 A.M.–11 P.M. Sat., noon–8 P.M. Sun.) is an upbeat brewpub with live music. Food here is mostly bar grub, stuff like pizzas and sandwiches. And oh, the hops: they have 24 beers (mostly Californian and West Coast microbrews) on tap to wash down that pub food. At least once a month, the Brick has bands playing Johnny Cash and classic rock; there's usually a small cover on those nights.

PJ's Roadhouse (5641 Mother Lode Dr., 530/626-0336, 7 A.M.–2 A.M. Mon.–Sat., 7 A.M.–10 P.M. Sun.) is known as a biker's bar, but don't be scared off by their scruffy reputation: All folks are welcome here. It is, however, most definitely a dive bar—one with a jukebox, pool tables, shuffleboard, occasional live music, and fried pub food. My advice is to come early and leave before the fun gets out of hand.

Another friendly bikers dive is **Bones Roadhouse** (4430 Pleasant Valley Rd., 530/644-4301, http://bonesroadhousebarandgrub.com, 11 A.M.–2 A.M. daily). Inside this low-slung building, you'll find tasty bar grub and genuinely nice bartenders; it feels more like a sports bar than a roadside hideout for the Sons of Anarchy.

If you're wandering around Placerville looking for a stiff drink, head for **The Liar's Bench** (255 Main St., 530/622-0494, 8 A.M.–2 A.M. daily). Now this is a dive. The low ceiling and dim light make the place feel like a cave with "stalactites" of crumpled dollar bills hanging

Creep through a real mine shaft at Old Hangtown's Gold Bug Park in Placerville.

from above. It's narrow, usually crowded, filled with people of various moods, and cocktails are cheap.

From the outside, the **Stadium Club** (1560 Broadway, 530/626-1689, 11 A.M.–2 A.M. daily) looks like an old cattle market. Inside, it's a dive with cold beer, stiff cocktails, and a pool table.

Casino

During the Gold Rush, prospectors often let loose with spirited card games that erupted in gunfire. Things have calmed down considerably at **Red Hawk Casino** (1 Red Hawk Pkwy., 888/573-3495, www.redhawkcasino.com). The casino is right off U.S. 50 between Shingle Springs and Placerville. Expect to find 2,100 slot machines, a poker room with seven tables, and dozens of table games. In California, Indian casinos can allow smoking but Red Hawk's second floor is smoke-free (although you can still smell cigarettes wafting from the other levels). Gambling can make you hungry;

the casino has seven cafés and restaurants, including the Waterfall buffet.

SHOPPING

Most shopping in Placerville happens downtown, where store owners have turned crumbling brick buildings into art galleries and boutiques. Seekers of antique bargains will have their hands full; new shops dealing in vintage trinkets appear every year. Start on Main Street and browse your way through the historic town center, keeping an eye open for bookstores, candy stores, and gift shops selling locally made handicrafts.

Antiques

Like many Gold Country towns, Placerville has its share of antiques shops, including **Empire Antiques** (432 Main St., 530/642-1025, 10:30 A.M.–5 P.M. daily), a co-op with more than 30 dealers selling vintage mementos and trinkets. **Placerville Antiques and**

WHY DO THEY CALL IT HANGTOWN?

Well, here's the short answer: They used to hang people here in the immediate years after James W. Marshall's discovery of gold in Coloma. The rush of 1849 brought miners seeking fortune, but it also beckoned gamblers and thieves. In those days, Placerville was known as Old Dry Diggins. Law enforcement didn't exist, and criminals often ambushed miners in broad daylight, robbing them of gold and sometimes killing them. Gamblers also relieved prospectors of their hard-earned dough by cheating other less-skilled players.

At some point in 1849, the townsfolk reached their limit. When five criminals attempted a holdup, the robbery went awry, and three gang members were caught. Mobs flooded the streets and quickly formed a street jury, convicting the robbers. "String 'em up!" shouted the crowd, and soon all were swinging from a large oak tree in the middle of Old Dry Diggins. According to some historians, another street hanging occurred in 1850 when a prospector accused a card dealer of cheating. Supposedly, the card dealer drew a large knife and killed the prospector. Another street jury formed, con-victed the card dealer, and strung him from that same tree.

Other hangings may have occurred, although the records don't give details. What is sure is that Old Dry Diggins became known as Hang-town after these executions. Hangtown was soon California's third largest town as more people arrived over the next few years. By 1854, some residents had decided the name was too scandalous and demanded a new moniker. That same year, Hangtown was incorporated as a city and received a new name: Placerville.

The hangman's oak tree was chopped down to a stump, and a saloon was built over it. For years, the Hangman's Tree was a roughneck bar on Main Street with a mannequin swinging from a noose on the building's facade. Customers came in to jaw with locals and hear stories about that notorious tree stump buried in the cellar. Sadly, the bar has since closed, and the building remained vacant throughout 2012. The poor dummy swinging from the noose disap-peared for a few years before mysteriously re-appearing in late 2011. Seems like some people can't let Hangtown's legacy die.

Collectibles (448 Main St., 530/626-3425, 10 A.M.–6 P.M. daily) will gift-wrap your purchase from this sprawling warehouse of cookware, furniture, vintage toys, and jewelry.

Art Galleries

Placerville's art scene is an established presence in town. **Gold Country Artist's Gallery** (379 Main St., 530/642-2944, www.goldcountry-artistsgallery.com, 11 A.M.–5 P.M. daily) show-cases works in a variety of mediums including oil, pastel, acrylic, and watercolor paintings, pottery, wood, glass, and photography. The art-ists are local, and the building is beautiful; a restored example of Gold Rush architecture. At the **Bennett Gallery** (6200 Pleasant Valley Rd., El Dorado, 530/621-1164, www.bennett-gallery.net, 10 A.M.–3 P.M. Mon.–Fri.), visitors can browse sculpture crafted by the Bennett family, who apparently have art running through their veins. Other local artists display blown glass, jewelry, paintings, and some-thing called "art humor." And the world's first **Kinkade Gallery** (262 Main St., 530/621-4453, 10 A.M.–5 P.M. Mon.–Sat., 11 A.M.–5 P.M. Sun.) displays works by the late Thomas Kinkade, a former Placerville resident known for his glow-ing depictions of bucolic small towns, cottages, and gardens.

Books

Who can resist buying something in a used bookstore? Fighting that temptation is even harder at **The Bookery** (326 Main St., 530/626-6454, 10 A.M.–5:30 P.M. Mon.– Thurs., 10 A.M.–7 P.M. Fri.–Sat., 10 A.M.–4 P.M.

Sun.). They sell a mix of used and new tomes in four packed rooms with shelves stacked to the ceiling.

Gifts

Can't find that perfect gift? Placerville's long Main Street is peppered with kooky shops selling everything from artisan olive oil to garden signs. For avant-garde trinkets to decorate the house, **Lighthouse** (451 Main St., Ste. 1, 530/626-5515, 9 A.M.–6 P.M. Sat.–Thurs., 9 A.M.–9 P.M. Fri.) has gifts from all over the world, including metal and cement art and wooden boxes, plus things for the garden like wind chimes. They also sell jewelry and greeting cards.

Another shop selling garden stuff is **Treehouse** (327 Main St., 530/295-0102, 10 A.M.–5:30 P.M. Mon.–Sat., 11 A.M.–4 P.M. Sun.), but they also have housewares like Christmas ornaments and Halloween decorations, candles, decorative canvas prints, and quirky dog toys.

Gourmet Goodies

If you need a gift basket, **Winterhill** (321 Main St., 530/626-6369, www.winterhillfarms.com, 10 A.M.–6 P.M. Mon.–Sat., 11 A.M.–5 P.M. Sun.) has a variety of artisan foods. They stock California olive oils and balsamic vinegars, plus chocolates, local honey, and preserves. A chunk of their products are made with organics. On the other hand, satisfy your sweet tooth at **CandyStrike: Old Tyme Candy & More** (398 Main St., 530/295-1007, www.candystrike.com, 11 A.M.–6 P.M. Mon.–Tues. and Thurs., 11 A.M.–8 P.M. Fri., 10 A.M.–8 P.M. Sat., 11 A.M.–5 P.M. Sun.) with goodies like black licorice, saltwater taffy, and fudge. For something heartier, get some great cheese and artisan bread from **Dedrick's Main Street Cheese** (312 Main St., 530/344-8282, www.dedrickscheese.com, 10 A.M.–6 P.M. Mon.–Sat., 11 A.M.–5 P.M. Sun.).

ACCOMMODATIONS

Placerville's old Gold Rush buildings have aged well, giving ambitious innkeepers plenty of vintage Victorian homes to convert into bed-and-breakfasts. This means visitors can be extra choosy when it comes to finding authentic digs for the night. Because many of Placerville's older homes once belonged to town fathers and Gold Rush merchants, staying in these 19th-century manors helps guests immerse themselves in the spirit of 1849. That may not be your thing, so Placerville also has comfortable budget motels that don't qualify for roach-coach status; these places are great options for families traveling with smaller children or pets.

Under $100

The **Mother Lode Motel** (1940 Broadway, 530/622-0895, www.placervillemotherlodemotel.com, $50–80) has clean and reasonably priced accommodations half-way between Placerville and Apple Hill. Don't get discouraged by the motel's cheap-looking sign; inside, the rooms are comfortable and tastefully decorated. If splurging on expensive bed-and-breakfasts isn't in your budget, the Mother Lode is a worthy alternative. Outside, there's a decent-size pool and lounge area that offer relief during the sweltering foothill summers. Inside the rooms, you'll also find modern amenities like free wireless Internet, microwave, mini-fridge, and private hot tubs.

Budget digs can be found at **National 9 Inn** (1500 Broadway, 530/622-3884, $60–90). This place is within a short drive of downtown Placerville and just a stone's throw from U.S. 50. The rooms are tidy and set up like most other corporate motels; simple furnishings, TV, microwave, and somewhat-comfortable bed. They do provide all rooms with air-conditioning and free wireless Internet. In the morning, chow down on the full breakfast before heading out to Apple Hill or Placerville's historic sights.

Best Western Plus (6850 Green Leaf Dr.,

530/622-9100, www.bwplacervilleinn.com, $90–200) has pretty standard motel lodgings for reasonable prices. Amenities include cable TV, table and chairs, fridge, microwave, and free wireless Internet. Some rooms also have a fireplace. When the mercury hits 90°F or higher during the summer, jump into the hotel's large swimming pool. Pets are welcome with an extra $25 tacked onto the rate.

Gold Country Inn (1332 Broadway, 530/622-3124, www.goldcountryinnplacerville.com, $75–95) has simple rooms and affordable rates. You'll find few frills, but each room does have a fridge, microwave, air-conditioning, and wireless access. Guests get a free continental breakfast every morning.

Innkeepers at **The Seasons Bed and Breakfast** (2934 Bedford Ave., 530/626-4420, www.theseasons.net, $90–180) bend over backward to make visitors feel at home. They give a quick tour of the verdant garden and lawns behind the main house, and help carry your bags from the car. The ancient stone and brick building (constructed in 1859) is one of Placerville's oldest, and retains an old-world vibe even though the interior has been thoroughly renovated. The four rooms have French-inspired decor, and are split between the main house and two cottages surrounded by rose gardens and picket fences. Inside, the rooms have antique 18th-century bed frames, French tapestries, and gleaming wood furnishings; the Moulin Rouge suite even has dual rain-forest showerheads in the bathroom. A gourmet French breakfast is served on your doorstep and typically includes quiche and pancakes. The Seasons may be quaint but still provides some modern conveniences; there's free wireless access and air-conditioning in every room. Kids and pets are welcome.

A Scottish highlander would enjoy staying at **Glen Morey Country House Bed and Breakfast** (801 Morey Dr., 530/306-3481, www.placervillebedandbreakfast.com, $84–135). Built in 1859, this stately manor lies hidden on 1.6 woodsy acres just outside of Placerville. Three elaborately decorated rooms, each with a Scottish theme, are swathed in lace curtains, stately antique furniture and bed frames, and wicker chairs; the Edinburgh room even has a marble fireplace. In the morning, expect hearty country fare of eggs and sausage for breakfast; veggies seem to be scarce, but the food is tasty. The Glen Morey has air-conditioning, and kids are welcome.

$100-150

Step back into the Gilded Age at the ◖**Albert Shafsky House** (2942 Coloma St., 530/642-2776, www.shafsky.com, $140–185), a cozy Victorian-era bed-and-breakfast built in 1902. Each room boasts luxurious handmade furniture and antiques from the late 19th century. You'll drool over the mouthwatering breakfast each morning, fixed entirely with local

the Albert Shafsky House

gourmet ingredients. New arrivals are treated with a complimentary bottle of El Dorado wine and an artisan cheese plate. Keep your eyes peeled before hitting the oh-so-comfortable sheets; the house was originally built for a wealthy Placerville businessman whose friendly ghost supposedly still haunts the guest rooms. The Shafsky House has only three delightful, decadent rooms so call well ahead to reserve.

You could picture Ernest Hemingway or Rudyard Kipling staying at **Eden Vale Inn** (1780 Springvale Rd., 530/621-0901, http:// edenvaleinn.com, $150–310). More safari resort than bed-and-breakfast, this renovated hay barn somehow combines a rustic foothill vibe with Napa-style luxury. The inn sits next to a fully stocked trout pond and exquisitely tended gardens that resemble a hidden Parisian park. Inside you'll find seven guest rooms named after native trees, each with gas fireplace and lavish amenities. Five of the rooms have private hot tubs and enclosed patios; soak away a long day in the Gold Country before slipping into unbelievably comfortable beds. If that's not decadent enough, book a relaxing massage or a facial at the on-site spa. In the morning, don't miss a homemade breakfast buffet made from locally grown ingredients and herbs from the inn's garden. The Eden Vale Inn is only a 10-minute drive from Coloma, and it's an excellent place to stay if you're river-rafting or visiting historic Gold Rush sites in the area.

The **Historic Cary House Hotel** (300 Main St., 530/622-4271, www.caryhouse. com, $100–160) is an imposing brick building right in the heart of downtown Placerville. Constructed in 1857, plenty of famous guests have slept here, including Elvis Presley and Mark Twain. The rooms are small but still bristling with character; the decor invokes the Gold Rush with period antiques and old tintype photographs hanging on the wall.

NORTHERN GOLD COUNTRY

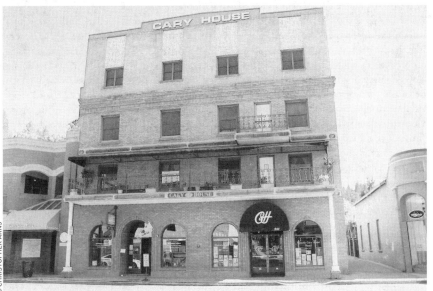

© CHRISTOPHER ARNS

the Historic Cary House in downtown Placerville

With over 150 years of history, it's not surprising that guests frequently report ghost sightings and other strange activity—the second floor is supposedly the most haunted. From the lobby, which is elaborately decorated with wooden paneling and plush furniture, take a ride on the 1920-style elevator if your room is upstairs. Amenities include free wireless Internet, continental breakfast, refrigerator, and cable television. While the hotel once boasted of having "a bathroom on every floor," past renovations made sure that every room now includes a private bath and shower. The Historic Cary House is just steps away from world-class restaurants and tiny boutiques; you won't find accommodations closer to the heart of Placerville.

For a backwoods vibe, stay at **The Davies Family Inn at Shadowridge Ranch** (3700 Fort Jim Rd., 530/295-1000, www.thedaviesfamilyinn.com, $135–170). This 19th-century log cabin is situated five miles east of Placerville on a working ranch. Four rooms have exposed wood beams across the ceiling and gnarled wood paneling on the walls. Guests might feel like they're on a hunting trip; each room has a stone hearth and a crackling wood-burning stove, homespun quilts covering queen or king beds, and sometimes even a mounted hunting trophy jutting from the wall. If you'd rather view wildlife outside the rooms, take a walk through the surrounding woods or the huge garden to spot woodpeckers, Steller's jays, and white-tailed deer. In the morning, expect to eat a homemade breakfast of yogurt, sausage, and apple cake. The inn allows children under "special circumstances," so call ahead if you're bringing little ones; pets are forbidden.

FOOD

Placerville sits squarely on U.S. 50, but it doesn't feel like a typical roadside town. You won't find a slew of fast-food restaurants choking downtown; instead, there's a surprising diversity to the cuisine here—from barbecue joints to upscale contemporary eateries serving fusion-style entrées.

American

The name says it all—◖ **The Shoestring** (1320 Broadway, 530/622-7125, 11 A.M.–8 P.M. Mon.–Sat., 11 A.M.–7 P.M. Sun., $10) is a roadside hole-in-the-wall that won't bust your budget. Serving savory fare like burgers, hot dogs, and culinary guilt-inducers like chili cheese fries, it's not the healthiest place—but your taste buds will love stopping here. If you need something less greasy, try a healthier option like one of the sandwiches. There's also a small children's menu, but most of the food here (cheeseburgers, corn dogs, chicken nuggets) is already kid-friendly. Since it's conveniently located near the northern tip of downtown Placerville, it makes an easy place to swing by on the way to Apple Hill. The Shoestring doesn't have public restrooms, so factor that into your plans before dropping in.

If the weather turns dark and stormy, head to **Z Pie Gourmet Pot Pies** (3182 Center St., 530/621-2626, www.z-pie.com/pv, 11 A.M.–9 P.M. daily, $8). They serve lots of different meats under each steaming-hot crust such as lamb, sausage, chicken, and steak. Along with potpies, you can order an organic salad or a soup. For dessert, try the berry pie with oatmeal crumble on top.

Inside **Bricks** (482 Main St., 530/303-3480, www.bricksonmainstreet.com, 11 A.M.–8:30 P.M. Sun.–Thurs., 11 A.M.–9 P.M. Fri.–Sat., $10–23), the walls have been stripped bare to reveal the original 19th-century—wait for it—red brick (what gave it away?). This contemporary pub has a fun atmosphere that's a step up from other sports bars. Photographs and large canvases by local artists hang on the old walls. There are a few flat-screen TVs (it's a great place to catch a game), but they don't dominate the place. The food is traditional pub grub so expect burgers, sandwiches, steaks, and slabs of grilled fish. Bricks doesn't take reservations, but they'll give you priority seating for calling ahead.

Get up early for a country-style breakfast at **Sweetie Pie's Restaurant** (577 Main St., 530/642-0128, www.sweetiepies.biz, 6:30 A.M.–3 P.M. Mon.–Fri., 7 A.M.–3 P.M. Sat., 7 A.M.–1 P.M. Sun., $5–12). The restaurant occupies a squat Victorian bungalow built in 1865 which has been thoroughly restored. Omelettes are the star on Sweetie Pie's menu (the smoked turkey and asparagus is amazingly good), and they're made with four belt-busting eggs—so come hungry.

For upscale American fare there's **The Independent** (629 Main St., 530/344-7527, http://independentplacerville.com, 11 A.M.–9 P.M. Sun.–Mon. and Wed.–Thurs., 11 A.M.–11 P.M. Fri.–Sat., $10–28). The menu describes itself as "American fusion," which apparently means surf and turf with a few tweaks. A typical entrée is the rosemary lamb or the grilled salmon. It's owned by the same folks who run the Heyday Café down the street, but the Independent is a little fancier.

Asian

If you're just looking for some quick Chinese takeout, there's **Golden Dragon Restaurant** (1341 Broadway, 530/621-1568, 11 A.M.–9 P.M. Sun.–Thurs., 11 A.M.–9:30 P.M. Fri.–Sat., $6–12).

Bakeries and Cafés

Located in the old Placerville Soda Works building, the **⊂ Cozmic Café** (594 Main St., 530/642-8481, http://ourcoz. com, 7 A.M.–6 P.M. Tues.–Wed. and Sun., 7 A.M.–8 P.M. Thurs.–Sat., $9) is probably one of the only coffee shops with a gold mine in back. Inside the weathered stone walls, this café serves locally farmed organic food and fair trade coffee. Yoginis will also love the weekly

Vinyasa classes held here, and musical acts play at least several times a month.

Barbecue

Expect finger-licking goodness at **Hog Wild BBQ** (38 Main St., 530/622-3883, http:// hogwildbbqca.com, 11 A.M.–9 P.M. Thurs.–Mon., $10). This place is small, but the rough wooden interior feels like an authentic Texas roadhouse. The food is made from scratch, and while it's probably not healthy, it sure is damn good. Menu items include smoked brisket, pulled pork, and platter after platter of chicken. There's live blues and bluegrass music on Saturdays, while every other Monday is Hot Rod Night when gearheads are encouraged to bring their rides.

Another barbecue spot is **Old Town Grill** (444 Main St., 530/622-2631, 11 A.M.–3 P.M. Mon. and Wed., 11 A.M.–8 P.M. Thurs.–Sat., noon–3 P.M. Sun., $8). Folks rave about the grass-fed exotic meats grilled here, like the buffalo and elk burgers. The black bean burger is also a favorite. Barbecue doesn't have a monopoly on the menu; you can order pasta like butternut squash ravioli or dig into a salad.

For an atmosphere that feels like an indoor summer cookout, there's **Poor Red's BBQ** (6221 Pleasant Valley Rd., El Dorado, 530/622-2901, 11:30 A.M.–9 P.M. Tues.–Thurs., 11:30 A.M.–10 P.M. Fri., 11 A.M.–10 P.M. Sat., noon–9 P.M. Sun., $6–21). It's a local favorite, although that's likely because the bar is so popular. The food is what you'd expect; spicy barbecue chicken, ribs, and steak at semi-reasonable prices.

Californian

⊂ The Heyday Café (325 Main St., 530/626-9700, www.heydaycafe.com, 11 A.M.–9 P.M. Tues.–Thurs., 11 A.M.–10 P.M. Fri.–Sat., 11 A.M.–8 P.M. Sun., $17–26) is one of the newer eateries in downtown Placerville, but it's quickly gained a reputation as one of the best. From the street, it's easy to miss Heyday's modest entrance; inside, the stripped-brick interior and rough-hewn wooden ceiling gives the café a rugged yet hip vibe. The food is California bistro style fused with Asian, Italian, and Mediterranean influences. Try the bacon artichoke pesto pizza or the lemon salsa skewers; pair with a crisp riesling from Apple Hill to sample the extensive wine list. If you aren't stuffed at that point, the dessert menu (molasses gingerbread cake and chocolate porter cake are just two of the mouthwatering options) is pure decadence.

Deli

The best place to find locally farmed and organic produce is **Placerville Natural Foods Co-op** (535 Placerville Dr., 530/621-3663, http://placervillecoop.org, 8 A.M.–7 P.M. Mon.–Fri., 9 A.M.–7 P.M. Sat., 10 A.M.–5 P.M. Sun., $5–10). This oversize health food store has a substantial produce section, a vitamin department, and bulk foods. The deli serves organic soups and salads, along with kick-ass sandwiches.

French

Serious foodies will enjoy ◀**Zachary Jacques Country French Cuisine** (1821 Pleasant Valley Rd., 530/626-8045, www.zacharyjacques.com, 4:30–8 P.M. Wed.–Sun., $18–35). This quaint restaurant is perfect for a romantic night out. The food is anything but quaint. Head chef John Evans is a culinary whiz, serving up savory meals like the sautéed salmon with Meyer lemon relish. The wine list is long and very distinguished with both French and local El Dorado vino.

Mexican

For upscale Mexican food in the heart of the Gold Country, grab a table at ◀**Cascada** (384 Main St., 530/344-7757, www.cascadaonmainstreet.com, 11 A.M.–8:30 P.M. Sun.–Thurs.,

11 A.M.–9:30 P.M. Fri.–Sat., $10–23). Located in downtown Placerville, Cascada is Mexican with a California bistro twist. Inside, like most of the region's more cosmopolitan eateries, the restaurant's historic building has been renovated to reveal rough brick walls and vaulted ceiling. You can find familiar Mexican favorites on the menu like burritos, tacos, and enchiladas, but if you're feeling adventurous, try something new: The pork medallions with raspberry chipotle sauce and the salmon stuffed with spinach are just two of the standouts. Since the restaurant is elegant-casual, you might want to freshen up before arriving, and reservations are probably a good idea.

INFORMATION AND SERVICES

Placerville is the largest town in El Dorado County and your best bet for major services. You can find gas stations, banks, ATMs, supermarkets, and a **post office** (3045 Sacramento St., 8:30 A.M.–5 P.M. Mon.–Fri., 10 A.M.–1 P.M. Sat.).

For local news, *Mountain Democrat* is one of the oldest daily newspapers in California and covers Placerville and El Dorado County. Many of the smaller towns also have their own weekly newspapers, and many are free. For arts and entertainment events information, pick up the free *Sierra Lodestar* (www.sierralodestar. com), which advertises upcoming concerts and cultural events.

For medical assistance, **Marshall Hospital** (1100 Marshall Way, Placerville, 530/622-1441, www.marshallmedical.org) offers an emergency room and a full range of hospital services.

GETTING THERE AND AROUND

Placerville is located at the intersection of Highways 50 and 49, 45 miles east of Sacramento. Stoplights on Highway 50 can

Apple Hill

cause traffic to back up on weekends, and winter snows can close the roads.

A commuter bus provides daily weekday service between Placerville and downtown Sacramento. The big blue **El Dorado Transit** (530/642-5383, www.eldoradotransit.com, $5) makes 11 return trips and includes stops in Shingle Springs, Diamond Springs, Cameron Park, and El Dorado Hills. **Amtrak Thruway** (Mosquito Rd. and Clay St., www.amtrak.com) has one daily bus between Placerville and the downtown Sacramento Valley Station.

Touring the Northern Gold Country by private plane? You can land at **Placerville Airport** (3501 Airport Rd., 530/622-0459, www.co.eldorado.ca.us/Airports) just three miles east of town.

APPLE HILL

Every fall during harvest season, you can follow the smell of freshly baked pies to Apple Hill (northeast of U.S. 50, between Placerville and Pollack Pines, 530/644-7692, www.applehill.com), a community of apple orchards, vineyards, and Christmas tree farms. There's just something about the air up here. Apple Hill's orchards grow their produce at an altitude of 3,500 feet, amidst a carpet of pine needles and black oak leaves. More than 50 farms open their gates to visitors for hayrides in late summer and into autumn. They also sell delicious pies, caramel apples, and ripe pumpkins. It's like a harvest fair that lasts from Labor Day until Thanksgiving. But unlike other fall celebrations, visitors to Apple Hill can also swing by some of El Dorado's best family-owned wineries tucked alongside the orchards. You can even cut down a Christmas tree during the holidays. Most of the action happens near the community of Camino (pop. 1,750), but Apple Hill itself isn't a town; it's the association of apple farmers that live in the area near Camino. Get there early in the morning to avoid throngs of tourists that clog up the windy two-lane country roads in fall.

Orchards and Farms

Believe it or not, Apple Hill wouldn't exist without pears, which local orchards grew almost exclusively until a blight in the early 1960s forced farmers to switch to something else. That's when farmers decided to put the apple into Apple Hill. These days, the hilly area around Camino is a patchwork quilt of apple orchards and woodsy valleys. To see the most of the area, download a map of the **Apple Drive Scenic Drive** (www.applehill.com) showing every vendor and produce stand. Fall is the best time to visit if you can stand the crowds, and it's the only time that many farms are open. Call ahead if you're passing through in either late August or early December to see what's open.

With a weekly craft fair, market, bakery, and pumpkin patch, **Boa Vista Orchards** (2952 Carson Rd., Camino, 530/622-5522, www.boavista.com, 9 A.M.–5 P.M. daily) is always buzzing come fall. It gives visitors that defining Apple Hill experience of pies and produce, with a carnival-like atmosphere. Boa Vista's open-air produce stand has huge bins of Red Delicious, Granny Smiths, and vegetables like club-stand stalks of brussels sprouts.

Hot, doughy, sugary apple cider doughnuts are the highlight at **Rainbow Orchards** (2569 Larsen Dr., Camino, 530/644-1594, http://rainboworchards.com, 9 A.M.–5 P.M. daily Labor Day–Thanksgiving weekend, some weekends in early Dec.). Buy a couple, buy a whole bag; you just can't stop eating these fried treats, made from real apple cider brewed on-site. Rainbow also sells pies, pumpkins, and colorful squash inside their reddish barn.

High Hill Ranch (2901 High Hill Rd., Placerville, 530/644-1973, 8 A.M.–5 P.M. daily Labor Day–Christmas Eve) sells freshly picked apples, pies, homemade caramel apples, and fritters. Wash it all down with their apple wine. And then there's this: High Hill has collected quite a few antique apple peelers dating back to 1850, along with a vintage popcorn wagon.

Kids can run amok at **Abel's Apple Acres** (2100 Hassler Rd., Placerville, 530/626-0138, www.abelsappleacres.com, 8 A.M.–6 P.M. daily Labor Day–Christmas Eve). There's a maze of 600 hay bales, pony rides, and a pumpkin patch. While kids tear around the maze, adults can browse for apple-themed trinkets at the craft fair. For lunch, get some barbecued grub (hot dogs, burgers, chicken, and sandwiches) from the grill. If you've saved room, try some homemade fudge or take home a pumpkin apple pie.

Grab a basket and get ready for stained fingers at **Patrick's U-Pick Berry Farm** (4455 Pony Express Trail, Camino, 530/647-2833, www.patricksmtngrown.com, berry patch 7:30 A.M.–5 P.M. Thurs.–Sun. June–early Sept.; store 9 A.M.–5 P.M. daily June–late Nov.). You

NORTHERN GOLD COUNTRY

© CHRISTOPHER ARNS

High Hill Ranch in Apple Hill

can pick blackberries and raspberries growing from the hillside before going home to bake a pie. Make sure to call ahead to see if the farm is open that day; sometimes the vines have to rest for a few days after picking.

Wineries

Some of the best vineyards in El Dorado County grow in Apple Hill. The higher elevation (around 3,500 feet), shallow soil, and good drainage make outstanding wine. Among the more polished outfits is **Boeger Winery** (1709 Carson Rd., 800/655-2634, www.boegerwinery.com, 10 A.M.–5 P.M. daily, tasting free) with award-winning barbera, cabernet franc, and zinfandel wines bottled almost entirely from estate grapes. The property has a stone wine cellar and distillery from the 1870s, when an Italian immigrant planted the first vineyard. Nowadays, Boeger grows 29 grape varieties on the estate, but they also make an "Old Clone" zinfandel from some of those old vines.

Whether it's the view (spectacular) or the reds (balanced), **Lava Cap Winery** (2221 Fruitridge Rd., Placerville, 530/621-0175, www.lavacap.com, 11 A.M.–5 P.M. daily, tasting free) is, bar none, among the most popular places in Apple Hill. The wine list features typical El Dorado classics such as barbera, syrah, cabernet sauvignon, and petite syrah. The winery has been owned by the Jones family since 1981; they named the outfit after the rare volcanic terroir that saturates their estate.

Named for the distinctive tree that grows abundantly at higher elevations, **Madroña Vineyards** (2560 High Hill Rd., Camino, 530/644-5948, www.madronavineyards.com, 11 A.M.–5 P.M. daily, tasting free) is an old-school El Dorado winery. The Bush family were among the first Apple Hill winemakers to produce Rhône and Bordeaux varietals such as barbera, cabernet franc, and a well-balanced zinfandel with raspberry, black pepper, and spice—typical for the El Dorado varietal.

Entertainment and Events

Problem: you're stuffed with Apple Hill pies and need to drop a few pounds. Sign up for the **Harvest Run** (3.5–8.5 miles, early Nov., 916/492-8966, www.applehillrun.org, $30–35, kids $16). The event began in 1979 when apple farmers wanted to extend the harvest season. They decided a footrace would be a good idea. These days, the event benefits Camino School, so all proceeds go to support local kids. The entry fee is kind of steep, but it includes parking, shuttle to and from the race, a long-sleeved T-shirt with a cool Harvest Run logo, and snacks after the race.

Once you've picked out pumpkins, scarfed down some pie, and braved Apple Hill's crowds, head to **Jack Russell Brewery** (2380 Larsen Dr., Camino, 530/647-9420, www.jackrussellbrewing.com, 11 A.M.–6 P.M. Mon.–Thurs. and Sat., 11 A.M.–8 P.M. Fri., 11 A.M.–5 P.M. Sun.) for a pint of English-style beer. Located behind an apple orchard, Jack Russell has handicraft vendors and live music on weekends. But the best thing about this place is the beer and the cider; if you try the sampler platter, it comes with taster cups filled with every Jack Russell brew.

Accommodations

Pickings are slim for sleeping in Apple Hill. After all, Placerville is just a short drive away. But if you can't leave the apple orchards behind, there's **Camino Hotel Bed and Breakfast Inn** (4103 Carson Rd., 530/644-1800, www.caminohotel.com, $60–150). It was built in 1888 as a barracks for loggers but has been spiffed up since then. The Pony Express and Wells Fargo stagecoaches used to charge by the inn, located on the historic Lincoln Highway. The nine cozy rooms have rustic wood paneling, comfy beds, a woodstove, and antique wooden furnishings. It's an old building, so not every room has a private bath—some are shared—so make sure to ask for one ahead of time. Before

© CHRISTOPHER ARNS

the Camino Hotel Bed and Breakfast Inn

heading outside in the morning, do sit down for a breakfast of quiche, French toast, or sausage. Because it's so close to wineries and orchards, Camino Hotel makes a perfect home base for seeing Apple Hill.

Food

Naming just a few places for food doesn't tell the whole story. Apple Hill's orchards have tons of food, like pies and produce, but they also serve up barbecue platters on weekends during the fall. For grub at other times, there's **Forester Pub and Grill** (4110 Carson Rd., Camino, 530/644-1818, 11:30 A.M.–9 P.M. daily, $8–19). This English-style pub serves Eastern European cuisine like stroganoff and schnitzel, along with good ol' American comfort food such as meatloaf. Sides include red cabbage kraut and spätzle, a pile of pea-size dumplings with gravy.

For touristy German food, there's **Bavarian Hills** (3100 North Canyon Rd., Camino, 530/642-2714, www.bavarianhills.com, 11 A.M.–5 P.M. daily Labor Day–Dec., $5–10). You can hear this place before you see it—as you come around the corner, strains of the Beer Barrel Polka waft through the pine trees. The restaurant is run by a German lady named Inge who bakes homemade apple strudel, pies, and apple almond cheese tortes inside this Bavarian-style shop. They also serve platters of bratwurst or schnitzel with a side of strudel. It's kind of kitschy, but fits with the rest of Apple Hill's attractions.

If you need a warm pastry to start the day, **Apple Blossom Coffee House** (4077 Carson Rd., 530/644-0284, 6 A.M.–2 P.M. Mon.–Sat., $2–10) serves espresso and pastries for breakfast. At lunch, order soups and savory empanadas.

Getting There and Around

To reach Apple Hill, turn off U.S. 50 two exits east of Placerville. Driving is the only way to

© CHRISTOPHER ARNS

a replica of the sawmill where gold was first discovered in Coloma

get around Apple Hill; download the Apple Hill Scenic Drive (www.applehill.com) maps and directions for specific routes, wineries, and orchards.

COLOMA

For many reasons, this sleepy hamlet (pop. 530) along the South Fork of the American River will always be stuck in 1848. That's the year one James W. Marshall, a foreman running a sawmill on the American, stumbled across a few pieces of gold in the water. The rush that followed would launch California into statehood and transform the West. Back in Coloma, Marshall never got rich, and tired prospectors eventually left town as goldfields petered out. Most of Coloma's Gold Rush buildings are now part of a state park dedicated to Marshall's discovery.

These days, a different rush has struck Coloma. Thrill seekers flock to the American River's frothy white water for rafting trips.

Outfitters have set up shop along the river's rocky banks to offer some of the most popular rafting adventures in California. A summer day can turn the American into an orange and yellow nylon quilt, as rafts pepper the rapids on daylong adventures. But with the adrenaline comes posh bed-and-breakfasts and wineries that welcome a different kind of traveler. Coloma may always be connected to the region's Gold Rush past, but this resilient town continues to reinvent itself.

◀ Marshall Gold Discovery State Historic Park

One day in 1848, a carpenter named James W. Marshall took a fateful stroll by the sawmill he was building for John Sutter on the American River and found gold specks shining in the water. Marshall's discovery sparked the Gold Rush and one of the greatest migrations in history. See where it all began at the Marshall Gold Discovery State Historic Park

(310 Back St., 530/622-3470, www.parks. ca.gov, 8 A.M.–7 P.M. daily in summer, $8 per vehicle). Start inside the visitor center for a quick lesson on the park's storied past, complete with artifacts from the native Nisenan and Miwok tribes that lived in the area before gold was discovered. You can even check out real gold nuggets on display. Outside the visitor center (10 A.M.–4 P.M. Tues.–Sun. Apr.–Nov.; 10 A.M.–3 P.M. Nov.–Mar.) history buffs will love the park's interactive exhibits—you can catch a live pioneer cooking demonstration or help load a real wagon with mining supplies like a true forty-niner.

Feel like recreating Marshall's discovery for yourself? Take a gold panning lesson at the park's Eureka Experience Center and then try your luck by the river. Kids will especially love getting elbow-deep in the mud for a chance to strike it rich.

Hiking

Marshall Gold Discovery State Historic Park provides nature walks and hikes through the scenic American River canyon. The **Gold Discovery Loop Trail** (3.6 miles) takes you right to the very spot where Marshall made his discovery. Surrounded by beautiful wildflowers in the spring, a full-size replica of Sutter's mill stands near several immaculately restored historic buildings, like the tiny one-bedroom Mormon cabin, the Chinese-operated Wah Hop and Man Lee stores, the old blacksmith shop and the Price-Thomas home. In summer, the park's towering oak trees help shade park visitors from the scorching sun, making a perfect spot for a picnic on a warm day.

The **Monroe Ridge Trail** (four miles, moderate) starts at the 1890 James Marshall Monument before climbing a series of tough switchbacks. There's a vista overlooking the park and the spot where James W. Marshall stumbled across gold nuggets in the South Fork of the American River. Hikers will pass an old

fruit orchard and a replica of Sutter's Mill before returning to the monument.

◖ White-Water Rafting

If you're looking for guided river trips, Coloma is the white-water capital of the Gold Country. From here, outfitters can take you to all three forks of the American River, including the rugged Class IV–V rapids of the North Fork and the more moderate Class III–IV white water of the Middle Fork. There are rafting trips designed for all experience levels, and you can even book overnight excursions; if you're a rookie rafter, try a more leisurely half-day trip down the lower section of the South Fork. The season usually runs from April to October except for trips on the North Fork, which usually last until May or June depending on weather and water levels. Check online for specific dates.

All-Outdoors Whitewater Rafting (925/932-8993, www.aorafting.com, $110–495) offers half-day, full-day and multi-day trips on the North, Middle, and South Forks of the American River. If you have time, a two-day or three-day jaunt involves camping in stunningly beautiful river canyons. Guides prepare all meals, and it's an excellent way to experience a different side of the Gold Country. You can also book full-day trips on any of the three forks if a multi-day expedition isn't feasible. If you have small kids or just want to calmly drift down the river, consider the full-day Tom Sawyer Float Trips along the rapids-free section of the South Fork.

Beyond Limits Adventures (530/622-0553, www.rivertrip.com, $100–300) offers mostly half-day and one-day excursions to the North, Middle, and South Forks; you can also take two-day trips on the South Fork with complimentary wine and beer served at dinner. Two-day trips also include a stop at a riverside resort where you can fish, play basketball, and try gold panning.

American Whitewater Expeditions (800/825-3205, www.americanwhitewater.com, $85–395) offers half-day, full-day, and multi-day trips to all three forks of the American River. All expeditions come with delicious meals, friendly guides, and jaw-dropping Sierra Nevada scenery.

O.A.R.S. (800/346-6277, www.oars.com, $110–360) also offers trips to all three forks of the American River. It's one of the most experienced rafting companies in the West, and the guides are extremely knowledgeable. O.A.R.S. offers full-day trips with a picnic on the Middle and North Forks; you can take half-day, full-day, and two-day trips with meals included on the South Fork. There's also a two-day wine and raft tour that includes side trips to several El Dorado County wineries.

Whitewater Connection (530/622-6446, www.whitewaterconnection.com, $95–340) offers the standard full-day trips to the North, Middle, and South Forks, along with multi-day expeditions. You can also book half-day trips on the South Fork if time doesn't allow a longer excursion. Whitewater Connection will do two-day trips combining one day on the North Fork with another day on either the Middle or South Fork.

ARTA River Trips (800/323-2782, www.arta.org, Apr.–Oct., $125–370) runs one- and two-day trips on both the Middle and South Forks of the American River. Expect good food and friendly company from the experienced rafting guides.

Entertainment and Events

A stuffed buffalo looks down from the wall as you walk into **Buford's** (835 Lotus Rd., 530/626-8096, www.sierranevadahouse.com, 5–10 p.m. Wed.–Sun.), the bar at Sierra Nevada House. Remodeled to look like an Old West saloon, you won't find dirty prospectors or gunslingers in this drinking establishment; the gleaming wooden interior and immaculate bar

give Buford's an upscale vibe. Still, it's a lively place to spend an evening after a day on the river if you're staying at the adjoining hotel. The bar offers an extensive list of local wines and beer, along with reasonably priced cocktails. Coloma's nightlife isn't exactly hopping, so Buford's is probably your best bet for evening fun in this tiny town. The bar closes at 8 p.m. in winter.

During the Gold Rush, mining camps attracted all kinds of roguish entertainers seeking to entrance bored and homesick prospectors with colorful melodramas. The **Olde Coloma Theatre** (380 Monument Rd., 530/626-5282, www.oldecolomatheatre.org, $10) is a throwback to those days. Built in a ramshackle cabin just down the street from where gold was discovered in 1848, the theater offers whimsical productions like *It Just Ghost to Show* and *There's Snow Time Like the Present.* The shows are family-friendly, and many productions are staged with kids in mind. Best of all, catcalls are encouraged—audience members can boo and yell at the actors, just like actual melodrama attendees did during the Gold Rush. While you shouldn't expect Shakespeare-level quality, the actors are locals and clearly enjoy performing, making any visit a lighthearted and memorable experience.

Accommodations

The **Coloma Country Inn** (345 High St., 530/622-6919, www.colomacountryinn.com, $125–235) has the white picket fence and wide veranda of a bucolic country ranch. Surrounded by willows and immaculate lawns on the bank of a small lake, the property is tucked back from the road and gives the place a secretive, private feel. Built in 1852, the inn has six rooms, each charmingly decorated with a 19th-century farmhouse theme. For a true farmhouse experience, book one of the two studios inside the property's original carriage house. Breakfast is a treat; if you're lucky, homemade blackberry pie will be waiting for you in the morning. The Coloma Country Inn is a short walk from the Marshall Gold Discovery State Historic Park and several of the town's historic buildings, including a crumbling cemetery that's almost 200 years old.

If you've tired of yet another Victorian inn, which seem ubiquitous in the Gold Country, check out **Bella Vista Bed and Breakfast** (581 Cold Springs Rd., 530/622-3456, www. discoverbellavista.com, $190–300). This palatial Mediterranean-style estate doesn't skimp on anything; the grounds are covered in plush lawns, fountains, and artificial waterfalls. On the back patio, there's a pool with sweeping views of the American River between groves of black oak trees. Each of the four rooms has large windows that overlook the river valley. The innkeeper is a contractor who renovated the house himself; walking into each room feels like stepping into a Parisian penthouse. Amenities can include a fireplace, spa, four-poster bed, mini-fridge, TV, and private bath.

The **Sierra Nevada House** (835 Lotus Rd., 530/626-8096, www.sierranevadahouse. com, $90–105) is just a stone's throw from the South Fork of the American River and offers six Western-themed rooms. The accommodations are charming and romantic, though a bit plain, and each room has a different Gold Rush decor. Overall, this roadside inn is actually more of a couples' retreat, and families with children might do best to stay elsewhere. The hotel is right on Highway 49 and can be somewhat noisy; if you stay in the Bordello Room, beware—your quarters are right above the bar. Otherwise, the location is conveniently close to the area's historic and recreational attractions; the price is also quite reasonable for the area.

For more casual accommodations, try camping at the **American River Resort** (6019 New River Rd., 530/622-6700, http://american-riverresort.com, cabins $150–280, campsites $25–35, RV hookups $45). More than just a drab RV park, the resort is right on the South Fork of the American River and gives visitors a chance to feel closer to nature. Bathrooms and showers are available near all 85 campsites, along with a swimming pool—although there's always the river if you're taking a dip. The riverside cabins have recently been remodeled; the kitchens are fully stocked with appliances and utensils, but bed linens are not provided.

Food

The **Café Mahjaic** (1006 Lotus Rd., 530/622-9587, www.cafemahjaic.com, 5–8 P.M. Wed.–Sat., $19–25) offers fine dining near the banks of the American River. Inside a historic brick building constructed in 1855, the restaurant's cuisine competes with anything you'd find in Napa or the Bay Area. The food is New American cuisine with a subtle Mediterranean touch, and menu items are served with natural and organic ingredients. The Hillbilly salad is a delicious twist on a traditional Greek favorite, and the grilled flatbread with tzatziki sauce and hummus is also wonderful. If you've been hankering for meat on your trips throughout the Gold Country, try the naturally raised New York steak or pork tenderloin. At Café Mahjaic, the white tablecloths and a decidedly cosmopolitan interior mean you'll want to spiff up before dinner. The Café Mahjaic is closed the first week of July and also the first two weeks of January, so make note if your travel is planned during those times. Every night, the last reservation is at 8 P.M., and do make sure you reserve a table, as this restaurant is very popular.

You can't go wrong with the cuisine at the **Sierra Nevada House** (835 Lotus Rd., 530/626-8096, www.sierranevadahouse.com, 5–10 P.M. Wed.–Sun., $8–23). It's mostly American steakhouse food and surprisingly good for a tiny Gold Rush town. If you're having trouble deciding on dinner, try the pear chutney pork chops sprinkled with chunks of blue cheese and pair it with a bottle of local zinfandel from El Dorado County. The haute fig chicken is also a treat, made with a tasty house fig and thyme jam. On the other hand, vegetarians might feel left out; the menu isn't exactly overflowing with meatless options, but the gourmet salads are meals by themselves. The restaurant is closed Monday and Tuesday, so plan accordingly.

The **Argonaut** (331 Hwy. 49, 530/626-7345, 10 A.M.–4 P.M. Tues.–Sun., $8) is a tiny shack just steps away from where James Marshall discovered gold in 1848. You can get homemade sandwiches, soups, chili, and pie from nearby Apple Hill. On sunny days, grab a picnic table out behind the Argonaut or just sit at one of the small tables on the café's side patio where you can see the South Fork of the American River. The food is reasonably priced, and the place is conveniently located across Highway 49 from the visitor center at the Marshall Gold Discovery State Historic Park.

Getting There and Around

Coloma lies almost nine miles north of Placerville on Highway 49; the Marshall Gold Discovery State Historic Park is the easiest landmark. It snows in Coloma from November through April, and sometimes even into May. If you're low on fuel and deep in the countryside, **Riverside Mini Mart** (7215 Hwy. 49, Lotus, 530/642-9715) provides gas for travelers in Coloma.

FAIR PLAY

The community of Fair Play still flies beneath the radar for most travelers, but enjoy this hidden gem while you can. The reddish soil and gently sloping hillsides make one hell of a place for wine, and Fair Play's wineries are quickly gaining recognition at California wine competitions. That distinctive landscape is also worth a trip, and while the lodgings are sparse here, they usually offer unparalleled views of unspoiled valleys and mountains.

Wineries

The Fair Play appellation is still fairly new. Most growers first planted their grapes within the last 20 years. But being the new kid on the block hasn't kept Fair Play down; even *Wine Spectator* has recognized the wineries here as among the best in the area. One of the first was **Fitzpatrick Winery and Lodge** (7740 Fairplay Rd., Somerset, 530/620-6838, www.fitzpatrickwinery.com, 11 A.M.–5 P.M. Wed.–Mon., tasting free), known for growing organic and sustainably farmed grapes. This place is eco-conscious to the core. The winery runs almost completely on solar energy while winemaker Brian Fitzpatrick loads up his tractor with biofuel.

Fitzpatrick's also has quite the view—on a clear day you can almost see Placerville. With the Gold Country's best vantage point, it's almost possible (but not quite) to forget about Fitzpatrick's Irish-themed wines and Rhône reds (like the Grenache Reserve), but don't make that mistake. At this winery, estate grapes are cultivated on different plots to enhance each varietal's diverse notes. The results will please your palate. The Irish theme is a popular one, and you can keep savoring it at the Fitzpatrick's bed-and-breakfast, which offers a delicious Ploughman's Lunch of smoked salmon, freshly baked breads, cheeses, veggies, and fruits.

The winemakers at **Skinner Vineyards** (8054 Fairplay Rd., 530/620-2220, www.skinnervineyards.com, 11 A.M.–5 P.M. Fri.–Sun., tasting free) have a Fair Play connection like no other. Their ancestor, a Scottish immigrant named James Skinner, planted one of the area's first vineyards in 1860. Those family roots inspired the current generation of Skinner winemakers to produce well-balanced Rhône varietals with complex aromas. The list includes typical Fair Play wines such as syrah, mourvèdre, viognier, and grenache.

Charles B. Mitchell Vineyards (8221 Stoney

© CHRISTOPHER ARNS

Staying at the Fitzpatrick Lodge means walking out to views like this every morning.

Creek Rd., 530/620-3467, http://charlesb-mitchell.com, 11 A.M.–5 P.M. Tues.–Sun., tasting free) produces Bordeaux-inspired wines from estate-grown grapes. After several years away from the winery named for him, Charles Mitchell bought back the outfit in 2010. Apparently, people can tell. Three varietals won Best in Class at the 2012 San Francisco International Wine Competition, including the Monsieur Omo—a delightful red produced in the style of beaujolais.

The wine at **Cedarville Vineyards** (6320 Marestail Rd., 530/620-9463, http://cedarvillevineyard.com, by appointment) has earned a top-flight reputation. *Wine Spectator* claims Cedarville's zinfandels are leading a taste revolution in the foothills. The smoky and well-balanced syrah, which notes of dark cherry and chocolate flavors, shouldn't be missed either. Cedarville prides itself on sustainable growing practices and recently converted the vineyards to organic grapes.

The reds at **Miraflores** (2120 Four Springs Trail, Placerville, 530/647-8505, www.mirafloreswinery.com, 10 A.M.–5 P.M. daily, tasting free) have also begun turning heads; *Wine Spectator* has consistently scored the zinfandel over 90 points. They produce muscular, focused reds from small lots of syrah and petite syrah. Whites include viognier and pinot grigio, both typical for the Fair Play terroir.

Accommodations

Unlike lodgings elsewhere in the Gold Country, overnight options in Fair Play seem more like country guesthouses than staid Victorian manors. Imagine staying with a friend out in the woods, and you'll have an idea. If the Irish-style wine was just too good to leave, **Fitzpatrick Winery and Lodge** (7740 Fairplay Rd., Somerset, 530/620-3248, www.fitzpatrickwinery.com, $90–165) takes its Celtic roots seriously—right down to the green eggs and ham served at breakfast. Inside, two of the five rooms have Irish-themed decor with Celtic-patterned cushions and Fitzpatrick family photos. Most of the rooms include a claw-foot tub and woodstoves, providing a comfortable homespun log cabin vibe that still feels lavish. Make sure to bring your camera; the inn is perched on a small hill, and you'll get miles of unbeatable views over the Fitzpatrick vineyards and surrounding pine woodlands. The log cabin theme continues inside the Great Room, which has a vaulted log ceiling and plush sofa set before a fireplace. Breakfast is homemade with ingredients from a local farmers market and the Fitzpatrick's own garden; try one of the delicious omelettes or frittatas in the morning after rousing from your comfortable bed. During steamy summer days, go outside and take a dip in the Olympic-length lap pool, or if it's cooler at night, you can ease into the lodge's hot tub for a relaxing soak. Smack-dab in the heart of Fair Play's wine region, the Fitzpatrick Winery and Lodge is a perfect starting point to explore El Dorado County and beyond.

One of the more homespun places to sleep is **Lucinda's Country Inn** (6701 Perry Creek Rd., 530/409-4169, www.lucindascountryinn.com, $175–225). This sprawling country home has been expanded to include five bedrooms, which might include a whirlpool tub, soft quilted bedspreads, a fridge loaded with complimentary snacks and drinks, and a flat-screen TV. After sleeping like a baby in microfiber sheets, walk out to breakfast—made-to-order omelettes, eggs Benedict, coffee cake, and fruits round out the menu. One of the best things about Lucinda's is the huge back deck. There's a roaring stone fireplace, and groves of oaks provide a shady respite during late afternoons. The inn's location is perfect for driving to Fair Play's only restaurant and several wineries that are located less than two miles away.

For a romantic getaway there's **The Barkley Historic Homestead** (8320 Stoney Creek Rd., 530/620-6783, www.barkleyhomestead.

com, $95–175). Built in 1915 and listed on the National Register of Historic Places, its six rooms have quilted queen or king beds, private baths and entrances, and views of the rolling hillside. The best thing about this place is the laid-back vibe you'll feel while relaxing on the patio overlooking the pond. Wake up to a gourmet breakfast every morning before walking out back to the regulation-size bocce ball court. Also, there are several hiking trails that lead to seasonal streams amidst the oaks and ponderosa trees.

Food

Fair Play's dining options are limited: There's just one restaurant serving dinner. From the outside, the **Gold Vine Grill** (6028 Grizzly Flat Rd., 530/626-4042, www.goldvinegrill.com, 11 A.M.–3 P.M. and 5–9 P.M. Wed.–Sun., $8–23) looks like a run-of-the-mill roadside café. But inside, the gleaming wooden tables and exquisite artwork give this restaurant a stylish vibe. Sure, it's one of the only eateries in the Fair Play area, but that fact takes nothing away from the food. It's mostly garden-variety California cuisine, with menu items such as blackened salmon with Cajun cream sauce, pork chops with jalapeño and honey, and macadamia-encrusted mahimahi; you can try any of those dishes and find that everything is all mouthwateringly good. If you're staying at any of Fair Play's bed-and-breakfasts, there's no need to drive into Placerville for dinner; Gold Vine is worth the stay.

For a quick espresso or a sandwich, stop by **Crossroads Coffee and Cafe** (6032 Grizzly Flat Rd., 530/344-0591, www.gr8espresso.biz, 6 A.M.–3 P.M. Mon.–Fri., 7 A.M.–3 P.M. Sat.–Sun., $9). This cozy café serves breakfast and lunch, along with excellent espresso drinks. There are about 20 different sandwiches to choose from on the menu; the Angry Angus hoagie with roast beef and pepper jack cheese is delicious. Almost all of the sandwiches come with meat, so vegetarians will probably need to stick to salads. If you're looking for a little live entertainment in the Fair Play area, come by the café every second Saturday of the month; Crossroads stays open in the evening for open mic night and a variety of local musicians usually play.

Getting There and Around

Fair Play lies up in Sierra Nevada foothills well off Highway 49. To reach Fair Play from Placerville, take Highway 49 out to Pleasant Valley Road. Follow Pleasant Valley Road east for about 10 miles to Pleasant Valley and head south on County Road 16 (also called Plymouth–Shenandoah Road). County Road 16 winds almost 30 miles up to Omo Ranch Road; turn east and then turn left onto Fair Play Road.

It's a good idea to have a full tank before you take on the winding country roads in this mountainous area. **Gray's Mart** (6713 Mount Aukum Rd., Melsons Corners, 530/620-5510) is the place to fill up near Fair Play.

THE SOUTHERN GOLD COUNTRY

The Southern Gold Country is a narrow belt of rugged high country straddling nearly 60 miles of Highway 49 from the Shenandoah Valley to Jamestown. Just about every major attraction is either on Highway 49 or a few miles off the road, making it easy to navigate the region southeast from Sacramento. This long corridor of wooded canyons and scenic valleys can be split up into several distinct sections.

At the northern end lies the Shenandoah Valley, home to award-winning Amador County wineries and gently rolling hills dotted with herds of sheep and horses. More than ever, the Shenandoah Valley is becoming a destination for food and wine lovers. Oenophiles seeking the next undiscovered Napa Valley will find

these family-owned vineyards worth the trip. As travelers sweep into former mining boomtowns such as nearby Plymouth and Sutter Creek, forward-thinking chefs have opened restaurants rivaling anything you might find in San Francisco or Los Angeles.

Jackson, a 15-minute drive south, is the area's largest town and a hub for visiting former boomtowns like Sutter Creek and Amador City; it's also a good jumping-off point for attractions like Indian Grinding Rock State Historic Park, the tiny town of Volcano, and the spring blooms of Daffodil Hill.

From Jackson, Highway 49 winds south to Calaveras County and the quirky towns of Arnold, Murphys, and Angels Camp. During

HIGHLIGHTS

LOOK FOR ◖ TO FIND RECOMMENDED SIGHTS, ACTIVITIES, DINING, AND LODGING.

◖ **Shenandoah Valley Wineries:** California's next premier wine region has rolling hills and family-owned wineries bottling delicious Rhône and Amador varietals (page 231).

◖ **Indian Grinding Rock State Historic Park:** Hundreds of crater-like grinding stones dot limestone formations covered in ancient petroglyphs—all that remains of Miwok Indian tribes, the Gold Country's first residents (page 250).

◖ **Daffodil Hill:** For a few brief weeks every spring, this remote farm bursts with botanic splendor as 300,000 blooming daffodils blanket an entire mountainside (page 251).

◖ **California Caverns:** Descend hundreds of feet through dark and mysterious subterranean chambers to gaze at mind-boggling crystalline formations hanging overhead (page 256).

◖ **Calaveras County Fair and Jumping Frog Jubilee:** This yearly event was inspired by Mark Twain's famous short story about a jumping frog. Now, every third week in May, you too can become a "frog jockey" or simply browse the warehouses full of craft and agricultural exhibits, watch a rodeo, and enjoy the rides and games on the midway (page 259).

◖ **White-Water Rafting:** Feel the adrenaline pumping while plunging through roaring Class III-V rapids on the Stanislaus and Tuolumne Rivers (pages 261 and 279).

◖ **Calaveras Big Trees State Park:** This awe-inspiring park is home to dozens of giant sequoias that rise 200 feet above the forest floor. Striding beneath these towering conifers is an almost religious experience (page 270).

◖ **Columbia State Historic Park:** At this living, restored gold-mining town, costumed docents serve sarsaparilla in real saloons and help visitors pan for gold. A working blacksmith, Mark Twain impersonators, and the largest collection of brick Gold Rush-era buildings make Columbia one of California's most fascinating attractions (page 274).

◖ **Railtown 1897 State Historic Park:** Take a ride on a real steam train as it chugs through the scenic Sierra Nevada foothills where Hollywood movies were filmed (page 284).

the Gold Rush, a motley crew of characters flocked here to find fortune in these peaceful oak woodlands—and few were more illustrious than Mark Twain, whose famous tall tale about a certain leaping amphibian of Calaveras County still inspires travelers to visit the annual Jumping Frog Jubilee in Angels Camp.

At the far end of the Southern Gold Country, Tuolumne County is home to bustling Sonora, rustic Columbia, and scruffy Jamestown. Here, the main attractions are relics of the region's

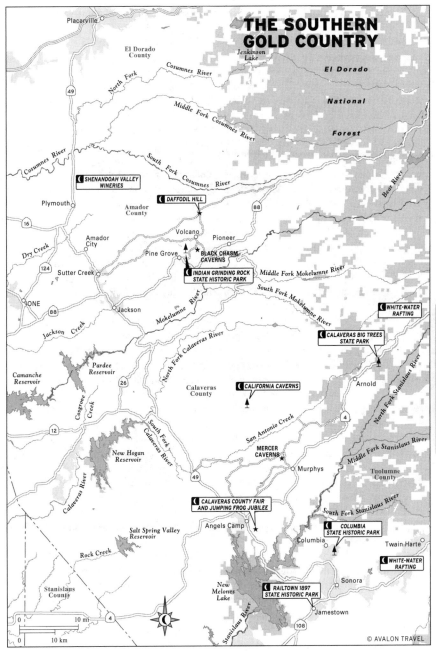

THE SOUTHERN
GOLD COUNTRY

SOUTHERN GOLD COUNTRY

Old West past, and there's none greater than Columbia State Historic Park—re-created to resemble its glory days during the Gold Rush. Watch costumed docents pan for gold or hammer iron at the blacksmith shop, try homemade candy at Nelson's Columbia Candy Kitchen, and sip locally brewed sarsaparilla at the Jack Douglass Saloon.

PLANNING YOUR TIME

The Southern Gold Country covers a large area, and it's best to plan your trip in advance. All of the towns in this region are strung along Highway 49, so a day trip can pass through most of the major attractions. Travel time varies depending upon the destination. Sonora is the town farthest from Sacramento—two hours from the capital and about 60 minutes from Modesto. Most of the other towns lie 30–45 minutes from one another, so you can skip from one place to the next without spending the entire day in the car. It would take a week to experience the entire region, but in 3–4 days you can visit most major attractions.

Trying to fit everything—and every place— into one day is simply not possible. Most people prefer to visit one town or spend the day doing a certain activity, like wine-tasting. **Plymouth, Sutter Creek, Amador City, Angels Camp, Murphys,** and **Jamestown** have an intimate, village-like vibe, and an overnight stay at any one is an enjoyable experience. Make one of these towns your home base and spend several days relaxing, wandering around town, and savoring Gold Country history.

Plymouth makes a fine center for exploring **Shenandoah Valley wineries,** which some wine lovers say feel like a smaller, down-home iteration of the Napa Valley. Farther south, near tiny Volcano, spend the night in a bark house at **Indian Grinding Rock State Historic Park** and discover petroglyphs and mortar holes that are 2,000 years old. At Angels Camp, explore

underground caves at **California Caverns** or visit in May to relive Mark Twain's tall tales at the **Calaveras County Fair and Jumping Frog Jubilee.** Adventurers can go **whitewater rafting** on the Class III–IV rapids of the North Fork of the Stanislaus River or the Tuolumne River. In Arnold, reserve a campsite at **Calaveras Big Trees State Park** and discover some of the world's oldest conifers. Sonora is a good base for exploring Tuolumne County. Wander through the Old West at **Columbia State Historic Park,** then meander south to Jamestown to appreciate the dozens of railcars and locomotives at **Railtown 1897 State Historic Park.**

ORIENTATION

Whether you are coming from Sacramento or Placerville, Highway 49 is the best way to tour the Southern Gold Country. From Sacramento, head southeast on Highway 16 for 40 miles to the junction with Highway 49.

The town of Plymouth lies about three miles northeast of the junction and acts as the gateway to the **Shenandoah Valley.** (You can also head 20 miles south on Highway 49 from Placerville to reach this region.) From Plymouth, Highway 49 continues south through Amador County, passing Drytown, Amador City, Sutter Creek, and Jackson. Tiny Volcano lies east of Sutter Creek on crooked and one-lane roads.

Angels Camp can be found 30 miles south of Jackson along Highway 49 where it enters **Calaveras County.** From Angels Camp, Highway 4 winds northeast about 10 miles to Murphys and another 12 miles to Arnold.

Continuing 15 miles south on Highway 49 you'll come to Columbia, Sonora, and Jamestown in **Tuolumne County.** From Highway 49 in either Jamestown or Sonora, Highway 108 climbs about 12 miles east into the craggy foothills of Twain Harte.

Shenandoah Valley

There's hardly a more pastoral experience than touring the rolling vineyards of the Shenandoah Valley. Spectacular in spring when fluffy herds of white sheep dot the velvety green hillsides, by summer the landscape turns into a golden Mediterranean dreamscape. Knowledgeable wine lovers claim the area resembles Napa or Sonoma before those places boomed; whether that's the case is purely subjective, but visitors will find small family-owned outfits producing Rhône-style varietals that are beginning to turn heads. To get your bearings, follow either Fiddletown or Shenandoah Road to find wineries; these two country lanes form a loop that's extremely easy to follow from downtown Plymouth.

The pristine Gold Country scenery is on full display as you drive through this rugged belt of high country where prospectors sought their fortune more than 150 years ago. You wouldn't know it, but there are miles of mysterious caverns and bottomless mine shafts in this area and some are open to visitors. The wineries follow along as you head farther south, although they become fewer and farther between past Sutter Creek. With the exception of Volcano, every town in this area is plopped right on Highway 49 and is pretty easy to navigate.

PLYMOUTH

Enjoy the sleepy town of Plymouth (pop. 1,000) while you can; folks like to boast this place is on the cusp of greatness. Indeed, Plymouth is the gateway to the rural Shenandoah Valley, where some of California's finest family-owned wineries are just 10 minutes from Main Street. Plymouth's unrefined downtown is refreshing thanks to a lack of the cluttered antiques shops

downtown Plymouth

SOUTHERN GOLD COUNTRY

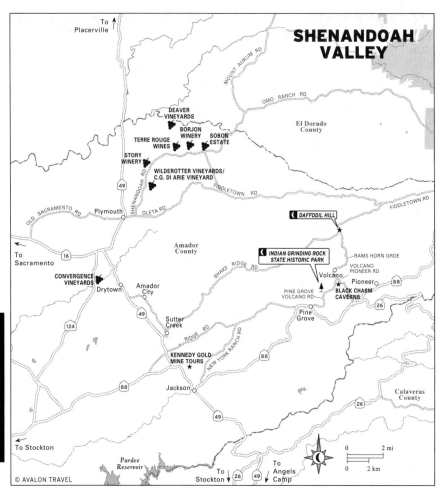

and overpriced boutiques found in other Gold Country towns. There's a hint of Mayberry innocence here, where business owners see nothing wrong with taking a few days off to go fishing. You won't find bustling dive bars or wannabe Wild West saloons, rather it's a great place to get away from the bustling traffic on Highway 49 and just kick back with a local bottle of award-winning barbera or primitivo.

Still, change is in the air. An award-winning restaurant opened on Plymouth's main street,

and locals grudgingly mutter about new casinos soon opening nearby. Now is the time to visit Plymouth and revel in the unvarnished vibe before the future inevitably changes this unpretentious village.

Plymouth's main appeal is the bucolic countryside of green vineyards and oak trees set against ocher hillsides. Make sure to take at least one drive along the entire distance of Shenandoah School Road to fully appreciate this area's beauty.

Amador Flower Farm

Even amid Shenandoah Valley's bucolic greenery, the sprawling Amador Flower Farm (22001 Shenandoah School Rd., 209/245-6660, www.amadorflowerfarm.com, 9 A.M.–4 P.M. daily) is a sight to behold. Every summer, thousands of daylilies carpet the farm in every color imaginable; Icy Lemon, Dallas Star, Octopus Hugs, and Canadian Border Patrol are just few varieties grown. Outside of the daylily season, the farm still has many flowers, herbs, and seasonal plants for sale, including more than 70 varieties of heirloom tomatoes. Purchases aside, the farm is a perfect place for a quiet stroll beneath gnarled oak trees or alongside the tranquil bullfrog pond. To get a feel for the place, take one of the tram tours around all 14 acres; call ahead for a packed lunch picnic. One thing to keep in mind: Although the farm seems like a good place to walk dogs, pets aren't allowed here.

rows of daylilies waiting to bloom at the Amador Flower Farm

Shenandoah Valley Museum

Take a few extra minutes while you're out wine-tasting and check out the Shenandoah Valley Museum (14430 Shenandoah Rd., 209/245-4455, www.sobonwine.com, 10 A.M.–4:30 P.M. daily, free). Some of the first wines in the Gold Country were produced here; the museum is part of the Sobon Estate, a winery that's been bottling Shenandoah Valley varietals since 1856. Exhibits include early winemaking tools, Gold Rush furniture, some vintage photographs, and a watermelon-size brass bell. Check out the original wine cellar, which has rock walls from local quarries and hand-cut wooden beams.

◖ Wineries

BORJON WINERY

Arguably one of the best new wineries in Amador County is Borjon Winery (11270 Shenandoah Rd., 209/245-3087, www.borjonwinery.com, 11 A.M.–5 P.M. Thurs.–Mon., tasting free). Founded less than a decade ago, this place cleans up at California's wine competitions with its gold medal–winning primitivo and barbera varietals. Still, the nice folks at Borjon haven't let success go to their head; the charismatic staff will warmly make you feel at home whether you're a serious oenophile or a wine newbie. The family's Mexican history carries over into their tasting room, and is a nice change from the endless parade of Mediterranean-style wineries, especially if you stop by for homemade salsa and wine pairings. Besides, how many other wineries have mariachi bands?

C. G. DI ARIE VINEYARD AND WINERY

Serious wine lovers should head to C. G. Di Arie Vineyard and Winery (19919 Shenandoah School Rd., 209/425-4700, www.cgdiarie.com, 11 A.M.–4:30 P.M. Fri.–Mon., tasting free). This up-and-comer was recently singled out by *Wine Spectator* for "raising the quality

SOUTHERN GOLD COUNTRY

standard" in the Shenandoah Valley—heady praise. Owner Chaim Gur-Arieh is like the Israeli Indiana Jones of winemaking; the former food executive has built a top-flight operation that easily rivals more established California wineries. The barbera and the primitivo shouldn't be missed, but make sure to try the "Southern Exposure" syrah—incredibly complex, starting with notes of blackberry, vanilla, tobacco, and hitting the palate with hints of black pepper, humus, and cedar.

CONVERGENCE VINEYARDS

One of Amador's new kids on the block is Convergence Vineyards (14650 Hwy. 124, 209/245-3600, www.convergencevineyards. com, 10 A.M.–5 P.M. Fri.–Sun., free), although visitors would never know it. Named for the confluence of three local creeks, this relaxed winery pours delicious Rhône varietals. The owners run their own tasting room and happily entertain guests with stories about the winery's background; the short version involves commutes from Napa to Amador every weekend until their first grape crush in 2004. Noteworthy wines here include a sparkling wine called Mr. Bubbles, zinfandel, primitivo, and carignane.

DEAVER VINEYARDS

Deaver Vineyards (12455 Steiner Rd., 290/245-4099, www.deavervineyard.com, 10:30 A.M.–5 P.M. daily) blends Napa-level quality with down-home Shenandoah Valley charisma. Winemaking goes way back in the Deaver family, which planted some of the first mission and zinfandel vines in Amador County about 150 years ago. You can taste that tradition in their specialty: full-bodied, layered zinfandels. They also produce 10 different varieties of port. Take a moment to absorb the stunning countryside and the Deaver's beautiful farm, surrounded by softly curving hills and serene lakes that attract all kinds of birds and wildlife.

SOBON ESTATE

It's worth stopping by Sobon Estate (14430 Shenandoah Rd., 209/245-4455, www.sobonwine.com, 9:30 A.M.–5 P.M. daily, tasting $5) to learn more about the winery's prominent place in Amador County history. Wine has been bottled here since 1856, and some of the original vines are still used for production; the winery is supposedly the oldest in California to continuously make zinfandel. The wines are just okay, but you do get some history with your vino.

STORY WINERY

Unpretentious and home to killer views of the Shenandoah Valley, Story Winery (10525 Bell Rd., 800/713-6390, www.zin.com, winter tasting hours: noon–4 P.M. Mon.–Fri., 11 A.M.–5 P.M. Sat.–Sun., summer tasting hours: 11 A.M.–5 P.M. daily, free) bottles one of the oldest varietals in California—the fabled mission wine, introduced in the 1700s by Franciscan and Jesuit missionaries. The winery also makes a medium-bodied zinfandel-mission blend called Miss Zin; with soft tannins and lingering finish, it's a definite crowd pleaser. Story's other wines aren't as spectacular, but the atmosphere—unpretentious hosts, laidback picnic area—is the main draw.

TERRE ROUGE WINES

Terre Rouge Wines (10801 Dickson Rd., 209/245-4277, http://terrerougewines.com, 11 A.M.–4 P.M. Fri.–Mon., tasting free) arguably bottles some of the better Rhône-style varietals in California. If you dig hearty, complex wines that take a few years to unwind, Terre Rouge is like dense, deep, layered nirvana. The specialty here is most definitely syrah (six different vintages) and the blends; the whites, especially the viognier and roussanne, are also good. There's also a second label produced here by the same winemaker called **Easton Wines,** which bottles traditional Amador-style zinfandels and barbera.

WILDEROTTER VINEYARD

Wilderotter Vineyard (21424 Shenandoah School Rd., 209/245-6016, 10:30 A.M.–5 P.M. daily, free) plants grapes in small plots and only produces 3,000 cases a year. The winemaker and owner, Jay Wilderotter, is one of Amador's most interesting vintners. Jay learned the craft at UC Davis before developing this label and recently expanded his vineyards to include tempranillos, petite syrah, and sauvignon blanc. Make sure to sample the estate Rhône varietals like the mourvèdre, viognier, and zinfandel.

Accommodations

Plymouth has few true options for discerning travelers. That said, it's tough to beat the pastoral setting at **Amador Harvest Inn** (12455 Steiner Rd., 800/217-2304, www.amadorharvestinn.com, $150–170). Amador Harvest Inn has a friendly, unpretentious vibe while still offering plush, decadent accommodations.

Each of the four rooms is named for different wine varietals—such as the Zinfandel room, the inn's master suite which has the best view—and has a private bath. Rooms overlook rolling vineyards, ancient walnut orchards, and glistening country lakes; at night, fall asleep to the soothing sound of croaking bullfrogs. Arrive hungry for breakfast, with at least two courses of hearty country fare like quiche and apple pancakes. The inn has modern amenities like wireless Internet, but does not allow pets and discourages guests with children under age 12. Amador Harvest Inn is owned by the Deavers, who also run the winery next door.

Romantic **Plymouth House Inn** (9525 Main St., 209/245-3298, www.plymouth-houseinn.com, $90–180) blends Amador wine culture with a dash of Gold Rush past. Seven Victorian-style guest rooms include quaint woodstoves, handmade antique furniture, and

The Plymouth House Inn is steps away from downtown Plymouth.

quilted linens along with ceiling fans, TVs, and air-conditioning. Underneath the building is an old mine shaft where gold was discovered in the late 1800s; you can still see the abandoned mine in the basement while visiting the inn's antiques shop. There's also a complimentary wine hour, a full breakfast in the morning, and plenty of country charm in the plush but understated common room. The ambience is perfect for couples, so you'll probably want to leave the kids at home—despite the vintage carousel sitting on the back lawn.

Rancho Cicada Retreat (10001 Bell Rd., 209/245-4841, www.ranchocicadaretreat. com, $85–159) is like summer camp for adults. Guests stay in rustic cabins by the Cosumnes River and join in fun activities like snorkeling, volleyball, tubing, fishing, and scrambling to various swimming holes—there's even a rope swing by the river for the adventurous. A big grassy area provides room for less taxing pursuits like croquet and tossing a Frisbee. Enjoy an evening meal on the huge redwood deck overlooking the Cosumnes River, chill out in the family-size hot tub, or relax in a hammock. The retreat has a commercial kitchen available during the week, but on weekends Rancho Cicada only caters meals for groups of 20 people or more. Individuals and small families are certainly welcome, but the retreat is really best for larger groups holding reunions or seminars.

A better option for families might be **49er Village RV Resort** (18265 Hwy. 49, 800/339-6981, www.49ervillage.com, $110–230), close to Plymouth's wineries and very conveniently located next to the highway. If you'd rather hang back instead of traipsing around town, there's a pool and a playground for young children, plus a fitness center for active travelers to keep in shape. The Village is your typical RV campground with dozens of spots, so you're a bit removed from nature; try staying in one of cabins for a more intimate experience.

Food

Restaurant pickings are slim, but at least the handful of eateries will stop visitors in their tracks. Without a doubt ◖**Restaurant Taste** (9402 Main St., 209/245-3463, http://restauranttaste.com, 4:30 P.M.–close Thurs.–Fri. and Mon., 11:30 A.M.–2 P.M. and 5 P.M.–close Sat.–Sun., $8–42) is one of the better restaurants. Set in a modest building off Plymouth's dusty main drag, this surprising bistro has a posh vibe with echoes of San Francisco. Chef Mark Berkner stocks the menu with gourmet food made from seasonal, healthy ingredients; try the mushroom cigars, a tasty combination of three different fungi wrapped in goat cheese and phyllo. The entrées are meat-heavy, upscale fare done to perfection; you can't go wrong with the roasted guinea hen with house-made ravioli. The wine list is a balanced selection of Amador wines and California varietals with some international labels sprinkled in. Vegans and those with gluten sensitivities should call ahead; the restaurant will happily create a special menu for your visit.

If you're planning a picnic, the **Amador Vintage Market** (9393 Main St., 209/245-3663, www.amadorvintagemarket.com, 10 A.M.–6 P.M. Wed.–Sun., $10) whips up gourmet sandwiches and takeaway cuisine in this downtown Plymouth eatery. The green awnings and brick wall exterior may resemble a New York hole-in-the-wall, but the interior has a down-home, rustic feel with plenty of local flavor. Try the Miner's Ruben for lunch, with pastrami and pepper jack cheese on grilled focaccia. Locals recommend the half-pound balsamic pork tenderloin along with the potato of the day. You can mix and match or ask the friendly staff to build a picnic for you.

If you're craving burgers, pop into **Marlene and Glen's Diner** (18726 Hwy. 49, 209/245-5778, 7 A.M.–2:30 P.M. daily, $4–14). This quirky roadside stop is like a scene from *Happy Days*—polished chrome and red leather seats at the counter, homey curios on the wall, and heaping portions of good ol' American diner food. For breakfast, choose from nine different variations of egg Benedict, including the steak Benedict with Cajun hollandaise sauce; your taste buds will thank you after they stop tingling. The menu offers plenty of greasy but tasty lunch choices; the Kelly Blue Cheese Burger is a standout, and there are several different kinds of fries. The service can slow down considerably on weekends, so either come early or be ready to wait.

Information and Services

Plymouth is a small town without many of the modern services found in larger cities. The best place for news and events is online (http://plymouthcalifornia.com). If you're planning to visit local wineries, a good place to start is the **Amador Vintner's Association** (9310 Pacific St., 209/245-6992, www.amadorwine.com, 10 A.M.–4 P.M. daily) to pick up brochures and directions. The **Amador 360 Wine Collective** (18590 Hwy. 49, 209/267-4355, www.amador360.com, 11 A.M.–5 P.M. daily) offers tastings and advice about smaller, boutique wineries that can be hard to find.

There aren't many bank branches in Plymouth, but you can find an ATM at the **El Dorado Savings Bank** (18726 Hwy. 49, 209/245-3000, www.eldoradosavingsbank.com, 9 A.M.–5 P.M. Mon.–Thurs., 9 A.M.–6 P.M. Fri.). Fill up your gas tank before heading into wine country at the **Shell** station (17699 Village Dr.) just south of town off Highway 49. You can find a **post office** at 9477 Main Street (9 A.M.–11 A.M. and 11:30 A.M.–4:30 P.M. Mon.–Fri.).

Getting There and Around

Plymouth is north of Jackson and Sutter Creek, just off Highway 49. From the north, follow Highway 49 south from Placerville for about 20 miles. From Sacramento, take Highway 16 southeast to Highway 49 and then head northeast. These highways are all two-lane roads and can become packed on weekends, so adjust your travel time accordingly.

Amador Transit (http://amadortransit.com, $2) runs buses between Plymouth and Sutter Creek, where you can catch connections to Jackson and other towns in the region.

DRYTOWN

Don't judge this place by its hard-luck name. Drytown (pop. 167) is the first place where gold was discovered in Amador County, and it's actually the oldest community in the area. During the town's heyday in the 1850s, there were 26 saloons, one post office, and one general store—sounds like the town's founders had their priorities straight. Today the town is essentially a working ghost town with a few antiques shops, a hotel, and an excellent winery. Drytown is easy to reach because Highway 49 passes right through; it makes a swift pit stop on the way to somewhere else.

Wineries

The best reason to stop in Drytown is **Drytown Cellars** (16030 Hwy. 49, 209/245-3500, www.drytowncellars.com, 11 A.M.–5 P.M. daily, tasting free). The view overlooks quintessential Gold Country: rolling hills covered in oaks and vineyards. Drytown bottles distinctive Amador County varietals such as zinfandel and barberas, and the proprietors are fun-loving, laid-back people who savor every minute of making wine. Wines tend to be robust and intense yet finely balanced between different flavors; try the Red-on-Red blend.

Shopping

Drytown has a few itinerant antiques shops, and that's about it. Most places seem to open and close rather quickly. One shop with staying power is **Miners Pick Antiques** (14207 Hwy. 49, 209/267-0848, www.minerspick.com,

11 A.M.–5 P.M. Fri.–Sun.). Ronnie and Connie Peterson are the proud curators of mining artifacts and antiques; their collection includes ore cars, signs and ads, tools, lamps, and books.

Accommodations and Food

Old Well Motel and Grill (15947 Hwy. 49, 209/245-6467, $65–80) is a basic motor court inn, and it's the only place to sleep in Drytown. Don't expect mind-blowing luxury, just basic amenities like air-conditioning, private bathrooms, TVs, and an outdoor pool. The adjoining **café** ($10) functions as the town's greasy spoon, serving American fare like prime rib, burgers, and clam chowder.

Getting There

Drytown lines the bottom of a narrow gulch on Highway 49, 3.7 miles south of downtown Plymouth and roughly 2.8 miles northwest of Amador City. There's very little signage to indicate the town—no stop signs or stoplights. A map of the area is advised.

AMADOR CITY

For such a tiny town, Amador City (pop. 200) packs quite the historical punch. The area's first gold quartz discovery happened here in 1851 when Baptist preacher S. A. Davison stopped for a drink at an icy-cold spring and found a chunk of the precious ore. Miners rushed to stake claims along Amador Creek next to the stagecoach road, which eventually became Highway 49. Later, prospectors built the prosperous Keystone Mine in town and started producing almost $500,000 in gold bullion per year—quite a sum in those days.

Flash-forward almost 150 years, and the gold is long gone. Amador City's new bonanza is the antiques trade; out of the 15 shops in town, at least one-third are dealers of vintage collectibles and rare items. Still, this town is so much more than a stop on the antiques trail. A handful of eccentric eateries serve up original fare,

especially in the Imperial Hotel's upscale dining room. Those looking for a quiet, romantic hideout will love Amador City's charm and historic ambience. If you're on a mission elsewhere, it's worth stopping for at least a bite to eat.

Amador Whitney Museum

The Amador Whitney Museum (14170 Old Highway 49, 209/267-5250, noon–4 P.M. Fri.–Sun., free) offers a peek into the lives of Amador's female inhabitants during 19th century. Check out replicas of a teacher's closet-size boarding room and a typical schoolroom desk; the (draconian) rules for female teachers are an eye-opener. The museum is located in the town's oldest building, constructed in 1860, and has lots of character in every creaky floor plank.

Shopping

Stick close to Main Street for Amador City's best shopping, which shouldn't be too hard—it's one of the only streets in town. Amid the usual assortment of antiques stores and funky boutiques common to most Gold Country towns, some shops here will surprise.

Tucked in a basement down a narrow alley, **Meyer's Antiques** (14183 Old Highway 49, 209/267-0315, 11 A.M.–5 P.M. Thurs.–Sun.) is like a peek into your grandfather's garage—if your grandfather had vintage slot machines, wooden crank telephones, Victor phonographs, arcade games, and a host of random mementos from days gone by. Meyer's also has a random section devoted to Celtic textiles and souvenirs.

Bellflower Home Decor and Art (10787 Water St., 209/267-1985, 10 A.M.–5 P.M. Wed.–Mon.) is actually three different stores. In addition to the eclectic housewares in the main shop, there's an outdoor area for avant-garde lawn sculptures and another smaller store carrying decorative garden knickknacks. The

© CHRISTOPHER ARNS

the Imperial Hotel in Amador City

selection of tasteful curios and random items is comparable to what you'd find at big-city boutiques.

A visit to **Victorian Closet Antiques** (14176 Old Highway 49, 209/267-5250, 11 A.M.–4 P.M. Wed.–Thurs., 10 A.M.–5 P.M. Fri.–Sun.) is like stepping into a stateroom on the *Titanic:* vintage Gilded Age gowns, brass-bound wooden chests and wedding dresses from several different eras. The selection of flapper-style dresses and hats is astounding, but the store also carries hundreds of smaller items like pince-nez eyeglasses and spools of fine lace. The clothing is all vintage, meaning people wore some of these pieces nearly 100 years ago.

Take a break from antiques shops and visit **Lanza Imports** (14215 Old Highway 49, 209/267-1234, 11 A.M.–4 P.M. Wed.–Mon.). This quirky shop has modern art, wooden furniture, and land decorations, some of which are made locally. Look for the swirling wind socks outside to know you're close.

Accommodations

The **Imperial Hotel** (14202 Old Hwy. 49, 209/267-9172, www.imperialamador.com, $105–190) looks pretty much like it did a hundred years ago: It's an ancient, boxy building with a rustic brick facade sprouting grass on the roof. In other words, it's pretty darn authentic if you're hunting for restored Gold Country digs. Upstairs, the six rooms offer cozy, comfortable accommodations with rough brick walls, high ceilings, and furnishings handmade by local artists. The Imperial feels more like a country inn or bed-and-breakfast, and the vibe is more intimate than at larger hotels. You will sacrifice some convenience for authenticity; each room has a private bathroom and free wireless Internet but no phone or TV. The upstairs rooms are a bit small; if that's a problem just stay up the road in one of the three "luxury suites," which are basically large apartments in the hotel's cottage. These rooms feature plush accommodations like hot tub baths, woodstoves, and canopy beds; there's also a porch where you can bask in the glow of Amador's beautiful sunsets.

Food

One thing Amador City does really well is spoil your taste buds. Though you only have three restaurants to choose from, each one is noteworthy. Start with **Andrae's Bakery** (14141 Old Hwy. 49, 209/267-1352, www.andraesbakery.com, 8 A.M.–4 P.M. Thurs.–Sun., $8), which feels like eating at a friendly grandmother's house. Locals swear by the gourmet sandwiches—the pesto salami is a standout, made with locally raised meat and cheese on a house-baked roll. For dessert, you absolutely must try one of the pastries; any of the cookies are dangerously good, but the seasonal scones (flavors like strawberry and peach in summer or cranberry in winter) are worth the trip in themselves. There's a fair amount of old-fashioned sodas in the drink case to wash down your sandwich. You can order to go at Andrae's, but a better alternative is to sit outside on the back patio. After lunch, browse the artisan salts and sauces on the café's shelves for a truly homemade souvenir.

The restaurant downstairs in the **Imperial Hotel** (14202 Old Hwy. 49, 209/267-9172, www.imperialamador.com, 5–8 P.M. Tues.–Thurs., 5–9 P.M. Fri., noon–2 P.M. and 5–9 P.M. Sat., noon–2 P.M. and 5–8 P.M. Sun., $13–30) is a grand ol' place to enjoy contemporary, upscale food. Ancient brick walls and polished wood floors give the place an authentic Gold Rush feel, while dishes like homemade pumpkin ravioli and grilled polenta compare favorably with anything you'd find in San Francisco. If there's a wait, grab a drink or challenge someone to a duel in the restaurant's **Oasis Bar,** a Wild West–style saloon with gas lamps, worn bar stools, and a creaky wooden floor.

At **Buffalo Chips Emporium** (14175 Hwy. 49, 209/267-0570, 9 A.M.–5 P.M. Wed.–Sun., 5–8 P.M. Fri., $8), you can't really order buffalo, um, droppings off the menu—just juicy, finger-licking burgers and other reasonably priced grub. Whatever you do, come with an appetite for blackberry pie, the house specialty.

Information and Services

Amador City only has a couple hundred residents; it's basically a working tourist town, so you're pretty detached from civilization once you get here. There are no banks, gas stations, or grocery stores. Drive a few miles south to Sutter Creek for any modern conveniences.

Amador City's merchant association does have a website (www.amador-city.com) with travel pointers for visiting the town and a list of upcoming events.

Getting There and Around

Amador City is technically on Highway 49, although the town is actually off the main road. From Plymouth, head south for about six miles and turn left on Old Highway 49; the town is another mile down the road.

There are two ways to reach Amador City from Sutter Creek; the easiest way is to follow Old Highway 49 north for two miles. If you're heading up the Golden Chain Highway, which is the more modern iteration of Highway 49, drive about four miles north from Sutter Creek and turn right at the sign for Amador City.

SUTTER CREEK

Before hordes of prospectors flooded Amador County during the frantic 1850s, there were already dozens of timber camps scattered throughout this small valley. In 1849, the world changed forever when James W. Marshall discovered gold in Coloma and "Sutter's Creek" camp became a stopover for miners working in the valley's many banks and gulches. The town didn't share in the boom until 1851, when surveyors found gold-rich quartz deposits just

© CHRISTOPHER ARNS

historic Sutter Creek

a half-mile away and touched off another rush to Sutter Creek.

Today, Sutter Creek stakes its claim on becoming a wine-tasting capital for the region. The town's festive Main Street is lined with several tasting rooms operated by family-owned Amador wineries, and you can also find mom-and-pop antiques stores, pricy boutiques, and an entertaining little theater company clinging to Main Street's narrow sidewalks. Sutter Creek certainly feels more genteel than the region's other former boomtowns, and businesses definitely cater to weekend tourists and wine lovers. A slew of spiffed-up Victorian inns line Sutter Creek's main drag, all within walking distance of tasting rooms; however, the town's culinary circuit has yet to embrace its full potential.

Monteverde Store Museum

One day in 1971, Sutter Creek's old general store shut down for a few days and never reopened. Twenty years later, historians took a peek and found ancient inventory like penny candy, canned food, hosiery, hardware, and many other dry goods untouched by time. Also left behind were more than 70 years of dusty store ledgers and records from the owners, all written in a spidery, old-fashioned handwriting. The city of Sutter Creek now keeps the Monteverde Store Museum (11A Randolph St., 209/267-1344, www.suttercreek.org) sealed like a time capsule, but visitors can call ahead to schedule a free tour. Docents will show you around and recant the store's history since it first opened in 1896. Keep an eye open for shelves of mysterious Mason jars; unopened for decades, not even the docents know what's inside.

Wineries

Wine-tasting in Sutter Creek is a different kind of experience. Unlike in El Dorado County or the Shenandoah Valley, vintners pour their

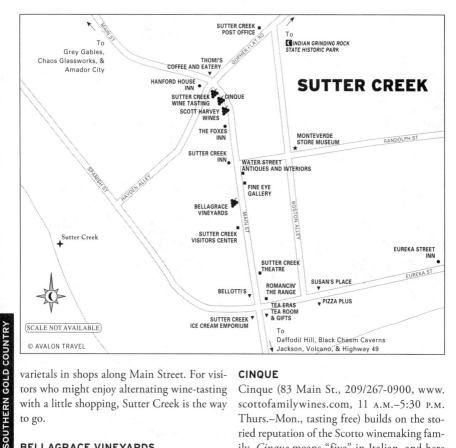

varietals in shops along Main Street. For visitors who might enjoy alternating wine-tasting with a little shopping, Sutter Creek is the way to go.

BELLAGRACE VINEYARDS

Remember this name: BellaGrace Vineyards (73 Main St., 209/267-8053, www.bellagracevineyards.com, noon–5 P.M. Thurs.–Mon., tasting free) is a rising star among Amador's wineries. Their 2010 barbera and 2011 grenache blanc won Best of California awards at the 2012 California State Fair. These two varietals will sweep even the most hard-boiled oenophiles off their feet. The grenache blanc is especially outstanding, carrying notes of lemon, anise, and green apple while staying evenly balanced with a long finish. Look for the white picket fence and the adorable white house to find the Sutter Creek tasting room.

CINQUE

Cinque (83 Main St., 209/267-0900, www. scottofamilywines.com, 11 A.M.–5:30 P.M. Thurs.–Mon., tasting free) builds on the storied reputation of the Scotto winemaking family. *Cinque* means "five" in Italian, and here the number represents both five generations of Scotto vintners and the amount of Scotto family labels poured at this tasting room. Try varietals from Sera Fina Cellars, Scotto Family Wines, Regio, Delta Luna, and Villa Armando—all labels produced by the Scottos.

SCOTT HARVEY WINES

Scott Harvey Wines (79 Main St., 209/267-0122, www.scottharveywines.com, 11 A.M.–5 P.M. Thurs.–Mon., tasting free) bottles some of Amador County's most expressive red wines, including spicy syrahs and understated barberas. Scott Harvey has decades of winemaking experience in the Napa and Shenandoah Valleys, and it clearly shows. The tasting room has a fun vibe where both wine newbies and seasoned oenophiles can learn about Gold Country varietals.

SUTTER CREEK WINE TASTING

Can't make up your mind? The friendly staff at Sutter Creek Wine Tasting (85 Main St., 209/267-5838, www.suttercreekwinetasting. com, 11 A.M.–6 P.M. daily) hosts three family-owned wineries in the same white clapboard house: Gold Hill, Le Mulet Rouge, and Sierra Ridge. You'll taste locally produced and estate-grown varietals from these three wineries, including several types of sparkling wine and champagne. If you can't find the place, just keep your ears open for the sound of laughter pouring out the tasting room's open door where guests are clearly enjoying themselves.

Entertainment and Events

Stop by the **Sutter Creek Theatre** (44 Main St., 916/425-0077, www.suttercreektheater. com, $17–25) for a bluegrass concert or a classic film showing. Nearly 100 years old, this adorable little bandbox has become Sutter Creek's main cultural hub. The exterior alone is a showstopper: A simple yet elegant facade beckons folks to pop in for a concert or a classic film. The shows are pretty eclectic, with lots of Elvis and Johnny Cash tribute bands, world music acts, and a fair amount of bluegrass and folk groups. You can also catch classic cinema here. Film buffs should take note: Sutter Creek Theatre is the only remaining theater in Amador County that once played silent movies.

Shopping

Sutter Creek's Main Street is a perfect place for window-shopping, wine-tasting, or finding an original handmade gift. At **Chaos Glassworks** (121 A Hanford St., 209/267-9317, www.chaosglassworks.com, noon–7 P.M. Wed.–Fri.,

10 A.M.–7 P.M. Sat., 10 A.M.–6 P.M. Sun.), owner Dave Hopman creates stunning works of original hand-blown glass. From ethereal teardrop-shaped vases to glowing sconces to shimmering glass floats, Hopman is quite the master, and you're sure to find a high-quality gift in his shop.

Water Street Antiques and Interiors (33 C Main St., 209/267-0585, www.waterstreetantiques.com, 10 A.M.–4 P.M. Mon. and Wed.–Fri., 10 A.M.–5 P.M. Sat., 11 A.M.–5 P.M. Sun.) is a huge warehouse filled with hardwood antiques like Colonial-style desks, solid teak armoires, and redwood chests. Discover a fine selection of textiles and decorative knickknacks for around the house.

At **Fine Eye Gallery** (71 Main St., 209/267-0571, www.fineeye.com, 10:30 A.M.–5:30 P.M. Mon.–Fri., 10:30 A.M.–6 P.M. Sat.–Sun.), visitors will find handmade jewelry, scarves, watches, and handbags along with gleaming artisan lamps, furniture, and garden sculptures.

Ladies, gallop down to **Romancin' the Range** (34 Main St., 209/267-9137, 11 A.M.–5 P.M. daily) for Western-style attire that's suitable for the big city. This isn't a novelty store; younger folks will dig the prairie boots, tops, and jewelry found here.

Accommodations

Sutter Creek is blessed with several inns right on Main Street, and there's a diverse price range for most budgets and tastes. The most glamorous place to stay is ◖ **Hanford House Inn** (61 Hanford St., 209/267-0747, www.hanfordhouse.com, $110–290). The stately red-brick manor has a prosaic, orderly look, more like a Gold Rush–era bank than a bed-and-breakfast. The real treat is inside: 14 luxurious rooms that feel like penthouse suites. The decor is minimalistic chic with a European flair that includes sleek leather lounge chairs, stainless steel gas fireplaces, and contemporary wood furniture. All linens are amazingly soft,

© CHRISTOPHER ARNS

Hanford House Inn

especially the complimentary robe for use during your stay. The meals are possibly the best part of a stop at Hanford House because many of the ingredients are local, including the eggs for breakfast, courtesy of the chickens out back. There's also a free wine and cheese hour in the evening with Shenandoah Valley and other Amador varietals. The inn has two separate bungalows where pets are allowed. Make sure to arrive between 3–6:30 p.m. for check-in or call ahead.

You might think **Grey Gables Inn** (161 Hanford St., 209/267-1039, www.greygables. com, $115–250) sounds like a country inn from an English novel, and you're not far off; each of the eight rooms is named for a British poet. Floral bed linens, claw-foot tubs, and antique wood furnishings give a distinctly English feel; tea and cake are served every afternoon and a full breakfast comes piping hot on fine bone china. The only thing missing is the queen herself, but the unpretentious welcome and warm

conversations you'll have in the fancy common room are even better. Don't fret if you're staying during the summer; each room has air-conditioning.

An evening at **Eureka Street Inn** (55 Eureka St., 209/267-5500, www.eurekastreetinn.com, $125–145) is like staying with old friends. This Craftsman-style manor was built in 1914 by an Italian stagecoach operator, and the current innkeepers have done a fine job of restoring the Victorian interior to its former glory. You can still see the inn's original rosewood and redwood wainscoting and beams, stained-glass windows, and a stunning rosewood staircase. Four comfortable rooms have quilted bedspreads, antique dressers and armoires, either a potbellied gas stove or a fireplace, private bathrooms, and dormer windows with views over the nearby hillsides. Innkeeper Chuck is a righteous dude who makes breakfast into art every morning; plates include frittatas, French toast, and yummy coffee cake. The downsides:

pets are not allowed, and there is a two-night minimum (although sometimes the innkeepers are flexible if they've just had a cancellation).

Claiming to be the first bed-and-breakfast west of the Mississippi, **Sutter Creek Inn** (75 Main St., 209/267-5606, www.suttercreekinn. com, $95–205) is a throwback to 19th-century boarding houses where guests ate meals around a long wooden table and played games in the parlor. Built in 1859, the main house is a rambling, New England–style building surrounded by shaded lawns and leafy patios where guests can spend hours relaxing on comfortable lounge chairs. Each of the 17 rooms has a private bath and air-conditioning along with antique furniture and bookshelves filled with dozens of titles. Looking for some movement in your relationship? Ask for one of the four rooms with a swing-bed if you enjoy rocking to sleep. In the morning, a full country breakfast is served with fruit and veggies from the inn's garden. While some of the rooms might feel a little gloomy from the lack of light, it's probably no big deal for an overnight stay. Please leave the kids and pets at home and know the rules (candles and rose petals are expressly forbidden) when you arrive.

With four-poster beds and decadent chandeliers, **The Foxes Inn** (77 Main St., 209/267-5882, www.foxesinn.com, $160–325) doesn't skimp on luxury. This is by far the most authentic Victorian bed-and-breakfast in Sutter Creek, and it's also one of the ritziest. All seven rooms offer either a queen or king bed, plush linens, complimentary robes and beverages, refrigerators, air-conditioning, and free wireless Internet; five of the rooms have fireplaces. In the morning, a two-course gourmet breakfast is made to order. If you need a bite later in the day, room service arrives on silver platters.

Food

Top-notch restaurants are hard to find in Sutter Creek, but these spots should satisfy your hunger. **Pizza Plus** (20 Eureka St., 209/267-1900, 11 A.M.–9 P.M. daily, $12–22) serves up the best pies in Amador County and some of the best ambience. Order your pizza at the counter by the old-fashioned cash register and grab a seat outside by the creek; if it's a sweltering summer day, duck into the old stone-walled basement downstairs where it feels like you're eating in a medieval castle. The pizza is great, but the cheese-covered breadsticks are just as famous. Vegetarians will be pleasantly surprised by the small mountain of tomatoes, olives, yellow onions, mushrooms, artichoke hearts, and green bell peppers on the Plus veggie pizza. You won't find big-screen TVs on the walls, making Pizza Plus the perfect place for families or anyone more interested in eating than watching the big game.

Locals swear that **Susan's Place** (15 Eureka St., 209/267-0945, www.susansplace.com, 11:30 A.M.–2:30 P.M. and 5–8 P.M. Thurs.–Sun., $20) is the best restaurant in town. With a patio shaded by wisteria and a wooden lattice, diners certainly have plenty of relaxing atmosphere. The menu advertises Mediterranean fare, although diehard Greek and Middle Eastern foodies would dispute that claim; most of the dishes are mainstream California cuisine. Susan's does have one major advantage: It's the only fine dining option in Sutter Creek. If you're in town for a romantic weekend, this restaurant should be on your itinerary.

Bellotti's (53 Main St., 209/267-5211, www. bellottis.com, 11:30 A.M.–close Tues.–Sun., $20) is your typical Italian trattoria with rich, meaty portions that would probably upset your cardiologist. Just reading the menu is enough to start your heart racing: Whiskey steak, veal scaloppine, and pot roast are a few of the guilty pleasures. For something lighter and a bit healthier, try the delicious flatbread with grilled chicken, apples, and gorgonzola. Besides the food, Bellotti's historic digs are worth appreciating; the building was completed in the

Pizza Plus

1860s, and stagecoaches would stop here during the Gold Rush.

If you can't go another minute in the Gold Country without clotted cream and a scone, stop by **Tea Eras Tea Room & Gifts** (34 Main St., 209/267-0333, www.teaerastearoom.com, 11 A.M.–3 P.M. daily). This charming tearoom harks back to elegant Victorian salons, with delicious pastries, exquisite lace tablecloths, and a mind-blowing amount of fine china on display. Meals include exotic tea flavors (try the chocolate macadamia), scones, salad, sandwiches, and cookies for dessert. Located on Sutter Creek's main drag, this is a convenient place to take a break from afternoon shopping. One word of advice: If arriving from outside Sutter Creek, call ahead to make sure the shop is open (the tearoom has been known to close unexpectedly).

Sutter Creek Ice Cream Emporium (51 Main St., 209/267-0543, 8 A.M.–6 P.M. daily, $5–10) is a chance to spoil your sweet tooth.

Nostalgia-seekers will dig the real sundae glasses and vintage Hamilton Beach shake machines at this old-fashioned ice cream parlor. Order ice cream treats, candy, or espresso, but don't skip the Emporium's homemade cobblers, cinnamon rolls, and banana bread.

Thomi's Coffee and Eatery (40 Hanford St., 209/267-1108, www.thomiscafe.net, 8 A.M.–3 P.M. Mon.–Wed. and Fri.–Sun., $10) serves hearty plates of breakfast and lunch; the egg salad sandwich is the best darn thing on the menu. The cuisine is a cross between Californian healthy fare, Mexican, and American diner food. Try to grab a spot on the patio when the weather is sunny.

Information and Services

The **Sutter Creek Visitors Center** (71A Main St., 209/267-1344, www.suttercreek.org, 11 A.M.–2:30 P.M. Mon.–Wed., 10 A.M.–5 P.M. Thurs.–Sun.) has a helpful website with loads of travel advice and tips on local sights, along with a list of upcoming events. Volunteers staff the center, and the daily hours may fluctuate; call ahead to make sure someone is there.

In Amador, the local paper *Amador Ledger-Dispatch* provides information about entertainment. Or, pick up a free copy of the *Sierra Lodestar* (www.sierralodestar.com).

Sutter Creek has ATMs and several bank branches, as well as a **post office** at 3 Gopher Flat Road (9 A.M.–4:30 P.M. Mon.–Fri.).

Getting There and Around

Sutter Creek sits directly on Highway 49, 10 miles south of Plymouth and roughly 5 miles north of Jackson. From Placerville, head south on Highway 49 for about 30 miles to reach Sutter Creek.

The local airport is **Westover Field-Amador County Airport** (12380 Airport Rd., Jackson, 209/223-2376, www.co.amador.ca.us), between Jackson and Sutter Creek.

Amador Transit (http://amadortransit.com, $2) runs several routes all over Amador County and to Sacramento.

JACKSON

Nope, it's not *that* Jackson; legendary singers Johnny Cash and June Carter were probably referring to a hardscrabble hamlet in Tennessee when they sang about "going to mess around" in Jackson. Based on the number of dive bars in this onetime mining camp, the tune actually applies quite well. Although you won't find gunslingers or desperadoes in today's Jackson (pop. 4,230), the town's Wild West cred goes back a long way. In 1854, a crooked judge named William Smith decided to make Jackson the Amador County seat even though a local election gave that honor to nearby Mokelumne Hill. Folks from Moke Hill sent armed gangs to find Smith, but he escaped and eventually shot the man in charge of counting the votes. Typical Jackson, locals will tell you.

Once everybody calmed down,

unimaginable wealth started flowing into the town's coffers. Three local claims, including the famous Kennedy mine, churned out more than 4.6 million ounces of gold from the 1850s until World War II, making up at least half of Amador County's total gold production. A fire destroyed Jackson in 1862, but the town's indomitable citizens bounced back by rebuilding, and 42 structures still stand from that era.

Modern Jackson has a bustling Main Street with friendly antiques stores, vibrant wine-tasting rooms, and a host of oddball shops selling everything from handmade stained glass to Native American handicrafts. Unlike other Gold Country towns that cater to wine tours and refined palates, Jackson hasn't changed much—it's still a rollicking mining camp at heart.

Historic Kennedy Gold Mine

The Historic Kennedy Gold Mine (Hwy. 49 and Hwy 88, 209/223-9542, www.kennedy-goldmine.com, 10 A.M.–3 P.M. Sat.–Sun. Mar.–Oct., adults $10, youth $7, children free) may not have been the richest strike in the Gold Country, but it's certainly the deepest—the main shaft plunges 5,912 feet into the earth. Of course, your surface tour won't descend into those depths, but visitors will enjoy strolling around the mine's old office building, steam boiler, mill wheels, and towering head frame that lowered miners into the shaft. You can also check out a slew of sepia photographs from the mine's working days. Guided tours are offered March through October.

Entertainment and Events

Visitors to Jackson can seek their fortune at a Gold Country casino, and why not—early prospectors spent much of their downtime playing cards while gambling away entire mining claims. Unlike those hard-luck miners, try not to lose the farm at **Jackson Rancheria Casino and Hotel** (12222 New York Ranch Rd.,

209/223-1677, www.jacksoncasino.com). You'll find 33 gaming tables, 9 card tables, and more than 1,500 slot machines. Need a break from the clamor of the casino floor? Take in a movie at the Rancheria's classic film nights; past showings have included James Dean's tragic performance in *Rebel Without a Cause,* timeless musicals like *Meet Me in St. Louis,* and definitive spaghetti Westerns like *The Good, The Bad and the Ugly.* From time to time, mainstream performers like Dierks Bentley and Sara Evans will perform here. If you're hungry, grab some chow at one of the casino's five restaurants and cafés like the Rancheria Buffet, which serves food at seven stations three times a day. To tell the truth, Jackson Rancheria has declined somewhat in recent years, and although a current renovation is underway, they need to address some lingering issues with customer service. One last thing: this casino is dry as a bone when it comes to alcohol—there is none served and none permitted inside the casino.

There are several dive bars in Jackson. About halfway down Main Street you'll find **Main Event** (105 Main St., 209/223-5775, 7 A.M.–2 A.M. daily), which pours cold beer and stiff drinks. There's a jukebox playing classic rock and country tunes, and patrons can rack 'em up on the bar's pool table.

Down by the old National Hotel building, **The Fargo Club** (2 Main St., 209/223-3859, 9 A.M.–10 P.M. Sun.–Thurs., 9 A.M.–2 A.M. Fri.–Sat.) is a corner bar with billiards, crusty local ambience, and inexpensive draught beer.

Shopping

Like most Gold Country towns, Jackson's commercial activity is primarily clustered around Main Street, where you'll find small shops selling oddball handicrafts, antiques, and local wines and olive oil. **Wierschem's Train Town** (139 Main St., 209/223-0250, 10 A.M.–5 P.M. daily) stocks everything a kid would want on Christmas morning. Besides model trains,

you can buy rockets, puzzles, Pez dispensers, wooden toys, and candy—lots and lots of candy. There's a wall of jelly beans, a full case of fudge, a pool-size table of saltwater taffy, and an ice cream parlor in the back of the shop. In such a large store, remember to check expiration dates on the candy before buying.

Gifted (8 Main St., 209/223-1558, 10 A.M.–5 P.M. Mon. and Wed.–Thurs., 10 A.M.–6 P.M. Fri.–Sat., 11 A.M.–4 P.M. Sun.) sells handicrafts made locally. You'll find knitted scarves, ceramic sculptures, and beauty products like oak milk lotion in this adorable little boutique; you can read artisan bios on a wall poster by the shop's front door.

Treasures Mercantile (122 Main St., 209/223-3095, 10 A.M.–5 P.M. daily) is owned by Lenny, a friendly ex-cowboy who still wears a Stetson to work. He's put together quite a store that spans different eras and tastes; you'll discover everything here, from vintage printing presses and gigantic 11 by 14 cameras to polished spurs and the odd Ouija board.

Hein and Company Bookstore (204 Main St., 209/223-9076, 9 A.M.–6 P.M. Mon.–Fri., 10 A.M.–6 P.M. Sat., 11 A.M.–6 P.M. Sun.) is comfortable, cavernous, and boasts thousands of rare and used tomes. Some used bookstores are crammed into tiny spaces without chairs or tables for browsing. Not at Hein, where readers can order coffee from the small café and sit at wooden library tables. It's also one of the best places to pick up books on California and Gold Country history.

Sports and Recreation

Sometimes I think golfing is the new Gold Rush in this region. The rolling terrain and stunning vistas create some of the most breathtaking layouts in the Southern Gold Country. Tee off at **Castle Oaks Golf Club** (1000 Castle Oaks Dr., Ione, 209/274-0167, www.castleoaksgolf.com, $20–52), and you'll find out why. At this 18-hole, par-71 course, golfers will find

the Mission-style El Campo Casa in Jackson

SOUTHERN GOLD COUNTRY

well-maintained fairways, beautiful greens, and five different tee boxes on every hole. For being in the foothills, Castle Oaks is fairly flat; there's an average amount of water, but too much to discourage weekend duffers. You can usually find specials on greens fees if you visit the course website.

The best place for camping and water sports in Amador is **Lake Camanche** (2000 Camanche Rd., Ione, 209/763-5121, www.camancherecreation.com). You can water-ski, wakeboard, or blast around the lake on Jet Skis. If you prefer a slower pace, the marina rents fishing boats and patio boats for a reasonable fee. There are also plenty of relaxing options for staying on shore, either to paddle around by the beach or fish. Once you're ready to crash for the night, the lake has 762 camping sites. Note: boat owners will need inspections for traces of invasive mussels before entering the water. You can also find plenty of swimming beaches and fishing spots at **Pardee Lake Recreation Area**

(4900 Stony Creek Rd., Ione, 209/772-1472, www.pardeelakerecreation.com).

Accommodations

You really won't find a whole lot of bed-and-breakfasts or country inns in Jackson. It's just not that kind of place. On the other hand, Jackson does a spectacular job with budget accommodations. For starters, **El Campo Casa** (12548 Kennedy Flat Rd., 209/223-0100, http://elcampocasa.com, $50–60) is a motel with old-world character. From the highway it might not appear that impressive, and it's certainly not lavish by any means, although that's not why El Campo Casa is worth a stay. If you're burnt out on Victorian-style inns or restored Gold Rush flophouses, pull into this white stucco rancheria for a change. The 15 rooms have ceiling fans, air-conditioning, and TVs; there's also an outdoor pool and shady patio area. For the price, it's actually quite reasonable and makes a perfect place to base your excursions into the Shenandoah Valley. On the downside, the rooms are somewhat spartan, and the bathrooms are a little too cozy. Note that El Campo Casa has central air-conditioning, which is great for cooling off during the sweltering Gold Country summers but also means there is no smoking in any of the rooms.

If you need a place with more modern conveniences, stay at the **Best Western Amador Inn** (200 S. Hwy. 49, 209/223-0211, www.bestwestern.com, $70–110). For a chain hotel, it's actually a homey place to crash after visiting the area's wineries. If you're visiting during the scorching summer months, take a dip in the outdoor pool by the laid-back patio area. Inside the rooms, you'll find a coffeemaker, air-conditioning, refrigerator, and cable TV; some rooms also have gas fireplaces. The continental breakfast is complimentary, and you can even make decently sized waffles. At this hotel, make sure to ask specifically for a nonsmoking room or you might end up with a room that smells rather smoky.

Jackson Rancheria RV Park (12222 New York Ranch Rd., 209/223-8358, www.jacksoncasino.com/lodging/rv-park, $40–45) is a surprisingly nice getaway. This place is spotless. You'll find tidy landscaping, a beautiful view of Amador's wildflowers and oak woodlands, and amenities like high-speed Internet, an outdoor pool with spa, a clubhouse and showers, plus a shuttle every 20 minutes to Jackson Rancheria Casino. The RV park is dog-friendly, so don't worry about bringing Fido along.

The **Holiday Inn Express** (101 Clinton Rd., 209/257-1500, $115–200) is a modern, comfortable, if somewhat sterile hotel just off Highway 49. The rooms are pretty well stocked with anything you'd need, including a microwave, mini-fridge, cable TV, and hair dryer. If you need a business center or fitness room, the Holiday Inn also has those amenities. In the morning, start your day with a trip to the hotel's complimentary breakfast buffet.

The Jackson Lodge (850 N. Hwy. 49, 209/233-0486, www.thejacksonlodge.com, $70–140) has rooms and cabins with a homey, Western ranch vibe. You'll find stone fireplaces, handmade wooden furniture, and kitchen areas with a large fridge and dining tables. The accommodations are a nice switch from mainstream chain motels, but still feel modern with amenities like microwaves, phones with voicemail, hair dryers, and in-room coffee. When you need to cool off during hot Gold Country summers, you'll find a spotless pool area with plenty of plastic lounge chairs and patio tables.

Jackson Rancheria Casino and Hotel (12222 New York Ranch Rd., 209/223-8358, www.jacksoncasino.com, $90–300) is a convenient place to stay if you're planning on burning some time at the Pai Gow tables. Unfortunately, this place seems to be perpetually under construction, which makes it somewhat tricky to walk the grounds and can make things noisy sometimes. It's a decent "last resort" kind of accommodation if Jackson's other lodgings are booked.

For a cheap last-minute place to stay there's also **Linda Vista Motel** (10708 Hwy. 49, 209/223-1096, $68–74), which has affordable, clean rooms with an outdoor swimming pool just off the highway.

Food

Good luck finding upscale cuisine options in Jackson. If that doesn't bother you, try the **Mother Lode Market and Deli** (36 Main St., 209/223-0652, 8 a.m.–3 p.m. Mon.–Sat., $5), a local institution that serves down-home meals and some local history. If you're walking around downtown Jackson, this quaint, rustic café is right in the middle of town and makes a perfect stop for coffee or a bite to eat. It feels a little bit like eating in a museum—the walls are lined with old photographs showing sepia-toned scenes from the town's past. The menu is filled with your standard Americana café fare—sandwiches, deli salads, and soups. It's nothing fancy, but everything is prepared from scratch. You can get a sandwich with freshly baked bread and a heaping pile of homemade potato salad; either the tri-tip beef or the Italian sausage sandwiches are excellent choices. Seasoned travelers will find that prices are reasonable here and it's one of the best options in Jackson for a home-style meal.

Thomi's Café (627 S. Hwy. 49, 209/257-0800, www.thomiscafe.net, 8 A.M.–9 P.M. Mon.–Sat., 8 A.M.–8 P.M. Sun., $10–17) is the kind of old-fashioned family restaurant you probably went to as a kid. You can get a meal pretty much any time of the day here, and make sure to come hungry; calling the portions hearty is an understatement. Try the plate-busting braised pot roast with mashed potatoes or the Cajun penne. Most of the food is typical American surf and turf, although Thomi also has an astonishingly good stir-fry menu. Locals dig the breakfast here, especially the California Benedict with eggs, tomato, bacon, and avocado. One thing you won't find is many vegetarian options other than some salads and a few meatless pasta dishes.

If you're looking for good takeaway food in Jackson, it's hard to beat the **Vinciguerra Ravioli Company** (225 Sutter St., 209/223-7654, 11 A.M.–6 P.M. Wed.–Sat., $8). There's no sit-down service here, just a window where you pick up buckets of mouthwatering ravioli to cook later. You'll need either a stove or a microwave because the ravioli comes frozen, but this hole-in-the-wall is a gem. Any of the different menu choices are excellent, although the pumpkin ravioli with sage butter sauce is ahead of the pack and the side of garlic bread is a tasty bonus. Everything is made from scratch, but since the ravioli is frozen when you buy it, bring an ice chest to keep the food chilled until you're ready to eat it.

The good folks at **Fat Freddy's** (4 Main St., 209/223-2525, 10:30 A.M.–3 P.M. Mon.–Sat.,

$5–10) have rules for eating your hot dog. Rule 1: Eat it with your hands. Sounds straightforward, but Freddy's has about a dozen tongue-in-cheek guidelines written on the wall to keep you honest. You'll find those kinds of quirks at this old-school hot dog joint, which also serves other fast food like juicy hamburgers, fish-and-chips, and brain-freezing milk shakes. Come for the food, and make sure to enjoy the classic Americana hung on the wall, from vintage photographs of old Jackson to Carl, the stuffed buffalo head mounted above the grill. If you can, grab a red leather stool at the wooden lunch counter and try to banter with Carlos, Freddy's gregarious owner behind the grill.

Mel and Faye's Diner (31 Hwy. 49, 209/223-0853, www.melandfayesdiner.com, 4 A.M.–10 P.M. Sun.–Thurs., 4 A.M.–11 P.M. Fri.–Sat., $8) is your typical roadside greasy spoon serving up burgers, omelettes, and steaks. This place is up and down in my book and service can be iffy; on the other hand, how many places are open at 4 A.M.?

The **Waffle Shop** (543 S. Hwy. 49, 209/223-4888, www.waffleshops.com, 5 A.M.–3 P.M. daily, $5–10) is a traditional diner where you'll probably end up with a food coma. Typical plates include the Special Omelette, a three-egg behemoth with four kinds of meat, two kinds of cheese, and a smattering of veggies. The Waffle Shop also serves burgers, sandwiches, and a decently sized salad selection; there's also a large "young at heart" menu for kids and seniors, although it's debatable if anything at the Waffle Shop is cardio-approved.

Information and Services

The **Amador Chamber of Commerce** (115 Main St., 209/223-0350, http://amadorcountychamber.com, 8 A.M.–4 P.M. Mon.–Fri., 10 A.M.–2 P.M. Sat.–Sun.) is also the visitors bureau in Jackson, and it's the best place to learn about what's happening in town.

Jackson is the nerve center for Amador

County politics, and the *Ledger-Dispatch* covers local government news. Cultural events can be found weekly in the pages of the *Sierra Lodestar* (www.sierralodestar.com).

Jackson is one of the region's largest towns and has plenty of services available, including ATMs, banks, gas stations, and supermarkets. There's also a **post office** at 424 Sutter Street (9 A.M.–4 P.M. Mon.–Fri., 10 A.M.–2 P.M. Sat.).

For medical emergencies and health needs, visit **Sutter Amador Hospital** (200 Mission Blvd., 209/223-7500, www.sutteramador.org).

Getting There and Around

Jackson lies near the intersection of two foothill highways and is fairly easy to reach by car. From the north or south, you can take Highway 49 to get to town; if coming from the Bay Area or the Central Valley, Highway 88 is your best bet. Note that both highways are two-lane roads that become congested during summer and on weekends. Jackson can also receive snowfall that can complicate your travel plans, so check traffic reports (www.caltrans.org) before setting out.

Aviation services can be found at **Westover Field-Amador County Airport** (12380 Airport Rd., 209/223-2376, www.co.amador.ca.us), just north of town. If you need a car, **Enterprise** (209/223-4200, www.enterprise.com) has rentals available.

Public transit options are limited in the area, but **Amador Transit** (http://amadortransit.com, $2) runs several routes between Sutter Creek and Jackson on weekdays.

VOLCANO

Getting to Volcano (pop. 115) is quite the odyssey. No, scratch that—with narrow one-lane roads that dip from rocky ridgelines into thickly forested ponderosa groves, it's more like a roller coaster. In other words, Volcano is kind of remote. Maybe that's why it's just now earning recognition as a cozy mountain burg

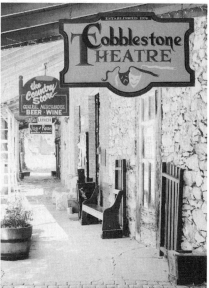

© CHRISTOPHER ARNS

"Downtown" Volcano has just a handful of shops.

with a ton of historical mojo. Volcano is the site of California's first lending library and first theater company, along with the state's oldest continuously operating grocery store. The town actually had a brief skirmish between Union and Confederate sympathizers during the Civil War—sure, no shots were fired, but the fracas did involve a cannon named Honest Abe that's still around. Budding volcanologists will be disappointed when they learn Volcano's name is a complete misnomer; 19th-century prospectors thought the bowl-shaped valley resembled a crater and that's how the name stuck. Those types of little quirks define Volcano's place in the pantheon of Gold Country tourist stops, and I highly recommend braving the hairpin road to get here.

◖ Indian Grinding Rock State Historic Park

You'll get chills visiting Indian Grinding Rock

Check out the "moonscape" at the Indian Grinding Rock State Historic Park.

© CHRISTOPHER ARNS

State Historic Park (14881 Pine Grove-Volcano Rd., 209/296-7488, www.parks.ca.gov, sunrise to sunset daily, $8 per vehicle). Left behind by Miwok Indian tribes, there are 1,185 mortar holes in the marbleized limestone outcroppings around this amazing state park, creating a pockmarked "moonscape" that remains unblemished for visitors to see. Along with the mortar holes, you'll find haunting petroglyphs of human feet, animal tracks, and geometric shapes etched into the rock; these decorative carvings are thought to be at least 2,000 years old. Park rangers have also re-created authentic tribal structures including a ceremonial roundhouse and several tepee-like bark houses. Inside the park's museum, make sure to check out exhibits with handwoven baskets, hunting tools, and Miwok dancing gear painstakingly made from hundreds of hawk and eagle feathers. Besides the historical attractions, you should really spend time exploring the park's grassy meadows and woodlands dotted with valley oaks. For the ultimate Grinding Rock experience, stay overnight in one of seven bark houses that accommodate up to six people; you'll need to reserve a spot at least six months in advance, but catching a sunrise over the mysterious landscape is unforgettable.

Black Chasm Caverns

If you're a first-time caver, Black Chasm Caverns (15701 Pioneer Volcano Rd., 866/762-2837, www.caverntours.com, 9 A.M.–5 P.M. daily, adults $14.95, children $7.95) is a fantastic place to start. Cavern newbies and experienced subterranean dwellers alike will enjoy plumbing Black Chasm's depths for the jaw-dropping sights around every mysterious corner. The cave's Landmark Room is famous for rare mineral deposits known as helictites, which resemble a latticework of shredded coconut growing from the cavern walls. No need to worry about bats in this cave, since Black Chasm's twisting tunnels are too narrow for the flying critters, but make sure to hold on to your belongings so they don't fall into the cavern's many nooks and crannies where they'll be lost forever. Docents offer two tours: One is underground through the cavern's many chambers and the other starts on the surface before leading visitors through rocky tunnels and passageways in the nearby forest. If you take this second tour, wear durable clothing and prepare to get a little dirty. Make sure to check out the new visitors center and watch a video on how the chasm inspired scenes from the *The Matrix* films.

◖ Daffodil Hill

More than 100 years ago, a Gold Country farmer and his wife began planting daffodil bulbs on their Amador County ranch. Thanks to their labor of love, Daffodil Hill (18310 Rams Horn Grade, 209/296-7048, http://suttercreek.org/daffodil-hill, late Mar.–mid-Apr.

daily, free) is blanketed every spring with a sea of white and yellow flowers for one of the area's most stunning attractions. The view is breathtaking—at least 300,000 bulbs and 300 varieties of daffodils grow on the farm, owned and operated by the McLaughlin family since 1887. Each year, around 6,000 daffodils are added to the ranch along with dozens of other beautiful flower and bulb varieties, creating a dazzling botanical wonderland that lasts for just a few weeks every year. Bring a picnic and a camera to fully experience this special place.

Daffodil Hill opens to the public *only* during daffodil season, but exact opening and closing dates vary each year. Call to get the latest information on this year's blooms.

Entertainment and Events

Why shouldn't this tiny town have its own theater group? The arts run deep in Volcano, where California's first performing company was founded in 1854. That group folded, but the **Volcano Theatre Company** (16140 Main St., 209/296-2525, www.volcanotheatre.org, shows 8 P.M. Fri.–Sat., 2 P.M. Sun.) has proudly carried on that tradition for more than 40 years. This vibrant amateur company might not win any Tonys, but they put up entertaining and earnest productions of plays like *Noises Off, The Odd Couple,* and *The Philadelphia Story.* Because the company has both an indoor and outdoor stage, you can watch shows year-round at the town's lovingly restored playhouse; look for the four distinctive green doors in the craggy stone building which marks the amphitheater. The indoor Cobblestone Theatre is directly across the street.

Volcano is pretty sleepy after dark, but you can find some fun at the **Union Inn and Pub** (21375 Consolation St., 209/296-7711, www.volcanounion.com, 5–8 P.M. Thurs. and Mon.,

Volcano's grassy outdoor amphitheatre hosts plays all summer long.

3–9 P.M. Fri., noon–9 P.M. Sat., 10 A.M.–8 P.M. Sun., $18). This small, friendly bar is one of the only spots in town for nightlife, and even then, it still closes early. On Sunday, local musical acts play everything from rock and country music to fiddle and banjo tunes. If you're into pub games, toss a few darts or try your hand at the Union's shuffleboard.

St. George Wine Room (16112 Main St., 5 P.M.–midnight Mon. and Fri.–Sat., 6 P.M.–midnight Wed., 5–11 P.M. Thurs., 3–9 P.M. Sun.) is more of a cheeky dive than a traditional wine bar. Besides the wine, which isn't much to speak of anyway, you can order bottled or canned beer and try your hand at karaoke or listen to live acoustic music. Then again, you can't be too picky here—besides the Union Pub, it's the only darn thing in town that qualifies as real nightlife.

Sports and Recreation

The course at **Mace Meadow Golf and Country Club** (26570 Fairway Dr., Pioneer, 209/295-7020, www.macemeadow.com, $8–32, carts extra) is a fun, quick adventure with surprisingly tough fairways. The cost is entirely reasonable for 18 holes, although there's a reason it's cheap: Seasoned duffers will notice the bunkers sometimes need a little TLC and the slightly worn condition of the course means Mace Meadow isn't in the same class as more expensive places. On the other hand, if you just want to enjoy some top-notch scenery while hitting the links, this unpretentious course is a fine place for a round.

Accommodations

Right now, you only have one option in Volcano, but it's a good one. For a budget hotel adventure deep in the northern Gold Country, head for the **Union Inn and Pub** (21375 Consolation St., 209/296-7711, www.volcanounion.com, $110–140). The lone hotel in this tiny town has only four rooms, but each

one is exquisitely decorated with a different luxurious theme. The building itself was originally constructed in 1880, but the renovated interior and the modern amenities include a flat-panel TV, radio with iPod dock, and DVD player. And even though the building dates back to the Gold Rush when most inns had shared bathrooms, every room at this hotel has private facilities; for a truly romantic stay, ask for a room with a sunken porcelain tub. In the morning, the Union serves up a gourmet breakfast (the owner is the chef at Restaurant Taste in Plymouth) with fresh fruit, homemade pastries, and usually something special that's whipped up just for that day. One word of advice: the Union is best for couples looking for a romantic getaway, and neither children nor pets are welcomed here.

Indian Grinding Rock State Historic Park (14881 Pine Grove-Volcano Rd., 209/296-7488, www.parks.ca.gov, mid-Mar.–end of Sept., $25) has a peaceful campground that feels miles away from everywhere even though Volcano is just a few minutes north. You'll find 22 campsites, picnic tables, fire rings, food lockers, and coin-operated showers.

Food

Volcano has slim pickins for dining, but what's here is special. Who'd expect gourmet food from a Wild West pub that's miles away from anywhere? The **Union Inn and Pub** (21375 Consolation St., 209/296-7711, www.volcanounion.com, 3–9 P.M. Fri., noon–9 P.M. Sat., noon–8 P.M. Sun., 5–8 P.M. Mon. and Thurs., $18) defies those expectations with seasonal dishes made from healthy, local food. The Union takes standard pub fare and surprises with goodies like the juicy lamb burger, dripping with Tunisian hot sauce, pickled carrots, and goat feta cheese. If that's too exotic for you, try the fried chicken with smoked cheddar macaroni and cheese. Take your meals over to the crackling stone fireplace on a chilly

© CHRISTOPHER ARNS

The Union Inn and Pub makes a mean lamb burger.

foothill night or grab a seat on the patio during warmer summer evenings.

Open since 1862, **The Country Store** (16146 Main St., 209/296-4459, 10 A.M.–6 P.M. Mon.–Sat., 11 A.M.–5 P.M. Sun., $4–7) is part museum and part working shop. It's California's oldest continuously operated grocery store and was actually portrayed in an 1948 issue of *Life.* Shelves are stacked with bottles, cans, and jars that probably haven't been opened in 100 years, so don't confuse them with your groceries! You can order sandwiches and burgers in the attached café, and all food is cooked on an indoor stone grill; draught beer is on tap along with sodas and juice. The store doubles as Volcano's visitor center, providing helpful information for visitors seeking theater reviews or tips about local sightseeing.

Information and Services

In Volcano you won't find much in the way of services; the closest bank branches or gas stations are located nearly four miles southwest in Pine Grove off Highway 88 or eight miles to the northeast in Pioneer. In Volcano, you'll find a **post office** at 16120 Main Street (8:30–4 P.M. Mon.–Fri.)

Getting There and Around

Volcano is on the eastern edge of the Gold Country where the elevation starts to climb among towering pine trees that blanket the hillsides. If you're arriving by car, take Highway 88 northeast from Jackson for about nine miles and turn left on Pine Grove-Volcano Road; Volcano will appear in about three miles. Because of the higher elevation, Volcano often receives heavy snowfall in winter, and chains can be required. Check weather and traffic reports (www.caltrans.org) before planning your trip.

Calaveras County

No one captured frontier Americana quite like writer Samuel Langhorne Clemens, known more famously as Mark Twain. Some of his wildest tales were inspired by this irrepressible stretch of Southern Gold Country. During the Gold Rush, outlaws and outcasts flocked to Calaveras County like frantic moths to a flame, including notorious bandits like Joaquin Murrieta and Black Bart; perhaps they were drawn to the mind-boggling wealth found in Calaveras mining camps, where the nation's largest gold nugget tipped the scales at 215 pounds in 1854.

Today, most Calaveras characters can be found in tasting rooms between Angels Camp and Murphys, where the region's next crop of iconoclastic winemakers have planted deep roots. Once here, you'll notice folks seem more authentic, distinctly homespun, and boldly more down to earth—perhaps taking after the famous writer himself.

ANGELS CAMP

You have to admire the founding fathers of Angels Camp (pop. 3,700). I mean, a jumping frog contest? Sure, Mark Twain obviously

A TALE OF TWO OUTLAWS: JOAQUIN MURRIETA AND BLACK BART

Almost overnight, the Gold Rush unleashed a stampede of pioneers and prospectors who swarmed across the frontier into California looking to strike it rich—some by nefarious means. As in other boomtowns across the West where the law was often nonexistent, mining camps in Calaveras County had their fair share of criminals. Some were simple crooks, while others left quite an impression with their notorious zeal for banditry. Newspaper writers of the time, desperate to sell copy, often romanticized these criminals as social revolutionaries caught on the wrong side of the law.

One such desperado was Joaquin Murrieta, known as the Mexican Robin Hood, who terrorized settlers and prospectors throughout Calaveras County with a violent crime spree in 1853. Legend has it, Murrieta supposedly turned to crime after white settlers brutally killed his wife, but that story is most likely a myth—most historians think Murrieta was a horse-thieving, bank-robbing murderer whose gang of fellow frontier thugs killed dozens of people. After exasperated law enforcement officials offered $6,000 to capture the outlaw, a posse caught up to Murrieta near Fresno and killed him; without DNA evidence or fingerprints, the posse

leader decided to prove Murrieta's demise by showing off the bandit's severed head in mining camps around the Gold Country.

A more lighthearted tale is the story of stagecoach bandit and poet Charles Bowles, known as Black Bart. Raised in England and displaying a genteel touch for crime, Black Bart wore a bowler hat and was terrified of horses. On foot, he held up 28 Wells Fargo stagecoaches all over the Gold Country without firing a shot. Black Bart's first robbery was in western Calaveras County near the town of Copperopolis; he walked away with only $160, but eventually stole thousands in later holdups. Stagecoach passengers were struck by his polite manner and the witty poems he left behind at crime scenes. After detectives finally nabbed him in 1883, Bart spent six years in San Quentin Prison near San Francisco. Upon his release, Black Bart told reporters that he was through with crime. The scribes asked if he would at least continue to write poetry. "Now, didn't I tell you I was through with crime?" he said, laughing. Indeed, Black Bart never robbed another stagecoach nor wrote another poem after leaving prison. He was never seen again.

Highway 49 winds through Angels Camp.

© CHRISTOPHER ARNS

deserves some creative credit for his famous short story, "The Celebrated Jumping Frog of Calaveras County," set in Angels Camp. Still, the sheer brilliance of turning this tall tale into a yearly event belongs to gutsy town officials who created the Jumping Frog Jubilee in 1928. Now frogs are everywhere in Angels Camp. From welcome banners on streetlights to brass plaques commemorating past Jubilee winners on Main Street, the little green critters literally have this town covered. There's a Jumping Frog Motel, a Frog's Tooth Vineyard, and the Frog Hollow landscaping company. (If you dislike frogs, maybe Angels Camp isn't for you.)

Aside from the leaping amphibians, Angels Camp is kind of a mishmash of Gold Country towns—there's wine-tasting, the usual smattering of antiques shops, a few offbeat mom-and-pop stores, and a beautifully restored marquee at the Angels 6 Theatre. Angels Camp works well as a jumping-off place (sorry, couldn't

help it) for experiencing local recreation, such as boating at New Melones Lake or clambering around California Caverns. Nearly every town claims to be the jewel or the gem of the Gold Country, but Angels Camp truly comes closest to earning that title.

◖ California Caverns

California Caverns (9565 Cave City Rd., Mountain Ranch, 866/762-2837, www.caverntours.com, 10 A.M.–5 P.M. daily Apr.–Oct., adults $14.75, children $7.50) has been welcoming underground explorers for more than 150 years. An army captain found the caves in 1850 when he noticed a strange breeze blowing from a rocky outcropping; since then, visitors such as Mark Twain and John Muir have gazed on the cavern's depths, spellbound at bizarre and beautiful formations. The basic tour is geared toward families and lasts just over an hour; a knowledgeable guide waxes on about the cavern's history and geology while

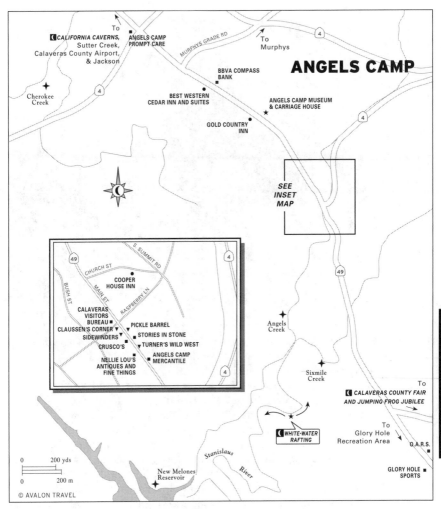

leading you through a wonderland of subterranean chambers. Kids will love gazing at the numerous stalactites, especially the vinelike formations in the **Jungle Room** cavern. You can also do some serious spelunking at California Caverns if you're not claustrophobic. Spend hours with a guide as you plunge into murky depths and raft across underground pools on the **Middle Earth Expedition** (four hours, $130); remember to look up at

the rare "helictite" formations of beaded crystal on the cavern ceiling. Make sure to bring hiking shoes or boots since the underground paths can be quite slippery, and wear clothes you won't mind getting muddy; some of the tours involve crawling through damp wormholes and crevices. Many of the tours can't be accessed in certain seasons, so call the caverns' visitor center or check the website for more information.

the visitors center at California Caverns

Angels Camp Museum & Carriage House

It doesn't look like much from outside, but the Angels Camp Museum & Carriage House (753 S. Main St., 209/736-2963, www.angelscamp. gov, 10 A.M.–4 P.M. Thurs.–Mon. Mar.–Nov.; 10 A.M.–4 P.M. Sat.–Sun. Nov.–Feb., adults $5, children 5–11 $2.50) has over three acres of displays packed inside a long narrow warehouse. Many of the exhibits are common to other Gold Country museums, like prospecting machinery and a re-created mining camp, although the carriage house is something special. More than 30 immaculate buggies line the warehouse in carefully arranged order, including hansoms, buckboards, wagons, and a 19th-century hearse. Carriages were once the Cadillacs of the West, and this museum has kept them in pristine condition. Outside, gearheads should check out the imposing Pelton wheel that once powered Calaveras County

gold mines; there's also a working stamp mill crushing fist-sized chunks of ore.

Entertainment and Events

If you'd like to catch a flick while in town, look for the glowing neon marquee at **Angels 6 Theatre** (1228 S. Main St., 209/736-6768, www.cinemawest.com/agl.html). This cinema has six small, cozy theaters with wall-to-wall silver screens, all showing the latest releases. The smaller confines aren't bad, and watching a movie at Angels 6 is a fun and intimate way to spend an evening.

Claussen's Corner (1208 S. Main St., 209/736-2593, 9:45 A.M.–1:45 A.M. Tues.–Sat., 9:45 A.M.–midnight Sun.–Mon.) is the unofficial capital of dive bars in Calaveras County. Bartenders take time to shoot the breeze with visitors inside this stripped down grungy little saloon. Locals tend to welcome outsiders with more vigor than normal for Gold Country dives. What else would you expect from a town that its loves frogs?

CALAVERAS COUNTY FAIR AND JUMPING FROG JUBILEE

And you thought the Calaveras County Fair and Jumping Frog Jubilee (209/736-2561, www.frogtown.org, every May, adults $7, children $5) was only a tall tale. Mark Twain's short story about a jumping frog named Dan'l Webster inspired this yearly event that's half folk tradition and half serious business. Anyone can step right up and become a frog jockey, which means wrapping your hands around a slippery bullfrog and coaxing the critter to leap. But I have to warn you, it's not easy holding those suckers. If frog jumping isn't your thing, the Jubilee is just one part of the county fair, and there are warehouses full of craft and agricultural exhibits, plenty of diet-busting carnival food, a rodeo, and a midway with games and rides. The fair happens every third week in May; since you'll be outdoors all day, bring plenty of sunscreen or a hat for the relentless Gold Country heat.

Shopping

There are just two city blocks of stores lined up along Main Street so window-shopping doesn't take too long. But just like everything else about Angels Camp, the downtown shops are one of a kind. Visiting **Stories in Stone** (1249 S. Main St., 209/736-1300, www.storiesinstones.com, 10 A.M.–5:30 P.M. Sun.–Fri.) is like stumbling across lost treasure. It's the only place with a fully intact cave bear skeleton; there's also the skull of a woolly mammoth and literally thousands of fossils, shells, crystals, and polished stones stacked from all over the world, like the cello-size Brazilian amethyst geodes. Owner Russ Shoemaker turned his personal rock collection into a magical store that feels like a secret vault at the Smithsonian. The huge selection means you could spend

thousands of dollars here or just a few bucks, no matter how exotic your taste. Kids will love the store's learning center, where Shoemaker gives presentations in a little auditorium; call ahead to find out the day's schedule.

Angels Camp Mercantile (1267 S. Main St., 209/890-7155, www.angelsmerc.com, 10 A.M.–6 P.M. Sun.–Mon., 10 A.M.–5 P.M. Wed.–Thurs., 10 A.M.–10 P.M. Fri., 10 A.M.–9 P.M. Sat.) is a gem of a store that defies expectations. Part coffee shop, part antiques store, there's live music almost every week and a gift shop with local products like olive oil, jam, mustard, and handmade games. Order some ice cream and hang out in the overstuffed chairs for a while; look up and gaze at the building's original tin ceiling from the 1860s. Workers at the "Merc" are volunteers who trade shifts for housing; the store itself is nonprofit, so every dollar spent here helps support folks in need.

Nellie Lou's Antiques and Fine Things (1254 S. Main St., 209/736-6728, 10 A.M.–5 P.M. daily) has a little bit of everything—porcelain dining sets, worn volumes of Shakespeare and Jack London, vintage necklaces and rings, and much more. Nellie Lou's specializes in classic cookware by Corning and Revere and offers shelves of cast-iron pans and enameled pots. This is definitely no dusty bargain bin; everything is in immaculate condition, and the prices certainly reflect Nellie Lou's fine quality.

Somehow, just walking into **Turner's Wild West** (1235 Main St., 209/736-4909, 10 A.M.–5:30 P.M. Mon.–Sat., noon–4 P.M. Sun.) makes you feel like a cowboy. Right away, the smell of musky rawhide hits you from the racks of Stetsons, leather dusters, and riding boots that line the wall. Two barn-size rooms mean there's a whole wagonload of different styles and options—everything from Clint Eastwood–wannabe to urban desperado.

If you're fishing, head to **Glory Hole Sports**

HOW TO JUMP A FROG

© CHRISTOPHER ARNS

The author with his frog, which failed spectacularly to advance into the finals.

Hold on there, frog jockey—you need to know the basics about the little leapers before you hop on over to the **Calaveras County Fair and Jumping Frog Jubilee** (www.frogtown. org), held every May in Angels Camp. Sure, I hear you: How hard can it be to make a bullfrog jump? Nonsense, my friend. Frog jumping is a serious business. If you're going to beat the world record of 21 feet, 5 3/4 inches, you need to learn a couple of things.

First off, it's okay to bring your own frog, but Jubilee officials will generously provide a rental amphibian for a few bucks. Second, make sure to hold the dang thing correctly: Grasp your frog firmly by pinching both sides of the hard cartilage protruding from its back. I know, you're worried about hurting the little guy, but the nice folks at the Jubilee say frogs aren't bothered by it. Now, if the frog starts squirming—and it will, because it wants to go right back into the Frog Spa where it came from—try stroking your leaper's hind legs until

they dangle limply. (The frog wastes too much energy if it gets riled up before jumping, and I hear this little trick calms them down.)

By now, the onstage announcer in the 10-gallon hat has called your name. Time to jump! Step out on the wide stage and look for a small disk of green Astroturf—that's the launching pad. Some old-timers say it's best to cover your frog's eyes at this point, like you're about to surprise him, and I'm sure that probably helps. Now, lower the frog until he's just a foot above the green pad and let go. Time to get hopping! You can tap your frog, blow on him, scream, or do whatever before the frog leaps, but after that first jump there's no touching allowed. Three leaps and it's all over; the judges record the frog's longest jump, and if he qualifies for the finals, you can do it all over again.

Winners are immortalized with a brass plaque on Main Street in Angels Camp, but world-record breakers get a cool $5,000. If you win, no need to thank me; just know I *toad* you so.

(2892 Hwy. 49, 209/736-4333, http://gloryholesports.com, dawn–dusk daily) before dropping a line at New Melones Lake. At this roadside oasis, you can pick up bait and tackle, rods and reels, wakeboards and water skis, and camping gear. Lose your boat plug last time out on the lake? Glory Hole (yes, that's really the name) also has basic boating hardware to keep you afloat. Don't forget to fill up; the store is also a full-fledged gas station with a deli and mini-mart.

Sports and Recreation

If you love water sports, rub your hands together in glee. Angels Camp is just a short drive from **New Melones Lake** (between Angels Camp and Sonora), one of the Gold Country's largest reservoirs. Most folks explore the more than 12,000 acres of surface water by boat, but hikers, equestrians, and anglers will also be enthralled. Start at the **visitors center** (0.25 mile south of Stevenot Stanislaus River Bridge, 209/536-9543, www.usbr.gov, 10 A.M.–4 P.M. daily Memorial Day–Labor Day; 10 A.M.–4 P.M. Wed.–Sun. Labor Day–Memorial Day) to get your bearings, pick up maps, and get the lowdown on boating regulations at the lake. Boat launching costs $10, and day use is $8 to hike or picnic around the lake. Waterskiing and wakeboarding are extremely popular, along with sailing and riding Jet Skis.

A simply awesome hike is the **Natural Bridges Trail** (3.7 miles south of Parrots Ferry Rd. and Hwy. 4, 1.5 miles, easy). Thanks to magical gnomes (boring geologists claim it was "erosion"), a secret tunnel burrows through 0.25 mile of bedrock where mysterious crystalline formations hang overhead. Known as a "karst," the cavern was created as Coyote Creek eroded the solid rock over time, leaving behind a twisting cavern. Make sure to wear hiking shoes with good traction for walking through the shallow but slippery creek in the tunnel. The trailhead is off Parrots Ferry Road. Visitors will see a sign that reads Natural Bridges; turn here and park by the restrooms.

Glory Hole Recreation Area (5.9 miles south of Angels Camp, 209/536-9094 or 209/536-9543, www.recreation.gov) has 30 miles of hiking and mountain bike trails. Hikers should explore either the **Carson Creek Trail** (2.3 miles, moderate) or **Buck Brush Loop** (1.3 miles, easy) for spectacular views of the lake. Looking for fat tire fun? Try either **Tower Climb** (1.3 miles, challenging), with lots of switchbacks and elevation changes, or **Frontier Trail** (1.3 miles, moderate). Download a trail map from the Bureau of Reclamation's website (www.blm.gov) before heading out.

◀ WHITE-WATER RAFTING

Angels Camp is another Gold Country town that's within a short shuttle ride of churning white water. Here the options change slightly from excursions in Northern Gold Country. You can still take guided tours on the South Fork of the American River, but the North Fork of the Stanislaus River is closer to Angels Camp and offers a greater number of intermediate to advanced trips through roaring Class III–IV rapids. The season is shorter on the Stanislaus and runs from mid-April through May, weather and river conditions permitting. Make sure to call ahead before booking your excursion.

All-Outdoors (925/932-8993, www.aorafting.com, $110–340) runs full-day trips to the North Fork of the Stanislaus. You can plunge through Class IV rapids with hair-raising names like Beginner's Luck, Rattlesnake, and Maycheck's Mayhem; the last rapid is a partial Class V drop. You can also take full-day and two-day trips on the calmer South Fork of the American River, if the Stanislaus is beyond your experience level.

O.A.R.S. (209/736-4677, www.oars.com, $110–360) also offers trips to the mighty North Fork of the Stanislaus River. Guides are knowledgeable and friendly, and lunch is provided. If you'd rather raft the South Fork of the American River, O.A.R.S. offers half-day, full-day, and two-day excursions.

Accommodations

It's impossible not to feel spoiled at the **Cooper House Inn** (1184 Church St., 888/330-3764, www.cooperhouseinn.com, $140–300), a renovated Victorian-era country home. Staying here is like taking a couples' getaway back to the Gilded Age with a few green upgrades. The three rooms are adorned with locally made linens, biodegradable bath kits, pillow-top bedding, and private showers, plus 21st-century conveniences like free wireless Internet and flat-panel TVs. (For a king-size bed, ask for the Chardonnay suite.) The only downside to the fabulously luxurious Cooper House is a lack of en suite bathrooms, which means you have to walk down the hall to find one. Downstairs, take a complimentary bottle of wine outside onto the patio and relax in the padded lounge chairs. Breakfast might include organic homemade frittatas, apple-chicken sausage, and foothill-grown produce. If you're looking for a cozy alternative to larger, less intimate accommodations, you'll fall in love with this charming bed-and-breakfast.

Best Western Cedar Inn and Suites (444 S. Main St., 209/736-4000, www.bestwesternangelscamp.com, $120–170) is a clean if somewhat sterile motel with modern amenities like granite countertops, free wireless Internet, microwave, hair dryers, and air-conditioning. Active travelers will stay fit with the stocked workout room and heated outdoor pool, and there's a continental breakfast every morning. If you'd rather not sample the seedier-looking accommodations around Angels Camp, this place is definitely a safer option.

A low-budget choice is **Gold Country Inn** (720 Main St., 209/736-4611, www.goldcountryinnangelscamp.com, $50–175). While

spartan might be too strong a word, this motel is a no-frills kind of place: clean and comfortable while offering basic amenities including cable TV, fridge, hair dryers, and microwaves. One of the best things about the Gold Country Inn is their pet policy, which only asks a nominal fee for furry friends. Outdoor enthusiasts also have ample space for boat parking in the motel's lot.

Who needs a stuffy motel room anyway? Sleep outside at **Glory Hole Recreation Area** (5.9 miles south of Angels Camp, 209/536-9094 or 209/536-9543, www.recreation.gov, standard sites $22, walk-in $18). Choose from 144 campsites on two different campgrounds with horseshoe pits, showers, campfire rings, and flush toilets. To reach the campground from Glory Hole Sports on Highway 49, turn west on Whittle Road and drive four miles to the recreation area.

Food

When it comes to food, Angels Camp is anything but hokey. If you stand long enough in front of **Crusco's** (1240 S. Main St., 209/736-1440, www.cruscos.com, 11:30 A.M.–3 P.M. and 5–9 P.M. Thurs.–Mon., $17–26), locals will inevitably stop to offer their glowing recommendation for the place. They're absolutely right, because this restaurant serves delicious homemade Italian food fixed with local ingredients. It's not your average spaghetti and meatballs kind of fare; Crusco's does Italian with a Californian flair, serving dishes like wild salmon with orange Madeira cream sauce and New York steak topped with crab and butter sauce. Save some room for the unreal chocolate truffle torte for dessert. The best part about this restaurant is the old-world hospitality and attentive service from the owner, who usually is on hand to greet you.

Just thinking about the **Pickle Barrel** (1225 S. Main St., 209/736-4704, www.pickle-barrel.com, 11 A.M.–3 P.M. daily) makes me hungry.

This is without a doubt the best place in town to get a sandwich, with grilled meats sizzling on the back porch and fresh homemade deli salads available to order. Along with sandwiches, you can sample stuffed wraps, steaming-hot paninis, and freshly made soup; wash it down with an old-fashioned soda from the drink case. Last but not least, you absolutely must try a slice of carrot cake—the recipe is from the owner's grandmother. Housed inside an old building with worn wooden floors and high ceilings, the deli feels like an Old West hole-in-the-wall without trying too hard; there are a few knick-knacks on the walls, but diners sit at simple cafeteria tables to enjoy their sandwiches.

Looking for something out of the ordinary? ◖ **Sidewinder's Café** (1252 S. Main St., 209/736-0444, 11 A.M.–8 P.M. Tues.–Sat., $10) serves all-natural food that's a mix of Californian, Mexican, and Basque cuisines. Belly up to the lunch counter to customize your order; there's an eye-popping amount of mostly organic and local ingredients to choose from. One top choice is the chili-lime chicken wrap with beer-battered fries and chipotle dip. If those fries make you thirsty, browse the stacked beer list for one of the many microbrews on tap. The relaxed decor means you can feel comfortable grabbing a table in flip-flops and a T-shirt. If there's a downside, it's the long line that can gather at night; try to call ahead if you're on the road or be prepared to wait.

Information and Services

In Calaveras County, begin your trip at the **Calaveras Visitors Bureau** (1192 S. Main St., 800/225-3764, www.gocalaveras.com, 9 A.M.–5 P.M. Mon.–Sat., 11 A.M.–4 P.M. Sun. in summer; 9:30 A.M.–4:30 P.M. Mon.–Fri., 10 A.M.–5 P.M. Sat., 11 A.M.–4 P.M. Sun. in winter). The newspaper of record in Angels Camp is the *Calaveras Enterprise* (www.calaverasenterprise.com), which comes out on Tuesday and Friday. For entertainment news and events,

check out the weekly *Sierra Lodestar* (www.sierralodestar.com).

Angels Camp has the **BBVA Compass** bank (479 S. Main St., 209/736-4561) with a 24-hour external ATM.

For urgent medical needs and health issues, go to **Angels Camp Prompt Care** (23 N. Main St., 209/736-9130, 8 A.M.–6 P.M. daily). Note that while Angels Camp Prompt Care can treat medical conditions such as broken bones or infections, it is not equipped to handle major emergencies.

Getting There and Around

Angels Camp is located right on Highway 49 in the heart of the Southern Gold Country, 75 miles southeast of Sacramento and 60 miles south of Placerville. From Sacramento, take Highway 16 east for 35 miles to its junction with Highway 49. From Highway 49, it's about 40 miles south to Angels Camp.

If you're lucky enough to have your own plane or access to one, you can fly into the **Calaveras County Airport** (3600 Carol Kennedy Dr., San Andreas, 209/736-2501).

There isn't much in the way of public transportation in Angels Camp, but **Calaveras Transit** (www.calaverastransit.com, $2) runs four routes to the surrounding area on weekdays, including trips to Arnold and Murphys.

MURPHYS

Few towns boast the charm and rugged vibe of Murphys (pop. 2,200), an old mining camp that's become another Napa-in-training. Murphys is the kind of place where horses still graze in front yards just a few feet from the main drag. During the Gold Rush, miners found unimaginable wealth in local gold deposits here; during one winter, prospectors claimed $5 million from the Sierra Nevada foothills. When gold claims finally went bust, Murphys still thrived as a timber town and ranching community while other Gold Country

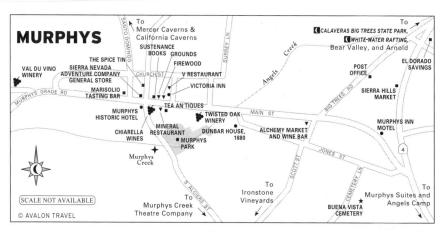

boomtowns withered and became dusty ghost towns. In the 1990s, Murphys began changing from a rural agricultural town into a more chic destination for foodies and wine lovers. That transition isn't complete, which isn't necessarily a bad thing if you prefer to avoid hordes of tourists.

Those familiar with Sonoma and the Napa Valley might recognize a miniature St. Helena or Calistoga as they cruise through Main Street's green tunnels of 100-year-old oak trees. The shopping district is adding more boutique shops and galleries alongside several tasting rooms. Murphys is unique in that the "downtown" area stretches for at least a half mile along Main Street's flat thoroughfare, so come prepared to walk.

Mercer Caverns

One day in 1885, Walter Mercer was looking for a cool drink on a sweltering afternoon when he found a small hole with a spooky breeze blowing from it. Taking his gold prospecting tools in hand, he expanded the hole and discovered Mercer Caverns (1665 Sheep Ranch Rd., 209/728-2101, www.mercercaverns.com, 10 A.M.–4:30 P.M. daily Jan.–May 25; 9 A.M.–5 P.M. daily Memorial Day–Labor Day, adults $13.95, children $7.95). Just like

Walter Mercer, visitors will find a subterranean world seemingly designed by Salvador Dalí. Surreal crystalline formations stretch toward the floor like glistening tentacles, taking on familiar shapes and faces as your imagination starts working. The caverns won a grand prize at the 1900 Paris World's Fair for the rare aragonite crystals that hang from the ceiling like sprays of white coral. As you walk through the Cathedral Room, keep an eye out for two transparent veil-like formations known as Angels Wings that hang nearly nine feet long. Out of the seven mysterious chambers, one of the most jaw-dropping is the 200-foot-long Gothic Chamber, where families can huddle together to gape at the towering ceiling nearly 60 feet above them.

Buena Vista Cemetery

If you like traipsing around old graveyards, Buena Vista Cemetery (Cemetery Lane, 209/728-2387, http://murphyscemetery.com) provides a certain morbid thrill. The macabre historical setting is a fantastic place to create gravestone rubbings. Hundreds of white marble headstones rise unevenly from the reddish hillside, each telling a different story in terse epitaphs; some date back more than 150 years to the early Gold Rush. While you won't find pastoral green lawns, the grounds are immaculately tended, and each plot has been weeded or raked. It's still very much a working cemetery, as evidenced by dates on the newer headstones, so please be respectful of where you walk. While the graveyard makes an interesting hike, it's easier to drive; most of the plots are on the gravel road winding through the cemetery and you can read headstones from the car.

Wineries

Not yet on par with Amador and the Shenandoah Valley, Calaveras winemakers are catching up. Murphys is bursting with fun tasting rooms that ring with excited voices on summer weekends. Since many of these outfits can be found along Main Street sidewalks, Murphys actually has one of the more accessible wine industries in the foothills.

CHIARELLA WINES

Ten years from now, you might look back and say Chiarella Wines (431 Main St., 209/728-8318, www.chiarellawines.com, noon–5 P.M. Fri.–Sun., tastings free) was an up-and-comer. The best varietals are bold, expressive reds like the sangiovese and the barbera. The very friendly tasting room staff obviously enjoys the job and goes out of the way to dispense tasting knowledge along with pouring great wine.

IRONSTONE VINEYARDS

The grande dame of the Calaveras wine country is Ironstone Vineyards (1894 Six Mile Rd., 209/728-1251, www.ironstonevineyards.com, 10 A.M.–5 P.M. daily, tastings $3). The wines are good, if not great, and the tasting room is usually fairly crowded. But you can cross Ironstone off your wine-tasting list by stopping for a glass or two.

Even if you don't enjoy wine-tasting, come for a concert at the stunning **Ironstone Amphitheatre** (www.ironstoneamphitheatre.net), which has hosted artists like Reba

McIntire, Kelly Clarkson, Tony Bennett, and John Fogerty.

TWISTED OAK WINERY

I'm not sure why the mascot for Twisted Oak Winery (4280 Red Hill Rd. at Hwy. 4, Vallecito, 209/736-9080, www.twistedoak.com, 11:30 A.M.–5:30 P.M. Sun.–Fri., 10:30 A.M.–5:30 P.M. Sat., tastings $5) is a rubber chicken, but it works. Twisted Oak is staffed by goofy people who are serious about wine, and they love sharing their knowledge. The bottling of Iberian and Rhône varietals like tempranillos and syrahs is only part of the Twisted experience, which puts on musical events and dinners for only a "twisted" few.

VAL DU VINO WINERY

In an area chock-full of young wineries, Val du Vino Winery (634 French Gulch Rd., 209/728-9911, www.valduvino.com, 11 A.M.–5 P.M. daily, tastings free) is already fairly polished. Housed in a 90-year-old barn set beneath gnarled oak trees, Val du Vino is Main Street's only working winery and produces award-winning reds like the Spanish Dragon Tempranillo. Like most of the Gold Country's smaller wineries, the tasting room is usually staffed by the owners, one of whom is a French chef, so ask about the winery's food events for a real treat.

Entertainment and Events

Drama is the new gold at **Murphys Creek Theatre Company** (580 S. Algiers St., 209/728-8422, http://murphyscreektheatre.org, $12–18), a professional group of actors performing deep in the foothills. The small company hosts wonderful productions of everything from Shakespeare's *Tempest* to contemporary shows like *Almost, Maine*. For years, the company only performed outside during the summer; they now have a permanent home at the **Black Bart Theatre** and put on shows

© CHRISTOPHER ARNS

The Murphys Historic Hotel is supposedly haunted.

year-round. During the warmer months, sit on the lawn at the Albeno Munari Vineyard and Winery and catch a play from the company's Under the Stars series. Make sure to bring a jacket; the summer foothill evenings can turn slightly balmy.

Care for a drink at the oldest pub in town? The **1856 Saloon in the Murphys Historic Hotel** (457 Main St., 209/728-3444, www.murphyshotel.com, 11 A.M.–11 P.M. Mon.–Thurs., 10 A.M.–2 A.M. Fri.–Sat., 10 A.M.–11 P.M. Sun.) probably hasn't changed much since the 1850s. Moose and elk heads glare down from the walls, and a vintage potbellied stove crackles during winter months. Behind the 30-foot-long wooden bar is a full arsenal of cocktails, local and international wine, and beer. The Saloon is standing room only on weekends when live bands or DJs sometimes play; otherwise most entertainment involves pushing quarters into the jukebox or catching 49er games on the big-screen TV.

Shopping

Rustic as Murphys might be, there's a bustling shopping district in the heart of this old mining town with antiques shops, small boutiques, and a few surprises. Most shops are between the parallel streets of Church and Main, with a few stores farther out along Highway 4. On weekends, parking can be a frustrating challenge along the town's Gold Rush–era streets, so arrive earlier in the day if you can.

The name says it all: **Tea an'Tiques** (419 Main St., 209/728-8240, 11 A.M.–5 P.M. Sun.–Fri., 10:30 A.M.–6 P.M. Sat.) serves tea while you browse their wonderful selection of old knickknacks and curios. Stepping through the bright yellow door is like stepping into an English country cottage, only with a self-serve tea bar stocked with 100 different varieties of fine tea. Take a freshly brewed cup with you while looking through the selection of antiques and handmade gifts.

Who says adventure is dead? At the **Sierra**

Nevada Adventure Company General Store
(448 Main St., 209/728-9133, www.snacattack.com, 10 A.M.–6 P.M. daily), you'll find gear for any kind of trek, climb, or walkabout imaginable. This is the perfect place to pick up hiking shoes, a new backpack, or a cool-weather fleece before heading into the foothills.

If you need a summer reading book or travel journal, stop by **Sustenance Books** (416 Main St., 209/728-2200, 11 A.M.–5 P.M. Mon. and Wed., 11 A.M.–6 P.M. Thurs.–Sun.). You can find both new and used tomes from every genre on the shelves here. Sustenance specializes in children's books; they also have a wide selection of nature books and volumes on sustainability.

Belly up to a different kind of bar at **Marisolio Tasting Bar** (488 Main St., 209/728-8853, www.marisolio.com, 10 A.M.–5 P.M. Wed.–Mon., noon–5 P.M. Tues.) for tastings of artisan olive oil and vinegars. The oils and vinegars are mostly from California, but the shop also sells imported products made with fair trade and sustainable ingredients from all over the world. Make sure to try either the white or the black truffle extra virgin olive oil, and if you taste the vinegars, don't miss the delicious black cherry.

Your nose will have no trouble finding the **The Spice Tin** (457 N. Algiers St., 209/728-8225, www.thespicetin.com, 11 A.M.–5 P.M. daily). Spices aren't the only goodies here; sauces, salts, dips, and rubs also line the tangy shelves. Pick up a grinder or mill and some Greek seasoning powder or the Black Bart BBQ spice to make a truly zesty gift.

Accommodations

For a little town, Murphys sure has a slew of choices. There's something for everyone, whether you hole up like a Wild West desperado or keep things modern out by the highway.

How many motels give out complimentary Oreos? That's what you'll find at **Murphys Inn Motel** (76 Main St., 888/796-1800, www.

centralsierralodging.com, $85–210), along with spotless rooms and modern amenities like microwaves, refrigerators, coffeemakers, and TVs; there's also an outdoor pool. If you plan on tasting wine, the motel is a convenient five-minute walk to downtown Murphys. Just like the rest of Murphys, this place is a little rough around the edges; don't expect a continental breakfast waiting in the morning, and most of the complimentary amenities are disappointingly cheap. But, why nitpick when they have cookies?

You won't have any complaints after a night at ◖ **Dunbar House, 1880** (271 Jones St., 209/728-2897, www.dunbarhouse.com, $200–275). This square-jawed New England–style farmhouse is spare, yet elegant and resembles something in New York's Hudson Valley. Your stay begins with complimentary cookies and port in the lobby, but the real treats are five luxurious rooms decorated with a colonial-country theme. Each room boasts a Norwegian woodstove and English towel warmers next to a claw-foot tub, perfect for warming up during a crisp foothill evening. In the morning, feast on breakfast dishes such as confetti enchurrito with fresh fruit or veggie frittata with zucchini muffins, served in your room, the dining room, or in the shaded garden area.

If you're tuckered out after a long day in Murphys, rest easy at **Victoria Inn** (402 H Main St., 209/728-8933, http://victoriainn-murphys.com, $130–385). This *Bonanza*-style ranch house may look like an outpost for the overland stage, but the interior is gussied up with soaking tubs, comfy beds, a huge contemporary kitchen, and roaring fireplaces. Choose from 19 rooms or condos, some with four-poster beds, high ceilings with exposed framing and beams, wet bar, spa, private bathroom, woodstove, down comforter, and a balcony overlooking the courtyard. In the morning, an extended continental breakfast awaits downstairs.

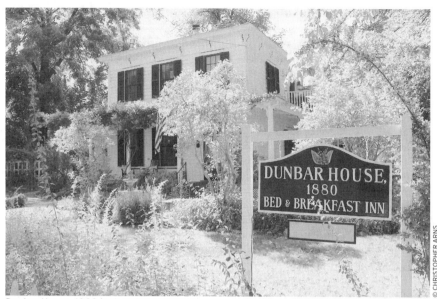

© CHRISTOPHER ARNS

Dunbar House, 1880 in downtown Murphys

According to legend, the outlaw Black Bart crashed at **Murphys Historic Hotel** (457 Main St., 209/728-3444, www.murphyshotel.com, $90–180) at least once. So did Mark Twain, Susan B. Anthony, J. P. Morgan, and John Wayne. With such an esteemed cavalcade of guests, this place just has to be haunted, right? Every ancient hotel in the Gold Country has at least one good ghost story, but the tales might be true at these ancient digs. Choose from original rooms with a shared bathroom and no air-conditioning, or sacrifice character to sleep in the newer, more modern wing. One thing to keep in mind is that the saloon can get noisy on weekends, and the clatter can rise to the floors above.

Murphys Suites (134 Hwy. 4, 209/728-2121, www.murphyssuites.com, $120–280) has modern facilities with a touch of high country character. Apparently the word has spread about the free Oreos, because this place goes even further by offering fresh mini-doughnuts

every morning. Once your sugar rush fades, crash in the comfy, well-appointed rooms with satellite TVs, individually controlled air-conditioning, microwaves, fridges, free wireless Internet, and magnifying makeup mirrors. But the hotel really goes all out downstairs with a fitness room, sauna, and outdoor pool with spa. In the morning, there's a complimentary continental breakfast and those oh-so-tempting doughnuts. Guests can also use the hotel laundry facility; rooms have a clothesline if you'd prefer to drip-dry.

Food

Along with progressive winemakers, Murphys also has attracted some very forward-thinking chefs who push the town's culinary envelope. Start at ◖**Grounds** (402 A Main St., 209/728-8663, www.groundsrestaurant.com, 7 A.M.–10:30 P.M. Mon.–Fri., 7 A.M.–11:15 P.M. Sat., 8 A.M.–11:15 P.M. Sun., $14–29), a contemporary bistro that holds its own among the Gold

Country's plethora of upscale eateries. Grounds was one of the first gourmet restaurants to open when Murphys began its renaissance in the 1990s, and it's still one of the best places to eat. The modern Californian cuisine features standard dishes, like a grilled eggplant sandwich or seared swordfish steak over linguini. At breakfast, make your own omelette from ingredients like sweet Italian sausage, black olives, and gouda or cheddar cheese. Grounds is one of the busiest restaurants in Murphys; reservations are recommended.

An eatery with a modern vibe is what you get at **Firewood** (420 Main St., 209/728-3248, www.firewoodeats.com, 11 A.M.–9 P.M. daily, $6–14). Just in case the name doesn't give it away, you're playing with fire at this place; from wood-fired pizzas to the ax handles that grace the front doors, the restaurant (housed inside a former fire station) has a fiery theme. You can't go wrong with the chicken pesto with basil and parmesan pizza, the the gorgonzola burger, or the fish tacos. A children's menu includes chicken strips and sweet potato fries, or the little ones can opt for pizza.

For a fancy steak dinner in Murphys, there's **V Restaurant** (402 V Main St., 209/728-0107, http://vrestaurantandbar-murphys.com, bistro 8 A.M.–10 P.M. daily, dinner 5:30–close Wed.–Sun., $28–42), an elegant dining room that dishes upscale American fare with plates like bacon-wrapped filet mignon and lamb T-bone. Call ahead on busy weekends to nab a table.

If you love veggies, come to █ **Mineral Restaurant** (419 Main St., 209/728-9743, www.mineralrestaurant.com, 5–8:30 P.M. Thurs., noon–8 P.M. Fri.–Sat., 10 A.M.–3 P.M. Sun., $10–16). Meat-eaters might grumble, but chef Steve Rinauros knows how to turn food into art at this mind-blowing restaurant serving vegetarian fare. The constantly changing menu includes dishes made with seasonal ingredients, and while the craft brew list isn't huge, you'll still be amazed at the selection of award-winning beers available.

Restaurant at Murphys Historic Hotel (457 Main St., 209/728-3444, www.murphyshotel.com, 7 A.M.–2:30 P.M. and 5–8 P.M. Mon.–Thurs., 7 A.M.–3 P.M. and 5–9:30 P.M. Fri.–Sun., $15–35) exudes a cool ambience inside this 150-year-old hotel. However, the combination of Italian and American steak house grub seems a little expensive for what you get.

Alchemy Market and Wine Bar (191 Main St., 209/728-0700, http://alchemymarket.com, 11 A.M.–8 P.M. Mon.–Tues. and Thurs.–Fri., 11 A.M.–10:30 P.M. Sat.–Sun., $12–25) is a hip bistro serving local vino, craft beer, and gourmet fusion fare on par with Sacramento's Midtown. Aim for the herb-crusted "scalone" (scallop and abalone medallions) or the cranberry-balsamic grilled salmon.

Information and Services

Murphys doesn't have much in the way of tourist services or a local newspaper; the best place for tourist information is online (www.visitmurphys.com). For financial needs, the **El Dorado Savings** (245 Tom Bell Rd., 209/728-2003, www.eldoradosavingsbank.com) has ATMs and banking services.

There are several gas stations in Murphys along Highway 4, the main thoroughfare in town. For groceries, head to **Sierra Hills Market** (117 E. Hwy. 4, 209/728-3402, 7 A.M.–8:30 P.M. Sun.–Thurs., 7 A.M.– 9 A.M. Fri.–Sat.).

You'll find a **post office** at 140 Big Trees Road (8:30 A.M.–4:30 P.M. Mon.–Fri.).

Locals in Murphys get their news from the *Calaveras Enterprise* (www.calaverasenterprise.com), the county's newspaper of record; editions come out on Tuesday and Friday. For entertainment, news, and events there's also the weekly *Sierra Lodestar* (www.sierralodestar.com).

Getting There and Around

Murphys lies 10 miles northeast of Angels Camp on Highway 4. The town is a far drive from Sacramento, 84 miles away, so it makes sense to combine a trip here with Angels Camp, Arnold, or Columbia (13 miles south).

For public transportation, **Calaveras Transit** (www.calaverastransit.com, $2) runs trips between Murphys and Angels Camp on weekdays.

ARNOLD

This rugged little town calls itself "Gateway to the Big Trees" and with good reason. Many visitors arrive here searching for Calaveras Big Trees State Park. But there's wonderful irony behind that nickname considering the area's first logging mill opened in Arnold (pop. 3,800) during the 1860s. Today trees are preserved here, not chopped down, and the mighty sequoias at the state park are tremendous. There is more to Arnold than giant conifers, though. As a pit stop on the old Ebbetts Pass route through the Sierra Nevada, Arnold built up a tidy hospitality industry centered around a few cozy mountain lodges. And the town claims some of the best outdoor recreation in the Southern Gold Country, where visitors can enjoy boating on nearby mountain lakes, skiing at Bear Valley, or tackling a hike on the Arnold Rim Trail.

◀ Calaveras Big Trees State Park

Quiet as a Gothic cathedral and just as imposing, Calaveras Big Trees State Park (Hwy. 4, three miles east of Arnold, 209/795-2334, www.parks.ca.gov, sunrise–sunset daily, $8) has one of the world's northernmost groves of sequoia redwoods. With shaggy reddish bark and trunks up to 25 feet thick, these conifers are more like beasts than trees. The tallest sequoia here is the Louis Agassiz Tree, towering 250 feet above groves of ponderosa pine,

incense cedar, and white fir. Make sure to walk through the Pioneer Cabin Tree, which has a tunnel carved through its burly trunk. The Calaveras Big Trees forest was first discovered in 1852, and as you stroll through the tranquil woodlands, it's easy to forget that California's first settlers weren't as careful about preserving these sequoias; one of the grove's largest trees died in 1854 after loggers stripped nearly 100 feet of bark from its trunk.

To really enjoy the grove's majestic splendor, hike along the **South Grove Trail** (five miles, easy) past the Agassiz Tree and the Palace Grove Tree, the two largest sequoias in the park. If you have time, the **North Grove Hike** (1.5 miles, easy) winds past other giants such as the Abraham Lincoln Tree, the Father of the Forest, and the Three Graces (named from Greek mythology). Take the **Bradley Grove Hike** (2.5 miles, easy) to check out a nursery of "young" (only 150 years old!) redwoods near a small meadow; the trail also passes a few other towering conifers like the Railroad Tree and the Lone Sequoia.

Sierra Nevada Logging Museum

Learn more about Arnold's logging legacy at the Sierra Nevada Logging Museum (2148 Dunbar Rd., 209/795-6782, http://sierraloggingmuseum.org, noon–4 P.M. Thurs.–Sun. Apr. 1–Dec. 1, free). Logging was actually the region's most successful industry before James W. Marshall discovered gold in 1848. The museum remembers that era with plenty of photos and exhibits, including a 1945 International truck for hauling lumber. Learn about the current economic and technological trends in Gold Country logging, including the environmental impact to the area.

Entertainment and Events

The Nugget Bar (75 Big Trees Rd., 209/728-3661, www.thenuggetbar.com, noon–2 A.M. daily) is Arnold's dive bar of record. Visitors should feel free to crash karaoke nights during the week and mingle with friendly locals, or rack 'em up at the pool tables.

Sports and Recreation

Arnold is perched on the roof of the Gold Country. At 4,000 feet in elevation, the steep mountain ridges and fresh air that comes with the town's remote location will be enchanting to outdoor enthusiasts. There are several alpine lakes where boating and fishing are popular during the summer.

BEAR VALLEY RESORT

Skiing at Bear Valley Resort (2280 Hwy. 207, Bear Valley, 209/753-2301, www.bearvalley. com, 9 A.M.–4 P.M. daily Dec.–Apr., adults $62, youth $49, children $19) is a good change from crowded runs near Lake Tahoe or Donner Summit. The attitude is a little bit more laid-back, even if the prices aren't. You'll find at least 75 runs, nine lifts, and lots of black diamond runs for advanced skiers; try Home Run for a hair-raising ride down the mountain's back side. Bear Valley's powder and deep snowfall (average base is well over 300 inches per year) tempt both beginning snowplowers and seasoned mountain tamers; experienced snowboarders will also love carving the Cub terrain parks.

Summer dries out Bear Valley's trails, leaving dusty hiking paths and single-track for mountain bikers. Some of the public roads are open to ATV use, but keep to the map provided by the resort. For truly hard-core outdoor folk, the Pacific Crest Trail and Tahoe-Yosemite Trail bisect Bear Valley from north to south, and you can amble up these rugged trails for a few miles before trudging back to the resort.

BOATING AND FISHING

The Calaveras high country is literally dripping with lakes. If you miss one, there's usually another just down the road. From Arnold,

visitors can drive about an hour east to reach a cluster of reservoirs and sparkling natural lakes cradled by craggy granite promontories. Many of these places are hard to reach for anyone but seasoned hikers and outdoor buffs, but a few just require sitting in the car for a little while. The largest and most noteworthy lake is **New Spicer Meadow Reservoir** (turnoff 21 miles east of Arnold on Hwy. 4; reservoir is 10 miles in from Hwy. 4). At roughly 6,000 feet, New Spicer Meadow is one of the highest lakes in California. Created by a 265-foot-high dam to provide water for towns in Calaveras County, this huge body of water offers fishing, kayaking, and limited boating along 22 miles of shoreline.

For fishing it doesn't get much better than **Lake Alpine** (Hwy. 4, two miles northeast of Bear Valley Village, www.lakealpine.com, Memorial Day–Labor Day). There's a free boat launch across the water from Lake Alpine Resort, although sometimes it's not advisable by late summer and early fall. Anglers have been known to catch huge trout from the shore, and those using bait have also had pretty good luck here. However, only polar bears would dip in Lake Alpine before mid-August when the water finally warms up. Waterskiing and any kind of speed boating are banned, and all watercraft must stay under 10 mph.

Local anglers also enjoy **White Pines Lake** (off Dunbar Rd., one mile northeast of Arnold). Most visitors pass over White Pines in their hurry to reach Big Trees or Lake Alpine, but this lake is closer and has more of a family atmosphere. There is a community park with picnic tables, barbecue grills, a beach, a playground, and a softball field near the waterfront. Anglers can bring either a fly rod or a bait rig and still catch trout at this lake.

For more information about local fishing reports, check with the good folks at **Ebbetts Pass Sporting Goods** (925 Hwy. 4, Arnold, 209/795-1686, www.ebbettspasssporting-goods.com).

HIKING AND BIKING

Outdoors enthusiasts should look into hiking the **Arnold Rim Trail** (Ebbetts Pass National Scenic Byway, http://arnoldrimtrail.org, 17.5 miles) in the Stanislaus National Forest. This rugged track, known as the ART to locals, is open to nonmotorized use only, which means mountain bikers, horseback riders, and hikers can use the trail. From the summit, the panorama is jaw-dropping with views all the way to Mt. Diablo in the East Bay and Mt. Lyell near Yosemite. Roughly 10 miles of trail are pure single-track that pass ancient strands of cedar, oak, pine and fir trees. Keep an eye open for a few random but glorious sights along the ART, like Indian grinding rocks, a waterfall, and a menagerie of wildlife. The ART runs from White Pines Lake to Sheep Ranch Road near Avery; volunteers hope to one day connect the trail to Calaveras Big Trees State Park.

Accommodations

Arnold has several places where visitors can crash for the night. There are several mountain lodges in town and some campgrounds farther to the east where you can gulp the bracing mountain air and experience a truly starry night far from the city.

Bring your tent to **Calaveras Big Trees State Park** (Hwy. 4, three miles east of Arnold, 209/795-2334, www.parks.ca.gov, $20–35) and sleep near some of the oldest redwoods in California. From here you can wander down the South Grove Trail or take a chilly dip in Beaver Creek, which winds beneath the towering conifers. Amenities are decent, with showers, bathrooms, picnic tables, and an amphitheater along with 129 campsites.

For a true mountain lodge experience there's **Black Bear Inn** (1343 Oak Circle, 209/795-8999, http://arnoldblackbearinn.com, $225–275). The five rooms have a contemporary theme that blends nicely with the rugged cabin environment. Amenities include private baths

with spas, complimentary bathrobes, free wireless Internet, flat-screen TVs, and pillow-top king beds. Make sure to relax with a book outside on the neatly trimmed lawns, or lie back in a hammock and enjoy a glass of Calaveras wine. In the morning, enjoy a gourmet breakfast whipped up by the innkeeper, who's also a trained chef.

Meadowmont Lodge (2011 Hwy. 4, 888/538-1222, http://arnoldlodgeca.com, $80–150) is a step up from other motor court motels. This log cabin–style lodge has 19 clean, basic rooms with just an extra touch of homespun comfort. Amenities include satellite TV, coffeemaker, microwave, refrigerator, and wireless Internet.

Food

Arnold is a long way from progressive eateries pushing the farm-to-table movement. The dining scene is made up of several mom-and-pop restaurants that make hearty, if somewhat predictable fare.

Snowshoe Brewing Company (2050 Hwy. 4, 209/795-2272, www.snowshoebrewing. com, 4–8:30 P.M. Mon., 11:30 A.M.–8:30 P.M. Tues.–Thurs., 11:30 A.M.–9 P.M. Fri.–Sat., 11:30 A.M.–8 P.M. Sun., $10) is a typical American sports pub with a family atmosphere. Snowshoe pours five of their own brews plus a few seasonal beers like Pumpkin Patch Ale, Pitch Black Porter, and Westridge Winter Ale. Order a pint to wash down a sandwich or juicy burger.

Serafina's Italian Kitchen (794 Hwy. 4, 209/795-9858, 5–9 P.M. Wed.–Sun. $10–25) is the most popular restaurant in town. The vibe mixes a rustic log cabin with a chic bistro theme. Expect traditional Italian pasta, such as calamari risotto, spaghetti with prawns, and veal scaloppine.

Looking for Chinese food high up in the Southern Gold Country? With **Arnold Chinese Restaurant** (2182 Hwy. 4, 209/795-6368,

11 A.M.–8:30 P.M. Mon.–Thurs., 11 A.M.–9 P.M. Fri.–Sat., 11 A.M.–8 P.M. Sun., $7–13), consider that mission accomplished. Arnold's serves traditional Chinese favorites such as chow mein, won ton soup, broccoli beef, and sesame chicken. Hard-boiled foodies might scoff, but this place could legitimately compete with any Bay Area eatery.

El Vaquero Mexican Restaurant (925 Hwy. 4, 209/795-3303, 11 A.M.–9 P.M. daily, $8–12) serves traditional and Cali-Mex cuisine. An evening here will satisfy cravings for chicken enchiladas and carne asada burritos, although the service could use a shot in the arm.

Information and Services

Arnold doesn't have the conveniences of a larger city, but visitors can still find banks, supermarkets, and gas stations in town. Fill up the car at **Arnold Chevron and Deli** (960 Hwy. 4, 209/795-1301) on the main highway. There's also a 24-hour ATM at **Bank of America** (1082 Hwy. 4, 209/795-1322). Visitors will find a **post office** at 997 Blagen Road (8 A.M.–4:30 P.M. Mon.–Fri.).

The **Greater Arnold Business Association** (209/795-4222, http://cometoarnold.com) doesn't have a brick-and-mortar location, but the website provides helpful travel tips and updated news about the region.

The *Calaveras Enterprise* (www.calaverasenterprise.com) is the county's newspaper of record and comes out on Tuesday and Friday. For breaking news, check the *The Pine Tree* website (http://thepinetree.net), which relies on community members to report headlines around Calaveras County.

Getting There and Around

From Murphys, it takes 20 minutes to drive northeast on Highway 4 to Arnold. There's very little public transportation in these parts, but **Calaveras Transit** (www.calaverastransit.com, $2) runs bus trips between Angels Camp and Arnold on weekdays.

Arnold sits at a 4,000-foot elevation and gets about 10 inches of snow every year. Every vehicle without exception needs chains during winter. Caltrans has a website (www.dot.ca.gov) for updated traffic info.

Tuolumne County

As you approach Sonora, the terrain becomes mountainous with fewer oaks and more ponderosas. One thing that stays constant is the amount of Gold Rush history in Tuolumne County hamlets and small towns, like the outdoor museum at Columbia. The opportunities for wine-tasting are fewer at this end of the Southern Gold Country, replaced by more chances for outdoor recreation. Expect Tuolumne towns to be a little scruffier and less touristy.

SONORA AND COLUMBIA

Luckily for Sonora (pop. 4,600), this town escaped the fate of nearby Columbia after

surviving a gut-wrenching cycle of booms and busts. After the roaring 1850s, depression hit Sonora fairly hard until a second gold discovery touched off another rush to Tuolumne County in the 1870s. But Sonora didn't experience true economic stability until 1925, when the U.S. Army Corps of Engineers built New Melones Dam and provided the town with a source of cheap hydroelectricity. As a result, timber and farming industries developed rapidly, and Sonora became one of the most prosperous towns in the Southern Gold Country.

Sonora and Columbia are just a couple of miles apart and seemingly blend into each other. There's a busy downtown district with

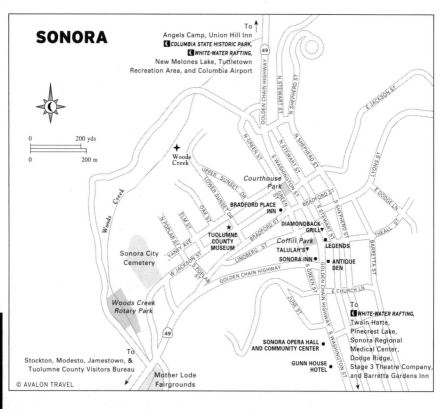

some cool shops in Sonora, although you might dislike the steady stream of cars from Highway 49, which runs right through town and creates traffic jams on the weekend. It's better to use Sonora as a base for day trips to Columbia State Historic Park, Railtown 1897, or New Melones Lake. When you come back at night to your (no doubt) luxurious inn, Sonora has usually calmed down, and you can enjoy a show at either of the town's two theater companies after feasting at a cosmopolitan eatery. For a more authentic Gold Rush experience, consider a stay at one of old Columbia's stately hotels just a few miles north.

C Columbia State Historic Park

If you could only visit one attraction in the Southern Gold Country, make it Columbia State Historic Park (11255 Jackson St., Columbia, 209/588-9128, www.parks. ca.gov, free). Hard-boiled travelers might scoff at Columbia as a tourist trap, but it's so much more than that. Many school kids fondly remember their first field trip to this old boomtown as a day filled with gold panning, candle-dipping, and stagecoach riding. Visitors will discover an outdoor museum and re-created mining town from the 1850s complete with costumed store clerks and docents. Nearly $150 million in Placer nuggets were pried from the town's "dry diggings" deposits between 1850 and 1900, which helped fund the Union Army during the Civil War. By the 20th century, gold mining had declined, and

the main street at Columbia State Historic Park

Columbia was falling apart when state park officials began renovating during the 1940s. Today, the park boasts the largest collection of Gold Rush–era buildings in California. Check out the contents of the Livery Stable, watch a blacksmith pound iron at the Parrott's Blacksmith Shop, or guzzle some sarsaparilla at the Jack Douglass Saloon.

Most of the action lies along Columbia's main street, which is flat and easily accessible for disabled visitors or parents pushing strollers. The town lies at a higher altitude and temperatures can vary greatly; dress accordingly and wear good walking shoes.

Tuolumne County Museum

Tuolumne County Museum (158 W. Bradford St., Sonora, 209/532-1317, www. tchistory.org, 10 A.M.–4 P.M. Sun.–Fri., 10 A.M.–3:30 P.M. Sat., free) is built in Sonora's old jailhouse, so you'll find plenty of historical background on what happened to Gold Rush miners who fell afoul of the law. And what better exhibit for a former jail than a display of Wild West firearms? Other exhibits include a description of the region's 19th-century wagon trails and a treasure trove of mining artifacts. This thoughtful little museum is still meaningful even if you've already checked out other Gold Country historical places; amateur historians and researchers will find plenty of material in the museum's archives, which are managed by the Tuolumne Historical Society.

Entertainment and Events

Gold Rush prospectors didn't spend all their time seeking fortunes in treacherous gold mines; after work, they spent hours playing card games in scruffy mining camps. While neither scruffy nor a mining camp, **Black Oak Casino** (19400 Tuolumne Rd. N., Tuolumne, 877/747-8777, www.blackoakcasino.com) is a fitting place to either find or lose a fortune.

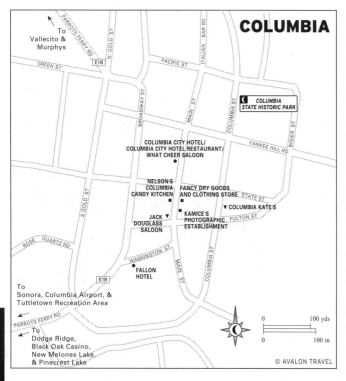

in 1857. If you need a drink, ask for a "Columbia Gold," the bar's most popular libation (but don't bother asking the bartender for the recipe; the ingredients are top secret). The saloon serves hard liquor (an eye-popping selection of cognacs and single-malt Scotch), along with beer and wine, so it's not really a family joint—the fun is mostly for adults.

In Sonora, you'll find a vibrant theater community producing some of the best entertainment in the foothills. At the **Stage 3 Theatre** (208 S. Green St., Sonora, 209/536-1778, www.stage3.org, 2 P.M. Thurs.–Sat., 7 P.M. Sun., $12–20), the regular season might include plays by Broadway heavyweights like Arthur Miller, David Mamet, and Neil Simon. Theater fans will love the surprisingly professional company, as well as folk and classical music performances featuring some of the top bands from the Southern Gold Country. Stage 3 is a small venue, which means you'll probably enjoy the intimate atmosphere; at the same time, note that tickets may sell out quickly for more popular plays.

Broadway might be miles away, but the nonprofit **Sierra Repertory Theatre** (13891 Mono Way, East Sonora, 209/532-3120, www.sierrarep.org, 2 P.M. Wed. and Sun., 7 P.M. Thurs.–Fri., 2 P.M. and 8 P.M. Sat., $20–32) stages

Owned by the Tuolumne Band of Me-wuk Indians, the casino boasts poker tables, 24 table games, and more than 1,200 slot machines. Don't want to gamble? Head to the 24-lane bowling alley or the arcade. If you're planning to go all night, grab a cup of joe at the smoke-free Jumping Coyote Espresso bar. When you're hungry, pop in to one of Black Oak's eight bars and restaurants for a bite to eat.

What's more fitting than finding a fortune? For a miner during the Gold Rush, it would be unwinding at the local saloon. You can follow in their footsteps at **What Cheer Saloon** (22768 Main St., Columbia, 209/532-1479, www.briggshospitalityllc.com, 3–9 P.M. Mon.–Fri., noon–10 P.M. Sat.–Sun.), the only full-service watering hole in town. The place still has the original cherrywood bar shipped from Boston

the Tuolumne County Museum in downtown Sonora

big-name hits in town. The performances by this small company are immensely enjoyable; it's worth traveling from the Bay Area to catch a show. Plays are performed at two different venues—-the East Sonora Theatre, a converted tin warehouse, and the Historic Fallon House up the road in Columbia. Seasonal shows have included *Oklahoma!, Hairspray,* and *Fiddler on the Roof.* If you like new twists on classic plays, the company has been known to get creative; they once staged *Romeo and Juliet* with a New Orleans theme.

Shopping

Looking for some Wild West mementos straight from the Gold Country? Columbia's old buildings are bristling with old-timey shops staffed by their costumed clerks. If Columbia feels too kitschy, head for Sonora's more refined downtown to browse the abundant boutiques and antiques shops along Highway 49. Exercise caution while driving through the city's narrow streets or searching for parking downtown; on crowded weekends, the two-lane main drag often feels like all of California is visiting.

For some fixings for the homestead, try the **Fancy Dry Goods and Clothing Store** (22733 Main St., Columbia, 209/532-1066, www.columbiacalifornia.com/fancy.html, 10 A.M.–5 P.M. Wed.–Sun. in winter or Wed.–Mon. in summer), where you can browse the "supplies" on hand like a true forty-niner. Everything in the store would have been in style 150 years ago, like the bonnets, calico dresses, and men's hats; you can also check out mock weapons and mining tools. Though it might feel like a museum, you can buy gifts for men, women, and kids, including sewing kits for quilting or knitting your very own Wild West wardrobe.

The next best thing to stepping back in time is visiting **Kamice's Photographic Establishment** (22729 Main St., Columbia, 209/532-4861, www.photosincolumbia.com,

MOANING CAVERN MOANS AGAIN

Contrary to some reports, the haunting sounds of **Moaning Cavern** (5350 Moaning Cave Rd., 209/736-2708, www.caverntours.com, 9 A.M.–6 P.M. daily in summer; 10 A.M.–4 P.M. Mon.–Fri., 9 A.M.–5 P.M. Sat.–Sun. in winter, adults $14.95, youth $7.95) can still be heard in this cave, the largest public chamber in California. More of a deep resonant thump than a moan, the noise is made by water dripping off stalactites into shallow puddles. When the drops strike the exact center of the puddle, it creates sound waves that make the stalagmites vibrate, turning the cavern into a subterranean tuning fork.

The sound disappeared after workers built a 235-step spiral staircase in the main chamber, and most people thought Moaning Cavern had gone silent. Turns out, construction on the staircase had accidently plugged the natural holes needed to catch water dripping from the stalactites. Once the holes were scooped out and water began pooling into puddles again, the cavern's deep bass booming noise returned.

Spring is the best time to hear Moaning Cav-

ern's "chamber" orchestra, when rainy weather guarantees plenty of underground dripping. Make sure to arrive early in the morning when the cave is still cool; body heat affects how the drips hit the puddles and you won't get Moaning Cavern's full effect. To hear the cavern's musical booms and thumps more clearly, stand at the top of the 100-foot-high spiral staircase and wait for the show to begin.

Of course, the cavern has other attractions besides the "moaning." Visitors can rappel 165 feet into the main chamber's yawning expanse, a trip that takes 45 minutes ($65). If you're really daring, sign up for the three-hour Adventure tour ($130 with rappel, $76 without rappel), a true spelunking odyssey involving muddy climbs and crawls through undeveloped tunnels hundreds of feet below the surface. Or try the 1,500-foot-long zip line ($39) along the ridge by the cave's visitor center. At speeds of 40 mph, the zip line is known to create its own moaning sounds—although it's probably just exhilarated visitors screaming in delight.

The cave still moans at Moaning Cavern.

10 A.M.–5 P.M. Thurs.–Tues., Wed. by appointment). Bring the family and snap a sepia-toned portrait while dressed like true pioneers. Kids will love putting on fake miner's outfits or posing with a six-shooter; you can even bring the family dog. Snapping an old-time photo at Kamice's is an especially great idea for couples, and there's a whole wagonload of suits and dresses to try on.

Don't leave town without visiting **Nelson's Columbia Candy Kitchen** (22726 Main St., Columbia, 209/532-7886, www.columbiacandykitchen.com, 9 A.M.–5 P.M. Mon.–Fri., 9 A.M.–6 P.M. Sat.–Sun.). Nelson's has been serving candy for more than 100 years, and they've just about perfected the recipes. Everything here is diet-busting, finger-licking good; try the homemade marshmallow bars or a piece of whipping cream fudge. Luckily, Nelson's also has a few sugar-free candies if you can't indulge your sweet tooth.

You'll quickly find that **Legends** (131 S. Washington St., Sonora, 209/532-8120, 11 A.M.–5 P.M. Wed.–Mon.) is a different kind of bookstore. Instead of the usual coffee bar, this fun little shop has an old-fashioned soda fountain. Grab some ice cream or a hot dog while browsing the rare books and antiques, or settle into the comfy bar stools for a sandwich. If you're lucky, someone might be banging out some tunes on the store's old piano.

If you've toured the Gold Country from top to bottom, you've probably breezed through quite a few antiques stores, but **Antique Den** (163 S. Washington St., Sonora, 209/533-1012, 10 A.M.–5 P.M. Mon.–Thurs., 10 A.M.–6 P.M. Fri.–Sat., 11 A.M.–4 P.M. Sun.) is one of the best. Antique Den is actually a collective of several antiques dealers, many specializing in vintage American and European furniture. For collectors, this place will yield all sorts of finds, like a German gun cabinet or a Victorian kerosene chandelier. Besides furniture, the collective has the standard lineup of antique glassware, porcelain, jewelry, and clocks.

Sports and Recreation

Anglers should cast their line at **New Melones Lake** (6850 Studhorse Flat Rd., Sonora, 209/536-9094, www.usbr.gov). It's kind of the go-to recreational spot for the area, and you can camp, fish, swim, or just lounge by the water. More adventurous lake visitors will find hiking and biking trails along the lake.

Another great spot for anglers is **Pinecrest Lake Recreation Area** (18 Pinecrest Lake Rd., Pinecrest, 209/965-3434, www.recreation.gov, 8 A.M.–8 P.M. daily), a tranquil mountain lake 30 miles east of Sonora that is stocked with rainbow trout. Boating is allowed, and the Pinecrest marina offers outboard craft for half- or full-day rentals. Travelers with polar bear blood can try taking a dip in the icy lake water, but you'll be one brave soul for doing so. Camping is also available; check with the U.S. Forest Service for reservations.

Just a few miles from Sonora, **Dodge Ridge** (1 Dodge Ridge Rd., Pinecrest, 209/965-3474, www.dodgeridge.com, 9 A.M.–4 P.M. daily Dec.–Apr., adults $64, youth $52, children $20) is an excellent alternative if you're trying to avoid Lake Tahoe's crowded slopes. There's just one mountain, but 12 lifts and 3 terrain parks usually satisfy most hard-core skiers and snowboarders, especially if you take Stagecoach for two rollicking miles through blue and black diamond runs. If you're into Nordic skiing, glide over to **Gooseberry** for some cross-country skiing, although beginners will find these trails rather difficult; there's also parking for about half a dozen cars, so arrive early.

◀ WHITE-WATER RAFTING

The Tuolumne River is a rushing, roiling torrent of white water that stays fairly unknown to rafters, which is strange considering these waters rise in Yosemite National Park. Ansel

Adams once aimed his lens at the river during his copious treks through the rugged backcountry. Most visitors probably pass over the Tuolumne's challenging stretch of rapids because other Gold Country waterways get more attention. But don't make that mistake. Few other American rivers pass through such deeply moving scenery. The Tuolumne even has its own Grand Canyon that begins below Tuolumne Meadows and drops through sheer granite cliffs dusted with chaparral, manzanita, conifers, and oaks that cling to the rock like howler monkeys. The river cascades through a series of Class III–IV white water, so even beginners can brave this nationally designated Wild and Scenic Waterway.

Outfitters usually take rafters on an 18-mile stretch of river from Meral's Pool to Ward's Ferry Bridge. Tuolumne trips usually take place on certain days of the week; check online for exact schedules. Some companies extend their season to run between March and October, which means tougher rapids in spring but more chilled-out excursions in fall.

Whitewater Voyages (800/400-7238, www. whitewatervoyages.com, May–Sept., $225–575) offers friendly, experienced guides and packed lunches on day trips; overnight trips include breakfast and evening barbecues.

Zephyr Rafting (22517 Parrotts Ferry Rd., Columbia, 209/532-6249, www.zrafting.com, Apr.–Sept., $215–555) also offers multiday trips with extra time allotted for hiking and swimming in natural whirlpools. All meals are provided on two- and three-day excursions.

Sierra Mac River Trips (Groveland, 800/457-2580, www.sierramac.com, Mar.–Oct., $235–585) has been charging through notorious rapids like Clavey Falls and Hells Kitchen for more than 40 years. Ambitious and experienced rafters can tack on nine extra miles to their expedition and brave Class V rapids through Cherry Creek and the Upper Tuolumne.

ARTA River Trips (24000 Casa Loma Rd., Groveland, 209/962-7873, www.arta.org, Apr.–Sept., $207–569) plunges through all 20 Class IV rapids and includes full- and multiday options. Ask about their "farm to river" excursion that includes food from local farmers on a three-day trip.

All-Outdoors Whitewater Rafting (925/932-8993, www.aorafting.com, Apr.–early Sept., $224–$579) also offers Class V adventures on the North Tuolumne and Cherry Creek, considered one of the most advanced commercially rafted rivers in the country.

O.A.R.S. (800/346-6277, www.oars.com, Mar.–Aug., $110–360) offers many of the same adventures as other outfitters. They take rafters out for full-day and multiday excursions.

Accommodations

Sonora offers a range of accommodations, most of which are renovated farmhouses or rambling town houses. If you're more into capturing the essence of what 19th-century boardinghouses were like, you can also find those accommodations in either Sonora or Columbia.

SONORA

Hole up like a desperado at the **Gunn House Hotel** (286 S. Washington St., 209/532-3421, http://gunnhousehotel.com, $80–115), where the area's first newspaper editor lived before angry mobs burned his printing press. That kind of history oozes from the walls at Gunn House, built in the 1850s as the area's first two-story adobe structure. It's been a getaway for miners, gunslingers, and Hollywood TV crews filming shows in the nearby hills. The rooms have a homey vibe and retain Victorian elegance without feeling stuffy; maybe it's the teddy bear slumbering on each bed. Amenities include private baths, air-conditioning, and comfortable king or queen beds. In the morning, enjoy a delicious full breakfast with quiche, fresh bread, and mouthwatering waffles before walking it off with a quick trip through nearby downtown Sonora.

◖ Barretta Gardens Inn (700 S. Barretta St., 209/532-6039, www.barrettagardens.com, $110–390) is a restored farmhouse with some of the most lavish digs in the Gold Country. Understated and elegant from the outside, inside the eight rooms you'll find serious luxury: Persian carpets, mahogany bed frames, polished antique furniture, and towering armoires. Mingle with other guests by walking into the downstairs living room and collapsing into one of the plush sofas. Take a glass of wine outside into the sprawling garden area that covers one full acre. Play croquet on the lawns or lounge in the comfortable lawn swing. Ecoconscious travelers will especially appreciate the inn's efforts to serve sustainable meals; most of the food comes straight from the garden and everything is composted.

Swanky enough to pamper, the **◖ Bradford Place Inn** (56 W. Bradford St., 800/209-2315, www.bradfordplaceinn.com, $140–265) still feels like an authentic Gold Rush home. First built in 1889 for a Wells Fargo agent, the house has been a bed-and-breakfast since the 1980s. The four rooms are decorated with Victorian-style floral wallpaper, plush furniture, and vintage wooden headboards—unless you're staying in the Bradford Room, which is graced by a French Empire four-poster bed. Worried about visiting during the hot foothill summer? Each room has private heating and air-conditioning. There's also a flat-screen TV, wireless Internet, and a phone (with digital answering machine!) in all four suites. Breakfast is arranged the night before; choose from the menu and have your entrée ready in the morning. Since there are only four rooms, call far in advance to book your stay.

Union Hill Inn (21645 Parrotts Ferry Rd., 209/533-1494, www.unionhillinn.com, $150–195) has four lovely guest rooms with custom linens, handmade beds, vaulted ceilings, spa tubs, and antique furniture; they also have three cabins set apart from the main hotel. This might be the only Gold Country lodging with its own chapel, which means Union Hill is often booked by wedding parties. You'll also find a beautiful yard ringed by lavender bushes, willow trees, and a pool.

Sonora Inn (160 S. Washington St., 209/532-2400, www.thesonorainn.com, $80–100) has basic rooms without much fluff. For a place built in 1896, guests might expect a little more old-school character, but the rooms bear a corporate chain vibe left over from when it was the Days Inn Sonora. Amenities include air-conditioning, fitness center, outdoor pool, and an elevator, with microwaves, refrigerators, and TVs in the rooms.

Just outside of town you'll find **Tuttletown Recreation Area** (Reynolds Ferry Rd., 9.5 miles from Sonora, 209/536-9094 or 209/536-9543, www.recreation.gov, standard sites $22, walk-in $18). The recreation area has 164 sites with showers, campfire rings, picnic tables, and toilets.

COLUMBIA

If you loved Columbia's state park and just can't leave, why not stay the night? There are two authentic Wild West hotels in town, and they've been restored in similar fashion. The **Columbia City Hotel** (22768 Main St., 209/532-1479, www.briggshospitalityllc.com, $120–150) is located near the north end of the park, just beyond the pedestrian zone. The **Fallon Hotel** (11175 Washington St., 209/532-1470, www.briggshospitalityllc.com, $80–150) is set near the park's southern boundary on the county road. The rooms in each hotel have been faithfully restored with Victorian-style wallpaper, handmade furniture, and vintage photographs from the Gold Rush. A night at the City or the Fallon guarantees visitors a true Old West experience, right down to the double beds and cozy quarters; if you need more space to stretch out, ask for one of the hall rooms with a queen bed. In the morning, walk down to the hotel parlor for a continental breakfast (included in the rate). Rumors abound that the City is haunted; if you want a spooky stay, come in winter when the hotel is almost empty. There's a strict pet policy at both hotels, so you'll have to leave the furry friends at home.

Food

Like the deep selection of plush accommodations in Sonora and Columbia, these two towns serve a gamut of different cuisines and tastes, and most visitors will find something to like.

SONORA

Start at the **○ Diamondback Grill** (93 S. Washington St., 209/532-6661, www.thediamondbackgrill.com, 11 A.M.–9 P.M. Mon.–Thurs., 11 A.M.–9:30 P.M. Fri.–Sat., 11 A.M.–8 P.M. Sun., $10), an upscale diner with food so good it will make your eyes roll back. The cuisine is made from scratch; meat and fish are smoked in-house by restaurant staff, all sauces and dressings are prepared on-site, and most menu items use farmstead products from ranches in Stockton and Modesto. Locals and tourists alike line up for hours to order Diamondback's famous burgers with sides like garlic or sweet potato fries. The long and narrow interior resembles a Manhattan bistro, but with unfinished shale rock walls, you'll never forget this family-owned eatery is all Gold Country.

Talulah's (13 S. Washington St., 209/532-7278, www.talulahs.com, 11:30 A.M.–2:30 P.M. and 5–8 P.M. Tues.–Thurs., 11:30 A.M.–2:30 P.M. and 5–8:30 P.M. Fri., noon–2:30 P.M. and 5–8:30 P.M. Sat., $14–20) serves piping-hot pasta like the ravioli sampler and homemade veggie lasagna stuffed with portobello mushrooms and eggplant; other entrées include gorgonzola chicken breast and meatloaf. Most ingredients are local and organic, and the

kitchen tries to serve seasonal dishes; gluten-free diners can substitute rice pasta for most items on the menu.

COLUMBIA

The **Columbia City Hotel Restaurant** (22768 Main St., 209/532-1479, 5–8 P.M. Fri.–Sun. in winter; 10 A.M.–2 P.M. and 5–9 P.M. Tues.–Sun. in summer, $20–36) is the place for gourmet meals in Columbia's historic district. During the Gold Rush, Columbia was the second largest city in California, and the City Hotel's elegant dining room befits a former boomtown. No baked beans and trail chow here—you'll find dishes like lobster whiskey in bourbon sauce and pan-roasted duck sautéed in a delicious red-wine sauce. If you're staying in the hotel, don't miss dinner or brunch in the elegantly decorated dining room. Even if you're just passing through Columbia, an evening at the City's restaurant shouldn't be missed.

With costumed bartenders, old-timey piano music, and a fully restored bar from the 1800s, the **Jack Douglass Saloon** (22718 Main St., 209/533-4176, 10 A.M.–6 P.M. daily, $5–10) feels like a place where duels might erupt. These days, the only conflict at the "JD" comes from deciding which homemade drink you'll have—either the sarsaparilla or the wild-cherry soda, both whipped up locally in Columbia. For lunch, order sandwiches, hot dogs, salads, or the gigantic nachos, a saloon specialty. If the sodas aren't your thing, ask for a glass of local wine or a cold beer.

Need some tea to whet your whistle? **Columbia Kate's** (22727 Columbia St., 209/532-1885, www.columbiakates.com, 11 A.M.–4 P.M. daily, $5–30) is a cozy English-style establishment with plenty of country hospitality. Stop for lunch or enjoy a full afternoon tea; make sure to order the thirst-quenching lavender lemonade along with your meal. I'd also recommend the chicken

© CHRISTOPHER ARNS

Grab a sarsaparilla at the Jack Douglass Saloon in Columbia State Historic Park.

potpie with a raspberry green salad if you're really hungry.

Information and Services

Sonora is one of the largest towns in the Southern Gold Country and has plenty of services, banks, and gas stations. For the central municipal visitors center, head for the **Tuolumne County Visitors Bureau** (542 W. Stockton St., Sonora, 209/533-4420, www.tcvb.com, 10 A.M.–5 P.M. Mon.–Sat., 10 A.M.–4 P.M. Sun.).

For local news during the week, the *Union Democrat* (www.uniondemocrat.com) publishes headlines Monday through Friday about Tuolumne County. There's also a local website (http://tuolumne.virtualsierra.com) that's jam-packed with plenty of recreation and travel advice about Sonora and surrounding towns.

In Sonora, the main **post office** sits at 781

North Washington Street (800/275-8777, 8:30 A.M.–5 P.M. Mon.–Fri., 10 A.M.–2 P.M. Sat.). In Columbia, the **post office** is at 22628 Parrotts Ferry Road (8 A.M.–4 P.M. Mon.–Fri.).

One of the few major hospitals in the area is **Sonora Regional Medical Center** (1000 Greenley Rd., Sonora, 209/532-5000, www.sonorahospital.org), which has an emergency room with a helipad for emergency access.

Getting There and Around

Sonora is at the tip of the Southern Gold Country, nestled among tall pine trees and rugged foothills. By car, it's about 15 miles south of Angels Camp on Highway 49. From Sacramento, take U.S. 50 east to Highway 16. Follow Highway 16 east 30 miles to the junction with Highway 49 and continue south on Highway 49 for 29 miles to Sonora.

There are several public transit options in Sonora. Don't miss a ride on the **Historic 49 Trolley** (www.tuolumnecountytransit.com/HistoricTrolley.html, adults $1.50, day pass $4, children under 13 free), an old-fashioned (but air-conditioned!) way to see local sights in Sonora, Columbia, and Jamestown. The trolley runs daily in summer and weekends only in winter. For bus rides during the week, **Tuolumne County Transit** (www.tuolumnecountytransit.com, adults $1.50, day pass $4) runs four bus routes from Sonora and the immediate vicinity.

Have your own plane? You can land at **Columbia Airport** (10723 Airport Rd., Columbia, 209/533-5685), about four miles north of Sonora. To rent a car, **Enterprise** (209/533-0500, www.enterprise.com) or **Hertz** (209/588-1575, www.hertz.com) can help you out.

JAMESTOWN

Probably best known for Railtown 1897 State Historic Park, Jamestown (pop. 3,400) has a funky backwoods vibe—it's like Country Bear

© CHRISTOPHER ARNS

the Rogers No. 3 locomotive at Railtown 1897 State Historic Park

Jamboree meets Gold Country. Walking past Main Street's rustic buildings adorned with wooden facades and block lettering, like the boxy-framed National Hotel, you really get the sense of an old mining camp. The railroad played an indispensible part in Jamestown's history; as gold miners dug deeper to find elusive quartz deposits, their operations required heavier equipment. Industrial tycoons choose Jamestown for an important steam engine depot that shipped quartz ore to the Central Valley for processing. Eventually the railroad was linked to other Gold Country towns, insuring Jamestown's prosperity with an economic lifeline that eventually reached to the rest of California.

Jamestown is rough around the edges compared to other Gold Country towns. You won't find the bevy of wine-tasting options common in other foothill hot spots, and it's not necessarily a fantastic shopping destination. History is the attraction here, and by visiting, you gain

the opportunity to experience Jamestown's delightful Gold Rush character.

◖ Railtown 1897 State Historic Park

Railtown 1897 State Historic Park (Hwy. 108, 209/984-3953, www.railtown1897.org, 9:30 A.M.–4:30 P.M. Thurs.–Mon. Apr.–Oct.; 10 A.M.–3 P.M. Thurs.–Mon. Nov.–Mar., $5) is a bona fide movie star: The park and its steam engines have appeared in numerous Western flicks, including *High Noon, Unforgiven,* and *Back to the Future: Part III.* You can still see leftover Hollywood props from the movies and TV shows produced here, but the biggest, most thrilling prop of all is the working steam train offering rides to visitors during warmer months. From April to October (11 A.M.–3 P.M. Sat.–Sun., adults $13, youth $6), steam out through oak trees and craggy foothills for a six-mile adventure aboard a real steam train. This ride is especially beautiful

the National Hotel in Jamestown

during spring wildflower blooms, when the hillsides are carpeted in California poppy and yellow mustard seed.

If you have kids who live and breathe *Thomas the Tank Engine,* they'll love watching the roundhouse spit out real-life locomotives; even hard-boiled adults will feel a surge of joy when they hear steam whistles start blasting. The park is sort of a work in progress with many trains undergoing renovation and maintenance, but seeing dissembled steel pistons, valves, scattered steam pipes, and fireboxes is also part of Railtown's attraction. Think of this park as the workshop for Sacramento's more polished California State Railroad Museum.

Sports and Recreation

A great place for boating, camping, and swimming is **Lake Tulloch** (14448 Tulloch Rd., 209/881-0107, www.laketullochcampground. com), southwest of Jamestown. On a map, this narrow reservoir resembles a squished spider, but from ground level visitors will find a marina, swimming holes, and decent beaches.

Accommodations

Many historic Gold Country inns claim to be haunted. At the **◖ National Hotel** (18183 Main St., 800/894-3446, www.national-hotel. com, $140), you can document your encounters with Flo, the hotel's mysterious ghost; each room has a notebook for visitors to record their paranormal experiences. Ask for an upstairs room and listen for slamming doors, sobbing, flickering lights, and thumping noises that sound like clothes being dumped on the floor. It may seem like a hassle, but fans of *Ghost Adventures* will be enthralled. Whether seeking the supernatural or not, guests stay in the hotel's elegant Victorian-style rooms outfitted with wrought-iron bed frames, plush linens, and private baths with tile showers and chain toilets. In the morning, fill your plate with piping-hot quiche, scones, and fresh oatmeal before heading upstairs to dine on the patio overlooking Main Street.

The **Victorian Gold B&B** (10382 Willow St., 888/551-1851, www.victoriangoldbb.com, $110–185) is a stunningly renovated Gilded Age mansion just off a quiet street in Jamestown. Built in the 1890s, the eight rooms have been charmingly decorated with modern amenities without losing their Victorian character. Each room has a private bath with either a shower or claw-foot tub; some rooms even have both. If you stay during the steamy summer months, no need to fret—the inn is fully air-conditioned to keep you cool. There's also free wireless Internet in every room. In the morning, don't miss the two-course homemade breakfast with fresh fruit and made-to-order omelettes. If you're traveling with family, the Victorian Gold has no qualms about children and will work to customize your room arrangements.

Royal Carriage Inn (18239 Main St., 209/984-5271, www.abvijamestown.com, $60–300) is a classic Victorian-style hotel with a charming lobby adorned by period furniture. The common areas share this homey vibe, but the somewhat smaller rooms may disappoint; make sure to stay in the hotel's main building. The staff is friendly and usually does everything possible to help guests enjoy a pleasant visit.

For camping near Jamestown, check out **Lake Tulloch** (14448 Tulloch Rd., 209/881-0107, www.laketullochcampground.com, campsites $23–35, cabins $100–150 in summer; campsites $20–30, cabins $50–75 in winter). Campsites include access to hot showers, flush toilets, and a clubhouse, although the amenities are a bit shabby.

Food

Know in advance that Jamestown is no culinary utopia. You won't be spoiled with seasonal farmstead ingredients, and vegetarians will be disappointed by the lack of choices. Instead, count on steaks, burritos, or standard diner fare while in town, but if you don't mind cowboy food, tuck in and enjoy.

At ◖ **Willow Steakhouse and Saloon** (Willow and Main Sts., 209/984-3998, 11 A.M.–9 P.M. Mon.–Fri., $20–35), you'll hear the ambience in every creak of the wooden plank floor. Some say the place is haunted; it was supposedly built over a collapsed mine shaft where numerous people died, and the restaurant has quite a reputation for spooky events. Of course, who wants to hear ghost stories on an empty stomach? The fine cuisine at Willow Steakhouse deserves most of the attention here, especially dishes like chicken cordon bleu and pepper steak; the cheese fondue is legendary and shouldn't be missed. After dinner, wander into the adjoining saloon and toss back a cocktail with genuine Jamestown locals. If the bar is full, read about the resident ghosts while you wait for a table—the restaurant displays several wall plaques detailing Willow's rumored supernatural residents.

Mother Lode Coffee Shop (18169 Main St., 209/984-3386, 7 A.M.–2:15 P.M. Mon.–Sat., 8 A.M.–2:15 P.M. Sun., $8) serves no-frills American cuisine and a hearty breakfast. At lunch, order sandwiches and burgers, but don't expect the food to arrive on silver platters—and don't be surprised if it comes with a little attitude. Just think of Mother Lode as your carb-fueling station before a full day of sightseeing, and your expectations will be properly set.

If you're in the mood for Mexican, **Morelia** (18148 Main St., 209/984-1432, 11 A.M.–9 P.M. daily, $12) won't disappoint. This is the best place in town for authentic burritos, enchiladas, Mexican hot wings with homemade habañero sauce, and fresh chips and salsa. The food usually arrives fairly quickly and comes with friendly service.

Information and Services

Jamestown doesn't have a visitor center, but you can find plenty of information online (www.jamestown-ca.com) with loads of travel advice and maps of the town.

Jamestown doesn't have many services, but you can still get gas and quick cash in town. To fill up your car, stop by **Chip's Chevron Mini Mart and Car Wash** (18151 Hwy. 108, 209/984-5245) on the main drag through town. There's also a 24-hour ATM at **Umqua Bank** (18281 Main St., 209/984-3971). If you need to mail something, there's a **post office** at 18303 Main Street (8:30–4:30 P.M. Mon.–Fri.).

Getting There and Around

By car, Jamestown is less than four miles south of Sonora on Highway 49.

Need to grab a bus? There are two routes that will take you from Jamestown and Sonora. For a more whimsical ride that families will especially love, hop on the **Historic 49 Trolley** (www.tuolumnecountytransit.com/HistoricTrolley.html, adults $1.50, day pass $4, children under 13 free) to ride during weekends; the trolley runs every day during summer. If you need public transit during the week, try **Tuolumne County Transit** (www.tuolumnecountytransit.com, adults $1.50, day pass $4).

TWAIN HARTE

The rustic foothill hamlet of Twain Harte (pop. 2,220) is an excellent day trip or overnight excursion from Sonora. Tucked high up among pine trees, Miwok tribes lived for millennia in small encampments next to Twain Harte Lake. The 1850s changed everything when gold-lusty prospectors started arriving in droves. The town was originally just a tollbooth on the road from Sonora to the gold-mining boomtown of Aurora, but settlers purchased 540 acres nearby and eventually subdivided the land. The first settlers named this area after legendary writers Mark Twain and Bret Harte, who lived in nearby Calaveras County during the Gold Rush.

By the 20th century, city dwellers from the Bay Area had built a lakeside community of weekend cabins to fish and enjoy the idyllic mountain lake. Twain Harte has now become a permanent town where you can hide out, plop a fishing line in the lake, paddle a canoe, or ride horseback through high mountain meadows.

Sports and Recreation

Twain Harte is all about getting away from traffic and city life to enjoy fresh, pine-scented air up in the Sierra Nevada high country. Do yourself a favor and get outside while you're here. At **Kennedy Meadows Resort and Pack Station** (Hwy. 108, Kennedy Meadows, 209/965-3900, www.kennedymeadows.com, 6 A.M.–6 P.M. daily, $25–90), visitors ride horseback through alpine meadows and forest groves on guided trips. You don't need experience for the shorter trips, which take about 75 minutes, but Kennedy does offer more rigorous excursions that last all day.

What better place to tee off than among towering conifers and gurgling streams? Unless you have a wicked slice, reserve a round at **Twain Harte Golf Club** (22909 Meadow Lane, 209/586-3131, www.twainhartegolf.com, $15–22). It's not a par-72 layout, but narrow fairways and stunning scenery make any round a memorable one at this challenging course.

Accommodations

Twain Harte has several lodging options, from low-rent motels to cozy mountain cabins. You won't find anywhere better than **McCaffrey House** (23251 Hwy. 108, 209/586-0757 or 888/586-0757, www.mccaffreyhouse.com, $150). This warm, country-style lodge has cheerful Craftsman decor with handmade Amish linens and furniture in all nine rooms. Each suite has a potbellied woodstove to warm your limbs on chilly mountain evenings, plus

MARK TWAIN, FROGS, AND POTHOLES

© CHRISTOPHER ARNS

a replica of Mark Twain's cabin on Jackass Hill

The crusty, acerbic wit of Mark Twain was honed in the goldfields of Calaveras County, where Twain started writing after failing miserably as a prospector. Twain headed to Angels Camp in 1864 with fellow writer Bret Harte, and the two men lived in a rough one-room cabin on a ridge called Jackass Hill. That's where Twain penned his first tall tale, "The Celebrated Jumping Frog of Calaveras County." It told the story of a saloon owner who is swindled after boasting his frog, one Dan'l Webster, could outleap any amphibian alive. The tale reflects Twain's experience with characters he found in mining camps, which often drew all kinds of showmen, con artists, and profiteers.

Twain didn't make up the story himself; miners had been telling the fireside classic for years before he arrived in Angels Camp. Twain, still rough around the edges as a writer, heard the tale from a bartender at the Angels Hotels in Angels Camp and rushed back to his tiny cabin to scribble it down. Chances are he had help; Harte was more polished as a scribe at that time and supposedly mentored Twain during their stay in Calaveras County.

The story put Twain and Calaveras County on the literary map, but ironically, the first frog jumping competition didn't happen until 1928 when Angels Camp needed to celebrate something much more prosaic: passing a bond to fix the town's potholes. Someone suggested a frog jump to commemorate the occasion, and the town has never looked back.

thermostats so you can control your own room temperature. Rooms feature flat-screen TVs, DVD players, complimentary robes, unbelievably soft sheets and pillowcases, and private balconies. In the morning, feast on delicious eggs Benedict and homemade pastries before heading off into Twain Harte for activities. To cap it all off, McCaffrey House is committed to reducing its carbon footprint with green energy; it's also pet-friendly.

Gables Cedar Creek Inn (22560 Twain Harte Dr., 209/586-3008, www.gccinn.com, $95–120) has intimate cabins tucked away in fragrant ponderosa and cedar groves. Each cabin has rustic pine paneling on the walls and piping-hot woodstoves or fireplaces, making visitors feel like they're roughing it in the woods. Some cabins have Murphy beds, while others have wrought-iron bedposts; most have kitchens where families can whip up meals instead of eating out.

Food

Alas, the fresh and local movement is still miles away from Twain Harte. Instead, bring your sweet tooth, and be ready to brave diet-destroying menus. **Sportsman Coffee Shop** (22978 Joaquin Gully Rd., 209/586-5448, 7 A.M.–2 P.M. daily, $5–10) is the mother ship calling all anglers to eat. Marlins, salmon, and other big fish gape from their wall mounts above red-checkered tables. Sportsman serves up a no-nonsense breakfast with hearty omelettes and buckwheat pancakes on spartan white plates so you can load up on calories before an early-morning fishing trip.

Alicia's Sugar Shack (24191 Hwy. 108, Sugar Pine, 209/586-5400, www.aliciassugarshack.com, 6 A.M.–2 P.M. daily, $5) is a small bakery with racks of fine pastries, muffins, cookies, and other goodies made fresh every morning. Wash it down with espresso; you'll need it, especially if you're up at the same time as Alicia's bakers.

Kennedy Meadows Resort and Pack Station (Hwy. 108, Kennedy Meadows, 209/965-3900, www.kennedymeadows.com, 6 A.M.–4 P.M. and 5–9 P.M. daily, $9–19) serves classic American cuisine of the meat and potatoes variety. You can order breakfast, lunch, and dinner, and there's a different meat special every night—choose from pot roast, prime rib, lasagna, and ribs. Reservations are suggested for Sunday evening dinner.

Looking for a candlelit dinner? Take your sweetie to **Villa D'oro** (23033 Joaquin Gulley Rd., 209/586-2182, www.villadororestaurant.com, 4:30 P.M.–close daily, $16–25), the best option for fine dining in Twain Harte. Choose from delicious entrées like fettuccine al carbonara, panko-encrusted calamari, and chicken marsala. Villa Doro also makes killer wood-fired pizzas.

Information and Services

For more information about the town, ring up the **Twain Harte Chamber of Commerce** (23000 Meadow Lane, 209/586-4482, www.twainhartecc.com, 10 A.M.–2 P.M. Mon.–Sat.). The website is a little cluttered, but does have loads of helpful tips and maps for the area.

Getting There and Around

Twain Harte is about 12 miles east of Sonora and Jamestown on Highway 108. A car is recommended, but if you've gotten this far with public transportation, there is one option; **Tuolumne County Transit** (www.tuolumnecountytransit.com, adults $1.50, day pass $4) runs five buses daily between East Sonora and Twain Harte; the trip takes about 30 minutes.

Since the town is perched at an altitude of 3,600 feet, Twain Harte most definitely gets a heavy dusting of snow every winter. Make sure you carry chains if traveling in this area during winter.

BACKGROUND

The Land

GEOGRAPHY

Sacramento lies in the middle of a 450-mile-long fold in the blanket of California's Central Valley, situated between the western peaks of the Coastal Ranges and the eastern hulk of the Sierra Nevada. This vast rift is actually two different valleys: The northern reach is the Sacramento Valley while the southern half is the San Joaquin Valley (each is named after the river that flows through it). Geologists believe these valleys started underwater and eventually rose above sea level as continental plates collided over millennia. This twist of tectonic fortune created a giant trough. Every year snowmelt cascaded down from the two mountain ranges into the valley and created an inland sea that enriched the soil with sediment; all that runoff created headaches for pioneers building a new settlement on the American and Sacramento Rivers. It's hard to say how many times those rivers swelled their banks and flooded Sacramento between 1850 and 1862, but it happened almost every year. Eventually settlers tamed the state's unruly rivers and wetlands with a watery spaghetti bowl of canals, levees, dams, and infill that dried out the

© CHRISTOPHER ARNS

ORIGIN OF THE WORD "SACRAMENTO"

Visitors fluent in Spanish will know that the word Sacramento means sacrament *en español*. Spanish explorer Gabriel Moraga rode into Northern California in 1808 and discovered a valley so beautiful that he claimed *"es como el sagrado sacramento"* ("it was like the holy sacrament"). Eventually the river, valley, and future city would all go by the name Sacramento.

For a city, it's a beautiful title, but locals love to shorten the moniker into fun nicknames. You might hear someone refer to the capital as "Sacto," "Sactown," or simply "Sac," as in, "I'm headed back to Sac tonight." Feel free to use all three nicknames when referring to the capital, even if they're not quite as romantic as "Sacramento."

valley. What remains is just a shred of the once mighty oak savannahs and woodlands of North America's largest riparian wilderness. Farms and ranches now pepper the flat valley floor where they reap the fruits of California's fertile soil to the tune of $25–30 billion per year.

Climbing into the Sierra Nevada foothills leads to a different story. Deep canyons, sparkling waterfalls, alpine lakes, and imposing granite massifs protrude from the continental spine. Gently sloping hills turn verdant green by early spring as flowers explode in hues of yellow, purple, orange, and white. Plenty of hiking and biking trails corduroy these hills, especially in the Auburn State Recreation Area or farther north in Nevada City. To the south, caverns tunnel deep below towns like Angels Camp and Murphys to carve out a bristling mess of crystalline formations and spooky wormholes. Some caves are abandoned mines from the Gold Rush, left over from a time when prospectors crept deep underground. Those old mining shafts have been closed for safety reasons, but many of the naturally formed caves are open for tours and sightseeing.

GEOLOGY

California's geological history started with a tectonic plate wreck about 150 million years ago when the Pacific Plate slammed head-on into the North American Plate, although it happened in slow motion over another 100

million years. Eventually the North American Plate buckled to create the Coast Ranges and sealed off California's Central Valley from the sea.

The Pacific Plate continued its collision with the North American Plate. Twenty-eight million years ago, this geologic fender bender created the San Andreas Fault, a seam in the earth's crust between the two plates. After the initial impact, the Pacific and North American Plates have continued sideswiping each other in what geologists call a "strike-slip" fault. The Pacific Plate is actually moving north at a fairly decent clip, about 1.5 inches per year, and often jolts ahead, moving several feet in mere seconds and causing an earthquake. The San Andreas Fault might concern visitors, but the Central Valley acts like a big buffer zone, insulating Sacramento and the Gold Country from much of the impact when earthquakes happen. Chances are very, very low that you'll feel a trembler during a visit here.

CLIMATE

The Sacramento Valley lacks proper seasons, basking in pure unadulterated sunshine 70–80 percent of the year with mild to moderate temperatures. In this Mediterranean-type climate, rolling golden hillsides are sprinkled with green bursts of oak trees. Spring seems to begin around mid-February when fruit trees start blooming brilliant shades of white and pink and those tawny hills glow a magnificent shamrock green. Summer weather arrives by mid-May, when temperatures climb into the 80s and 90s, and lasts through the beginning of October. By mid-October, Sacramento's thick canopy of leaves begins melting from the branches into piles of molten orange, yellow, and red. By December, the trees are finally bare, and winter (if you can call it that) lasts from December through February; this is when Sacramento receives the bulk of its annual rainfall. (Sacramento averages about 18 inches of rain per year.) It doesn't snow in Sacramento (except for a very light dusting every several years), and only Gold Country towns above 2,000 feet in elevation—like Nevada City, Grass Valley, Twain Harte, and Arnold—get the white stuff on a regular basis.

Temperatures swing wildly between summer and winter months. Sacramento is famous for blistering heat from late June through September when the mercury can hit triple digits, but things cool off significantly by late December and January. Rough averages for Sacramento are 75°F in spring, 90°F in summer, 70°F in fall, and 55°F in winter. However, a spring day in March could be 65°F and then rise two months later to 90°F in mid-May. Gold Country burgs at lower altitudes (Auburn, Placerville, Angels Camp, and Sonora) are usually five degrees cooler than Sacramento; higher elevations are about 10 degrees lower.

Sacramento rarely suffers from crazy weather, so things stay pretty predictable in these parts. No hurricanes, maybe a few thunderstorms, the odd tornado every so often. But the Central Valley often plays a wild card that keeps things interesting. In summer, cooler air from nearby wetlands randomly creates a "delta breeze" that relieves scorched Sacramentans during the summer. Winter is a different story. When frigid mountain air spills into the valley like a giant bowl and mixes with warmer air, it creates a thick mist called "tule" fog; this happens most often after a rain when the humidity rises. Visibility can drop to 100 feet and create nightmarish road conditions in which drivers can barely see in front of them.

Flora and Fauna

FLORA

Thanks to a mild climate, California has more than 5,000 native plant species, a whopping 32 percent of all vascular plants in the United States. The Sacramento Valley is a great place to observe this abundance of plantlife. Five different varieties of **oak trees** grow around the capital and the Gold Country, including blue oak, black oak, interior live oak, canyon live oak, and the massive valley oak that live up to 600 years. Visitors might unpack a picnic beneath ponderosa and ghost pines, pass big leaf maples on a hike, or catch patches of dogwoods glowing a bright yellow in fall.

In March, wildflowers blanket the Sacramento Valley with a vibrant quilt of gold, purple, ivory, and orange; it's common to see fields turn bright yellow during April with blooms of Spanish mustard seed. The state's official flower is the **California poppy.** State law bans the picking of all wildflowers on any land you don't own, including state property, unless permission is obtained from the owner. Offenders can be fined $1,000 and may receive six months in jail.

FAUNA

The California **grizzly bear** once roamed in large numbers throughout the lower Sierra Nevada foothills and Central Valley. Sadly, the grizzly (also known as the California golden bear) had a taste for livestock and landed on settlers' bad side during the Gold Rush. California grizzlies became extinct in 1922 when the last bear was shot in Tulare County; they now only exist on the California state flag.

Plenty of California **black bears** live at higher elevations and are harmless when left alone; however, all that changes that when there's food left in sight. In wilderness areas and campgrounds, lock up any food items in special bear-proof containers to avoid an encounter.

Bears might be harmless, but **mountain lions** are a different story. The rural areas of the Gold Country include cougar territory; these animals are most active at dawn and dusk, and they usually avoid groups of people. If you spot a mountain lion while in the backcountry or are concerned you might, contact the California Department of Parks and Recreation (1416 9th St., Sacramento, 916/653-6995, www.parks.ca.gov) or Department of Fish and Wildlife (1740 N. Market Blvd., Sacramento, 916/928-5805, www.dfg.ca.gov) for updates on mountain lion activity.

Arguably the most dangerous critter in California can't even walk. **Rattlesnakes** are named for the noisemaker on their tail that warns bystanders to back off. Rattlesnakes are poisonous, and their bites can be fatal if left untreated. Watch for them on dusty trails on hot summer days where they enjoy basking in the blazing sunlight. Most rattlesnakes will avoid humans; don't poke them or rile them up, but instead give them a wide berth and room to retreat.

Another animal you might encounter on the trail, **coyotes** are a wild canine related to gray wolves. Coyotes are everywhere in California (I've seen them running through the American River Parkway in Sacramento.). They tend to avoid humans and usually hunt small mammals and reptiles or even midsize livestock like pigs and sheep. Never feed a coyote, no matter how doglike they may appear; a tame coyote is a dangerous animal that no longer fears humans.

California has a menagerie of less threatening but still fascinating creatures. At last count, 195 species live in California and 54 of those critters are endemic, so you won't find them anywhere else. Keep an eye out for mule deer, elk, bobcats, raccoons, wild turkeys, gray squirrels, golden and bald eagles, gray foxes, black-tailed hares, bats, badgers, and skunks. Lucky visitors might also glimpse rare species such as river otters, California condors, and Sierra Nevada red foxes.

History

JOHN SUTTER

In 1839, a man named John Sutter staggered off a cargo brig in San Francisco. Sutter soon talked California's Mexican governor into giving him 44,000 acres between Sonoma and the Central Valley. The Swiss immigrant built a fort where the Sacramento and American Rivers converged, but his holdings stretched all the way to Fort Ross, a onetime Russian outpost that Sutter purchased in the early 1840s.

After settling his ranch near the Sacramento River, Sutter turned his attention to several new business projects, including a sawmill on the South Fork of the American River. In 1848, one of Sutter's employees discovered gold near Coloma. The Swiss land baron was wary about what might happen if people found out, but the secret got out when Sutter's employees started paying for groceries in gold. The store owner, a man named Sam Brannan, also published a San Francisco newspaper called the *California Star*. Brannan decided to open a new line of stores specializing in mining equipment. Before the stores opened, Brannan went back to San

Francisco and ran around the city streets waving a bottle filled with gold nuggets. "Gold! Gold! Gold from the American River!" he shouted.

Brannan's performance worked like a charm. San Francisco emptied almost overnight as the city's residents rushed toward the Sierra Nevada foothills. At Sutter's fort, the employees quit work to join the stampede for more gold. These "forty-eighters" were the first prospectors to ply the Gold Country for precious metal; most were either California residents or settlers from nearby Oregon territory. By December, U.S. President James Polk told Congress about the new discovery and it became official: There were riches for the taking in California. The Gold Rush was officially on.

THE GOLD RUSH

By 1849 settlers were pouring into California despite the long and dangerous journey from the East Coast. These were the "forty-niners," the gold-mad pioneers who rode wagons on the California Trail from Missouri and Kansas through rugged country to reach the West Coast. San Francisco's population swelled from 1,000 people to more than 25,000. Boomtowns sprang up all over the territory as prospectors built cabins wherever they could dip a gold pan and pull precious nuggets from the mud. The S.S. *California* began regular service between San Francisco and Sacramento to ferry pioneers farther upriver. By some estimates almost 100,000 new settlers galloped into California during 1849, including thousands from China, Australia, Europe, and Latin America. The Gold Country was rolling in saloons, gambling halls, bordellos, and hastily built hotels. By 1850, California settlers applied for statehood in the Union. The Compromise of 1850 approved that application, and California became the 31st state.

The first prospectors had it easy: They could find placer deposits (loose gold nuggets in river gravel) by simply using a pan. More industrious forty-niners started using complex sluices and boxes to sift through larger amounts of gravel. Added together, all the gold these placer miners found between 1948 and 1953 equals roughly 12 million ounces, or around $21 billion in 2012 prices. Prospectors then began blasting hillsides with water to loosen hidden gravel, a process known as hydraulic mining; another 11 million ounces was found over the next 30 years using this process.

THE RAILROAD

Gold fever didn't really subside until the early 20th century, but the initial madness was over by 1855. Mining changed from simple placer prospecting to industrial hard-rock mining. Hydraulic mining continued until the 1880s when farmers complained about the silt building up in the California Delta, which caused devastating floods. In 1884 a U.S. district court banned the practice and ended large-scale hydraulic mining, although Congress passed a law several years later that legalized it. Instead, dredging river bottoms became lucrative. Large waterborne tractors scooped gravel in huge shovels and dumped them on barges and riverbanks. At least 20 million ounces of gold were found this way, worth around $35 billion today!

More pioneers and settlers wanted to reach the Sacramento Valley, but the journey was unbelievably difficult. Many travelers choose to sail 18,000 nautical miles south around Cape Horn in South America and up the long Pacific coastline. Most pioneers traveled six months by land through the country's tough, arid Western frontier where they faced a number of dangers like disease, starvation, floods, and attacks by Native American tribes. As the Gold Rush changed from placer prospecting to industrial deep-shaft mining, a new means of transportation was desperately needed to bring heavy capital to the mines. A Connecticut engineer

© CHRISTOPHER ARNS

The "iron horse" transformed California.

named Theodore Judah decided that California needed a railroad linking the Golden State with the East Coast.

Judah was a visionary, but he had trouble convincing investors to believe in his project. As the chief engineer for the Sacramento Valley Railroad (California's first rail line, which ran from Folsom to the capital), the ambitious young man surveyed additional routes through the Sierra Nevada. In 1862, Judah persuaded four Sacramento merchants—Leland Stanford, Charles Crocker, Mark Hopkins, and Collis P. Huntington—to invest in the new Central Pacific Railroad. Judah then traveled to Washington DC and successfully lobbied Congress to authorize the project. After planning the railroad's course, convincing wealthy investors to buy in, and securing the U.S. government's consent, Judah stood on the brink of wealth and fame. But those Sacramento merchants, known as the Big Four, cut him out. Charles Crocker took over as construction chief in 1863 and oversaw the project. The First Transcontinental Railroad was completed when the Central Pacific was linked to the Union Pacific at Promontory Summit, Utah in 1869. A foreman hammered a ceremonial golden spike into the last railroad tie, symbolically tying the railroad back to the Gold Rush and opening the West for a new influx of East Coast settlers. Now the journey took just a few days instead of months.

Government, Economy, and People

POLITICS

As California's capital, Sacramento is where the buck stops. Here the bicameral California State Legislature, made of 80 Assembly Members and 40 Senators, meet for two-year sessions at the State Capitol. While California has often elected Republican governors, the state is staunchly Democratic. Both of California's U.S. senators are Democrats, as is Governor Jerry Brown, who was elected in 2010 after eight years of Arnold Schwarzenegger's gubernatorial reign. Brown is serving his second stint as the state's chief executive after completing two terms between 1974 and 1982.

California has a reputation for dysfunctional politics. The state's constitution requires a two-third majority vote to raise taxes, but voters can approve statewide ballot measures by a simple majority. In other words, it's easier to spend money than to raise it. Democrats might control the California State Legislature, but they don't have enough votes to raise taxes. Things bog down at the Capitol every year as politicians wrangle over billions in gaping budget holes. In 2012, a new law redrew the state's political districts in the hopes of shaking things up; the effect is supposed to encourage moderate politicians to run and work together to reduce logjams at the Capitol.

THE FIVE CAPITALS OF CALIFORNIA

Before Sacramento became the Golden State's political hub, four other cities claimed the title. The Spanish colonial capital and headquarters for California's 1849 statehood constitutional convention was Monterey, a beach town on the coast made famous later by John Steinbeck's novel, *Cannery Row*. After the first elections were held in Monterey, the constitutional convention decided to make San Jose the first state capital of California. From 1850 to 1851, the California State Legislature met in that southern Bay Area city—right about the same time Sacramento was experiencing its first disastrous flood. San Jose's capitol building was a two-story adobe hotel; the Senate met on the lower floor and the Assembly met on the top.

After just one year, the legislature moved to the east Bay Area town of Vallejo where former Mexican general Mariano Vallejo donated land for a new state capitol. The next session in 1852 was a disaster; buildings weren't finished, there was nowhere to stay, and the often dreary Bay Area weather made lawmakers miserable. They fled to Sacramento for the rest of the year.

The next year in the legislature's fourth session, things were pretty much the same. The lawmakers moved to Benicia, another eastern Bay Area town named for General Vallejo's wife. Even though the legislature had a decent two-story brick building for their chambers, apparently the rest of the town couldn't handle the influx of journalists, lawmakers, and other political flacks.

Finally, desperate to resolve this itinerant wandering from town to town, the legislature received an invitation from Sacramento to use the county courthouse while a more permanent situation was found. The lawmakers were so desperate they apparently didn't mind moving to a cholera-plagued, flood-prone city that had also proved to be a firetrap.

By 1854, the legislature moved for the last time. The permanent Neoclassical Capitol building, modeled after the U.S. Capitol, was constructed between 1861 and 1874, finally completing the migratory journeys of the first four sessions of the California State Legislature.

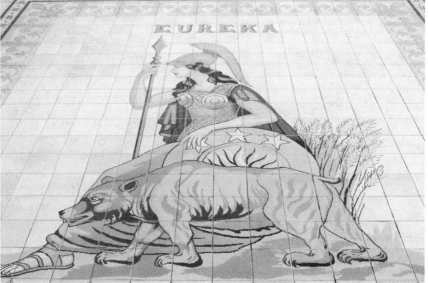

California's official seal graces the floor in the State Capitol.

© CHRISTOPHER ARNS

WINE INDUSTRY

Wine is a huge part of California culture, and Sacramento is Shangri-la for wine enthusiasts. Franciscan friars planted grapes here more than 200 years ago to make wine for Mass at their missions, and Gold Rush settlers from Europe planted vineyards throughout the valley. Some of the Gold Country's original grapes still grow in places like Amador County, although they are quite rare.

In the Gold Country, award-winning varietals are emerging in Fair Play, Murphys, Camino, and the Shenandoah Valley. The California Delta's wine trail leads to buttery chardonnays, subtle tempranillos, and chenin blancs with hints of melon and lime. Gold Country vintners often host their own tasting rooms where they can elucidate the fine art of bottling great vino for visitors. Unpretentious, surrounded by gorgeous scenery, and the home of rising stars in the wine industry, this wine mecca is just a short drive from Sacramento.

PEOPLE AND CULTURE

Sacramento's cultural heritage reflects California's broad diversity. The city's character is a rich stew of Latino, European, and Mediterranean influences, as seen in both the city's architecture and its people. Visitors might even detect notes of New Orleans in the capital's affinity for jazz, a legacy of Sacramento's Gold Rush steamboats and Prohibition paddle wheelers.

Demographics

Sacramento and the Gold Country have completely different demographics. Based on 2011 estimates from the U.S. Census Bureau, Sacramento is roughly 34.5 percent Caucasian, 26.9 percent Hispanic, 18.3 percent Asian, 14.6 percent African American, 7.1 percent two or

POLITICAL MAVERICKS

Jerry Brown's official portrait, by artist Don Bachardy

Something about California politics seems to draw iconoclasts. Some are activists, while others have been movie stars.

UPTON SINCLAIR

Sinclair was a Progressive muckraking journalist and Socialist political candidate. (Sinclair wrote *The Jungle*, which sparked the creation of the U.S. Food and Drug Administration.) In the 1920s, Sinclair ran for Congress twice unsuccessfully as a Socialist and earned the Democratic nomination for governor in 1934; his Socialist past was considered a major liability and he lost to Frank F. Merriam.

RONALD REAGAN

Reagan was an anti-Communist crusader who was successfully voted to the governor's office twice and to the White House twice. Reagan traveled to California in 1937 as a radio announcer for the Chicago Cubs and entered the movie business instead; between 1937 and 1964, his filmography included more than 60 movies. Reagan was never a major star, but he went on to become president of the Screen Actors Guild and eventually gave a 1964 campaign speech that turned heads within the Republican Party; two years later, he was elected as the 33rd governor of California. And of course, he was president of the United States from 1981–1989.

ARNOLD SCHWARZENEGGER

Schwarzenegger became the second governor of California with movie star roots. Elected in 2003 after then-Governor Gray Davis was recalled, the former bodybuilding champion and box office megastar came into office as a huge celebrity, promising to "terminate" budget deficits like his movie character terminated cyborgs. Schwarzenegger honed his brash style at the Capitol—he bought a huge gilded grizzly bear to adorn the hallway outside his office and put up a smoking tent where he could puff stogies outside. Schwarzenegger soon became frustrated with the glacial pace of Sacramento politics. (He once famously sent a metal sculpture of bull testicles to the state's Democratic leader urging the man to, ahem, grow a pair and pass the budget.) After leaving office, the "Governator" returned to making action movies.

JERRY BROWN

Brown is the only California governor to serve two different terms: 1975–1983 and another starting in 2010. Jerry Brown's father was Governor Pat Brown, who served from 1959–1967. Jerry Brown rose through the state's political ranks before winning his first gubernatorial election in 1974 when he served two terms. As a bachelor, Brown famously dated singer Linda Ronstadt and kept an apartment, instead of living in the Governor's Mansion. (Brown's nickname, Moonbeam, was given to him by ex-girlfriend Ronstadt, and it became a derisive way for journalists to mock his efforts to build a state space academy.) In 1982, he ran for a California U.S. Senate seat and lost.

Brown then traveled around the world, studied Buddhism, hung out with Mother Teresa, and returned in 1988. He ran for the Democratic presidential nomination in 1992 and lost to Bill Clinton; many thought his political career was over. But in 1999, Brown began a slow climb back to the State Capitol, serving as mayor of Oakland, district attorney of California, and finally winning the 2010 gubernatorial election.

more races, 1.4 percent Native Hawaiian/ Pacific Islander, and 1.1 percent American Indian/Alaska Natives. Women claim a small majority with 51.3 percent of the population. The capital is a fairly young city with 60 percent of all residents under the age of 40. Primary age groups are: 17 percent 20–29 years, 14.4 percent 30–39 years, 14.2 percent 0–9 years, 13.8 percent 10–19 years, 12.9 percent 40–49 years, 12.2 percent 50–59 years, 8 percent 60–69 years, 4.3 percent 70–79 years, and 3.2 percent above 80 years.

The Gold Country is much less ethnically diverse. A rough average of six counties (Placer, Nevada, El Dorado, Amador, Calaveras, and Tuolumne) are 75.4–86.2 percent Caucasian, 8.9–13.3 percent Hispanic, 1.2–6.3 percent Asian, 2.9–3.8 percent two or more races, 0.5–2.8 percent African American, 1.1–2.2 percent American Indian/Alaska Native, and 0.1–0.3 percent Native Hawaiian/Pacific Islander. The population in the Gold Country is also older, with 50–60 percent of residents older than age 40.

Language

English is the predominant tongue in Sacramento and the Gold Country, followed by Spanish. Beyond those two major languages the capital has tremendous linguistic diversity. A fascinating survey by the U.S. Centers for Disease Control (CDC) found 91 languages spoken at home in Sacramento County. The CDC discovered that Hmong, Chinese, Vietnamese, Tagalog, and Russian are the next most common languages after English and Spanish.

Visitors won't find the same diversity in the Gold Country, where the most common languages besides English and Spanish are German, French, Italian, Tagalog, Portuguese, and Japanese.

ESSENTIALS

Getting There

BY AIR

The region's major airport is **Sacramento International Airport** (SMF, 6900 Airport Blvd., 916/929-5411, www.sacramento.aero/smf), located just a few miles north of downtown Sacramento. Flying into Sacramento is easy; most major cities on the West Coast have direct flights into the capital, as do New York and Chicago. The airport just completed a $1 billion upgrade in late 2011 and now has two modern terminals with an expanded parking garage. Most of the time, traveling through SMF is a breeze. Lines are fast and not too long, and it seems like the baggage crews do a fine job getting luggage quickly from the aircraft to the conveyor belts. Occasionally the airport gets busy, such as on Friday and Sunday afternoons when lines for the security checkpoint always seem longer than normal. Try to arrive at least 90 minutes before your flight to make sure everything goes smoothly.

Reaching the Gold Country by air is more difficult. Visitors must either fly their own plane or rent private aircraft; commercial airlines do not service the foothills. Most of the airports in

© CHRISTOPHER ARNS

the Gold Country are general aviation fields for small single and twin-engine planes.

Airport Transportation

One thing the Sacramento airport could improve is public transportation between the airport and the city. Only a handful of hotels offer free shuttles, which means visitors will have several options: rental cars, private taxis, **SuperShuttle** (www.supershuttle.com, about $13), or a public bus bound for downtown. Plans for light-rail service are supposedly in the works but don't appear likely anytime soon. Cabs cost between $35–50 for rides between Sacramento and the airport.

BY TRAIN

Traveling by train is a fantastic and leisurely way to go. **Amtrak** (www.amtrak.com) has four routes that chug into the **Sacramento Valley Station** (401 I St., 800/872-7245, www.amtrakcalifornia.com). There are also four routes that pass through Sacramento and parts of the Gold Country: The *California Zephyr* runs service between San Francisco and Chicago with a daily stop in Davis, Sacramento, Colfax, and Reno; the *Capitol Corridor* is a commuter train with daily service between Auburn and San Jose with stops in Sacramento and Davis; the *Coast Starlight* runs daily between Los Angeles and Seattle; and the *San Joaquin* runs multiple trains from Sacramento to Bakersfield.

BY BUS

Plenty of coach routes run from the capital to other destinations in California; however, it's more difficult to continue into the Gold Country. **Amtrak** (www.amtrak.com) runs Thruway bus service between Sacramento and the foothill cities of Auburn, Colfax, and Placerville. **Greyhound** (www.greyhound.com) makes stops and picks up passengers in Sacramento, Colfax, and Isleton.

BY CAR

Driving a car is the easiest way to reach the Sacramento region. The capital sits squarely at the intersection of three major thoroughfares: I-80 and U.S. 50 both travel the length of the continental United States to reach the East Coast, while I-5 spans 1,400 miles north-south from Canada to Mexico. All three freeways pass through the city of Sacramento, so it's easy to drive a straight shot between the capital and the Bay Area or Los Angeles.

Rental Cars

Most major rental car companies have offices at **Sacramento International Airport** (SMF, 6900 Airport Blvd., 916/929-5411, www.sacramento.aero/smf) or downtown. The Gold Country is a different story, and there are fewer options for renting a car. In the Northern Gold Country, the Nevada County Airport (13083 John Bauer Ave., Grass Valley, 530/273-3347, www.nevadacountyairport.com) rents cars through **Hertz** (530/272-7730, www.hertz.com) and **Enterprise** (530/274-7400, www.enterprise.com). At Auburn Municipal Airport (13626 New Airport Rd., 530/386-4211), visitors can rent a vehicle through **Enterprise** (530/823-5500). In Columbia in the Southern Gold Country, you can rent a car from **Enterprise** (209/533-0500) or **Hertz** (209/588-1575).

TAXIS

The Sacramento region has numerous cab companies to pick up customers in the Gold Country and deliver them to the airport in Sacramento, although this service is pretty expensive. The cheapest option is **SuperShuttle** (www.supershuttle.com, $50–100 one-way ride).

Getting Around

BY AIR

There are a smattering of general aviation airports throughout the Sacramento region, but commercial airlines don't operate between the capital and the Gold Country. Some visitors may fly their own aircraft or arrive in Sacramento on a charter flight at **Sacramento Executive Airport** (SAC, 6251 Freeport Blvd., 916/875-9035, www.sacramento.aero/sac). Sacramento Executive is a general aviation facility with three paved runways (two lighted), a fixed-based operator, and free 72-hour parking. Better yet, downtown is only 10 minutes away. You can also rent planes here.

Private aircraft also fly from **Sacramento Mather Airport** (3745 Whitehead St., 916/875-7077, www.sacramento.aero/mhr). This former army base has been converted into a cargo and general aviation airfield with two runways, a fixed-base operator, and maintenance crews. Parking is free for the first 72 hours, and downtown is a 20-minute drive.

Franklin Field (12480 Bruceville Rd., 916/875-9035, www.sacramento.aero/f72) is owned by the county and mostly sees flight-training duty. There's no air traffic control tower, so call the county for more details if you're interested in landing here.

Private Aircraft

Pilots with their own plane or rental aircraft will be able to fly between towns in the Sacramento Valley. In the Northern Gold Country, the **Nevada County Airport** (13083 John Bauer Ave., Grass Valley, 530/273-3347, www.nevadacountyairport.com) accommodates private aircraft. Pilots can also fly into **Auburn Municipal Airport** (13626 New Airport Rd., Auburn, 530/386-4211), and **Placerville Airport** (3501 Airport Rd., Placerville, 530/622-0459, www.co.el-dorado.ca.us/Airports).

In the Southern Gold Country, there are three airfields: **Westover Field-Amador County Airport** (12380 Airport Rd., Jackson, 209/223-2376, www.co.amador.ca.us), **Calaveras County Airport** (3600 Carol Kennedy Dr., San Andreas, 209/736-2501), and **Columbia Airport** (10723 Airport Rd., Columbia, 209/533-5685), about four miles north of Sonora.

BY BUS

Sacramento Regional Transit (www.sacrt.com) has a great bus and light-rail network for getting around the capital. It's really easy to go anywhere within the capital's greater metropolitan area for just a couple of bucks.

The Gold Country does not have anything comparable to Sacramento's extensive bus network. Instead, most foothill towns rely on daily weekday commuter buses for traveling to and from Sacramento. These services include: **Placer Commuter Express** (530/885-2877 or 916/784-6177, www.placer.ca.gov, $4.75), which operates between foothill towns in Placer County and Sacramento; **El Dorado Transit** (530/642-5383, www.eldoradotransit.com, $5), which makes 11 return trips between Placerville and downtown Sacramento; and **Amador Transit** (http://amadortransit.com, $2), which runs several routes between Sutter Creek and Sacramento.

A few companies do operate limited service between other Gold Country towns. For transport between Nevada County and Auburn, there's the **Gold Country Stage** (http://new.mynevadacounty.com/transit, adults $1.50–3, children under 6 free, day pass $4.50). **Amador Transit** (www.amadortransit.com, $2) operates routes from Sutter Creek to Plymouth, Ione, Jackson, Mokelumne Hill, and east into the high country. Farther south, **Calaveras**

SACRAMENTO DRIVING DISTANCES

FROM SACRAMENTO TO:

Auburn	33 miles
Placerville	45 miles
Sutter Creek	46 miles
Jackson	48 miles
Volcano	57 miles
Nevada City	61 miles
Angels Camp	76 miles
Sonora	92 miles

Transit (www.calaverastransit.com, $2) runs four weekday routes to Arnold and Murphys, while **Tuolumne County Transit** (www.tuolumnecountytransit.com, adults $1.50, day pass $4) runs during the week between Twain Harte, Columbia, and Jamestown.

BY CAR

Sacramento lies at the busy intersection of I-80, I-5, U.S. 50, and Highway 99. I-80 is the main route into Sacramento from the San Francisco Bay Area. From Sacramento, **I-80** continues northeast to the Northern Gold Country town of Auburn, where you can take Highway 49 north and south. **Highway 49** is the gateway to the Northern Gold Country, stretching north to Nevada City and Grass Valley, or winding south through Auburn and Coloma to meet U.S. 50 in Placerville.

From Sacramento, **U.S. 50** leads east to the Northern Gold Country town of Placerville, where it meets Highway 49. Apple Hill also lies along this stretch of road, while Fair Play is farther south. Follow Highway 49 south to enter the Southern Gold Country towns of Plymouth and Sutter Creek.

I-5 serves a straight shot north to Red Bluff, Redding, and the Shasta region; heading south, I-5 passes through the Central Valley and Stockton. **Highway 99** is a suburban

thoroughfare that parallels I-5 for much of its route.

Sacramento's traffic congestion isn't too bad just yet, but an influx of public workers clogs the capital's freeways every weekday. For that reason it's a good idea to stay off downtown freeways during morning and evening rush hours.

To explore the Gold Country, take U.S. 50 or I-80 to one of the larger foothill towns (Auburn or Placerville) and then drive north or south on scenic Highway 49. A few other east-west highways bisect the foothills, including Highway 20, Highway 88, and Highway 4. Traffic jams and accidents are common on these twisting two-lane roads, especially during wet and snowy weather between December and February. Make sure to check road conditions online at the **California Department of Transportation** (Caltrans, www.dot.ca.gov). A good map is a necessity when traveling in the Gold Country; GPS may not always be accurate.

Seasonal Access

Winter months will throw a wrinkle into travel plans, especially for trips headed into the higher reaches of the Gold Country. The worst months for driving are between December and February. Much of Sacramento's yearly rainfall seems to drench the Sacramento Valley during this three-month stretch, and it sometimes appears to fall at once during torrential storms. Sacramento's rather flat topography means it's not unusual for creeks to rise and drains to back up, creating huge puddles that may shut down intersections. Contact the **City of Sacramento** (916/264-5011 or dial 311 in Sacramento) to report flooding or to find out if any streets have closed.

Slick roads can be a problem at lower elevations. Most drivers need only worry about icy conditions when ascending above 2,000 feet, which includes most of the Gold Country.

Snow makes things even worse. **Caltrans** (800/427-7623, www.dot.ca.gov) may shut down traffic on I-80 and U.S. 50 if blizzards roar into the Sierra Nevada. Bring chains if you plan on driving into the mountains during winter; trying to buy chains in a snowstorm is pure misery. You'll be glad to have them.

In the Gold Country, snowstorms can dump anywhere from a few inches to a couple of feet within 24 hours. Major freeways like I-80 and U.S. 50 are the roads most often affected, although Highways 88 and 4 in the Southern Gold Country also get buried in snow during the winter; Highway 20 in the Northern Gold Country also passes through blizzard country. If weather reports mention snow, check the Caltrans website (www.dot.ca.gov) before heading out to see if any freeways have closed. Even if roads are open, drivers should carry chains if traveling through the upper Gold Country. Caltrans will usually provide updates about whether chains are required in certain areas.

Tips for Travelers

CONDUCT AND CUSTOMS

California might have a slacker rep, but folks in Sacramento are all business. Workers in the state capital spend long feverish hours shaping policy and passing new laws, which means downtown is often packed with journalists, lawmakers, and legislative aides all jostling to grab their piece of the political pie. Sometimes visitors can be taken aback by the decidedly cold reception to tourists around the Capitol. Don't take it personally; the state legislature can get testy during budget season when Republicans and Democrats take off the gloves.

Attitudes stay down to earth in the Gold Country—living among such beautiful scenery would make anyone chipper. Don't be surprised if people wave when you drive by or say hello in the street. Locals happily turn on the country charm whenever they see an unfamiliar face, especially in places like Auburn or Nevada City. And apparently it's genuine. Expect a hearty Gold Country welcome when you arrive.

Smoking

Smokers often complain of California's "draconian" smoking laws, and they are pretty strict. As a general rule, smoking is banned inside public buildings, restaurants, bars, and within 20 feet of an open door. Since 2008, it is illegal to smoke in moving vehicles with children under 18; as of 2011, landlords can ban lighting up in rental units. Only 13 percent of California's population smokes, so most locals don't mind, but visitors who smoke should be aware of these regulations.

Tipping

Sacramento is very proud of its restaurant industry, which unfortunately depends on overworked and underpaid service workers to stay successful. Try to tip somewhere between 15 and 20 percent when dining out. Take that same philosophy to the bars, but tip your server or bartender at the beginning of the night instead of at the end. And don't forget the friendly valets ($2), hotel bellhops ($1 per bag), and the taxi you're taking home (15 percent).

ACCESS FOR TRAVELERS WITH DISABILITIES

Sacramento is fairly easy for disabled visitors to get around. California law also makes it easy to sue for damages if businesses aren't accessible for wheelchair use and disabled parking, so many buildings around town have the required ramps and designated parking spaces.

The Gold Country is another matter. Many of the 150-year-old buildings cannot accommodate a wheelchair ramp or larger restroom, and those that are registered historic places are excluded from having to do so. Towns like Nevada City have steep or cobblestone sidewalks and steps that are very tricky to navigate, and most Gold Rush–era buildings are walk-ups with no elevators. Expect the easiest access in towns like Auburn and Grass Valley, which have some off-street parking with designated spaces for travelers with disabilities.

TRAVELING WITH CHILDREN

Children are welcomed by every bistro, café, and eatery in Sacramento's restaurant scene. Most of Sacramento's foodie impresarios have small children or grandchildren themselves and often go out of their way to make sure parents feel welcome. Some of the best places to bring kids include Selland's, Tapa the World, Paragary's, and Crepeville. These restaurants all have high chairs and friendly servers with strict orders from management to treat their littlest customers with respect. Many restaurants have children's menus, but it's rare to find anything beyond basic stuff like burgers, mac n' cheese, chicken nuggets, and pizza. Nicer restaurants, like Ella Dining Room and Bar, will make something special just for your kids if they have unique dietary restrictions.

The Gold Country has a similar attitude when it comes to welcoming kids. There's more room to play and run around outside at places like the Auburn State Recreation Area, South Yuba River State Park, Apple Hill, and New Melones Lake. When traveling in the Gold Country, plan ahead and bring toys, books, and plastic bags for those long car rides. (While parents might enjoy the scenic drives down winding Highway 49, it's a carsick kid's worst nightmare.)

WOMEN TRAVELING ALONE

Women can travel alone safely in Sacramento and the Gold Country. However, the capital is a large city with plenty of large-city problems. Be advised not to walk alone at night in urban areas and try to avoid parking on poorly lit streets. One word of caution: the FBI believes Sacramento to be one of the country's five worst cities for sex trafficking and has worked hard to break up forced prostitution rings in North Sacramento.

SENIOR TRAVELERS

Sacramento is a great place for seniors to visit. Nearly every hotel and attraction offers a discount of 10–25 percent for senior travelers (most often, travelers between the ages of 55 and 65). For more information about discounts and travel advice, contact **AARP** (www.aarp.org). **Road Scholar** (800/454-5768, www.roadscholar.org) offers planned trips throughout Sacramento and the Gold Country, such as music festivals, wine-tasting in Amador and El Dorado Counties, and train rides from Sacramento to Reno.

When traveling in the Gold Country, be aware that many historic buildings and sites require quite a bit of walking or climbing stairs; elevators are infrequently found in all but the most modern accommodations.

GAY AND LESBIAN TRAVELERS

Sacramento provides a welcoming atmosphere for gay and lesbian visitors. Every year the city's GLBT community hosts a parade in Midtown and downtown Sacramento to raise AIDS awareness and foster connections with other civic groups in town. The unofficial hub for gay and lesbian life in Sacramento is 20th Street between K and L Streets. The **Sacramento Gay and Lesbian Center** (1927 L St., 916/442-0185, http://saccenter.org. noon–9 P.M. Mon.–Fri.) is located here and often helps coordinate upcoming events in the capital. Just down the street are several gay and lesbian bars like Faces, The Mercantile, The Depot, and Badlands. Some refer to this area as Lavender Heights because so many members of the GLBT community live and work here.

Unfortunately, the vibe up in the Gold Country isn't as welcoming. These areas are older, more conservative, and are less comfortable with GLBT sexual orientation. To prevent unwanted confrontation, avoid dive bars in the smaller towns. While things are getting better, it's not uncommon for some locals to vocalize disapproval toward GLBT visitors if they witness any PDA.

Health and Safety

FIRE SEASON

Fire is a danger in the Gold Country. By July and August, the region's oak woodlands and pine forests turn into miles of dry kindling, and it doesn't take much to spark blazing infernos. Simply flicking a cigarette out the window can lead to forest fires that burn thousands of acres of national forestland. Fireworks are banned across much of the foothills for this very reason; if visiting on the Fourth of July, don't bring any pyrotechnics. Setting them off is illegal in places like Placer and Amador Counties. Those who do could be fined and may receive jail time for violating the law. Campers should also take care to extinguish any campfires at night and before leaving the tent site.

SAFETY IN RIVERS

Travelers should exercise caution when visiting nearby waterways during the summer, especially while rafting or swimming in open water. Every year people drown in the capital's seemingly calm rivers. Alcohol plays a large

Park rules are often clearly posted.

© CHRISTOPHER ARNS

role, along with hidden currents that can pull weak or impaired swimmers underwater. This risk increases in the Gold Country. Watch out for submerged rocks around swimming holes, especially where cliff jumping is popular. Brave white water only on guided trips, or if you're an experienced rafter with excellent swimming skills.

THINGS THAT BITE

There are four notorious critters in Sacramento and the Gold Country: mosquitoes, rattlesnakes, deer ticks, and black widows. Along with these dangerous critters, remember that wild animals often carry rabies. Creatures more likely to carry this deadly virus include skunks and bats, but can also include rats, squirrels, raccoons, wild dogs, feral cats, and possums. Rabies is a terrible disease with fatal results if left untreated. You're more likely to find rabid animals in the foothills than in Sacramento, but always stay away from wild animals no matter the location.

Black Widow Spiders

The black widow spider is an ugly-looking thing—eight spindly legs, a bulbous abdomen bearing a wicked-looking red hourglass pattern, and thick sticky webs distinguish this critter. They're about the size of a paper clip and are usually not aggressive, fleeing from people when discovered. Black widows love nooks and crannies, either inside or outside, and are most commonly found under or behind a box that has rested in one place for a while. Though they rarely bite, when they do a black widow's venom is *15 times* more potent than a rattlesnake's poison. Symptoms include muscle aches, nausea, and difficulty breathing. People with weak immune systems, like children and seniors, are at risk from black widow venom and in some cases have died from the bites. If bitten, seek a doctor for treatment immediately.

Deer Ticks

Stay watchful for deer ticks, especially during spring in the Gold Country. Deer ticks love to climb new grass and brush, making it easier to cling to whatever passes by (i.e., you). These annoying pests can carry Lyme disease, an extremely painful affliction that causes headaches, fever, fatigue; more serious symptoms can attack the heart, joints, and central nervous system. The most common symptom is a reddish bull's-eye–shaped rash; see a doctor immediately if you discover this rash on your skin. Fortunately, early treatment usually cures Lyme disease. Pets can also contract the disease; make sure you check dogs and horses for ticks after a day outside in the Gold Country.

Mosquitoes

One of the most common pests in the Sacramento Valley is the mosquito, which easily breed in small amounts of standing water and may carry West Nile virus. Even though Sacramento County rarely sees human cases of this disease, every year officials spray pesticides from crop dusters to control the mosquito population. If you plan on staying in Sacramento for a few days during the summer, bring mosquito repellent and slather it on before dusk when the little bloodsuckers are most active.

Rattlesnakes

Mosquitoes are mostly a nuisance, but rattlesnakes will flat out ruin your day. Visitors who spend any length of time hiking, golfing, swimming, biking, or horseback riding through the Gold Country foothills will probably stumble across these bad boys, which are California's only poisonous snake. The most common species is the Northern Pacific rattlesnake (*Crotalus oreganus oreganus*). Like all rattlesnakes, this species is poisonous and eats small rodents, other reptiles, and insects. Rattlesnakes are shy, retiring creatures that bite people only when provoked. The California

Poison Control Center reports about 800 bites a year with only a couple of fatalities. Not every bite is poisonous; snakes do not inject venom in 25 percent of their bites. If you or someone else you are with is bitten, don't panic. Keep the bitten area below level with the heart and wash the area gently with soap and water. Move slowly so that the poison does not spread quickly throughout the body. Common symptoms include nausea, swelling, extreme pain, and weakness. A swift dose of antivenom is the best thing, so visit a doctor immediately.

CRIME

Sacramento is a fairly safe city. According to the city's police department, violent crime declined in 2011 and through the early part of 2012.

When the Gold Country is added in, the area appears even safer. In 2009, the FBI ranked the greater Sacramento area at No. 90 on their list of metropolitan crime rates (a higher number indicates lower crime). Although Sacramento has less crime than cities such as Houston, Oakland, and St. Louis, there's enough crime to warrant a friendly reminder to skip certain areas on the city's scruffier outskirts. Simple steps like securing your belongings and parking in well-lit areas will also help visitors avoid becoming victims of petty crimes like car theft or break-ins.

If you are a victim of a crime while in the Sacramento area, contact the **Sacramento Police Department** (5770 Freeport Blvd., Ste. 100, 916/264-5471). In an emergency dial either 911 or 916/732-0100.

Information and Services

EMERGENCY SERVICES

As always, call **911** in case of emergencies. Before heading into the Gold Country during the winter make sure to check **Caltrans** (800/427-7623, www.dot.ca.gov) for current highway conditions and closures. If you have a nonemergency situation or need assistance on the road, call the **California Highway Patrol** (800/835-5247, www.chp.ca.gov) or local law enforcement agencies, including these sheriff departments: **Sacramento County Sheriff's Department** (916/874-5115, www.sacsheriff.com), **Nevada County Sheriff's Office** (530/265-7880, www.mynevadacounty.com), **Placer County Sheriff's Department** (530/886-5375, www.placer.ca.gov), **El Dorado County Sheriff's Department** (530/621-5655, www.edcgov.us), **Amador County Sheriff's Office** (209/223-6513, www.amadorsheriff.org), **Calaveras County Sheriff's Department** (209/754-6500, http://sheriff.co.calaveras.ca.us), and **Tuolumne County Sheriff's Office** (209/533-5855).

There are three different area codes to remember for the region. The greater Sacramento metropolitan area uses 916, while Davis and the Northern Gold Country use 530. The northern San Joaquin Valley and the Southern Gold Country use 209.

COMMUNICATIONS AND MEDIA
Cell Phones

Cell phone reception is wonderful in the Sacramento Valley and includes both 3G and 4G service. The Gold Country can be trickier. Most of the larger towns like Auburn, Nevada City, Placerville, Jackson, and Sonora have decent coverage (although smartphone owners will notice slower download speeds). Smaller towns are less reliable. Highway 49 has spotty coverage between Auburn and Placerville and in some parts of the Southern Gold Country. Figure on losing those precious bars as you drive higher into the foothills, where cell phone towers struggle to beam their signals into canyons and between rugged hillsides.

SACRAMENTO QUICK FACTS

- **Founded:** 1849
- **Population:** 466,488 (2010 U.S. Census Bureau)
- **Area:** 99 square miles
- **Size:** Sixth-largest city in California; 35th most populous city in the United States
- **Time zone:** GMT/UTC -8 (Pacific Time Zone)
- **Demographics:** 34.5 percent Caucasian, 26.9 percent Hispanic, 18.3 percent Asian, 14.6 percent African American, 5.7 percent "other"
- **Median home price:** $275,000 in 2012
- **Sales tax:** 7.75 percent
- **Average climate:** Sacramento has 265 days of sunshine annually

- **Average temperature:** winter: 53-38°F; summer: 92-59°F
- **Average rainfall:** 17.93 inches annually
- **Major employers:** City of Sacramento, Elk Grove Unified School District, Intel, Kaiser Permanente, Mercy/Catholic Healthcare, Sacramento City Unified School District, Sacramento County, San Juan Unified School District, State of California, Sutter Health, UC Davis Health System
- **Colleges:** American River College, Cosumnes River College, Folsom Lake College, Pacific McGeorge School of Law, Sacramento City College, Sacramento State, Sierra College, UC Davis, Woodland Community College

Internet Access

Internet access is available at **FedEx Office** stores throughout Sacramento and the Gold Country's larger towns; computer rentals usually cost roughly $0.20–0.50 per minute. You can also try any of the Sacramento Public Library's 28 locations or public libraries in towns throughout the region. For laptop users, most coffee shops and hotels offer fast, free, and reliable wireless Internet anywhere you go (even at older bed-and-breakfasts in the Gold Country, where free wireless Internet is becoming the norm rather than the exception). Need to check email one more time before catching a flight? The **Sacramento International Airport** has both free and faster premium wireless Internet service.

Newspapers and Magazines

The **Sacramento Bee** (www.sacbee.com) is the most prominent daily newspaper for the region, specializing in covering city and state politics. Most newsstands sell the *Bee* in just about every town. For stories on music and local culture, you can't beat the free **Sacramento News and Review** (www.newsreview.com/sacramento), which can also be found throughout the region. Each of the major Gold Country towns produces either daily or semi-daily newspapers that cover local sports and politics.

Sacramento has two glossy monthly magazines. **Sactown** (www.sactownmag.com) and **Sacramento Magazine** (www.sacmag.com) usually profile local celebrities, offer recipes, and highlight cultural trends in the capital. In the Gold Country, **Sierra Heritage** (http://sierraheritage.com) offers thoughtful commentary on how to eat, drink, and paddle your way through the foothills.

Postal Services

Sending a letter or postcard from Sacramento and the Gold Country is easy and costs less than $0.50. Package post depends on weight unless you ship via Priority Mail, which has standardized rates if you choose certain boxes provided by the U.S. Postal Service. Even the smallest burgs in the foothills have a tiny post office off the main drag; they're usually the most official-looking business in town, flanked by those telltale blue drop boxes and a tall flagpole.

UPS, FedEx, and OnTrac are available in Sacramento, but you might have a tough time shipping through these carriers in the Gold Country. You'll have to locate a FedEx Office outlet or UPS Store, which are few and far between in the smaller towns but are fairly common in places like Auburn, Grass Valley, and Placerville.

MAPS AND TOURIST INFORMATION

The best place to pick up maps of the Sacramento Valley is at the **Sacramento Convention and Visitors Bureau** (1608 I St., 916/808-7777, www.discovergold.org). The friendly staff will happily offer tips on dining, accommodations, and regional sightseeing. You can also print detailed, colorful maps of the city and the greater Sacramento area right off the bureau's website.

Most of the larger towns and county seats in the Gold Country have chambers of commerce offices that double as tourist information centers. Smaller towns usually lack these services, so your innkeeper or hotel manager is usually the best fount of local info. Almost all of the region's most heavily visited towns have free area maps, which you can find at hotels, shops, sights, and tourist information centers. Stick with these local maps over anything created online through mapping websites, which are often inaccurate for remoter areas.

RESOURCES

Suggested Reading

Brand, H. W. *The Age of Gold: The California Gold Rush and the New American Dream.* New York, NY: Doubleday, 2003. This fascinating history explores the Gold Rush and its iconic characters while showing how California helped shape the nation's destiny.

Burg, William. *Sacramento Then and Now.* Charleston, SC: Arcadia, 2007. The author uncovers a trove of vintage photographs that span decades of the capital's history.

Hayes, Derek. *Historical Atlas of California: With Original Maps.* Berkeley, CA: University of California Press, 2007. The author uses almost 500 historical maps and illustrations to create a stunning visual perspective on the Golden State's history.

Holliday, J. S. *The World Rushed In.* New York, NY: Simon and Schuster, 1981. This gripping volume looks past California's wealthy magnates to honor the first forty-niners who braved overland migration to strike it rich. Based on diaries and letters from actual Gold Rush prospectors.

Hurtado, Albert. *John Sutter: A Life on the North American Frontier.* Norman, OK: University of Oklahoma Press, 2006. In one of the most thorough accounts of Sacramento's founding father, the author takes a courageous and unblinking look at Sutter's successes and many failings.

Kimbro, Edna, Julia G. Costell, and Tevvy Ball. *The California Missions: History, Art and Preservation.* Los Angeles, CA: J. Paul Getty Trust, 2009. This comprehensive work offers a riveting look at California's missions with gorgeous illustrations and photos, including a balanced account of early history, subjugation of the native peoples, and modern preservation projects.

Rayner, Richard. *The Associates: Four Capitalists Who Created California.* New York, NY: W. W. Norton and Company, 2008. This entertaining and unflinching tome reveals the men behind the Big Four railway tycoons who built the First Transcontinental Railroad.

Secrest, William B. *When the Great Spirit Died: The Destruction of the California Indians 1850–1860.* Fresno, CA: Craven Street Books, 2003. A startling account of California's native people and the brutalities inflicted upon them by European settlers. The author narrowly focuses on one decade, but it's arguably the most fateful era for California Indians.

Stapp, Cheryl Anne. *Disaster and Triumph: Sacramento Women, Gold Rush through the Civil War.* Sacramento, CA: 2012. This wonderful tome shines light onto Californian women and their place in the state's long history.

Steinbeck, John. *The Harvest Gypsies*. Berkeley, CA: Heyday, 2002. This compilation of seven magazine articles by the author in 1936 includes an eyewitness account of California's Dust Bowl refugees living in squalor; 22 photos by famed photographer Dorothy Lange.

Stone, Irving. *Men to Match My Mountains*. New York, NY: Berkley Trade, 1987. The author frames the story of America's western expansion like a Homeric epic, vividly describing the prominent pioneers who helped settle the West, including John Sutter, John C. Frémont, Brigham Young, and Kit Carson.

Twain, Mark. *Great Short Works of Mark Twain*. New York, NY: HarperCollins, 2004. This collection includes "The Jumping Frog," about a notorious leaping amphibian in Angels Camp that loses a bet for his owner.

Varney, Philip. *Ghost Towns of Northern California*. Stillwater, MN: Voyageur Press, 2001. This amazing work uncovers Northern California's forgotten Gold Rush villages and explains where to find them. The author's clear and ringing prose revives a lost era that's often hidden in plain sight.

Internet Resources

California State Parks
www.parks.ca.gov
Official site for California State Parks which includes information on parks, hiking trails, camping, hours of, information, and accessibility.

California Tourism
www.visitcalifornia.com
Official site for state tourism providing maps, guidebooks, photos, reservations for hotels, tickets for attractions, airport info, and everything else related to a visit in the Golden State.

Center for Sacramento History
www.cityofsacramento.org/ccl/history/
default.asp
Photos and archives from Sacramento's history.

Gold Country Visitors Association
www.calgold.org
Main site for Gold Country tourism bureaus.

Old Sacramento
http://oldsacramento.com
Includes general information for Old Sacramento.

Sacramento Bee
www.sacbee.com
An informative site for local entertainment, wine, culture, capital politics, local sports, calendar of events, and Sacramento weather.

Sacramento Convention and Visitors Bureau
www.discovergold.org
Premier site for tourism in Sacramento.

Sacramento History
www.sacramentohistory.org
Photos of Sacramento's transportation and agricultural history.

Sacramento News and Review
www.newsreview.com/sacramento
A comprehensive and entertaining source for local music, art, city politics, environmental news, restaurant and movie reviews, with profiles on Sacramento bands, weekly schedules for live music, and a calendar of events.

Sacramento 365
www.sacramento365.com
A comprehensive and thoughtfully organized calendar of events for Sacramento.

Index

List of Maps

www.moon.com

MOON.COM is ready to help plan your next trip! Filled with fresh trip ideas and strategies, author interviews, informative travel blogs, a detailed map library, and descriptions of all the Moon guidebooks, Moon.com is all you need to get out and explore the world—or even places in your own backyard. While at Moon.com, sign up for our monthly e-newsletter for updates on new releases, travel tips, and expert advice from our on-the-go Moon authors. As always, when you travel with Moon, expect an experience that is uncommon and truly unique.

KEEP UP WITH MOON ON FACEBOOK AND TWITTER
JOIN THE MOON PHOTO GROUP ON FLICKR

MAP SYMBOLS

▦ Expressway	⟨ Highlight	✗ Airfield	⚲ Golf Course
Primary Road	○ City/Town	✗ Airport	ⓟ Parking Area
Secondary Road	◉ State Capital	▲ Mountain	⛰ Archaeological Site
Unpaved Road	⊛ National Capital	✛ Unique Natural Feature	⛪ Church
Trail	★ Point of Interest		
Ferry	• Accommodation	≀ Waterfall	⛽ Gas Station
Railroad	▾ Restaurant/Bar	▲ Park	Glacier
Pedestrian Walkway	▪ Other Location	⬛ Trailhead	Mangrove
Stairs	Λ Campground	⛷ Skiing Area	Reef
			Swamp

CONVERSION TABLES

°C = (°F – 32) / 1.8
°F = (°C x 1.8) + 32
1 inch = 2.54 centimeters (cm)
1 foot = 0.304 meters (m)
1 yard = 0.914 meters
1 mile = 1.6093 kilometers (km)
1 km = 0.6214 miles
1 fathom = 1.8288 m
1 chain = 20.1168 m
1 furlong = 201.168 m
1 acre = 0.4047 hectares
1 sq km = 100 hectares
1 sq mile = 2.59 square km
1 ounce = 28.35 grams
1 pound = 0.4536 kilograms
1 short ton = 0.90718 metric ton
1 short ton = 2,000 pounds
1 long ton = 1.016 metric tons
1 long ton = 2,240 pounds
1 metric ton = 1,000 kilograms
1 quart = 0.94635 liters
1 US gallon = 3.7854 liters
1 Imperial gallon = 4.5459 liters
1 nautical mile = 1.852 km

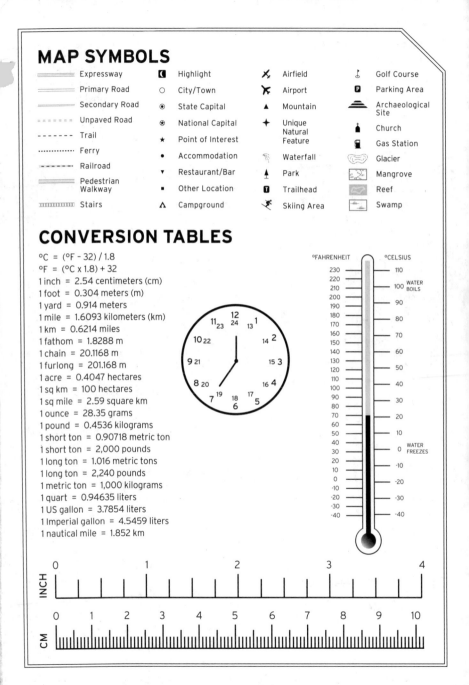

MOON SACRAMENTO AND THE GOLD COUNTRY

Avalon Travel
a member of the Perseus Books Group
1700 Fourth Street
Berkeley, CA 94710, USA
www.moon.com

Editor: Sabrina Young
Series Manager: Kathryn Ettinger
Copy Editor: Ashley Benning
Graphics Coordinator: Tabitha Lahr
Production Coordinator: Elizabeth Jang
Cover Designer: Tabitha Lahr
Map Editor: Albert Angulo
Cartographers: Kaitlin Jaffe, Chris Henrick, Heather Sparks, and Andy Butkovic
Indexer: Greg Jewett

ISBN-13: 978-1-61238-516-7
ISSN: 2325-517X

Printing History
1st Edition — June 2013
5 4 3 2 1

Title page photo: © Christopher Arns

Interior color photos: p. 1-8 all © Christopher Arns; p. 9 (top left) Lynn Bendickson/123rf.com, (top middle) © Christopher Arns, (top right) © iofoto/123rf.com, (bottom) © Christopher Arns; p. 10-11 all © Christopher Arns; p. 12 © John Painting/123rf.com; p. 13 © Randy Miramontez/123rf.com; p. 14-19 all © Christopher Arns; p. 20 (top) © sarahjanet/123rf.com; (bottom) © Christopher Arns; p. 21-24 all © Christopher Arns

Printed in Canada by Friesens

All recommendations, including those for sights, activities, hotels, restaurants, and shops, are based on each author's individual judgment. We do not accept payment for inclusion in our travel guides, and our authors don't accept free goods or services in exchange for positive coverage.

Although every effort was made to ensure that the information was correct at the time of going to press, the author and publisher do not assume and hereby disclaim any liability to any party for any loss or damage caused by errors, omissions, or any potential travel disruption due to labor or financial difficulty, whether such errors or omissions result from negligence, accident, or any other cause.

Front cover photo: Sacramento Old Town and Sacramento River *Delta King* sternwheeler © John Elk III / Alamy

---

KEEPING CURRENT

If you have a favorite gem you'd like to see included in the next edition, or see anything that needs up **32953011926641** p us a line. Send your comments via em   s above.